THE THEOLOGY OF RENEWAL FOR *HIS CHURCH*

The Theology of Renewal for *His Church*

The Logic of Vatican II's Renewal in Paul VI's Encyclical *Ecclesiam Suam* and Its Reception in John Paul II and Benedict XVI

DOUGLAS G. BUSHMAN, STL

☙PICKWICK *Publications* • Eugene, Oregon

THE THEOLOGY OF RENEWAL FOR *HIS CHURCH*
The Logic of Vatican II's Renewal in Paul VI's Encyclical *Ecclesiam Suam*, and Its Reception in John Paul II and Benedict XVI

Copyright © 2024 Douglas G. Bushman, STL. All rights reserved. Except for brief quotations in critical publications or reviews, no part of this book may be reproduced in any manner without prior written permission from the publisher. Write: Permissions, Wipf and Stock Publishers, 199 W. 8th Ave., Suite 3, Eugene, OR 97401.

Pickwick Publications
An Imprint of Wipf and Stock Publishers
199 W. 8th Ave., Suite 3
Eugene, OR 97401

www.wipfandstock.com

PAPERBACK ISBN: 978-1-6667-3125-5
HARDCOVER ISBN: 978-1-6667-2356-4
EBOOK ISBN: 978-1-6667-2357-1

Cataloguing-in-Publication data:

Names: Bushman, Douglas G.

Title: The theology of renewal for his church : the logic of Vatican II's renewal in Paul VI's encyclical ecclesiam suam and its reception in John Paul II and Benedict XVI / Douglas G. Bushman, STL.

Description: Eugene, OR: Cascade Books, 2024. | Includes bibliographical references.

Identifiers: ISBN 978-1-6667-3125-5 (paperback). | ISBN 978-1-6667-2356-4 (hardcover). | ISBN 978-1-6667-2357-1 (ebook).

Subjects: LSCH: Theology, doctrinal—Roman Catholic. | Vatican Council (2nd : 1962–1965 : Basilica di San Pietro in Vaticano. | Catholic Church—Pope (1963–1978 ; Paul VI)—Ecclesiam Suam. | Pope John Paul II. | Pope Benedict XVI. | Catholic Church—Doctrines.

Classification: BX2110 B97 2024 (print). | BX2110 (ebook).

Except where otherwise noted, all biblical quotations are taken from Revised Standard Version of the Bible—Second Catholic Edition (Ignatius Edition) Copyright © 2006 National Council of the Churches of Christ in the United States of America. Used by permission. All rights reserved worldwide.

Excerpts from the English translation of the Catechism of the Catholic Church for use in the United States of America Copyright © 1994, United States Catholic Conference, Inc.—Libreria Editrice Vaticana. Used with Permission. English translation of the Catechism of the Catholic Church: Modifications from the Editio Typica copyright © *1997*, United States Conference of Catholic Bishops—Libreria Editrice Vaticana.

Nihil obstat
Rev. Lawrence C. Brennan, SThD
Censor, November 27, 2019
Imprimatur
Most Rev. Michael J. Sheridan, SThD
Bishop of Colorado Springs, December 4, 2019

Contents

Abbreviations ix
Introduction 1

PART I *Ecclesiam Suam*: **A Path for Vatican II**

1 "To Walk according to the Will of Christ" | 19
2 *Ecclesiam Suam*: Prolegomena to an Analysis | 38
3 The First Path: Awareness | 54
4 The Second Path: Renewal | 62
5 The Third Path: Dialogue | 83
6 Implications of the Analysis | 120

PART II Complementary Themes

7 Two Themes of Pope John XXIII on the Renewal of Vatican II | 129
8 Pope Paul VI on Fidelity to God and Fidelity to Man | 135
9 Pope John Paul II on Fidelity to God and Fidelity to Man | 168

PART III *Ecclesiam Suam*: **A Path for the Church**

10 Three Paths of Renewal and Three Dimensions of Formation | 209
11 How Are the Three Dimensions of Renewal/Formation Related? | 223
12 Cardinal Wojtyła/Pope John Paul II on Faith | 277
Conclusion: *Ecclesiam Suam*, the Logic of Renewal, and the Spirit of Vatican II | 319

Epilogue: A Parable and Its Explanation | 329
Appendix: Three Paths of Renewal | 345
Bibliography | 367

Abbreviations

AA	Second Vatican Ecumenical Council. Decree on the Apostolate of the Laity, *Apostolicam actuositatem*. November 18, 1965
AAS	*Acta Apostolicae Sedis* (Official Acts of the Holy See)
AG	Second Vatican Ecumenical Council. Decree on the Mission Activity of the Church, *Ad gentes*. December 7, 1965
AS	*Acta Synodalia Sacrosancti Concilii Oecumenici Vaticani II*. Vatican City: Typis Polyglottis Vaticanis, 1970
CCC	*Catechism of the Catholic Church*. 2nd ed. Washington, DC: Libreria Editrice Vaticana, 2016
CD	Second Vatican Ecumenical Council. Decree concerning the Pastoral Office of Bishops in the Church, *Christus Dominus*. October 28, 1965
CL	Pope John Paul II. Post-Synodal Apostolic Exhortation on the Vocation and Mission of the Lay Faithful in the Church and in the World, *Christifideles laici*. December 30, 1988
CT	Pope John Paul II, Apostolic Exhortation on Catechesis in Our Time, *Catechesi tradendae*. October 16, 1979
CTH	Pope John Paul II. *Crossing the Threshold of Hope*. New York: Knopf, 1994
D-R	*The Holy Bible* (Douay-Rheims Version). New York: Kenedy & Sons, 1914

DCE	Pope Benedict XVI. Encyclical Letter on the Love of God, *Deus caritas est.* December 25, 2005
DeV	Pope John Paul II. Encyclical Letter on the Holy Spirit in the Life of the Church and the World, *Dominum et Vivificantem.* May 18, 1986
DFT	*Dictionary of Fundamental Theology.* Edited by René Latourelle and Rino Fisichella. New York: Crossroad, 1994
DH	Second Vatican Ecumenical Council. Declaration on Religious Liberty, *Dignitatis humanae.* December 7, 1965
DM	Pope John Paul II. Encyclical Letter on Divine Mercy, *Dives in misericordia.* November 30, 1980
DV	Second Vatican Ecumenical Council. Dogmatic Constitution on Divine Revelation, *Dei Verbum.* November 18, 1965
EAm	Pope John Paul II. Post-Synodal Apostolic Exhortation on the Encounter with the Living Jesus Christ: The Way to Conversion, Communion and Solidarity in America, *Ecclesia in America.* January 22, 1999
EO	Pope John Paul II. Post-Synodal Apostolic Exhortation on Jesus Christ and the Peoples of Oceania: Walking His Way, Telling His Truth, Living His Life, *Ecclesia in Oceania.* November 22, 2001
ES	Pope Paul VI. Encyclical Letter on Paths of the Church, *Ecclesiam Suam.* August 6, 1964
EN	Pope Paul VI. Apostolic Exhortation on the Annunciation of the Gospel, *Evangelii nuntiandi.* December 8, 1975
FR	Pope John Paul II. Encyclical Letter on the Relationship between Faith and Reason, *Fides et ratio.* September 14, 1998
GCD	Sacred Congregation for the Clergy. *General Catechetical Directory.* Washington, DC: United States Conference of Catholic, 1971

GDC	Congregation for the Clergy. *General Directory for Catechesis*. Washington, DC: United States Conference of Catholic Bishops, 1998
GE	Second Vatican Ecumenical Council. Declaration on Education, *Gravissimum educationis*. October 28, 1965
GS	Second Vatican Ecumenical Council. Pastoral Constitution on the Church in the Modern World, *Gaudium et spes*. December 7, 1965
ITC	International Theological Commission
LG	Second Vatican Ecumenical Council. Dogmatic Constitution on the Church, *Lumen gentium*. November 21, 1964
MCC	Pope Pius XII. Encyclical Letter on the Mystical Body of Christ, *Mystici corporis Christi*. June 29, 1943
NJB	*The New Jerusalem Bible*. Edited by Henry Wansbrough. New York: Doubleday, 1985
NMI	Pope John Paul II. Apostolic Letter at the Close of the Great Jubilee Year 2000, *Novo millennio ineunte*. January 6, 2001
OT	Second Vatican Ecumenical Council. Decree on Priestly Training, *Optatam totius*. October 28, 1965
PA	Pope John XXIII. Encyclical Letter on the Need for Practice of Interior and Exterior Penance, *Paenitentiam agere*. July 1, 1962
PDV	Pope John Paul II. Post-Synodal Apostolic Exhortation on the Formation of Priests in the Circumstances of the Present Day, *Pastores dabo vobis*. March 15, 1992
PO	Second Vatican Ecumenical Council. Decree on the Ministry and Life of Priests, *Presbyterorum ordinis*. December 7, 1965
QIA	Pope Paul VI. Apostolic Exhortation after Five Years, *Quinque iam anni*. December 8, 1970
RH	Pope John Paul II. Encyclical Letter on the Redeemer of Man, *Redemptor hominis*. March 4, 1979

RMat	Pope John Paul II. Encyclical Letter on the Blessed Virgin Mary in the Life of the Pilgrim Church, *Redemptoris Mater*. March 25, 1987
RMiss	Pope John Paul II. Encyclical Letter on the Permanent Validity of the Church's Missionary Mandate, *Redemptoris missio*. December 7, 1990
RP	Pope John Paul II. Post-Synodal Apostolic Exhortation on Reconciliation and Penance in the Mission of the Church Today, *Reconciliatio et paenitentia*. December 2, 1994
RSV	*The Holy Bible* (Revised Standard Version; Second Catholic Edition). San Francisco: Ignatius, 2006
SA	Pope John Paul II. Encyclical Letter on the Apostles of the Slavs, *Slavorum apostoli*. June 2, 1985.
SC	Second Vatican Ecumenical Council. Constitution on the Sacred Liturgy, *Sacrosanctum Concilium*. December 4, 1963
SR	Karol Wojtyła. *Sources of Renewal: The Implementation of Vatican II*. Translated by P. S. Falla. San Francisco: Harper & Row, 1979
SS	Pope Benedict XVI. Encyclical Letter on Christian Hope, *Spe salvi*. November 30, 2007
ST	Thomas Aquinas. *Summa Theologica*. Translated by Fathers of the English Dominican Province. New York: Christian Classics, 1981
SCG	Thomas Aquinas. *Summa contra Gentiles*. Translated by Anton Pegis et al. New York: Hanover, 1955–57
TDNT	*Theological Dictionary of the New Testament*. 10 vols. Edited by Gerhard Kittle and Gerhard Friedrich. Translated by Geoffrey W. Bromiley. Grand Rapids: Eerdmans, 1984
TMA	Pope John Paul II. Apostolic Exhortation on the Coming of the Third Millennium, *Tertio millennio adveniente*. November 10, 1994
UR	Second Vatican Ecumenical Council. Decree on Ecumenism, *Unitatis redintegratio*. November 21, 1964

VD	Pope Benedict XVI. Post-Synodal Apostolic Exhortation on the Word of God in the Life and Mission of the Church, *Verbum Domini*. September 30, 2010

Except where otherwise noted, all biblical quotations are taken from the RSV—Second Catholic Edition. The following abbreviations are used for books of the Bible:

Acts	Acts of the Apostles
Amos	Amos
Bar	Baruch
1 Chr	1 Chronicles
2 Chr	2 Chronicles
Col	Colossians
1 Cor	1 Corinthians
2 Cor	2 Corinthians
Dan	Daniel
Deut	Deuteronomy
Eccl	Ecclesiastes
Eph	Ephesians
Esth	Esther
Exod	Exodus
Ezek	Ezekiel
Ezra	Ezra
Gal	Galatians
Gen	Genesis
Hab	Habakkuk
Hag	Haggai
Heb	Hebrews
Hos	Hosea
Isa	Isaiah

Jas	James
Jer	Jeremiah
John	John
1 John	1 John
2 John	2 John
3 John	3 John
Job	Job
Joel	Joel
Jon	Jonah
Josh	Joshua
Jdt	Judith
Jude	Jude
Judg	Judges
1 Kgs	1 Kings
2 Kgs	2 Kings
Lam	Lamentations
Lev	Leviticus
Luke	Luke
1 Macc	1 Maccabees
2 Macc	2 Maccabees
Mal	Malachi
Mic	Micah
Mark	Mark
Matt	Matthew
Nah	Nahum
Neh	Nehemiah
Num	Numbers
Obad	Obadiah

1 Pet	1 Peter
2 Pet	2 Peter
Phil	Philippians
Phlm	Philemon
Prov	Proverbs
Pss	Psalms
Rev	Revelation (Apocalypse)
Rom	Romans
Ruth	Ruth
1 Sam	1 Samuel
2 Sam	2 Samuel
Sir	Sirach (Ecclesiasticus)
Song	Song of Solomon
1 Thess	1 Thessalonians
2 Thess	2 Thessalonians
1 Tim	1 Timothy
2 Tim	2 Timothy
Tit	Titus
Tob	Tobit
Wis	Wisdom
Zech	Zechariah
Zeph	Zephaniah

Introduction

THE FOCUS OF THIS study is the first encyclical of Pope St. Paul VI, *Ecclesiam Suam* (hereafter, *ES*), inasmuch as it can serve as a hermeneutical key to understand the true spirit of Vatican II and the idea of renewal in the subsequent magisterium. For this is precisely what Pope Paul intended it to be. He did not propose it as an authoritative clarification of the doctrine, morals, or social teaching that the Council was in the process of formulating.[1] Certainly, as the Successor of Peter it was his prerogative to do so, and he would exercise this prerogative in the course of the Council. But his purpose in *ES* is to make known, particularly to those participating in the Council, how he understands the Council's goal to foster profound renewal of the Church, based on the apostolic deposit of faith, and in view of a revitalization of the Church's mission. He seeks "to impart closer cohesion and deeper joy to that unity in faith and charity which ... binds us together" and "thereby to inject new vigor into our sacred work" (*ES*, 7). For Pope Paul, *ES* is an invitation to come together in a common vision for the renewal of Vatican II and, rooted in this vision, to collaborate in a common spirit in which its goals are to be pursued and its renewal undertaken.

More than fifty years after the close of Vatican II, the question of how to interpret the Council is as lively as ever. At the same time, the call has been sounded for new attention to "the council's central insights [which] have not yet received sufficient attention."[2] To complement the enormous body of studies on particular Conciliar teachings and texts, Gilles Routhier thinks it is time to attend to "the council's central intuitions that

---

1. Taking the name Paul VI, Cardinal Montini was elected to succeed John XXIII on June 21, 1963. He did not complete and promulgate *ES* until August 6, 1964.
2. Routhier, "Vatican II," 541.

should still be nourishing us today."³ What he has in mind is "a more adequate reading [that] demands a grasp of the whole, a synthetic approach that highlights the central axes, the load-bearing structures."⁴ He calls for a study of the approach or method with which the Council addresses the questions before it,⁵ "a holistic reading of the council's work rather than remaining at a microanalytic reading of pronouncements."⁶ Regarding this,⁷ the Second Extraordinary Assembly of the Synod of Bishops appears prescient:

> The theological interpretation of the conciliar doctrine must show attention to all the documents, in themselves and in their close inter-relationship, in such a way that the integral meaning of the Council's affirmations—often very complex—might be understood and expressed. Special attention must be paid to the four major Constitutions of the Council, which contain the interpretative key for the other Decrees and Declarations.⁸

Here the Synod is echoing some elements of theological efforts to propose an adequate hermeneutic of the Council.⁹

Despite the fact that Pope Paul proposes *ES* precisely as the kind of framework for the interpretation for which Routhier pleas, as far as I am aware, no serious attention has been given to *ES* as a hermeneutical source in the discussion about interpreting Vatican II. This neglect of *ES* is symptomatic of a more general neglect of the theological thought of Paul VI, as one scholar remarks, "The historical and theological silence about Giovanni Battista Montini/Paul VI . . . is a very clear sign of the theological *Zeitgeist* in the Catholic Church of today."¹⁰ While this is certainly an exaggeration regarding Paul VI and his influence on the Council,

---

3. Routhier, "Vatican II," 540.
4. Routhier, "Vatican II," 541.
5. Routhier, "Vatican II," 542–46.
6. Routhier, "Vatican II," 542.
7. Routhier is not alone in this sentiment. John O'Malley similarly writes of "the big, but altogether common hermeneutic mistake of resting content with examining the documents individually, one by one, and failing the crucial further step of examining them as a single corpus" ("Hermeneutics of Reform," 541).
8. 2nd Extraordinary Assembly of the Synod of Bishops, "The Church," I.5.
9. See, for example, Thils, "En pleine fidélité au concile du Vatican II"; Pottmeyer, "Continuité et innovation dans l'ecclésiologie de Vatican II." On this subject, also see Dupont-Fauville, "Une herméneutique pour Vatican II."
10. Faggioli, "The Future of Vatican II," 272.

and specifically regarding *ES*,[11] the silence is indeed nearly total when it comes to attention given to *ES*, taken as a whole, as a hermeneutical key to Vatican II. The purpose of this study is to make the case that *ES* has an unparalleled contribution to make to an understanding of the Council's central insights, intuitions, "load-bearing structures," and architectonic method. It thereby remediates, if only partially, the silence about Paul VI, while at the same time it contributes to the current discussion about the interpretation of Vatican II.

Paul VI sets forth his vision for a renewal of the Church by articulating the relationships among doctrine, personal and institutional conversion, and mission. The first and third of these—doctrine and related questions regarding doctrinal unity, and mission and related questions regarding its new challenges and methods—have been the subjects of voluminous theological reflection. Equally impressive, quantitatively, is the volume of studies on the institutional reforms initiated by the Council. In contrast, and impressive by reason of the contrast, the decisive role of personal renewal through conversion (*metanoia*) in Pope Paul's synthesis has received comparatively little attention. I am in complete agreement with Fr. John Kobler, who observes that Pope Paul's call for a thoroughgoing moral renewal on the part of the Church's members—a call, it should be observed, that Pope Paul inherited from his predecessor[12]—has been

---

11. See Peri, "Appunti per un'indagine sull'ecclesiologia di Paolo VI"; Camadini, *"Ecclesiam Suam" première lettre encyclique de Paul VI*; Chadwick, "Paul VI and Vatican II"; Chenaux, *Giovanni XXIII e Paolo VI*; Famerée, "XIII International Study Interview"; Barroso, "Ecclesiam suam (1964–2014)."

12. That John XXIII thought of the Council in these terms is evident in his encyclical, *PA*, issued just three months prior to the opening of the first session. And it is of greatest significance that he sees the renewal of Christian life as the prerequisite for the success of the Church's mission: "The salutary results we pray for are these: that the faith, the love, the moral lives of Catholics may be so re-invigorated, so intensified, that all who are at present separated from this Apostolic See may be impelled to strive actively and sincerely for union, and enter the one fold under the one Shepherd" (*PA*, 25); "Renewal of Christian life which is one of the principal aims of the coming Council . . . that we may bring back to him our wayward human race that wanders aimlessly without a guide" (*PA*, 27). One month closer to the Council, Pope John sounds a similar theme, this time strictly linking what in his Opening Address he would call "doctrinal penetration" to a renewal that yields a greater fervor of Christian life. By seeking intimate communion with Jesus in faith, hope, and charity, he states, is the way in which the faithful "make your contribution to the success of the Ecumenical Council, which intends to be a Council of updating [*aggiornamento*] primarily in deeper knowledge and love of the truth revealed in the fervor of religious piety, holiness of life" ("General Audience, August 1, 1962").

largely overlooked in the fifty years since the Council.[13] Indeed, attention to Pope Paul's theme of personal conversion and, therefore, to an essential dimension of Vatican II's renewal, does not appear to be commensurate with the attention paid to other dimensions.[14]

If there is little question that this aspect of Pope Paul's synthesis in *ES* has been nearly completely overlooked by scholars, the same cannot be said about his successors. Indeed, both Pope St. John Paul II and Pope Benedict XVI faithfully follow their predecessor's outline for the renewal of Vatican II. Not only do they place a priority on the call to holiness and the related necessity of conversion, they also explicitly refer to *ES* as their source.

This study intends to address this scholarly neglect of Paul VI and of *ES* as a hermeneutical key, in particular, and to propose that there is no more penetrating, comprehensive, and authoritative text than *ES* as a source for understanding the true spirit of Vatican II and subsequent magisterium. The study will entail a commentary on *ES* and will enlist complementary texts of Paul VI and his successors in order to delineate,

---

13. Kobler, "Introduction to the Thought of Vatican II," 86: "Much of the interpretation of Vatican II in the post-Conciliar era seems to have missed this call to moral greatness. In the Church today, there are endless squabbles about liturgy, feminism, collegiality, celibacy, biblical interpretation, and so on.... Part of this confusion is due to the neglect of the thought of Pope Paul VI."

14. Ormond Rush's contributions to a collection of reflections on Vatican II are perhaps representative. He identifies the spiritual reception of Vatican II for the sake of greater fidelity to the Gospel, that is, to Jesus Christ and the Holy Spirit, which is in essence a response to the call to holiness, as the Council's pastoral goal. He calls this purification. Yet, in the end, his discussion of conversion has less to do with the perfection of charity, which is the Council's definition of holiness and the primary focus of John Paul II, and more to do with the Church's new ecclesiological way of relating to God. His emphasis is on the institutional dimension of conversion. For example, he observes that the Council's teaching on the Holy Spirit is not reflected in the treatment of the governing office in the 1983 *Code of Canon Law*, and that structures of participation are inadequately developed in acknowledgement of the *sensus fidelium*. See Ormond Rush, "Toward a Comprehensive Interpretation of the Council and Its Documents," and Ormond Rush, "Ecclesial Conversion After Vatican II: Renewing the 'Face of the Church' to Reflect 'the Genuine Face of God,'" both in Schultenover, *50 Years On*. While it is certain that the Council initiated a number of institutional changes, it is equally certain that it understood these institutional changes as means to the end of promoting the personal conversion that is a hallmark of taking up the call to holiness. The whole point of Vatican II is to show that the call to holiness, understood as it always has been as participation in divine life of charity, is as actual as ever and that it can be lived out in contemporary cultural contexts.

to clarify, and to develop the principal themes of *ES* and the relationships among them.

THE USE OF POPE PAUL VI'S *ECCLESIAM SUAM* FOR INTERPRETING THE COUNCIL

The turn to *ES* as a hermeneutical key to Vatican II and subsequent magisterium is not the result of a direct, personal discovery. Rather, it is the fruit of having found that it is the central point of reference for Pope John Paul II in his determination to make the interpretation and implementation of Vatican II the defining goal of his pontificate. To accomplish this task, he turns to his predecessor's first encyclical, which, like a road map, provides the essential direction in which the Church must journey in order faithfully to live the graces of the Council. Among his first words, which make known the program of his pontificate,[15] he writes: "Let me refer first of all to this Encyclical and link myself with it in this first document that, so to speak, inaugurates the present pontificate."[16]

This study will show that this initial reference to *ES* by Pope John Paul II is neither isolated nor merely a polite deference to a predecessor. Rather, Pope Paul's encyclical shapes the way that John Paul understands Vatican II, both prior to his election to the See of Peter and throughout his pontificate. Substantiating this and exploring its meaning is one of

15. John Paul refers to his first encyclical as establishing the program of his pontificate in *RMiss*, 4. In doing so, he quotes from *RH*, 14: "the Church's fundamental function in every age, and particularly in ours, is to direct man's gaze, to point the awareness and experience of the whole of humanity toward the mystery of Christ." The program, then, is phrased Christologically. It is clear, however, from the first part of *RH*, that his program is to direct the gaze of men to the mystery of Christ by taking this as the program of Vatican II and by faithfully following the Council's pastoral manner of doing so.

16. John Paul II, *RH*, 3: "Paul VI selected this present-day consciousness of the Church as the first theme in his fundamental Encyclical beginning with the words *Ecclesiam Suam*. Let me refer first of all to this Encyclical and link myself with it in this first document that, so to speak, inaugurates the present pontificate. The Church's consciousness, enlightened and supported by the Holy Spirit and fathoming more and more deeply both her divine mystery and her human mission, and even her human weaknesses—*this consciousness is and must remain the first source of the Church's love, as love in turn helps to strengthen and deepen her consciousness. Paul VI left us a witness of such an extremely acute consciousness of the Church*. Through the many things, often causing suffering, that went to make up his pontificate he taught us intrepid love for the Church, which is, as the Council states, a 'sacrament or sign and means of intimate union with God, and of the unity of all mankind'" (emphasis added).

the principal aims of this study. For John Paul, the three paths of the Church, expounded in *ES*, recapitulate the true spirit of Vatican II. He sees in the Council, inseparable from and as expounded in *ES*, a precious inheritance over which he is called, as Pope Paul's successor, to exercise a responsible stewardship. *ES* delineates the *paths* that the Church must follow in order to be faithful to her Founder and to the mission that he has entrusted to her, that is, in order to live up to her vocation as the Church understands this vocation and presents it in the teaching of Vatican II. John Paul thoroughly makes his own Pope Paul's understanding of the three paths that the Church must trod in order to follow the one and unique Path that the Church must travel in order to renew herself for the missionary tasks awaiting her in the Third Millennium. That Path is better known as the Way, Jesus Christ (John 14:6).

> When we penetrate by means of the continually and rapidly increasing experience of the human family into the mystery of Jesus Christ, we understand with greater clarity that there is at the basis of all these ways that the Church of our time must follow, in accordance with the wisdom of Pope Paul VI (*ES*), one single way: it is the way that has stood the test of centuries and it is also the way of the future. Christ the Lord indicated this way especially, when, as the Council teaches, "by his Incarnation, he, the Son of God, in a certain way *united himself with each man*" (*GS*, 22). The Church therefore sees its fundamental task in enabling that union to be brought about and renewed continually. The Church wishes to serve this single end: that each person may be able to find Christ, in order that Christ may walk with each person the path of life, with the power of the truth about man and the world that is contained in the mystery of the Incarnation and the Redemption and with the power of the love that is radiated by that truth. Against a background of the ever-increasing historical processes, which seem at the present time to have results especially within the spheres of various systems, ideological concepts of the world and regimes, Jesus Christ becomes, in a way, newly present, in spite of all his apparent absences, in spite of all the limitations of the presence and of the institutional activity of the Church. Jesus Christ becomes present with the power of the truth and the love that are expressed in him with unique unrepeatable fullness in spite of the shortness of his life on earth and the even greater shortness of his public activity.

> Jesus Christ is the chief way for the Church. He himself is our way "to the Father's house" (John 14:2) and is the way to each man. On this way leading from Christ to man, on this way on which Christ unites himself with each man, nobody can halt the Church.[17]

John Paul's intense focus on Christ, or his "Christocentrism" is entirely consistent with that of Pope Paul. For example, a similar intensity is evident in the remark by Pope Paul about the unique grace that marks the post-Conciliar period:

> Fidelity to Christ—this is everything. We can only repeat the words of St. Peter, of whom we are the humble but true successor, at whose tomb we now gather: "Lord, to whom shall we go? You have the words of eternal life" (John 6:68–69). Fidelity to Christ—this must be the essence of the post-Conciliar period.[18]

For Pope Paul, *ES* is the mature fruit of years of reflection on the Council, beginning from the time that Pope John declared his intention to convoke it. Germinal versions of some of the themes of *ES* can be detected in his Pastoral Letter to the faithful of the Archdiocese of Milan, for Lent, 1962, and the main themes of *ES* are already manifest as well as in his first address, as pope, to those participating in Vatican II, to open the second session (September 29, 1963). Noteworthy is his emphasis on a renewal for the sake of deepening the Church's relationship with Christ. What, he asks, is the starting point for the path[19] we must follow, and what is our goal? Though in *ES* Pope Paul identifies three paths for the Church, it is clear that in reality there is only one path, and that is Jesus Christ. He is the one, simple answer to the questions about the starting point, path, and goal of Vatican II.

> At this very hour we should proclaim Christ to ourselves and to the world around us; Christ our beginning, Christ our life and our guide, Christ our hope and our end.
>
> O let this council have the full awareness of this relationship between ourselves and the blessed Jesus—a relationship which is at once multiple and unique, fixed and stimulating, mysterious and crystal clear, binding and beatifying—between

---

17. John Paul II, *RH*, 13.
18. Paul VI, "General Audience, July 15, 1970."
19. The Italian uses two words, *camino* and *via*, to which the corresponding Latin words are *iter* and *via*.

> this holy Church which we constitute and Christ from whom we come, by whom we live and toward whom we strive.
>
> Let no other light be shed on this council, but Christ the light of the world! Let no other truth be of interest to our minds, but the words of the Lord, our only master! Let no other aspiration guide us, but the desire to be absolutely faithful to him! Let no other hope sustain us, but the one that, through the mediation of his word, strengthens our pitiful weakness: "And behold I am with you all days, even unto the consummation of the world" (Matt 28:20).[20]

Eleven months later, Pope Paul will make known his definitive synthesis for understanding the renewal of Vatican II in terms of the three paths of renewal expounded in *ES*. This will be equally Christocentric and thereby display a profound continuity with Pope St. John XXIII's Christocentric vision for Vatican II.[21]

This study begins by presenting the evidence that Pope John Paul II, and to a lesser extent Benedict XVI, take *ES* as their guide for interpreting Vatican II. An in-depth analysis of *ES* follows, elucidating each of the three paths of renewal and providing further indications of the Encyclical's influence on Pope Paul's successors, thereby reinforcing its importance for an accurate grasp of these popes' understanding of the renewal of Vatican II and of their own pontificates.

The journey begins along the first path of "doctrinal penetration," as Pope John XXIII described it, regarding the person and teachings of Jesus Christ, especially his union with his Body, the Church and the Church's participation in his mission. Pope Paul's term for describing this first path is "awareness." His conviction is that only a mature doctrinal awareness can provide the necessary foundation for a real transformation in the life of the Church and in the faithful, because only this kind of faith-awareness can produce a personal renewal or *metanoia* that has God's vision for the Church as its objective measure. Naturally, the first path leads to

---

20. Paul VI, "Address for the Opening of Session Two of Vatican II," 5; emphasis added.

21. One month prior to the opening of the Council, John XXIII spoke of the Council in profoundly Christocentric terms: "What, in fact, is an Ecumenical Council if not the Church's renewal of itself in this encounter with the presence of the risen Jesus, the glorious and immortal king, radiating outward from the whole Church, with salvation, with joy, and with splendor for all mankind?" ("Radio Message, September 11, 1962"). It should be noted that this exhibits the same movement from an interior renewal to an exterior witness that characterizes his thought in *PA* (see n12 above).

the second path of conversion, along which Christ's disciples cooperate in their own transformation in order to be more fully conformed to him, participating more fully in his twofold love, for the Father and for men. This ardent participation in Christ's life cannot fail to produce the fruit of a correspondingly ardent participation in his mission: "the internal drive of charity [fruit of the first and second paths] . . . expresses itself in the external gift of charity [third path]" (*ES*, 64). The term Paul uses for this "external gift" or third path is "dialogue." Part I of the study ends with a brief consideration of some of the implications of this analysis, with special emphasis on the order inherent in the paths and the core significance of this order.

Part II shows how the three paths of renewal are evident in other themes found in John XXIII, John Paul II, and Benedict XVI. One theme in particular, fidelity to God and fidelity to man, will be seen as a complementary summary of the three paths found in *ES*. For Pope Paul's successors, fidelity to God conveys the permanence of the Church's identity, based on the unchanging deposit of faith, and fidelity to man conveys the Church's mode of presenting doctrine for the purpose of dialogue with her contemporaries, who are immersed in diverse cultures. This twofold fidelity is another way of conveying what the hermeneutic of reform in continuity means. This is the *aggiornamento* of John XXIII, which, very importantly, he and his successors understand to entail more than the new modes of expression and adaptation of institutions, above all the personal, spiritual updating through conversion for the sake of a full, conscious, and active participation in the mystery of Christ on the part of the faithful. Just as awareness of the place of the Church in God's plan of salvation (first path) leads to conversion into a fuller conformity to God's vision of the Church (second path) and this bears the fruit of participating in a dialogue of salvation with the world (third path), so, too, fidelity to God (corresponding to the first two paths) bears the fruit of fidelity to man through mission (third path). The three paths and the law of twofold fidelity entail a profoundly theological, that is God-centered, vision of ecclesial renewal. Ongoing renewal (reform, conversion, *aggiornamento*) is a law of the Church's life, but this can be separated neither from the doctrine upon which it depends and which gives renewal its objective standards, nor from conversion's fruit of revitalized mission.

Based on the earlier analysis of *ES* and the paths' complementary themes, Part III demonstrates the intimate connection between the three paths of renewal and the Church's life. It thereby shows that Pope Paul's synthesis is less a theological construction and more a theological phenomenology of the Church's life. The three paths of renewal recapitulate and systematize an order or pattern that can be discerned in Scripture and in the Church's life, for example: the faith of Mary at the Annunciation; the order of the Mass; and the catechetical tradition.

Of particular significance is the potential of the three paths of renewal to serve as a hermeneutical key to unlock a deeper understanding of the three dimensions of formation—doctrinal (or intellectual, or theological), spiritual, and pastoral—that the Church invariably proposes for every category of her members, most notably, for priests, deacons, religious, and catechists. Part III does not propose that the threefold structure of programs of formation explicitly takes *ES* as a guide. I am not aware of any evidence that would corroborate such a claim. But it does propose that the logic according to which the three paths of renewal are interlocked elucidates the relations among the three dimensions of formation. In this light, the threefold structure of programs of formation can be taken as an indication of the reception of Vatican II. As far as I am aware, there is no precedent for such a claim.

Finally, the Conclusion indicates the relevance of *ES* for defining the authentic spirit of Vatican II. This Conclusion is followed by a parable which serves as the Epilogue, the chief lesson of which is that for the Church to live up to her vocation to continue Christ's mission as Servant of humanity she must begin by renewing herself.

The comprehensive goal of this study is to demonstrate that *ES* has served as the point of reference for the post-Conciliar popes' understanding of the spirit of Vatican II and their hermeneutic of reform in continuity. For Paul VI and his successors, there can be no authentic reform or renewal unless it is based on divine revelation, and in particular God's vision for the Church (ecclesiology). Nor can a renewal be authentic without conversion and the requisite critical judgment, which necessarily entails a distinction between what is essential and thus necessarily continuous, and what is contingent and subject to change. Finally, in order for a renewal of mission to be authentic, it must be based on fidelity to the content of the Gospel that shows its power through the transformation of the human condition, bearing fruit in witness to its transforming power, and loving dialogue that invites people to leave behind their worldly vision of happiness in order to convert into God's vision of a fully human life by participation in the mystery of Christ.

SEVERAL CLARIFICATIONS

To my knowledge, this is the first and only study on the three paths of the Church in *ES* as a hermeneutical key to Vatican II and the subsequent magisterium. This novelty results in several features to which the reader should be alerted. The first is that, without being able to presuppose a detailed knowledge of *ES*, this study does three things: It introduces the main lines of the thought of Paul VI in *ES*; it presents an in-depth analysis of the ways in which the three paths of renewal interrelate; and it explains the relevance of that analysis for the interpretation of Vatican II by the popes of the Council—Paul VI, John Paul II, and Benedict XVI—and how the three paths of renewal are reflected in the life of the Church. If these three goals were broken into separate works, then an important element of continuity between Conciliar and post-Conciliar magisterium would be lost, and to manifest this continuity is one of the major goals of this study. To pursue these three goals and to maintain this sense of continuity is the first reason for a study that is admittedly lengthy. Further, and similarly at the service of demonstrating this continuity, Parts II and III contain numerous references to and brief summaries of the main lines of thought in *ES* and of the analysis set forth in Part I.

A second feature of the originality of a study seeking to remedy the total neglect of *ES* as a hermeneutical key to Vatican II and post-Conciliar magisterium is the absence of directly relevant scholarly research upon which to draw and with which to dialogue. To be sure, there are numerous works on interpreting Vatican II, but these are related to the thesis of this study only in a general way.[22] In order to avoid distracting the reader from the main points of this study and making it even longer, interaction with other scholarly work on the hermeneutic of Vatican II occurs only when it contributes to the elucidation of those main points or when it is helpful to indicate considerations that are proximately related to them.

A final clarification concerns what might appear as insufficient theological attention to the use of texts drawn upon to support the thesis. Throughout this study there is a constant interaction among numerous authors and texts that are temporally distant from one another and that vary in degrees of theological weight. This is especially conspicuous, for example, when the *Catechism of the Catholic Church* (hereafter, *CCC*) is enlisted in order to summarize important points, to shed further light on

---

22. See, for example, Rush, *Still Interpreting Vatican II*; Routhier, *Vatican II*; Faggioli, *Vatican II*; Faggioli and Vicini, *The Legacy of Vatican II*.

passages of Vatican II, and to demonstrate the Council's genuine, pastoral character (the spirit of Vatican II).[23] The issue of the validity of such an approach also arises when texts of John Paul II and Benedict XVI are similarly enlisted.

Whether this is considered a breach of proper theological methodology or a justifiable procedure will depend on whether the reader subscribes to a hermeneutic of continuity. Just as some see Vatican II as a rupture with a so-called pre-Conciliar Church, so some see the pontificates of the post-Conciliar popes as a rupture with Vatican II. For these, the period from 1978–2013 is a time of repression (and thus regression),[24] if not a betrayal, of what they understand to be the teaching and spirit of Vatican II. On such a view, especially the pontificates of John Paul II and Benedict XVI are seen as impediments to the reception of Vatican II. This study takes them as valuable contributors to that reception and reinforces their value by demonstrating their essential continuity with Paul VI.

As will be set forth in the first chapter, my conviction is that a hermeneutic of continuity is a corollary deriving from faith in the essentially unchanging identity of the apostolic Church. The constancy of this identity is the fruit of the realization of Christ's promise to continue to be with his Church and the guidance of the Holy Spirit, on one hand, and on the other hand it is the fruit of the collaboration of the Church's members as they exercise "reason [in] its sphere of responsibility for acting

---

23. Regarding this, it is significant that John Paul II refers to the *CCC* as the final document of Vatican II ("Address, December 22, 1992," 3) and as the Catechism of Vatican II ("Address, October 11, 2002," 1). John Paul elaborates on the link between the *CCC* and Vatican II in the Apostolic Constitution, *Fidei depositum*, that promulgates the *CCC*. The *CCC* "aims at presenting an organic synthesis of the essential and fundamental contents of Catholic doctrine ... in light of the Second Vatican Council and the whole of the Church's Tradition" (*CCC*, 11).

24. Faggioli writes of a period of thirty years marked by a "theologically activist papacy" that reversed the "victory" of Vatican II's "new definition of the role and theology of bishops in the Church," resulting in a "weakening or destroying [of] a delicate balance of power within the Church" (*A Council for the Global Church*, 93–94). For Faggioli, the resignation of Benedict XVI marks the end of papal guidance regarding the interpretation of Vatican II while the pontificate of Francis marks a relinquishing of interpretation to historians and theologians along with an emphasis on accelerating reception and implementation of the Council. Faggioli interprets this as "not only a new start in the life of the Church along the trajectories drawn by Vatican II," but also "a rediscovery of the profound historical nature of Christianity and of the Catholic Church in particular" (3).

within history,"[25] as this was assigned by the Lord Jesus himself. While it is true that John Paul II and Benedict XVI enjoy a particular authority by reason of their papal office, the continuity between their teaching and the teaching of Vatican II and Pope Paul's vision for Conciliar renewal is readily demonstrable. For them, Vatican II is not a dead letter, but a major milestone along the Church's pilgrimage of faith. They recognize the need constantly to return to the Conciliar corpus[26] in order to guide the Church in a Marian pondering of her own mystery.[27] And this includes

25. Ratzinger, *Jesus of Nazareth*, 1:126.

26. John Paul II was indefatigable in his commitment to implement Vatican II. As archbishop, he wrote *Sources of Renewal: The Implementation of Vatican II* as a handbook to guide the Synod of the Archdiocese of Cracow. As pope, in his first encyclical he takes Vatican II as the great sign of the times indicating the direction in which the Holy Spirit is guiding the Church, and dedicates his pontificate to Conciliar implementation (*RH*, 2–3). Two years later he repeats his commitment: "in the present phase of the Church's history we put before ourselves as our primary task the implementation of the doctrine of the great Council" (*DM*, 1). In 1985, John Paul II convoked an Extraordinary Assembly of the Synod of Bishops in order "to promote knowledge and application of it" (*Fidei depositum*, I). During the Jubilee Year he called for and participated in an assembly to reflect on the status of the reception of Vatican II (see his "Address, February 27, 2000"). An element of the examination of conscience that was central to his preparation for the celebration of the Jubilee of the Year 2000 concerned fidelity in receiving and implementing the Council (see *TMA*, 36). A homily preached during the Jubilee recapitulates his determination to lead the Church in being a good steward of the gift of what the Spirit is saying to the Church through Vatican II: "Thirty-five years after its conclusion, I say: *we must return to the Council.* We must once again take the documents of the Second Vatican Council in hand to rediscover the great wealth of its doctrinal and pastoral motives" ("Homily, November 26, 2000," 3; cf. *NMI*, 2, 39, 44, 55, and especially 55). The day following his election, Benedict XVI discloses his "determination to continue the commitment to implement the Second Vatican Council" because, in his judgment, "the conciliar documents have not lost their current importance; on the contrary, their teachings reveal themselves particularly pertinent in relation to the new needs of the Church and of the present globalized society" ("First Message"). In his well-known Christmas Address of the same year, he indicates that while the Council brought "new thinking" to the perennial problem of "the relationship between the faith of the Church and certain essential elements of modern thought," that new thought is "only roughly traced in the conciliar texts." Nevertheless, "this determined its essential direction, so that the dialogue between reason and faith, particularly important today, found its bearings on the basis of the Second Vatican Council" ("Address, December 22, 2005"). This should make it clear that for John Paul and Benedict Vatican II is not a dead letter and that the Church needs to re-read it in order to apply what it roughly traced to the challenges that the New Evangelization (which according to John Paul II and Benedict XVI, began with Vatican II) faces in differing cultures in the Third Millennium.

27. For John Paul II, Tradition is "the task assumed by the Church of transmitting

being alert to the distinction between what is historically contingent and conditioned in the Conciliar magisterium and what is essential and unchanging with respect to the apostolic deposit of faith.

The conviction here is that the *CCC* and the pontificates of John Paul II and Benedict XVI relate to Vatican II in a manner that is analogous to the way in which the Fathers of the Church relate to divine revelation. I consider John Paul and Benedict to represent the maturing fruit of the Council, and this is the justification for turning to them as authentic interpreters of the teaching and spirit of Vatican II—not to mention the fact that both were active participants in the Council and, as such, are eye-witnesses.[28] With this *apologia* in mind, the reader will, hopefully, understand my decision not to burden the text with details about the differences among texts regarding their nature (addresses, encyclicals,

---

[in Latin, *tradere*] the mystery of Christ and the entirety of his teaching preserved in her memory?" (Wojtyła, *Memory and Identity*, 149). He calls this memory "maternal," thus linking it to Mary, as the Council itself does, by making two references to Mary remembering the events of Jesus's infancy and childhood (see Luke 2:19, 51) in *DV*, 8. While in *Memory and Identity* John Paul emphasizes that the Marian memory of the Church is motivated by maternal love—"The Church is a mother who, like Mary, treasures in her heart the story of her children, making all their problems her own" (Wojtyła, *Memory and Identity*, 151)—and ordered to the mission of the Church— "Mary's memory and the Church's memory enable man to rediscover his true identity at the dawn of a new millennium" (Wojtyła, *Memory and Identity*, 152), in *RMat* the accent is on the confirmation and new light that Mary experiences throughout her pilgrimage of faith. Vatican II was a Marian pondering by the Church of her own mystery, in cooperation with the Holy Spirit, who is the Church's living memory (*CCC*, 1099). This corresponds to the first path of renewal. Like Mary, the Church knows herself as loved by God, having a place and a mission in the economy of salvation, which is to be the servant of the mystery of Christ.

28. It should be admitted that some scholars do not believe that John Paul II is "an authentic interpreter of Vatican II." For example, in *A Council for the Global Church*, Massimo Faggioli declares: "But during the pontificate of John Paul II, a staunch defense of the council in the name of the personal experience of the pontiff as a council father did not exclude a sometimes casual labeling of phenomena, movements, and theological insights as the direct 'fruit of Vatican II,' thus endorsing a kind of Vatican II nominalism coming from John Paul II" (48). In other words, Faggioli believes that Vatican II was simply a label or name that John Paul used to endorse his own agenda. Later, in the same work he returns to this claim: "It is also true that in the post-Vatican II years, there was a tendency to label with Vatican II much or everything that was being enforced in the Church by the magisterium. In other words, a kind of 'Vatican nominalism' was evident, so that at some point, the reference to Vatican II in official magisterial documents became a litmus test and not a real marker of the theological references of that document" (333). In reality, for Faggioli this is a postulate and not something he demonstrates.

apostolic exhortations, etc.) and historical context. In my view, these differences neither eclipse nor attenuate the discernible continuity between Vatican II and the post-Conciliar sources drawn upon in this study. Quite the reverse, they serve to make all the more manifest the essential continuity between Vatican II and the post-Conciliar sources enlisted in this study.

PART I

Ecclesiam Suam: A Path for Vatican II

1

"To Walk according to the Will of Christ"

IN THE FIRST ARTICLES of his first encyclical, John Paul II discloses in very personal terms how he situates his pontificate in historical context. He tells us that he is deeply conscious of having been entrusted with the ministry of St. Peter, and that he will take as the fundamental mission statement of his pontificate the task of implementing the Second Vatican Council. To accomplish this task, he turns to the first encyclical of his predecessor, Paul VI, as the map that provides the essential direction in which the Church must journey in order be a faithful steward of the gift of Vatican II, saying: "Let me refer first of all to this Encyclical [*ES* of Paul VI] and link myself with it in this first document that, so to speak, inaugurates the present pontificate."[1]

As this study will show, this is not an isolated reference to *ES* by John Paul II. In fact, *ES* shapes the way he thinks about Vatican II, from before his election to the See of Peter and throughout his pontificate. Substantiating this will be the task of later chapters. The purpose of this chapter is to provide a first introduction to *ES* and, most importantly, to that which makes this Encyclical so attractive to John Paul II, namely, the three dimensions of renewal that it discusses. For John Paul, these three dimensions express the true spirit of Vatican II and constitute the "path" that the Church must take into the Third Millennium. In addition, by reproducing short summaries of *ES* from John Paul II and Benedict XVI, this first chapter both prepares for the in-depth analysis of *ES* in chapter

---

1. John Paul II, *RH*, 3.

2, and gives an initial indication of the Encyclical's influence on Pope Paul's successors and thus of its importance for an accurate grasp of their understanding of the renewal of Vatican II and their own pontificates.

POPE PAUL INTRODUCES *ECCLESIAM SUAM*

On August 5, 1964, Pope Paul VI announced that he had finally completed his first encyclical and that its official date of promulgation would be the following day, August 6, the Feast of the Transfiguration.[2] He identifies it as an exhortatory encyclical, because its purpose is not to clarify points of doctrine but "to reinforce sentiments and purposes of Christian life in those who receive it, and to strengthen the ties of discipline, union, and fervor, which must inwardly unify the Church and support it in its spiritual mission."[3]

Since the pope is, as Vatican II would declare in its *Dogmatic Constitution on the Church*, "the perpetual and visible principle and foundation of unity of both the bishops and of the faithful,"[4] Pope Paul sets forth in *ES* his feelings and thoughts, his preoccupations and convictions, in order to make these known to his brother bishops and to the faithful. This, he judges, will foster communion in a faith-based vision and attitudes in relation to the Church and in particular in relation to the great ecclesial event that was underway, the Second Vatican Council.[5]

> We say what we think the Church should do today in order to be faithful to her vocation and to be fit for her mission. We speak of the methodology that the Church, in Our view, should follow to

---

2. Santiago Díez Barroso convincingly argues that Paul VI's first encyclical was anticipated by an evident and explicit love for Christ and his Church during his episcopacy in Milan. Three texts that are exemplary of this love were his Pastoral Letter for Lent, *Pensiamo al Concilio*, 1962; his homily for Pentecost, *Amare la Chiesa*, 1962; his homily to priests on Holy Thursday, *Amare Cristo e la Chiesa*, 1963. For more on this precedent, see Barroso, "*Ecclesiam suam* (Part I)," 89–138.

3. Paul VI, "General Audience, August 5, 1964."

4. Vatican II, *LG*, 23.

5. See *ES*, 8: "This encyclical intends neither to claim a solemn and strictly doctrinal function, nor to propose particular moral or social teachings, but merely to communicate a fraternal and informal message. In fact, through this document we wish simply to fulfill our duty of revealing our mind to you in order to impart closer cohesion and deeper joy to that unity in faith and charity which, thank God, binds us together."

journey according to the will of Christ the Lord. We can call this encyclical: the paths of the Church.[6]

The final sentence in the above quotation not only provides a focus for those about to read the text; it also occasions a departure from the custom of naming papal documents. Typically, encyclicals are named by their first two (or three) Latin words, and English translations reflect this. For example, John Paul's encyclical, *Rich in Mercy*, corresponds word for word to the Latin, *Dives in misericordia*. In the case of *ES*, however, Paul VI himself suggests a title that conveys the subject matter of the Encyclical, *Paths of the Church*, even though this does not correspond to the Latin, *Ecclesiam Suam*, which means "His Church." Nevertheless, *Paths of the Church* is the title by which *ES* is most widely known by English readers.

Because Latin is an inflected language, its syntax is highly manipulable. This facilitates the intention to begin official documents with two (or three) words that are chosen, for example, to convey something of the document's subject. By leading with "His Church," Pope Paul introduces a Christocentric, ecclesiological theme from the outset. Whatever else may be said about the Church's mission, it is hers only by participation in Christ's mission.[7] This mission, as will be seen, is properly Christ's, and for this reason it has an objective content and goal that cannot be altered

---

6. Paul VI, "General Audience, August 5, 1964." The Italian of the final phrase here is "le vie della Chiesa." "Vie" is the plural of *la via*, which can mean: way, route, road, street, path, or track. In English translations of later ecclesiastical documents, such as those of John Paul II, which refer to *ES* based on the popular title suggested by Paul VI, the most common rendering is "way" or "path." Because "way" and "path" are not theologically technical terms, readers must be attentive to the context as well as proximate references to *ES* in the texts of John Paul II in order to verify that the presence of "way(s)" or "path(s)" is an intentional reprise of the theme from *ES*.

7. The Council richly develops the concept of participation in *LG*. In teaching that the Church is the messianic people of God (*LG*, 9), it means not only that Christ, the Messiah, founded or established the Church, but also that he continues his threefold mission as Prophet, Priest, and King through the Church. He does this by bestowing on the faithful a participation in his mission and thus in his three messianic offices. Communion with Christ is communion in *his* mission. During the conciliar sessions, drafts of texts included unofficial Latin titles of each article in order to facilitate the location of subjects. The unofficial titles for articles 34–36 on the laity contain the word *participatio*: participation of the lay faithful in the common priesthood; participation of the lay faithful in the prophetic function; participation of the lay faithful in royal dignity. Within the final version of *LG*, key assertions on participation are found in articles 10, 12, 19, and 28.

and that are the criteria for the renewal, conversion, and adaptation that the Council promoted.

English translations of the first sentence of *ES* faithfully convey the intended Christocentricity, but they do not convey the emphasis on the Church in the same way that the Latin does. Pope Paul and the participants in Vatican II engaged in a re-centering on Christ, which would become a principal aspect of the hierarchy of truths. While a Christ-centered presentation of the faith facilitates ecumenical dialogue, this is not the only or even the primary reason for the Council's re-centering on Christ.[8] Its re-centering reflects the fruits of the renewal in biblical and Patristic studies prior to Vatican II. The best way to understand the Church is in light of its place in the plan of God, the divine economy of salvation, which culminates and is recapitulated in the mystery of Christ. To view the Church from the perspective of faith—which is God's own perspective, revealed to us so that we may know in faith what God wishes to make known of his hidden wisdom—is to see that in Christ the Church

---

8. Keeping in mind that the outline of *ES* is already present in the "Address for the Opening of Session Two of Vatican II", what Joseph Ratzinger writes about the impact of this address's Christocentricity is equally applicable to *ES* itself: "What most impressed me was how Christ-centered it was. The words of the liturgy, *Te, Christe, solum novimus* ('Only you, Christ, do we know'), were especially stressed. Reference to Christ as the *only* mediator, as the hope that guides our vision and our work, carried strong conviction. And the pope movingly evoked the painting in the apse of St. Paul Outside-the-Walls. In this mosaic, Christ the Pantocrator stands upright, and prostrate before him is Pope Honorius III, 'small and insignificant, throwing himself down to kiss the feet of Christ, who infinitely surpasses him in greatness. This scene,' the pope went on to say, 'repeats itself here, we believe, not in the manner of artistic representation, but, in reality, here in our gathering.' The ancient mosaic, reflecting as it does early Christian awareness of Christ's primacy, interpreted the present age and, as the pope saw it, served as a yardstick by which to measure events. All human greatness was dwarfed before the vision of the Lord. The pope's address ended on a note that again evoked this theme. *Christus praesideat*, the pope exclaimed: 'May he, the Lord himself, be the real president of this Council'" (Ratzinger, *Theological Highlights of Vatican II*, 40). Ratzinger's attentiveness to Christocentricity is already set forth in the short preface to this work: "This renewal [of Vatican II] has rather a twofold intention. Its point of reference is contemporary man in his reality and in his world, taken as it is. But the measure of the renewal is Christ, as scripture witnesses him. And if the renewal seeks to think through and to speak the Gospel of Christ in a way understandable to contemporary man—i.e., in a contemporary fashion (*aggiornamento* means bringing up to date), then the objective is precisely that Christ may become understood" (2). The lasting impression of the Christocentric nature of *ES* is evident in Pope Benedict's Angelus address, in which he quotes *ES*, 35: "The first benefit which We trust the Church will reap from a deepened self-awareness, is a renewed discovery of its vital bond of union with Christ" ("Angelus, October 2, 2011").

is the goal of God's plan of love. Drawing from witnesses to the Catholic tradition, the *CCC* teaches that "the Church is the goal of all things,"⁹ the realization of the idea that God had in mind even "before the foundation of the world" (Eph 1:4; 1 Pet 1:20). To take Christ seriously is to take seriously his mission and its enduring effect, that is, the Church and the mission that he has entrusted to her.

The English version of *ES* that carries the title, *Paths of the Church*, is not alone. Other translators, for example, who rendered it in Italian and French, were also aware of the General Audience in which Pope Paul himself suggested a title that would convey more than the official Latin title. The salutation of *ES*, in the Latin text and translations faithful to it, includes the theme of "paths" or "ways" and thereby confirms the title that Pope Paul put forth in his General Audience:

> To My Venerable Brethren the Patriarchs, Primates, Archbishops, Bishops, and other Local Ordinaries who are at Peace and Communion with the Apostolic See, to the Clergy and faithful of the entire world, and to all men of good will: On the Paths on which the Church Must Carry Out Its Mission in the Contemporary World.[10]

Like the Second Vatican Council itself, the focus of *ES* is on the revitalization of the Church's mission in the modern world. The paths that it outlines indicate the direction the Church must take in order to fulfill the vocation to extend the mission of Christ into the modern world.

POPE PAUL OUTLINES PATHS OF THE CHURCH

In the same "General Audience, August 5, 1964," Pope Paul follows his suggestion that the Encyclical could be entitled "Paths of the Church" by explaining why this is appropriate. In doing so, he gives a brief summary of the Encyclical.

> We talk about the methodology that the Church . . . must follow in order to walk according to the will of Christ the Lord. We can perhaps entitle this Encyclical: The Paths of the Church. And the paths We indicated are three. The first is spiritual. It

---

9. *CCC*, 760.

10. Among the versions available on the Vatican website, only the Italian and Portuguese include this salutation. The Spanish translation totally obscures the theme of "path" or "way."

concerns the *consciousness* of itself that the Church must have and nourish. The second is moral. It concerns the ascetic, practical, canonical *renewal*, which the Church needs in order to conform to the consciousness just mentioned, in order to be pure, holy, strong, and authentic. The third path is apostolic, and We have designated it with a term in vogue today: *dialogue*. This path concerns the manner, art, and style that the Church must infuse into her ministerial activity to meet the dissonant, changing, diverse voices of the contemporary world. Consciousness, renewal, and dialogue are the paths that today are opened before the living Church, and they form the three chapters of the Encyclical.[11]

Noteworthy in this text are the two "in order to" clauses. These are important indicators regarding how Pope Paul understood the ways in which the three paths of the Church are related to one another. Since this will be the object of a more detailed analysis in a later chapter, here it suffices to indicate that the first path precedes the second path as envisioning a goal or ideal precedes the actions undertaken to realize it. The doctrine of the Church is the objective measure of the renewal that results in the Church conforming more perfectly to that doctrine.

Pope Paul's delineation of the ways in which the three paths of renewal are related systematically orders the desire of John XXIII, whose vision for the Council was that it engage in "a doctrinal penetration and a formation of consciousness in faithful and perfect conformity to the authentic doctrine."[12] As this renewal advances, the Church becomes more fully what she is called to be. Pope Paul conveys this finality of renewal with the four adjectives that convey something of the realized goal. As a

11. Paul VI, "General Audience, August 5, 1964." It could be argued that the three paths were already in his mind while bishop of Milan. Two years prior to his encyclical we hear him anticipating the work of the Council with his faithful in the pastoral letter *Pensiamo al concilio* (English translation mine): "Vale a due che immetterà nella Chiesa nuova coscienza, nuova energia, nuovo impegno, nuova carità. Darà alla Chiesa intima consapevolezza di ciò che essa è e di ciò che essa deve fare; e da questa profonda e interiore impressione essa caverà nuova capacità di espressione: nella predicazione, nell'apostolato, nella testimonianza, nella sofferenza, nella bontà, nell'arte, nella santità" (51) (Moreover, [the Council] will bring into the Church a new consciousness, new energy, new commitment, new charity. It will give the Church intimate awareness of what she is and what she needs to do; and this deep, inner sense will give rise to new means of expression: in preaching, in the apostolate, in testimony, in suffering, in kindness, in art, in holiness.).

12. John XXIII, "Address for the Opening of Vatican II." This address is known by its first three Latin words, *Gaudet Mater Ecclesia*.

result of efforts to conform more fully to God's vision for the Church, she will be pure, holy, strong, and authentic. The apostolic path, dialogue, follows on this even as action is rooted in and follows upon being (*operatio sequitur esse*).

Pope Paul's brief summary of *ES* familiarizes us with the theme of the three paths that he insists the Church "*must* follow in order to walk according to the will of Christ the Lord," the three "ways in which the Church *must* carry out its mission."[13] Reading *ES* with this awareness leads to the discovery of two passages within it that provide very concise summaries of the Encyclical.

> It is truly difficult for us to specify such thoughts, because we ought to derive them from the attentive meditation of the teaching of God . . . always keeping in mind those words of Christ: "My doctrine is not so much mine as that of him who sent Me" (John 7:16). Further, we ought to apply our thoughts to the present situation of the Church at a time when both energy and toil characterize its internal spiritual experience as well as its external apostolic efforts. Finally, we ought not to ignore the contemporary state of humanity in the midst of which our mission is to be accomplished. (*ES*, 12)[14]

The three paths are not mentioned here by the names that are by now familiar. Nevertheless, the realities that these names signify are readily identified. The "doctrine" of Christ, the truth he revealed about the Church, is the essential content of the Church's *consciousness*. The "internal spiritual experience" is the *renewal* by which the Church strives to conform more perfectly to that doctrine. Finally, "external apostolic efforts" and "mission" correspond to *dialogue*.

A second text from *ES* even more incisively sets forth the three paths of the Church, and in the same order, though with a variation in vocabulary.

> She must learn to know herself better, if she wishes to live her own proper vocation and to offer to the world her message of brotherhood and of salvation. (*ES*, 25)

---

13. Paul VI, "General Audience, August 5, 1964"; emphasis added.

14. Because it is generally more accurate than the version available on the Vatican website, the translation used throughout this study traces its roots to the National Catholic Welfare Conference publication in 1964 and can be found at https://www.papalencyclicals.net/Paul06/p6eccles.htm and https://www.newadvent.org/library/docs_pao6es.htm.

Clearly, knowing herself better corresponds to the doctrine of the previous paragraph and to *consciousness*, living her vocation corresponds to internal spiritual experience and *renewal*, and bringing her message to the world corresponds to mission and apostolic efforts, and thus *dialogue*.

It is noteworthy that the order of the three dimensions always remains the same. Also, the first text indicates that the three thoughts or paths are intricately interrelated. A principal goal of this study is to examine the foundations for this order and these interrelationships. The focus here is only to set the stage with a brief examination of the interest of later popes in *ES*.

POPE PAUL VI'S SUCCESSORS LOOK BACK TO *ECCLESIAM SUAM*

At the time of its promulgation, *ES* was largely eclipsed by the proceedings and texts of the Council regarding which *ES* purports to provide a general framework of interpretation. The Council had already concluded two of its four sessions (fall of 1962 and fall of 1963). Nearly one-third of the final documents were either already promulgated or so far along that they would be definitively approved just three months later.[15] In fact, the Council itself refers to the Encyclical only twelve times[16] and never quotes it. In several of these, *ES* is one in a list of several ecclesiastical documents given to show that an assertion has precedents in papal or conciliar teaching. The exceptions are three references to *ES* to identify it as a source for the theme of dialogue. Yet even these do not draw on the Encyclical to support something like a definition or examination of the notion of dialogue; they only alert the reader to the source of the theme.

Taking all this into account, it cannot be said that *ES* had a direct influence of discernible significance on the promulgated texts of the Council.[17] Neither does it appear that post-Conciliar commentators have

---

15. Vatican II's *SC* and *IM* were promulgated before *ES*, on December 4, 1963. *LG*, *UR*, *OE* were promulgated shortly after *ES*, on November 21, 1964. For a more developed discussion of the influence of *ES* on Vatican II, see Evangelista Vilanova's contribution, "The Intercession (1963–1964)" in Alberigo and Komonchak, *History of Vatican II*, 3:448–57.

16. Vatican II, *GS*, 21, 23, 40; *CD*, 13; *PO*, 3, 9; *OT*, 9, 15, 16, 19; *DH*, 11; *GE*, 11.

17. Evidence of indirect influence is seen in the references to *ES* in support of various interventions by the Council Fathers. See, for example, the interventions of Stefan Cardinal Wyszynski (September 16, 1964; *AS* III/1, 441), and José Cardinal Bueno y

looked to *ES* as a source for comprehensive principles for interpreting the Council. The reason is that virtually all of the attention to *ES* has focused on the third path of dialogue. Andrea Riccardi is correct in pointing out, "All too often, the first two parts have been overlooked, thus presenting a reductive, second-hand interpretation."[18] Yet, as he also indicates, the first two paths of *ES* are indispensable, since "without self-awareness and renewal there can be no serious relationship with the world." Indeed, as he insightfully explains, because dialogue with the world presupposes a sense of identity on the part of the Church, which entails awareness of her distinction from the world—as Pope Paul explicitly indicates in *ES*, 58–63—dialogue cannot be effective without this doctrinal awareness. Indeed, from its promulgation until today, the focus of attention to *ES* has been almost exclusively on the third path of dialogue.

Not only did the timing mitigate the influence of *ES* on the Council, but the very nature of the Encyclical also played a role. The general principles or paths of *ES* did not lend themselves to being incorporated, as such, into any one of the particular documents because each dealt with a specific subject matter, not with the Council itself—except for the cursory mention of the Council's goals, which are briefly identified, for example, in *SC*, 1, *PO*, 12, and *LG*, 1.[19] At Vatican II, the Church desired to

---

Monreal (September 29, 1964; *AS* III/III, 11). Ralph Wiltgen mentions these two interventions in *The Rhine Flows into the Tiber*, 154, 174. Other references, culled from the five-volume *History of Vatican II* include: Bishop De Smedt (*AS* IV/V, 104); Cardinal Garrone (*AS* V/I, 553); Bishop Jaeger (*AS* III/III, 195).

18. Riccardi, "40th Anniversary of *Ecclesiam Suam*," 4. One would certainly expect to find evidence of looking to *ES* as a whole from which to derive principles of interpreting Vatican II, as well as references to relevant literature on that subject, in the publication of papers and discussions of an international colloquium on *ES*, sixteen years after its promulgation and fifteen years after the close of the Council. Such an expectation is not met in Camadini, *"Ecclesiam Suam" première lettre encyclique de Paul VI*. The same conclusion results from reviewing the multiple references to *ES* in Dhanis, *Acta Congressus Internationalis de Theologia Concilii Vaticani II*. René Latourelle's article on *ES* confirms this virtually exclusive focus on dialogue when treating *ES*. See *Dictionary of Fundamental Theology* (hereafter *DFT*). Dialogue is the context for half of the thirty plus references to *ES* in volumes III, IV, and V of the *History of Vatican II*. Other references are general in nature or refer to specific themes of *ES*, such as: the ecclesiological emphasis of *ES*; what it says about the relation of pope to bishops (or to the Council); the Church of the poor; re-centering on Christ. In the five volumes of Vorgrimler, *Commentary on the Documents of Vatican II*, twenty-two of the twenty-five references to *ES* are in the context of the theme of dialogue.

19. Summarizing the view of Yves Congar, Vilanova explains the "scant use" of *ES* in the texts of Vatican II by "the fact that the encyclical dealt with the spirit of the

make known to the faithful and to the world how she viewed herself, her mission, and her place in history, especially in relation to the advances in science, contemporary political systems, and other religions.[20] The Council intended to be a pastoral exercise of the magisterium, but it did not tell us precisely what that means, except in *GS*.[21] This is why studies seeking to grasp the pastoral nature of the Council tend to look to sources other than the sixteen promulgated documents.

A comparison with the juridical directives that put order in the Council's proceedings may be helpful. Certainly, the Council needed a set of rules of order in order to conduct its business efficiently and fairly, but its purpose was to set forth the Church's teachings on a number of subjects, not to make known the juridical disciplines that governed it. Similarly, the Council needed a set of overarching, guiding principles to put unity and order in what it taught. At the time of the Council and since, various terms have been enlisted to signify this set of guiding principles, most prominently: the spirit of Vatican II; *aggiornamento*; pastoral council. The selection of the subjects the Council treated and the way in which they were set forth were determined by the prevailing understanding of the Council's spirit, its pastoral character, and the need for *aggiornamento*, so that these are reflected in its documents. Nevertheless, the Council's goal was not to teach about its own spirit but about the subjects that were judged to be of importance at that time.

One might object that the three paths of *ES*, which this study takes as defining the spirit, pastoral character, and *aggiornamento* of Vatican II, are present in the Council's sixteen documents. Indeed, the Council's primary focus was the Church's understanding of herself, that is, the doctrine of the Church and her mission—and this is the first path of *ES*. Equally demonstrable is the presence in the official texts of the themes of renewal (or reform) and dialogue—and these are the second and third

---

Council (the spirit of dialogue and openness to humanity) but did not outline its ecclesiology" ("The Intercession," 454). Similarly, referring to *ES* in relation to *GS*, Vilanova accounts for the fact that "from as early as 1965 the encyclical received hardly any mention in the immense bibliography on the ecclesiology of Vatican II" by referring to the character of *ES*: "This can be explained by the fact that *ES* intended simply to offer a direction, whereas *Gaudium et spes* gave concrete form to the dialogue" (456). An indication of how little attention *ES* has received since Vatican II is the limited number of sources from which Vilanova draws.

20. These are the three broad subjects that Benedict XVI identifies as the focus of Vatican II in his first Christmas address to the Roman Curia (December 22, 2005).

21. See the note accompanying the title of *GS*.

paths of *ES*. So, it would appear, the Council did incorporate the overarching, guiding principles that constitute its spirit, pastoral character, and *aggiornamento*.

The response to this objection takes us to the very heart of the present study. While the presence of the three paths of the Church in the texts of Vatican II can be verified, the ways in which they relate to one another are not. Yet, it is precisely the interrelationships among the three paths that determine the spirit, pastoral character, and *aggiornamento* of Vatican II. It was important, indeed, that those participating in the Council, in keeping with their human dignity, act out of a precise consciousness of the goals and principles that identify Vatican II as the unique and unrepeatable actualization of the Church that it is.[22] Pope Paul's project in *ES* is to provide a framework in light of which the Conciliar participants could engage in their proceedings with this self-awareness, while the purpose of the Council was to act out of this self-awareness in addressing the great issues of the day rather than to consider this self-awareness for its own sake.[23]

The question of the spirit of the Council was posed from its opening as participants sought clarification and direction in their deliberations. After the proceedings of the first and second sessions of 1962 and 1963, and thus by the time that *ES* appeared, this question had been largely settled, more as a working understanding than in precise, theological terms. This does not mean that the *ideas* set forth in *ES* had only a negligible impact on the Council. Well before the *ES* was made public, the main lines of Pope Paul's thought in the Encyclical had already contributed to defining the spirit of the Council. As an influential cardinal, months before the first session, Montini played a significant role in promoting

---

22. Cardinal Wojtyła would make the concepts of self-consciousness, self-determination, and self-realization central to his understanding of the Council. These three properties of the human person as a freely acting subject also characterize corporate acts that engage human freedom and responsibility. With profound perspicacity and incisiveness, Peter Simpson unites these ideas, drawing from Cardinal Wojtyła's exposition of the anthropology of Vatican II in *The Acting Person*, by saying that the Council could be thought of as "The Acting People of God." See Simpson, *On Karol Wojtyła*, 71.

23. Given the inseparability of being and action (*operatio sequitur esse*), the Church's self-consciousness is present in the final documents as the cause is present in its effect. In the synthesis of Wojtyła/John Paul II, this self-consciousness may be understood as the fully internalized spirit of Vatican II.

a comprehensive plan or strategy to order the Council's work.[24] Once elected to succeed Pope John, it was by his very office that he led the Council to its conclusion. Of prime importance is his address to open the second session, in which the main lines of *ES* are already present.[25]

Despite the fact that *ES* was to a certain extent overshadowed by the Council itself, by no means was this Encyclical overlooked by two men who participated in the Council and who would later follow Paul VI in the See of Peter. Both John Paul II and Benedict XVI took it upon themselves to oversee a faithful interpretation and implementation of the Council, and to this end drew attention to *ES* and gave brief summaries of its content.

In an Angelus address on the eve of the new millennium, John Paul II summarized *ES* for the faithful, saying:

> In *Ecclesiam Suam*, this great Pontiff indicated the paths of an inspired ecclesial journey towards the third millennium. The first is a spiritual path and refers to the awareness the Church must have of herself to conform to the vocation entrusted to her by the Redeemer. The second is the moral path and concerns the authentic ascetic, practical and canonical renewal she needs to carry out her mission in the world. The third is the way of the apostolate. For the ecclesial community, the method of dialogue is becoming the way in which to work to bring the Lord's comforting message of salvation everywhere.[26]

This text of John Paul II calls for several comments regarding vocabulary. First, regarding the first way or path, the English version of Pope Paul's general audience (on the Vatican website) translates the Italian, *coscienza*, as "consciousness" while the text of John Paul renders the

---

24. On this, see Suenens, "A Plan for the Whole Council," 88–105. According to Cardinal Suenens, John XXIII solicited the support of other cardinals for the pre-Conciliar outline that he, Suenens, had drawn up at the Pope's request. Essential elements of this plan became fully public through the speeches to the Council Fathers of Cardinals Suenens and Montini on December 4 and 5, 1962. Cardinal Suenens also tells us that a letter Cardinal Montini sent to John XXIII just one week after the opening of the Council contains certain elements of this plan and that these anticipate the themes of *ES* (91).

25. Telling evidence of this is the four-part structure adopted by the editors—Hans Küng, Yves Congar, and Daniel O'Hanlon—of *Council Speeches of Vatican II*. They tell us that this was inspired by Paul VI's opening speech for Session Two. The affinities between this speech of September 29, 1963 and *ES* (August 6, 1964) will be discussed in chapter 2.

26. John Paul II, "Angelus, August 8, 1999."

same word, *coscienza*, as "awareness." "Consciousness" and "awareness" are synonyms, so there is no difference in meaning. This observation is important for those students of Karol Wojtyła/John Paul II, who, while recognizing that "consciousness" links the Polish Pope's thought and writings to the philosophical school of phenomenology, do not see that it also links him in an important, theological way, to Pope Paul VI. It should also be observed that the Italian language does not have two separate words for "conscience" and "consciousness," as English does. The context determines whether *coscienza* should be understood as "consciousness" or "conscience." Pope Paul explicitly recognizes this in *ES* when he distinguishes between "psychological awareness" and "moral conscience" (*ES*, 21).[27]

Theologically, these two terms are quite distinct. Those who read texts closely will come across English translations of texts of Paul VI and John Paul II that render *coscienza* as "conscience" when the context clearly calls for "consciousness." Conscience signifies "a judgment of reason whereby the human person recognizes the moral quality of a concrete act."[28] For Paul VI, an interior dialogue takes place in the conscience. The terms of this dialogue are freedom, good and evil, and thus the relation of considered acts to man's own human nature, to his vocation to find fulfillment in love and ultimately to God, the Author of human nature.[29] Consciousness is "the state of being aware." When Paul VI refers to "psychological awareness," he is not taking psychology to refer to the science of psychology. Rather, he is thinking of the fundamental dynamisms of the soul, the psyche, at work in self-knowledge or self-awareness.

The second consideration relating to vocabulary is the word "renewal." In the summaries of Paul VI and John Paul II, renewal signifies the second path or way that the Church must follow. Some texts, however, refer to the entire three-part process as renewal. So, both the whole

---

27. The same distinction is found in Cardinal Montini's Pastoral Letter for Lent 1962 (*Pensiamo al concilio*), which he dedicated to the subject of the upcoming council. There he writes of "the divine-human consciousness" (*coscienza divino-umana*) of the Church that will be voiced at the Council (n28). Here he refers to the letter to the Churches to announce the decision of the Council of Jerusalem, in which the apostolic Church expresses its faith-awareness of the theandric nature of its action (see Acts 15:28). At another place (n38), he writes of a "universal examination of conscience" (*esame di coscienza universale*) in which all are invited to participate as they prepare for the Council.

28. *CCC*, 1778.

29. See Paul VI, "General Audience, July 12, 1972."

process and one of its parts can be signified by the same name. The goal of Vatican II was to initiate a great renewal in the life of the Church, and all three dimensions or paths outlined by Paul VI contribute to this. It is perhaps an indication of the central importance of the second path that it carries the same name as the entire process.

Third and finally, in discussing the third path, Pope Paul describes it adjectively as "apostolic" and John Paul employs the substantive, "apostolate." Paul VI also employs the term "ministerial activities" to describe the same path. Both popes understand and describe this path in terms that refer to the Church's mission. It should also be observed, however, that Vatican II, the *CCC*, and John Paul II systematically reserve the term "minister" and "ministry" to signify those who are ordained and the activities related to their clerical office. There are a few noteworthy exceptions. For example, husbands and wives are the proper ministers of the sacrament of Matrimony, and certain liturgical functions are properly called ministries and those who perform are properly called ministers. Best known among these are extraordinary ministers of the Eucharist.

Pope Paul does not intend to be restrictive when referring to "ministerial activities." This is clear from the fact that he also uses the more general adjective, "apostolic," when discussing the third path of the Church, that is, dialogue. He clearly intends to include all aspects of the Church's mission. For this reason, readers will encounter a rich variety in the vocabulary employed in the discussion of the third path: mission, ministry, service, apostolate, and pastoral activity. "Dialogue" refers to the manner in which the Church's mission—and thus all of the ways in which it is realized—is carried out.[30] John Paul calls it the "method of dialogue," while Paul refers to it as the "manner, art, and style" in which the Church conducts her mission.

The second text adduced to demonstrate the conviction of Pope Paul's successors regarding the enduring relevance of the three paths of *ES* for a theological understanding of the renewal of Vatican II comes from Benedict XVI.

> With that first Encyclical the Pontiff sought to explain to all the Church's importance for humanity's salvation and, at the same time, the need to establish a relationship based on mutual knowledge and love between the ecclesial community and

---

30. In chapter 5 it will become clear that Paul VI develops a genuinely theological understanding of "dialogue" that is much richer than the common understanding of the term.

society.... "Consciousness,"[31] "renewal," "dialogue"; these were the three words that Paul VI chose to express his principal "thoughts,"[32] as he himself describes them, at the beginning of his Petrine ministry, and all three concern the Church. First of all comes the need for her to increase her self-awareness: of her origins, nature, mission and final destiny; secondly, comes her need to renew herself, to cleanse herself by looking at her model, Christ. Lastly there is the problem of establishing relations with the modern world.... Dear friends... how can we fail to see that the question of the Church, of her necessity in the plan of salvation and of her relationship with the world, still remains absolutely central today? And, indeed, that the developments of secularization and globalization have made it even more essential, in the confrontation on the one hand with the disregard for God and on the other with the non-Christian religions? Pope Montini's reflection on the Church is more relevant than ever.[33]

This paragraph identifies the historical and theological context of *ES*. It thus situates the three paths of the Church in relation to Vatican II and its all-embracing goal, namely, to revitalize the Church's mission to make her a more effective instrument through which the mission of Christ continues in the modern world. The Second Vatican Council was the occasion for the Church to become more profoundly conscious of her vocation to serve mankind by responding to the need of all men and women for Christ.

The preoccupation with effective mission is a manifestation of what the Council called pastoral charity.[34] Without using that term, Pope Benedict nonetheless draws our attention to Pope Paul's interior motives, with a strongly Christocentric missionary motif.

---

31. The English translation on the Vatican website has "conscience" here.

32. The English translation of Benedict XVI's homily on the Vatican website has "policies" here. The Italian is "*pensieri*," as in the Italian of *ES*. The Latin version of *ES* has "*consilia*."

33. Benedict XVI, "Homily, November 8, 2009."

34. In the documents of Vatican II, "pastoral charity" signifies the interior motivation for the ministry of those who are ordained. See *LG*, 41; *PO*, 14–17. The more general expression, "soul of the apostolate" (see *LG*, 33; *AA*, 3), signifies the charity that impels all the Church's members actively to fulfill their vocations as a way to exercise responsibility for and to foster the Church's mission. When speaking of the spirit of Vatican II and taking "spirit" as a synonym for "soul," charity is the spirit, that is, the life-giving, animating force of Vatican II and for the Church's mission, as it is for the Church of all times.

In all the seasons of his life, from the early years of his priesthood until his pontificate, Giovanni Battista Montini had particularly at heart the Church's encounter and dialogue with mankind in our time. He dedicated all his energy to serving a Church that would conform as closely as possible to her Lord Jesus Christ, so that in encountering her contemporaries, men and women, she might encounter him, Christ, because their need for him is absolute. This was the basic desire of the Second Vatican Council, to which Paul VI's reflection on the Church corresponds. He wanted to expound programmatically on some of her salient points in his first Encyclical, *Ecclesiam Suam* of 6 August 1964, at a time when the conciliar Constitutions *Lumen gentium* and *Gaudium et spes* had not yet been written.[35]

Love for Christ and for the Church are inseparable from love for mankind, and this gives rise to a solicitude to see the Church's mission be as efficacious as possible. Similarly, John Paul II praises Pope Paul for his love for the Church and his concern to reinvigorate the Church's mission: "A strong and mild Apostle, Paul VI loved the Church and worked for her unity and to intensify missionary action."[36]

ECCLESIAM SUAM AND THE SPIRIT OF VATICAN II

In themselves, the summaries of *ES* by John Paul II and Benedict XVI are nothing more than a paraphrase of Pope Paul's own summary in his General Audience of August 5, 1964. Their value resides not in any new light that they shed on the three paths the Church must take in order to renew herself for the sake of more effective mission, but in the witness they give to the conviction of Pope Paul's successors regarding the enduring importance of *ES* for a correct understanding of Vatican II.

For Popes John Paul II and Benedict XVI, Paul VI personified the spirit of Vatican II, and more than any other document, *ES* is a theological conceptualization of this spirit. If the Angelus address of John Paul II and the homily of Benedict XVI are not a directive to turn to *ES* as an interpretive key for understanding Vatican II and the Church's mission in the context of the secularization that characterizes much of contemporary culture, they are at least an endorsement of the Encyclical as a source of wisdom regarding the renewal of Vatican II and the vocation

---

35. Benedict XVI, "Homily, November 8, 2009."
36. John Paul II, "General Audience, June 25, 2003," 3.

and mission of the Church in our age. Together, these texts constitute an invitation to study *ES* in order better to grasp the vision of Paul VI for the renewal of the Church undertaken by Vatican II and the revitalization of her mission—what John Paul II would popularize as the New Evangelization—in the context of the challenges the Church faces in the modern world.

For Pope John Paul, *ES* does more than just expound the spirit of Vatican II; it is an interpretive key to his understanding of Vatican II and of his own pontificate. Positively, John Paul's concern is to respond with appropriate responsibility to the gift of the Council, a gift from the Holy Spirit who, through the Council, continues to speak to the Church.[37] Negatively, his insistence on the proper interpretation of Vatican II was occasioned, at least in part, by a concern that a partial or unilateral reading of the conciliar texts and a failure to grasp them as a unified whole continued to produce interpretations that were opposed to the Council's letter and spirit.[38] What is needed might be called a hermeneutic of integrity or totality, according to which individual documents and passages within them are not isolated from the whole comprised by all the documents and unified by the stated goals of the Council.[39] *ES* provides the principles for precisely such a hermeneutic.

Here we can see a parallel between what Vatican II teaches regarding the interpretation of Scripture and the challenge of interpreting the

---

37. "The Second Vatican Council has been a gift of the Spirit to his Church" ("Address, February 27, 2000," 1). "We can say that in its rich variety of teaching the Second Vatican Council contains precisely all that 'the Spirit says to the Churches' (cf. Rev. 2:29; 3:6; 13:22) with regard to the present phase of the history of salvation" (*DeV*, 26).

38. See the Final Report of the 2nd Extraordinary Assembly of the Synod of Bishops, which identifies a partial or selective reading of the texts as a cause of inadequate interpretations. John Paul returned to this during the Jubilee Year 2000: "the genuine intention of the Council Fathers must not be lost: indeed, it must be recovered by *overcoming biased and partial interpretations* which have prevented the newness of the Council's Magisterium from being expressed as well as possible" (John Paul II, "Address, February 27, 2000," 4). He could also speak of "unilateral interpretations" ("Address, May 22, 1992," 3; see also "Address, October 9, 1998," 3). In the same vein, see Benedict XVI, "Homily, June 7, 2012."

39. The four main goals of Vatican II are identified in the first sentence of the first document approved by the Council and promulgated by Paul VI, *Sacrosanctum Concilium*: "This sacred Council has several aims in view: it desires to impart an ever increasing vigor to the Christian life of the faithful; to adapt more suitably to the needs of our own times those institutions which are subject to change; to foster whatever can promote union among all who believe in Christ; to strengthen whatever can help to call the whole of mankind into the household of the Church."

Council itself. Scripture, the Council's *Dogmatic Constitution on Divine Revelation* tells us, "must be read and interpreted in the same Spirit in which it was written."[40] The significance of this reference to the Holy Spirit[41] lies in four assertions that *DV* makes about the activity of the Holy Spirit, who "constantly brings faith to completion by his gifts,"[42] and the relevance of each of these for interpreting texts of Scripture. The first is that because the Holy Spirit has inspired "the books of both the Old and New Testaments in their entirety, with all their parts,"[43] "attention must be given to the content and unity of the whole of Scripture if the meaning of the sacred texts is to be correctly worked out."[44] Second, the nature of the Spirit's graces of inspiration is such that he makes use of the human authors' powers and abilities, which are historically and culturally conditioned. Consequently, the interpreter seeks to ascertain the human authors' intended meaning through understanding the literary forms employed and the "styles of feeling, speaking and narrating which prevailed at the time of the sacred writer."[45] Third, the Holy Spirit guides the whole Church in the development of the Apostolic tradition,[46] so that the Church's life becomes a commentary on how she understands the Scriptures. Fourth, the Holy Spirit assists those entrusted with the task of "authentically interpreting the word of God" for the Church.[47] A thorough investigation into the meaning of a biblical text, then, will take all of these into account.

An important fifth aspect of reading Scripture in the same Spirit in which it was written is the implication this has for the disposition of the one seeking to know what God has revealed. Pope Benedict XVI puts it this way: "holiness in the Church constitutes an interpretation of Scripture which cannot be overlooked. The Holy Spirit who inspired the sacred authors is the same Spirit who impels the saints to offer their lives for

---

40. Vatican II, *DV*, 12.

41. Readers should be attentive to a serious flaw in the English translation on the Vatican website of the first clause of the first sentence of *DV*, 12. Inexplicably, it has "sacred spirit" where the original Latin and faithful renderings in other languages read "same Spirit."

42. Vatican II, *DV*, 5.

43. Vatican II, *DV*, 11.

44. Vatican II, *DV*, 12.

45. Vatican II, *DV*, 12.

46. See Vatican II, *DV*, 8.

47. Vatican II, *DV*, 10.

the Gospel. In striving to learn from their example, we set out on the sure way towards a living and effective hermeneutic of the Word of God."[48]

All five of these principles of interpretation of Scripture are applicable to the interpretation of Vatican II. The application of the first entails reading the conciliar documents as a whole. Above all, this means keeping in mind that all of the texts are united by a common goal, which could be summed up as renewal *ad intra* (interior) for the sake of reinvigorated mission *ad extra* (exterior). The second necessitates research into the sources that have the potential of shedding light on what the authors of the final texts intended to communicate. Among these sources, the *Acta Synodalia* carry the greatest weight.[49] The applicability of the fourth principle is obvious, though it should be restated that because of the architectonic nature of *ES* the Encyclical did not lend itself to being a source of authoritative papal teaching on particular doctrinal subjects. Pope Paul was explicit in avoiding doctrinal, moral or social pronouncements in *ES*, and he tells us the reason: he does not want to restrain the deliberations of the Council on particular subjects.[50]

The third and fifth principles are the most significant for this study. Their relevance will become clear through an analysis of *ES* in the following chapters, and in the elaboration of conclusions in a later chapter. This analysis and the conclusions will focus especially on *the order* of the three paths of renewal—doctrinal awareness, spiritual renewal through conversion, mission through dialogue—and the ways in which these three paths relate to one another. The contention of this study is that Pope Paul identifies what could be called a threefold logic or law of the Church's life, the way she receives, understands, and lives the revelation of God's love in Jesus Christ, and that this is what gives *ES* its enduring relevance.

Although Pope Paul's successors do not put it precisely this way, *ES* may be viewed as embodying the essentials of the spirit of Vatican II as a pastoral council. It thus provides the key to a proper interpretation of the event of Vatican II, the Conciliar magisterium, and the New Evangelization championed by Pope John Paul II. Given its key role for interpreting these different events, it will prove useful to look more closely at the encyclical.

---

48. Benedict XVI, *VD*, 49.

49. Archbishop Marchetto makes this point on several occasions in his reviews of literature on Vatican II. See Marchetto, *The Second Vatican Ecumenical Council*.

50. See Paul VI, *ES*, 6–7.

2

Ecclesiam Suam: Prolegomena to an Analysis

SOMETHING OF THE SPIRIT and content of *ES* can be discovered by attending to what Pope Paul says about his first encyclical being a disclosure of three thoughts that preoccupied him at the time of composing it, and by attending to what he means when he writes of "methods" in relation to the revitalization of the Church's mission through dialogue. Before embarking on a close analysis of the three paths that Pope Paul proposes, it will be beneficial to draw attention to certain key terms, and the method and focus at work in Pope Paul's thought. These preliminary remarks and distinctions help to create a profitable disposition for better understanding Paul's thought on the paths of the Church and the ways in which the three paths of the Church relate to one another.

POPE PAUL DISCLOSES HIS THOUGHTS

Pope Paul tells us that the purpose of *ES* is "to communicate . . . some of the dominant thoughts in our heart which seem useful as practical guidelines at the beginning of our service as Pope" (*ES*, 4).

The Latin for "thoughts" is *consilia*, from *consilium*, which can have a range of meanings: consideration, thought, counsel, determination, plan, design, deliberation, advice. With the nuance of looking ahead to some action, it can mean purpose or intention. A word that combines both the intellectual and the volitional elements is "strategy." A thought of this kind is ordered to action; it is a plan of action. Given the personal tone and style of *ES*, "preoccupation" conveys something of Pope Paul's sense of the weightiness of his subject. All of this is congruent with the context of the Second Vatican Council. Not only is this an ecclesial event of great importance. As a pastoral council, Vatican II's concern is with a plan for renewal for the sake of reinvigorating the Church's mission in the modern world. The purpose of the Council is to construct a strategy aimed at making the Church's mission more effective, and to do so by deriving that strategy from the doctrine about the Church, that is, from what God has revealed about the Church's nature, vocation, and mission.

One of the best ways to decipher what Pope Paul means by referring to his *consilia* is to consult the Vulgate, the standard Latin version of the Bible that his generation read and studied, and which provides his foundational theological vocabulary. God directs history and fulfills his promises by assuring the realization of his eternal plan or purpose, his *consilia* (see Acts 2:23; 20:27; Eph 1:11).[1] Men also conceive plans to direct their activities, in which case there is nothing essentially theological about the term. As beings endowed with reason and freedom, it is natural for men to project their vision for the future, whether short or long term, into their actions. The fruit of deliberation is a plan of action, an internal blue print of what one intends to do. Whether the designs of men be wise and prudent or foolish and vicious is determined ultimately by their concordance with God's own thoughts and designs.

ES speaks of God's plan(s) or dispensation several times.[2] That three of these come in the prologue and first part on consciousness is no accident. Pope Paul's intention is to set forth his own thoughts in a genuinely theological perspective. "Theological" can mean "of or pertaining to the science of theology," or, it can mean "God-centered." This latter sense is in play when speaking of faith, hope, and charity as the three theological virtues. Certainly, because in writing *ES* Pope Paul draws from the theology he studied throughout his life, it bears the marks of this theology and is therefore theological in the first sense. Since, however, theology is faith seeking understanding, it must always be theological in the primary sense of God-centered. *ES* is the fruit of Pope Paul's living faith reflecting

---

1. See also Pss 32:11; 105:13; 107:11.
2. See Paul VI, *ES*, 2, 9, 18, and 56.

on the *consilia Dei*, the thoughts, plans, or dispositions of divine wisdom regarding the Church.³

Pope Paul's intention, then, is that his three *consilia*, corresponding to the three paths the Church must follow at the Second Vatican Council, conform to, contain, and convey the *consilia* of God regarding the Church's mystery, vocation, renewal, and mission. He clearly and concisely conveys this in his Pastoral Letter for Lent 1962, in which he writes of the "divine-human consciousness" that as never before will express itself in the Council.

ECCLESIAM SUAM AND METHODOLOGY

The preceding consideration of Pope Paul's fidelity to the *consilia Dei* is important because one of the methodologies that he employs in *ES* is to employ vocabulary that will resonate in the minds of modern men. The two most conspicuous examples of this are his use of "consciousness" or "awareness" and "dialogue." His own standard of fidelity to the *consilia Dei*, which concretely means fidelity to the entire Catholic Tradition, requires on the part of anyone reading *ES* a presumption of continuity between these and what he writes. The same is true of Vatican II.

The term, "methodology," occurs once in *ES*, while "method" occurs five times.⁴ The contexts indicate that Pope Paul uses this term in one of two senses. One takes method to signify a step-by-step, practical set of guidelines. These are so many strategies to guide the Church's pastoral charity in the exercise of her mission. This concerns general principles of pastoral wisdom derived from experience, so that one may speak of concrete methods of preaching, pastoral care for the elderly, etc. This sense of "method" is especially evident in the third part on dialogue, and this is confirmed by what he says in his general audience introducing *ES* to the Church. Under the heading of dialogue he has in mind what

---

3. This is precisely what Paul VI says about his predecessor, John XXIII, referring to the latter's decision to convoke Vatican II as "doubtless under divine inspiration" and "as if by divining heavenly counsels [*consilia*]" ("Address for the Opening of Session Two of Vatican II").

4. In the version used for this study, the term "methodological" occurs in *ES*, 17 (*ES*, 18 in the Italian version). "Method" occurs five times in the Italian (*ES*, 12, 56, 68, 95, 110). The English articles corresponding to these are: *ES*, 11, 54, 66, 91, 106. The English renders the Italian or Latin as "method" in *ES*, 41 (Latin: *disciplina*; Italian: *scuola*), 67 (Latin: *vias/rationes*; Italian: *stile* or *indirizzo*), 81 (Latin: *ratio*; Italian: *modo/modi*).

"concerns the manner, art, and style that the Church must infuse into her ministerial activity to meet the dissonant, changing, diverse voices of the contemporary world."[5]

The second sense of "method" or "methodology" refers to more general implications of overarching theological principles for the life of the Church, and in particular for the renewal of Vatican II. Pope Paul employs "method" in this theological sense when he informs readers of *ES* that he is writing of the Church's duty "to find the method to achieve wisely so sweeping a renovation" (*ES*, 11)[6] undertaken by Vatican II. He also alerts readers that in this Encyclical he limits himself "to some methodological considerations concerning the life of the Church" (*ES*, 17). This is the meaning of "method" that is most important for this study, which has as its goal precisely to identify and to analyze the methodology of renewal for the sake of reinvigorating the Church's mission in the modern world. Before examining this method, it will be helpful to indicate the principal sources drawn upon here in order to elucidate Pope Paul's thought.

SOURCES FOR THIS STUDY

There are two categories of sources from which to draw in order to grasp Pope Paul's thinking on the three paths set forth in *ES*. The first is comprised of those that are historically proximate to *ES*. Above all is the Encyclical itself, and within it one can distinguish the introductory summary (articles nine through fourteen) from the rest of *ES*, which develops each of the paths in greater depth. Other proximate sources include Pope Paul's addresses for the opening and closing of the second, third, and fourth sessions of the Council. Pope Paul himself indicates, for example, that his address for the opening of session two may be considered a verbal and in-person presentation of the main lines of thought of *ES*.[7]

---

5. Paul VI, "General Audience, August 5, 1964."

6. The English version here reads "way" rather than "method."

7. "It had been our intention, as hallowed custom prescribes for us, to send to all of you our first encyclical letter. But why, we ask ourself, entrust to writing that which, by a singular and happy opportunity—that is, by means of this ecumenical council—we are able to declare by word of mouth? Certainly we cannot now say by word of mouth all that we have in our heart and all that more easily could be poured forth in writing. But for this time let this present address be a prelude not only to the council, but also to our pontificate. Let the living word take the place of the encyclical letter, which, if

Though the address for the closing of the Council does not display so clearly the theme of the three paths of the Church, nevertheless it reflects the threefold plan of renewal while expressing in the clearest terms possible what Pope Paul understood to be the animating spirit of Vatican II. The second category of sources includes numerous post-Conciliar documents, audiences, homilies, and speeches of Pope Paul that take up the themes related to the renewal of Vatican II.

The following summary and analysis of *ES* will draw on all of these sources. The attention is not on the chronological development of Pope Paul's thinking, but on what is essential to his understanding of the three paths of renewal. If it is possible to detect some variation in vocabulary, images, or emphasis with respect to one or another of his major lines of thought, this is an indication of the richness and depth of the mystery upon which he is reflecting, not of a significant theological development. Drawing on all of these sources, it is hoped that the following summary and analysis will serve to bring that richness and depth to light.

These sources disclose Pope Paul's "thoughts" on the three dimensions of renewal prior to, during, and after the Council, and the "method" he used to convey them. Equipped with these preliminary considerations, we can now turn to Pope Paul's principal focus.

Christ, the Hermeneutical Key

Article five of *ES* reinforces the preceding consideration of Pope Paul's desire to align his *consilia* with the divine *consilia*. It contains a kind of summary of the Encyclical, with a strongly Christocentric focus that leads from Christ to the Church. Pope Montini turns to a text of John's Gospel in which Jesus discloses his internal disposition in relation both to the truth that he has come to reveal and to his heavenly Father.[8] Jesus acknowledges that the Father is the source of his teaching and that he must be faithful to his Father by being faithful to the truth received from him. Pope Paul adopts this disposition that is simultaneously one of

---

it please God, we hope to address to you once these toilsome days are past" (Paul VI, "Address for the Opening of Session Two of Vatican II").

8. In his first encyclical, John Paul II gives this disposition of Christ a name: a sense of responsibility for the truth. *ES*, 5 may be the source of inspiration for this theme's presence in John Paul's inaugural encyclical and thus an indicator of the continuity between the two pontificates. See *RH*, 4, 12, 13, and 19. In *RH*, 4 and 19, he quotes the parallel passage of John 14:24; in *RH*, 12, he quotes John 7:16.

indebtedness, humility, and fidelity, stating that his three thoughts derive from a divine source, "the teaching of God," and that his concern is to be faithful to that source.

> It is truly difficult for us to specify such thoughts, because we ought to derive them from the attentive meditation on the divine teaching, . . . always keeping in mind those words of Christ: "My teaching is not mine but his who sent me" (John 7:16).[9] Further, we ought to apply our thoughts to the present situation of the Church at a time when both energy and toil characterize its internal spiritual experience as well as its external apostolic efforts. Finally, we ought not to ignore the contemporary state of humanity in the midst of which our mission is to be accomplished. (*ES*, 5)

Pope Paul's three thoughts, his *consilia*, are oriented first to Christ as the source of divine teaching, then to the Church's interior life of communion in the life of Christ, and finally to participation in Christ's mission in historical context.[10] For, the whole endeavor of Vatican II is premised on the Council being a guide for "everyone who wishes to be a docile follower of Christ" (*ES*, 9). As the opening line of *ES* indicates, in every way the Church is Christ's; it is his Church—*Ecclesiam Suam*.

Pope Paul's opening address for session two of the Council contains a similar Christological trilogy:

> These three very simple and at the same time very important questions have, as we well know, only one answer, namely that here and at this very hour we should proclaim Christ to ourselves and to the world around us; Christ our beginning, Christ our life and our guide, Christ our hope and our end.[11]

---

9. This translation of John 7:16 amends that found in the English text of *ES*.

10. A strikingly similar personal disclosure about his thoughts being directed to Christ comes early in John Paul II's first encyclical: "THE REDEEMER OF MAN, Jesus Christ, is the center of the universe and of history. To him go my thoughts and my heart in this solemn moment" (*RH*, 1). "It was to Christ the Redeemer that my feelings and my thoughts were directed on 16 October of last year, when, after the canonical election, I was asked: 'Do you accept?'" (*RH*, 2).

11. Paul VI, "Address for the Opening of Session Two of Vatican II."

Christ, the Source of Truth about the Church

Repeatedly, Pope Paul qualifies that the content of the Church's consciousness regarding her own mystery comes from what Christ has revealed. He refers to "the ideal image of the Church just as Christ sees it, wills it, and loves it" (*ES*, 10). The disposition that gives rise to the desire for renewal is "the desire to see the Church of God become what Christ wants her to be, one, holy, and entirely dedicated to the pursuit of perfection to which she is effectively called" (*ES*, 41). This disposition entails "a stronger determination to preserve the characteristic features which Christ has impressed on the Church" (*ES*, 47).

The revealed truth about the Church is that she is a mystery by reason of her indefectible bond with Christ. To say "Church" is to say "Christ," and vice versa. Twenty years after the Council, the Extraordinary Synod of 1985, called by John Paul II to engage in an act of ecclesial consciousness about the reception and implementation of Vatican II, incisively summed up the Council's Christocentric ecclesiology:

> The Church makes herself more credible if she speaks less of herself and ever more preaches Christ crucified (cf. 1 Cor 2:2) and witnesses with her own life.... The whole importance of the Church derives from her connection with Christ.[12]

Pope Paul is no less emphatic when he writes, "the first fruit of the deepened consciousness of the Church regarding herself is a renewed discovery of her vital bond with Christ" (*ES*, 37).[13] In the end, the renewal of Vatican II is rooted in a profound awareness that the Church "needs to experience Christ in herself" (*ES*, 25). With solicitude regarding the encroachment on the Church's members of the values of an increasingly secular society, Pope Paul states, "it seems to us that to check the oppressive and complex danger coming from many sides, a good and obvious remedy is for the Church to deepen her awareness of what she really is according to the Mind of Christ" (*ES*, 26).

The whole purpose of the act of ecclesial consciousness is to "put on Christ" (Gal 3:27; cf. Rom 13:14), and in particular to put on "the mind of Christ" (1 Cor 2:16) regarding the Church.

---

12. 2nd Extraordinary Assembly of the Synod of Bishops, "The Church," II.A.2.

13. This translation follows the Italian and Latin more closely than the English version used in this study.

Christ, the Source of Renewal within the Church

The goal of renewal through conversion is to "render [the Church's] following of Christ more genuine" (*ES*, 51). This is essentially a moral issue, which Pope Paul calls "the great moral problem which is uppermost in the life of the Church, a problem which reveals what she is, stimulates her, accuses her, and sustains her" (*ES*, 41). It is rooted in "the desire to see the Church of God become what Christ wants her to be, one, holy, and entirely dedicated to the pursuit of perfection to which she is effectively called" (*ES*, 41). Because "Jesus Christ himself call[ed] for the Kingdom of God to be received interiorly . . . his whole pedagogy [is] an exhortation, and initiation to the interior life" (*ES*, 21).

The goal of this renewal is that "the presence of Christ, his very life will become operative in each one and in the whole of the Mystical Body by reason of the working of a living and life-giving faith" (*ES*, 36). Put another way, the goal of the renewal is a reawakening of the life of Christ in the Church's members, and this "for acquiring that sanctity which Christ teaches" (*ES*, 41).

Christ, the Source of the Church's Mission within the World

A foundational truth about the Church is that it is "the Divine Institution by which Christ continues his work of salvation in the world" (*ES*, 30). For those with "the desire to see the Church of God become what Christ wants her to be," Christ's missionary mandate cannot remain some merely factual datum known about the Church. This desire gives rise to a sense of duty: "The duty consonant with the patrimony received from Christ is that of spreading, offering, announcing it to others. Well do we know that 'going, therefore, make disciples of all nations' (Matt 28:19) is the last command of Christ to his Apostles" (*ES*, 64). By the act of ecclesial consciousness this truth is more penetratingly known. Then, it becomes a criterion for ecclesial examination of conscience and conversion. Finally, it becomes more fully lived as the Church engages in a mission of dialogue, which is nothing other than the continuation in the modern world of the "conversation of Christ among men" (*ES*, 70). The goal of this "mission is none other than making men brothers by virtue of the kingdom of justice and peace inaugurated by Christ's coming into the world" (*ES*, 16). Since he is that kingdom, the mission is to "invite all men to make a living, profound and conscious act of faith in Jesus Christ Our Lord" (*ES*, 23).

The nature of the spiritual renewal, which is the center of Pope Paul's vision for Vatican II, is such that its fruit is a more perfect participation in the life of Christ. "Only the man who is completely faithful to the teaching of Christ can be an apostle" (*ES*, 88). As a result, the mission must be conducted "according to the example and commandment that Christ left to us" (*ES*, 87), that is, in a spirit of Christ-like service. Pope Paul identifies other qualities of Christ's life and mission that will become qualities of the Church's life and mission as her members follow him more closely. She must make her own Christ's spirit of poverty (*ES*, 54), charity (*ES*, 56), obedience (*ES*, 51, 114), and humility (*ES*, 81).

The teaching of Christ that will be the main subject of *ES* is the doctrine of the Church. Pope Paul's goal is not to define doctrine as past councils have. Rather, presupposing that heritage of doctrinal clarification, his goal is to highlight the implications of doctrine for the Church's "internal spiritual experience as well as its external apostolic efforts" (*ES*, 5). Here we encounter the duality of *ad intra* and *ad extra* that is at the heart of the self-consciousness of Vatican II.[14] Clearly, "internal spiritual experience" corresponds to the second path of renewal through conversion, and "external apostolic efforts" corresponds to the third path of mission through dialogue. Just as clearly, and of foundational importance for this study, the same thoughts that constitute the Church's self-consciousness carry over into and govern the second path of renewal and the third path of mission.

ES considers the same doctrinal truth, the doctrine of the Church, from three perspectives. First, in relation to God, the Church can and must say with Christ, "My teaching is not my own." The key theme here is fidelity and accuracy in thinking about the Church within God's plan for man, so that the *consilia* of men correspond to the *consilia* of God. Second, this teaching is the content of the Church's internal spiritual experience. It defines the Church for herself, and it constitutes the objective measure of her efforts to conform to the vocation she has received from God. The

---

14. The *ad intra/ad extra* duality became a helpful way for the Council Fathers to understand their work. It appears in the important memo of Léon-Josef Cardinal Suenens in response to the request of John XXIII for a framework for understanding the order among the large number of draft documents. See Suenens, "A Plan for the Whole Council," 88–105. The important point about this duality for the present study is that it became shorthand for conveying that the Church must renew her own life (renewal *ad intra*) as a condition for her dialogue with the world (renewal *ad extra*).

key theme here is fidelity in the form of conversion into God's will,[15] that is, a more perfect participation in the life of Christ (*ES*, 41, 58–61). Third, this teaching defines how the Church should relate to the world, namely, through service and mission that take the form of dialogue. In this way, the Church fulfills the missionary mandate received from Christ (*ES*, 64) by perpetuating the "conversation of Christ among men" (*ES*, 70). Here the key theme is that fidelity to God and to her own vocation entails for the Church being faithful to man through her mission.[16] The same truth that the Church comes to know more deeply through an act of faith (awareness), namely, that God is love, also spurs her to strive to measure up to it (renewal) and to fulfill her mission to communicate this love to the world (dialogue).

The movement from the first to the third path is entirely Christological. Knowledge of the mystery of Christ is the foundation for a greater doctrinal penetration into the mystery of the Church, which is "the whole Christ." This doctrinal penetration is already a greater conformity to Christ, a deeper communion with him in the truth that he reveals, the truth that he is. At the same time, this communion on the level of knowing is the foundation for renewal through conversion that brings about a yet more complete conformity and more profound communion, not only in thought but in life, in word and in deed. Communion with Christ necessarily entails taking up the mission, his mission, in which he makes us participants.

Reversing the order, mission with Christ presupposes and is the fruit of communion with him, and this communion is built on the foundation of faith in what he has revealed. This reproduces the order of the gospels, in which Christ calls his disciples, first to be with him, in order that he might then send them (see Mark 3:14). In turn, these two dimensions of communion with Christ, being with him and being sent by him, correspond to the *ad intra/ad extra* duality, to which we now turn.

---

15. The use of "into" here intends to convey the dynamic nature of conversion as a movement, and its goal of deeper participation in divine life and the mystery of Christ. Imagined spatially, conversion is not just a movement toward Christ but a movement by which man enters into his mystery so as to participate in it.

16. Chapters 8 and 9 will elaborate on this theme of fidelity to God and to man to show that it is a bipartite recapitulation of the tripartite plan of three paths of renewal.

THE AD INTRA/AD EXTRA DIMENSIONS OF RENEWAL

In the view of Pope John Paul II, the paths of renewal of *ES* can be ordered according to the *ad intra/ad extra* duality. The first path of doctrinal consciousness concerns the interior life of the Church, being directed to those who already believe, while the mission of dialogue clearly concerns the outward projection of the Church's interior life toward the world. It is an indication of his conviction that *ES* is a hermeneutical key to understanding Vatican II that he refers to the "two fronts that Paul VI already indicated in his first encyclical, *Ecclesiam Suam*." After quoting summary passages from *ES* on the first and third paths, he states: "Here we find the two directions of this path of the Church: both *ad intra* and *ad extra*, because these dimensions are complementary; they are, so to speak, organically united. Indeed, the Second Vatican Council has corresponded to these expectations."[17]

Interpreting *ES* in this way, as a movement from renewal *ad intra* to mission *ad extra*, is not an innovation of John Paul II. In the general audience during which he introduced *ES* to the world, Pope Paul himself stated that he was aware that the Encyclical concerns itself more with matters pertaining to the Church *ad intra*, yet it does not neglect matters pertaining to the Church *ad extra*.[18] Long before the promulgation of *ES*, the *ad intra/ad extra* duality had become a helpful way for the Council Fathers to understand their work. It appears in the important memo of Léon-Josef Cardinal Suenens in response to the request of Pope John XXIII for a framework for putting order into the large number of draft documents.[19] The important point about this duality for the present study is that it became shorthand for conveying that the Church must renew its own life (renewal *ad intra*) as a condition for her dialogue with the world (renewal *ad extra*).

In his Radio Message, just one month prior to the opening of the Council, John XXIII makes use of the *ad intra/ad extra* duality in order to express an aspect of his vision for Vatican II. He says that Vatican II corresponds to the Church's desire "to be what she is, especially in her

---

17. John Paul II, "Address, June 28, 1986." In the original Italian, the references are to *ES*, 10 and 67.

18. "e se riguarda di preferenza la *Ecclesia ad intra* non ignora la *Ecclesia ad extra*" (Paul VI, "General Audience, August 5, 1964").

19. See Suenens, "A Plan for the Whole Council," 88–105.

internal structure—her vitality *ad intra*—in the action of re-presenting, first of all to her own children, the treasures of illuminating faith and sanctifying grace." He then proceeds to discuss the Church's "vitality *ad extra*, that is, the Church before people's conditions and needs," her "external activity" and "apostolic activities," which are motivated by the realization that "the world in fact needs Christ: and it is the Church that must bring Christ to the world."[20]

Pope John's Radio Message greatly influenced the first "document" of Vatican II, the Council's Message to Humanity, issued just nine days into the first session. In this Message the Council Fathers state that they "wish to inquire how we ought to renew ourselves, so that we may be found increasingly faithful to the gospel of Christ." This renewal *ad intra* bears the fruit of mission *ad extra*: "We shall take pains so to present to the men of this age God's truth in its integrity and purity." The logic of the movement from renewal within the Church to mission directed outward becomes obvious when mission is conceived in terms of witness. The same Message to Humanity states: "we as pastors devote all our energies and thoughts to the renewal of ourselves and the flocks committed to us, so that there may radiate before all men the lovable features of Jesus Christ, who shines in our hearts 'that God's splendor may be revealed.'"[21]

The lasting impression of the *ad intra/ad extra* duality is evident in what Joseph Ratzinger writes about the Council, twelve years following its completion. In the year that Pope Paul makes him a cardinal (1977), he is keen to emphasize that an interior *aggiornamento* for the Church is not only not closed off from mission but actually contains the spiritual élan that cannot fail to produce a greater missionary commitment.

> The concentration on what is Catholic, which seems at first glance to be directed exclusively inward, thus is revealed in its original impulse to be an emphatic orientation toward those today who are searching. . . . Only when we see this clearly can we rightly understand the purpose of Vatican Council II, which, in all its comments about the Church . . . was not primarily concerned with how the Church envisaged herself, with the view from within, but with the discovery of the Church as sacrament, as the sign and instrument of unity. . . . And we come here upon something unexpected; rightly understood, the path that leads

---

20. John XXIII, "Radio Message, September 11, 1962."
21. Vatican II, "Message to Humanity."

men within and the path that draws them together are not in conflict; on the contrary, they need and support one another.[22]

As Pope Benedict XVI, Ratzinger returns to this theme on several occasions. "Evangelization," he states, "thus appears not simply a task to be undertaken *ad extra*; we ourselves are the first to need re-evangelization."[23] Keeping in mind that the New Evangelization began with Vatican II, he adds,[24] "Although this task [of New Evangelization] directly concerns the Church's way of relating *ad extra*, it nevertheless presupposes first of all a constant interior renewal, a continuous passing, so to speak, from evangelized to evangelizing."[25]

Self-Evangelization

The *ad intra/ad extra* dynamic can be conveyed through the term "self-evangelization." The 1985 Extraordinary Synod takes up the theme:

> Evangelization does not regard only the missions in the common sense of the word, that is, *ad gentes*. The evangelization of non-believers in fact presupposes the self-evangelization of the baptized and also in a certain sense, of deacons, priests and bishops. Evangelization takes place through witnesses. The witness gives his testimony not only with words, but also with his life.[26]

Given the inheritance that John Paul II received from Paul VI and the attention the 1985 Extraordinary Synod gave to the theme of self-evangelization, it is to be expected, then, that this theme will appear in John Paul's writings.

The theme is found in the post-Conciliar popes, which they use to summarize the three dimensions of renewal of *ES*, by using two closely related terms: "self-evangelization" and "being evangelized in order to

---

22. Ratzinger, *Principles of Catholic Theology*, 50, 52.

23. Benedict XVI, "Address, November 26, 2011."

24. "The period of the New Evangelization began with the Council; this was basically the intention of John XXIII. Pope John Paul II strongly emphasized the 'need' for it in a world that is undergoing great changes" (Benedict XVI, "Inflight Interview with Journalists").

25. Benedict XVI, *Ubicumque et semper*. See also Benedict XVI, "Address, February 3, 2007."

26. 2nd Extraordinary Assembly of the Synod of Bishops, "The Church," II.B.1.b.

evangelize." A passage from *EN* of Pope Paul VI is the point of reference for this theme. In this passage, Pope Paul gives a virtual recapitulation of *ES* when he writes of the need for the Church to evangelize herself in order effectively to evangelize others.

> The Church is an evangelizer, but she begins by being evangelized herself. She is the community of believers, the community of hope lived and communicated, the community of brotherly love, and she needs to listen unceasingly to what she must believe, to her reasons for hoping, to the new commandment of love. She is the People of God immersed in the world, and often tempted by idols, and she always needs to hear the proclamation of the "mighty works of God" (cf. Acts 2:11; 1 Pet 2:9), which converted her to the Lord; she always needs to be called together afresh by him and reunited. In brief, this means that she has a constant need of being evangelized, if she wishes to retain freshness, vigor and strength in order to proclaim the Gospel. The Second Vatican Council recalled (cf. *AG*, 5, 11–12) and the 1974 Synod vigorously took up again this theme of the Church which is evangelized by constant conversion and renewal, in order to evangelize the world with credibility.[27]

The Church listens anew to what she already believes (first path) in order to purify herself from temptation in order more fully to convert to the Lord (second path). The fruit of this is newly refreshed vigor and strength for mission (third path).

The first time that John Paul employs "self-evangelization" he indicates that *EN* is his source. "There exists therefore for Europe the problem that was defined in *Evangelii nuntiandi* as 'self-evangelization.'" Such self-evangelization is the prerequisite for the Church to respond to the alarming signs of the times, that is, the "negation of religion, the movements of the 'death of God,' of programmed secularization, of organized militant atheism," which characterize European culture.[28] On another occasion, this time with an explicit reference to *EN*, 15, he proclaims that "everyone in the Church of Christ is called to 'self-evangelization,' of course in union with the teaching ministry of pastors. Only those evangelize the world in a credible and effective way who have previously evangelized themselves through a constant deepening of the truths of faith and life

---

27. Paul VI, *EN*, 15.
28. John Paul II, "Homily, June 20, 1979," 3.

in love of God and neighbor (cf. Paul VI, *Evangelii nuntiandi*, 15)."[29] The mention of "truths of faith" and "the teaching ministry of pastors" indicate the pope's awareness that doctrinal penetration or awareness is the first step in self-evangelization.

Reflecting Vatican II's emphasis on the ecclesial and missionary dimension of every vocation, what John Paul says about the contribution of religious to the New Evangelization—which, it is timely to recall, he sees beginning with Vatican II, and the term as coined by Paul VI in *EN*—applies as well to all the Church's members. All "are called to manifest the unity between self-evangelization and witness, between interior renewal and apostolic fervor, between being and acting, showing that dynamism arises always from the first element of each of these pairs."[30] One of the fruits of the Special Assembly of the Synod of Bishops for Europe is the realization that the commitment to a New Evangelization is "a necessary work of courageous 'self-evangelization.'"[31] Similarly, for Benedict XVI, a "new self-evangelization through an encounter with Christ" makes it "unthinkable that a person should accept the word and give himself to the Kingdom without becoming a person who bears witness to it and proclaims it in his turn."[32]

In the pontificates of John Paul II and Benedict XVI, the terminology of "first being evangelized in order to evangelize" is far more frequent than "self-evangelization." Since the two terms convey precisely the same reality, presenting further texts is not necessary. The point for this study is that this terminology manifests the enduring impact of *ES* on Pope Paul's successors. Indeed, having shown that emphasis on "self-evangelization" as the prerequisite to evangelizing others recapitulates the three dimensions of renewal of *ES*, it can now be concluded that *ES* may also be read in light of this movement from renewal *ad intra* to mission *ad extra*. Accordingly, the first two paths concern the *ad intra* dimension of renewal—the Church's renewal of herself, her self-evangelization through doctrinal penetration and conversion—and the third path concerns the *ad extra* dimension of renewal, the revitalization of the Church's service to mankind, the first and most fundamental realization of which takes the form of witness to the transforming power of God's love.

---

29. John Paul II, "Homily, June 13, 1987," 7.
30. John Paul II, *Vita consecrata*, 81.
31. John Paul II, "Address, April 16, 1993," 4.
32. Benedict XVI, *Ecclesia in Medio Oriente*, 85, quoting *EN*, 24.

Once it is seen that renewal *ad intra* comprehends the first two paths of renewal, the movement from renewal *ad intra* to renewal *ad extra* is seen precisely to correspond to the framework for the Council proposed by Cardinal Suenens, adopted by John XXIII, and elaborated upon by Paul VI in terms of the three dimensions of renewal set forth in *ES*. This is the inheritance of Pope Paul's successors in their commitment faithfully to implement the Council by reading it above all as great impetus to spiritual renewal in Christ.

3

The First Path: Awareness

POPE PAUL TELLS US that Vatican II is the historical context for his reflections in *ES*. The Council is the occasion for the Church to reflect anew on her own mystery. Though at the outset this is asserted as a postulate, later it becomes clear that Pope Paul sees this as a continuation of the preceding seventy-five years of papal magisterium. As an act of ecclesial self-consciousness, Vatican II is the continuation of a process of deepening self-understanding that is characteristic of the Church's life. Besides the expected reference to John XXIII, he mentions Leo XIII, Pius XI, and Pius XII as pontiffs who had already led the Church into a deeper understanding of herself. The influence on Paul VI of Pius XII, and especially his encyclical on the Mystical Body of Christ, is evident in Paul's own singling out of *Mystici Corporis Christi* in *ES*, 30, and the multiple references to the Church as the Mystical Body of Christ in *ES*.[1] For Pope Paul, he and his brother bishops are the beneficiaries of a certain momentum in the Church's efforts to plumb the depths of her own mystery. Vatican II is the opportunity to continue this effort at deeper self-awareness.

---

1. Not only did Paul VI significantly draw from the ecclesiology of Pius XII, but the teaching of Pius XII had more influence on Vatican II than any other pope prior to the Council. "*The Council drew much from the experiences and reflections of the immediate past*, especially from the intellectual legacy left by Pius XII" (John Paul II, *TMA*, 18). There are 167 quotations of or references to the teaching of Pius XII in the sixteen documents of Vatican II.

THE FIRST PATH: AWARENESS

Pope Paul goes further and roots this effort in the very nature of the Church. He asserts, "such an act of reflection can look to the very manner chosen by God to reveal himself to men" (*ES*, 19). From the Church's origin it is a property of her life that she progress in her understanding of the faith. Pope Paul develops this via the biblical theme of vigilance. Acknowledging that in the Gospels this theme has an eschatological dimension, having to do with man's final destiny, it also concerns "close and immediate things," things that determine man's daily actions (*ES*, 21). The Church's life is one of "gradual development" into a fuller "awareness of her own vocation, of her own mysterious nature, of her own doctrine, of her own mission" (*ES*, 22). Here Pope Paul quotes St. Paul: "And it is my prayer that your love may abound more and more, with knowledge and all discernment" (Phil 1:9).[2] By striving to develop a more perfect self-awareness, the Church is being faithful to her own nature. Since God is the Author of that nature, she is thereby being faithful to God as well.

Pope Paul tells us that there are several reasons for his "boldness to invite [the Church] to this act of ecclesiastical awareness" (*ES*, 23), but "they all derive from the profound and key demands of the unique moment reached by the life of the Church" (*ES*, 24). This unique moment is one at which the Church desires to reinvigorate her mission "to offer to the world her message of brotherhood and of salvation." The precondition for this is that she "learn to know herself better" by reflecting on herself so as "to feel the throb of her own life," which is "to experience Christ in herself" (*ES*, 25). Here, still in the first section of *ES* on the path of awareness, it is clear that awareness cannot be separated from the other two paths of renewal through conversion and mission through dialogue.

Very importantly, a deepened consciousness of the Church's mystery, vocation, nature, and mission is also a remedy against errors (*ES*, 26), precisely the errors that can arise when efforts are made to adapt for the sake of more effective missionary dialogue. In terms of the concepts that will be developed in the following chapter, a deepened consciousness of the doctrine of the Church is the condition for remaining faithful to God while striving to promote pastoral *aggiornamento* of structures and methods for the sake of being faithful to man.

---

2. Paul VI often employs the image of the growth of a plant or a tree to convey the continuity in the identity of the living subject that becomes more fully what it is. See, for example, Paul VI's Addresses on October 29, 1964, September 8, 1971, and December 20, 1976.

A deepening of the Church's understanding of her own mystery is possible because what God has revealed about the Church is "a doctrine never sufficiently investigated and understood." Pope Paul calls this revealed truth about the Church "a mysterious storehouse, or, in other words, a treasury of the mysterious plans of God" (*ES*, 9). In his opening address for the second session, Pope Paul puts it this way: "The Church is a mystery; she is a reality imbued with the divine presence and, for that reason, she is ever susceptible of new and deeper investigation."[3] Later in the Encyclical, he returns to this theme of the apostolic deposit of faith being a storehouse or treasury by referring to Jesus's saying about the wise scribe who knows how to draw from his treasury things both new and old.[4] This anticipates what Vatican II would teach in *Dei Verbum* regarding the development of the apostolic tradition in the Church.[5]

Developing the Church's consciousness cannot be a mere verbatim repetition of divine revelation or compilation of prior expressions of her consciousness. In such a case, there would be no development of Sacred Tradition. Since this Tradition does develop as the Church continues her historical pilgrimage, it cannot suffice simply to repeat what the Church herself has already declared by authoritative teaching regarding this mystery. As Pope Paul puts it, taking up an image previously used by his predecessor, the Church is not a museum of memories, in which one finds only past expressions and the remnants of past centuries.[6] The work of erudition and compiling of previous formulations is certainly a very helpful, even indispensable, part of the process. But the goal of doctrinal penetration, as Pope John XXIII called it in his opening address, cannot be reduced to pure erudition. Genuine *ressourcement* is not an end it itself. Rather, it is at the service of doctrinal *aggiornamento*.[7]

---

3. Anderson, *Council Daybook*, Sessions I and II, 146 (bottom of first column).

4. See Matt 13:52 and Paul VI's use of the biblical text to elucidate the renewal of Vatican II with regard to doctrinal *aggiornamento* in Bushman, "Pope Paul VI on the Renewal of Vatican II."

5. See Vatican II, *DV*, 8.

6. Paul VI, "General Audience, November 25, 1964." Other texts: "Tradition is not a museum, a cemetery, an archeology. It is a plant that blooms every spring, a sap that is continually renewed" ("Address, September 8, 1971"). "The Church is not ... a museum; it is a garden where every plant always has a new spring" ("Address, June 22, 1967").

7. See D'Ambrosio, "*Ressourcement* theology," esp. 532. See also Flynn and Murray, *Ressourcement*.

Neither is genuine *ressourcement* an exclusively intellectual exercise. The reason is that "the mystery of the Church is not a mere object of theological knowledge; it is something to be lived, something that the faithful soul can have a kind of connatural experience of, even before arriving at a clear notion of it" (*ES*, 37).[8] Connatural knowledge of the Church is knowledge that goes beyond merely factual information about the Church, no matter how extensive and accurate that information is. It is this knowledge enriched by a profound experience of and love for the Church.[9] *ES* begins on this theme of loving the Church:

> Since Jesus Christ founded his Church to be the loving mother of all men and the dispenser of salvation, it is obvious why she has always been specially loved and cherished by those with the glory of God and the eternal salvation of men at heart. (*ES*, 1)

Love for the Church is the reason Pope Paul gives for the ecclesiological focus of *ES*, in which he turns his "thoughts with love and reverence towards Holy Church" (*ES*, 2). He returns to this later in the encyclical, stating: "We must serve the Church and love her as she is" (*ES*, 47).[10]

This loving, connatural knowledge of the Church's mystery is the interior, experiential reality that correlates to the doctrinal, propositional assertions about the Church. It gives rise to the supernatural instinct of faith, the *sensus fidei*.[11] This auto-critical faculty, which can never be

---

8. The term, "connatural experience," corresponds precisely to the Italian: "quasi connaturata esperienza." The Latin, rendered here as "a kind of connatural experience of," is "quasi experimento naturae suae consentaneo." Literally, it is: "as by a kind of meet [or: agreeing or fitting] experience of the Church's nature."

9. John Paul II links connaturality with the gift of wisdom. See *FR*, 44.

10. Love for the Church is a major theme of the most important magisterial text on the Church prior to Vatican II, *Mystici Corporis Christi* of Pius XII (June 29, 1943). See *MCC*, 66, 91, 95, 100, 104, 106, and 109.

11. That the quality of judgments, both moral and speculative, is influenced by the state of one's will is a fundamental anthropological reality. Aristotle realized that in deliberations about the concrete demands of justice, those of a just man will be qualitatively different than those of a person lacking justice. In its document of 2014 on the *sensus fidei*, the International Theological Commission (ITC) affirms the general principle in terms of connaturalization: "Every virtue connaturalises its subject, in other words the one who possesses it, to its object, that is, to a certain type of action" (ITC, "Sensus Fidei," 51). "The *sensus fidei fidelis* arises, first and foremost, from the connaturality that the virtue of faith establishes between the believing subject and the authentic object of faith" (50). Because faith is informed by charity, "the intensifying of faith within the believer particularly depends on the growth within him or her of charity, and the *sensus fidei fidelis* is therefore proportional to the holiness of one's life"

separated from the authoritatively taught doctrine of the Church, assures that the deepening of consciousness can never be merely an application of logic to revealed data in order to draw from them new theological corollaries, or nothing more than an echo of cultural values that have had more influence than the divinely instituted sources of truth and grace. The *sensus fidei* also assures that the necessary critical judgment, which comes with the second path of renewal through conversion, is not a cheap, extrinsic criticism by one who remains distant but the fruit of a commitment of love that is willing to take upon itself the price of renewal through conversion. This is why John Paul insisted, "The saints have always been the source and origin of renewal in the most difficult moments in the Church's history."[12] Cardinal Ratzinger also demonstrated the same conviction when he remarked, "Saints, in fact, reformed the Church in depth, not by working up plans for new structures, but by reforming themselves."[13]

In light of the preceding, it is clear that the second path of renewal through conversion has its own reciprocal influence on the consciousness of faith. Pope John Paul makes this point:

> The Church's consciousness, enlightened and supported by the Holy Spirit and fathoming more and more deeply both her divine mystery and her human mission, and even her human

---

(57). The ITC does not quote, refer to, or integrate two significant texts of John Paul in which he discusses St. Thomas Aquinas's understanding of knowledge by connaturalization. In *VS*, 64, connaturality is the source of "true judgments of conscience." Mere "knowledge of God's law in general is certainly necessary, but it is not sufficient: what is essential is a sort of 'connaturality' between man and the true good." *FR*, 44, quotes St. Thomas Aquinas to the effect that "the gift of wisdom enables judgment according to divine truth." These judgments are based on a kind of connatural knowledge, since "wisdom comes to know by way of connaturality." The link of connaturality to the gift of wisdom and to the *sensus fidei* suggests that the judgments of the *sensus fidei* regarding faith and morals are the same as the judgments of wisdom. The question whether wisdom perfects those judgments or should be considered identical to the *sensus fidei* cannot be addressed here. The ITC also links the *sensus fidei* with the intellectual gifts of the Holy Spirit: "By means of these gifts of the Spirit, especially the gifts of understanding and knowledge, believers are made capable of understanding intimately the 'spiritual realities which they experience', (78) and rejecting any interpretation contrary to the faith" (58). After giving *DV*, 8 as the reference to the quoted words, note 78 confirms the close relation of the *sensus fidei* to the intellectual gifts of the Holy Spirit: "In the theology of the gifts of the Spirit that St. Thomas developed, it is particularly the gift of knowledge that perfects the *sensus fidei fidelis* as an aptitude to discern what is to be believed. Cf. Aquinas, *ST*, IIa-IIae, q. 9, a. 1 co. et ad 2."

12. John Paul II, *CL*, 16. The *Catechism* quotes this text in article 828.

13. Ratzinger and Messori, *The Ratzinger Report*, 53.

weaknesses—this consciousness is and must remain the first source of the Church's love, as love in turn helps to strengthen and deepen her consciousness.¹⁴

Greater holiness, the fruit of conversion, deepens connaturality, which in turn enriches the *sensus fidei* and the "growth in the understanding of the realities and the words which have been handed down . . . through a penetrating understanding of the spiritual realities which they [the faithful] experience."¹⁵ The result is a more penetrating act of ecclesial self-consciousness. As the ITC confirms, "by keeping the commandments and putting faith into practice, the believer gains a deeper understanding of faith."¹⁶ The ecclesial consciousness of the *sensus fidei* also serves as an internal, auto-critical principle when making the critical judgments that renewal through conversion presupposes. In Christological terms, a mature participation in Christ's paschal love for the Church is required in order for the faithful to make the kind of sacrifices that are required to promote the renewal through conversion. If this love is lacking, the temptation to equate renewal (*aggiornamento*) with the manipulation of institutional structures will be great.

Returning to *ES*, and to bring this discussion of the first path to a close, Pope Paul indicates that it is natural, in the order of grace, to desire to know the mystery of the Church more fully. This is motivated by love for the Church. What the *Catechism* says about St. Anselm's well-known assertion that faith seeks understanding applies not only to God, but to the Church:

> It is intrinsic to faith that a believer desires to know better the One in whom he has put his faith, and to understand better what He has revealed; a more penetrating knowledge will in turn call forth a greater faith, increasingly set afire by love. The grace of faith opens "the eyes of your hearts" (Eph 1:18) to a lively understanding of the contents of Revelation: that is, of the totality of God's plan and the mysteries of faith, of their connection with each other and with Christ, the center of the revealed mystery.¹⁷

---

14. John Paul II, *RH*, 3.

15. Vatican II, *DV*, 8.

16. ITC, *"Sensus Fidei,"* 59. This passage goes on: "Putting faith into practice in the concrete reality of the existential situations in which he or she is placed by family, professional and cultural relations enriches the personal experience of the believer. It enables him or her to see more precisely the value and the limits of a given doctrine, and to propose ways of refining its formulation."

17. *CCC*, 158.

A more penetrating knowledge of what God has revealed gives rise to a dilation of the heart,[18] that is, to a more ardent love because the central content of divine revelation is the truth about God's love. Moreover, because God's love is effective, the central content of divine revelation is the Church. God makes his love known not only by words but also by acts of love. A response of faith, then, is both assent to the truth about this love and a *fiat* or consent to being loved. By faith an encounter takes place in which God's love effectively transforms the one who is loved. The result of this is communion of God and man in truth and love. This communion is the Church, which precisely as communion is the goal of all things.[19] The believer not only knows about God and his love, but knows them by experience, and this produces a return of love.

To know and to love the Church produces a spontaneous desire to engage in doing what one can in order to bring about the fullest and purest participation in the mystery of the Church in one's life. Like God, the Church can be both known and loved, yet unlike God, the Church can also be built up and renewed. In the language of Thomistic epistemology, the Church is a "doable"; it can be built up. As such it can be the object of acts of the practical intellect directed toward building up the Church.[20] These are acts of renewal or *aggiornamento*, both personal and

---

18. Scriptural foundations for the dilation of the heart or soul include: Ps 118:32; Isa 60:5; 2 Cor 6:11, 13. From Scripture, several saints develop the theme, for example, St. Bernard of Clairvaux: "The soul must grow and expand, that it may be roomy enough for God. Its width is its love, if we accept what the Apostle says: 'Widen your hearts in love' (2 Cor 6:13). The soul, being a spirit, does not admit of material expansion, but grace confers gifts on it that nature is not equipped to bestow. Its growth and expansion must be understood in a spiritual sense; it is its virtue that increases, not its substance. Even its glory is increased. And finally it grows and advances toward 'mature manhood, to the measure of the stature of the fullness of Christ' (Eph 4:13). Eventually it becomes 'a holy temple in the Lord.' The capacity of any man's soul is judged by the amount of love he possesses; hence he who loves much is great, he who loves a little is small, he who has no love is nothing, as Paul said: 'If I have not love, I am nothing' (1 Cor 13:2)" (*Sermons on the Song of Songs*, 27.6.10). See also Benedict of Nursia, *Holy Rule*, Prologue; Teresa of Avila, *The Interior Castle*, 4.3.8.

19. See *CCC*, 760.

20. This is the epistemological foundation for considering pastoral theology as existential ecclesiology. A study on the nature of pastoral theology and its fundamental principles will come in a future work.

institutional or structural,[21] and guided by pastoral prudence.[22] These acts constitute the second path of *ES*.

Looking back at Vatican II on the day of its closing, Pope Paul shows that he continues to understand the Council in terms of the three paths of *ES*. He underscores the purpose of the act of ecclesial self-consciousness and its inseparability from renewal through conversion. The doctrinally based self-consciousness is not "an end in itself," he states, or an act of merely human understanding ordered to merely natural ends. It is, rather, a thoroughly supernatural exercise with three outcomes: for the Church "to find in herself, active and alive, the Holy Spirit, the word of Christ; and to probe more deeply still the mystery, the plan and the presence of God above and within herself; to revitalize in herself that faith which is the secret of her confidence and of her wisdom, and that love which impels her to sing without ceasing the praises of God."[23] This revitalization of faith within the Church is the second path of *ES*, to which we now turn.

---

21. Because the Church is a personal subject, the personal dimension of *aggiornamento* must have the primacy. The Church is a supernatural society of men. Just as men are built up and become more fully human through immanent activity, so too it is primarily through immanent activity that any society develops. Aristotle's political philosophy bears this out. Constitutions, which order the governmental structure of human societies, are at the service of promoting the order of justice and through that order the order of friendship, which is the order of participation in the common good through virtuous activities. John Paul II develops this most elaborately in his encyclical on human work, *Laborem exercens*. The Church is built up essentially by the holiness of her members. This is why the Blessed Virgin Mary is preeminent among all of the faithful of all time and precedes the apostles in faith, not only temporally but also in terms of perfection. This has important implications for ecclesiology. In cultures that emphasize the authority of office there is a tendency to equate active participation in the Church's mystery with the holding of ecclesiastical office. This is a subordinate and limited authority, which is proportionate only to the subordinate common good of ecclesiastical order. The higher authority, which correlates most directly to human dignity and perfection, is the authority of personal influence, which works through exemplary causality and the instrumental causality of intercession. The authority of holiness is the power of the good to be diffusive of itself, both through example and through personal participation in Christ's mediation by charity.

22. Pastoral prudence is to the supernatural society of the Church what political prudence is to the natural society. Most properly the virtue of those who are responsible for the common good of each of these societies, the citizens of both the natural and the supernatural society conduct themselves virtuously by exercising the virtue of prudence regarding those matters in which they act for the common good by determining the best way to perform the acts that they are obligated to accomplish and by exercising their gifts and freedom to take initiatives for the sake of the common good.

23. Paul VI, "Address, December 7, 1965."

4

The Second Path: Renewal

THE SECOND PATH OF renewal is the path of conversion, and it has two elements. First, there must be a critical judgment, the essence of which is a comparison of the divine ideal for the Church with the present reality, which in some ways falls short of that ideal. This judgment is based on and thus presupposes the deepened consciousness that constitutes the first path. Second, this critical judgment gives rise to a humble effort to measure up to the divine ideal. Pope Paul calls this effort *renewal, reform, aggiornamento* and *metanoia*.[1] While the last of these refers exclusively to personal, spiritual conversion, the other three have both a personal and an institutional dimension. Both structures and persons are in need of renewal, reformation, and updating, and this always entails a critical judgment by way of comparing the present reality to the divine ideal in order to identify what falls short of that ideal. Still, Pope Paul's emphasis falls on the personal dimension of renewal through conversion, as he writes of the Church "interiorly assimilating her true spirit of obedience to Christ" and coming to "greater maturity and wisdom" through "faithfulness, effort, mortification and sacrifice," and the "moral energy" and "supernatural motives" that this renewal entails (*ES*, 51).

---

1. In the Italian text, *riforma* (or its plural, *riforme*) appears nine times, in articles 12, 46 (three times), 48 (twice), 49, 50 (twice). *Rinnovamento* or the related verb appears twelve times, in articles 12 (twice), 37, 43 (title), 47 (twice), 53, 55, 58, 61, 86, 97. *Metanoia* appears once, in article 53, where it is a synonym for *rinnovamento*. *Aggiornamento* appears thee times, in articles 45 and 52 (twice).

In the years following the Council, Pope Paul found it necessary to insist on the Council's emphasis on the personal dimension of renewal:

> It should be noted that for many the interest in renewal was directed to the external and impersonal transformation of the ecclesiastical edifice . . . rather than to the first and principal renewal that the Council desired, namely, a moral, personal, interior renewal that should rejuvenate the Church in the consciousness of her mystery, her adherence to Christ, her invigoration by the power of the Holy Spirit.[2]

The ecclesial awareness of the first path is an act of faith (*ES*, 24) by which the Church comes to a deeper understanding about the Church. The Church is both the believing subject and the content of this act of faith.[3] This identity of subject and content is the foundation for "the spontaneous desire to compare (Italian: *confrontare*)[4] the ideal image of the Church just as Christ sees it, wills it, and loves it . . . with the actual image which the Church projects today" (*ES*, 10). This confrontation bears a twofold fruit, the first being a critical judgment regarding the discrepancies between the divine ideal and current reality, and the second being the efforts of renewal through conversion that have as their goal the eradication of those discrepancies.

THE NECESSARY CRITICAL JUDGMENT

In the introductory section of *ES*, Pope Paul links the first path of deepened consciousness of the Church's mystery, vocation, and mission to what could be called a derivative consciousness of not measuring up to this divine ideal. This second consciousness results from placing what God has revealed about the Church side by side with the actual state of

---

2. Paul VI, "General Audience, January 15, 1969." Cardinal Wojtyła echoes this: "The Council does not merely outline an external plan for the renewal of the Church, based on new structures that correspond more completely to the present-day demands of communal sociology; it also outlines a real plan for the enrichment of faith" (*SR*, 218).

3. This language of subject and object captures the thought of Paul VI, though it comes from Cardinal Wojtyła: "It was impossible to treat the Church merely as an 'object': it had to be a 'subject' also" (*SR*, 35); "We ourselves are the Church, and at the same time we believe in it; it is the object of our faith, and it is ourselves. The whole movement of the Council must be a reflection on this reality" (*SR*, 38).

4. See the discussion of this term in the next chapter.

the Church. Such a comparison results in a critical judgment of the actual state of the Church and the identification of deficiencies that need to be amended.

> From this enlightened and effective consciousness[5] there arises the spontaneous desire to compare the ideal image of the Church just as Christ sees it, wills it, and loves it as his holy and immaculate spouse (Eph 5:27), with the actual image which the Church projects today. . . .
>
> But the actual image of the Church is never as perfect, as lovely, as holy or as brilliant as that formative Divine Idea would wish it to be. (*ES*, 10)

The reason why a deeper understanding of the Church's mystery spontaneously leads to a critical judgment, which Pope Paul understands as an act of moral conscience, is that the identity of the faithful is inseparable from the mystery of the Church.[6] Because by baptism the faithful participate in the mystery of the Church, the truth about the Church is necessarily also truth that shapes their self-identity, vocation, and mission. Pope Paul conveys this by employing the imagery of looking in a mirror.

> Hence there arises the unselfish and almost impatient need for renewal, for correction of the defects which this conscience denounces and rejects, as if, standing before a mirror, we were to examine interiorly the image of Christ which he has left us. (*ES*, 11)

Pope Paul's image of a mirror applies first and foremost to individual members of the Church and secondarily to the Church's structures. He emphasizes the personal dimension of growth in holiness, that is, the perfection of charity, through conversion. Nevertheless, structures should be both the fruit of holiness and the means to promote holiness.[7]

---

5. "Consciousness" here is an amendment of the English translation used in this study, which has "realization" for the Italian *coscienza*. Certainly, "realization" can be a synonym of "awareness" or "consciousness," as in: "I finally realized that I was lost." For the sake of accurately conveying the continuity in Paul VI's vocabulary and thought, and especially in order to show the connection between the first and second paths, "consciousness" is the preferred rendering of *coscienza* here.

6. Cf. Paul VI, *ES*, 37, quoted above.

7. Speaking of ecclesiastical institutions, Benedict XVI asserts that these institutions "are intended to be expressions of the love of God for humanity" ("Address, September 8, 2011").

The combination of acts and fruits of personal holiness, on one hand, and of institutions that are transparently the fruit and means of this holiness, on the other hand, contributes to the Church being an effective sacrament, that is, sign and instrument, of God's love at work in the world. The Church's vocation is to cooperate with that love first of all with respect to herself, to allow it to work a transformation into the divine ideal: "the Church should tend towards becoming perfect in the real expression of her earthly existence. This is the great moral problem which is uppermost in the life of the Church, a problem which reveals what she is" (*ES*, 41). This confirms, once again, the priority of doctrinal consciousness in the process of ecclesial renewal. For, the "impatient need for renewal" at both the personal and institutional levels presupposes the objective criterion of revealed doctrine against which the comparison with the present reality is made and a critical judgment is formed.

The interpenetration of the self-identity, vocation, and mission of the Church, on one hand, and of the faithful, on the other hand, is rooted, ontologically, in the participation of the faithful in the mystery of the Church brought about by baptism.[8] Experientially, it takes the form of the consciousness and related connaturality that Pope Paul takes as the first and foundational path of renewal. This is the foundation for the spontaneous critical judgment and examination of conscience that comprise the second path of renewal. By its very nature, an examination of conscience has the living, free, and responsible subject as its focus of attention, not some object exterior to the subject. A sign of a mature and penetrating act of ecclesial consciousness, and of a well-developed *sensus fidei* is that a deeper understanding of the mystery of the Church elicits an act of self-examination regarding the exigencies of personal participation in that mystery and regarding the transparency and efficacy of ecclesiastical institutions.

VATICAN II AS AN EXAMINATION OF CONSCIENCE

The obvious moral context that Pope Paul has in mind in *ES*, 11 (quoted just above) is the reason for translating *coscienza* here as "conscience" rather than "consciousness." In *ES*, 41 and in a general audience that will be quoted shortly, Pope Paul makes this moral dimension explicit. Before

---

8. "The lay apostolate, however, is a participation in the salvific mission of the Church itself" (*LG*, 33).

turning to that, however, it is instructive to consider the consistency of this moral dimension in Pope Montini's understanding of the renewal of Vatican II. In fact, his focus on moral conscience and conversion predates the Council. While still Archbishop of Milan, in his Pastoral Letter for Lent 1962, he refers to Vatican II as a great examination of conscience on the part of the Church.

> This pre-Conciliar vigil is a time for a universal examination of conscience, to which everyone feels invited to participate. Who is without consciousness of some need for some improvement, some advancement in perfection, regarding Catholic religious life?[9]

After this, the theme found its way into the plan for the Council submitted to Pope John XXIII by Cardinal Suenens in July of 1962.[10] Five years after the Council, Pope Paul returned to this theme, speaking of "the examination of conscience that the Council initiated."[11] In manifest continuity with this, John Paul II called for an examination of conscience as the way to prepare for the graces of the Jubilee Year 2000, and specified that a key element of this examination should be the reception of Vatican II.[12]

Because this examination of conscience is at the heart of Vatican II, its teachings are rightly seen as the fruit of this an examination. This is vital for any interpretation (hermeneutic) of the Council, the teachings of which cannot be fully understood and received if they are subject to a merely objective, scientific examination. To the extent that they remain merely the object of historical, philological, psychological, and

---

9. Montini, *Pensiamo al concilio*, 38 (author's translation). It is illustrative to notice the relative neglect that this letter receives by scholars particularly interested in pre-Conciliar history. Perhaps the most sympathetic attention to this text is found in Hebblethwaithe, *John XXIII*, but this sympathy is lacking in more recent works such as Alberigo and Komonchak, *History of Vatican II*; Alberigo, *A Brief History of Vatican II*; Bulman and Parrella, *From Trent to Vatican II*; Gaillardetz and Clifford, *Keys to the Council*; Wicks, *Investigating Vatican II*. In contrast, Montini's pastoral letter is unfavorably cited in Amerio, *Iota Unum*, 720, and for this reason alone is quoted in Faggioli, *Vatican II*, 93.

10. On this, see Suenens, "A Plan for the Whole Council," 97. Given the communication between Cardinals Suenens and Montini, it is not improbable that the Lenten Pastoral Letter, or Cardinal Montini personally, had some influence on the plan drawn up by Cardinal Suenens.

11. Paul VI, "General Audience, January 14, 1970."

12. See John Paul II, *TMA*, 36; also 27 and 34.

sociological analysis, their authentic meaning cannot be ascertained, for the very same reason that the full meaning of Sacred Scripture cannot be determined by historical methodologies alone.

While historical and philological approaches are valid, they cannot be isolated from the kind of formation of consciousness and resulting examination of conscience that Pope Paul goes to great lengths to set forth in *ES*.[13] Living faith, then, is a foundational element of the spirit of Vatican II, without which it is impossible to interpret the Council according to the same spirit in which it was written.[14] The entire patrimony of divine revelation and sacred tradition constitutes the content for this examination of conscience, and once the Council was completed, it takes its place within sacred tradition so that from then forward an examination of conscience must bear upon it as well. Thus, Pope Paul can say, eight years after the Council: "if we want to make a frank and calm examination of conscience, we cannot say that that *aggiornamento* has yet fully achieved the goals to which bishops (*CD*, 17), priests (*PO*, 13) and laity (*AA*, 6, 8, 14) are called."[15] An examination of conscience is required of diocesan directors of social media regarding the implementation of conciliar norms in *Inter mirifica*.[16] Moreover, Pope Paul challenges the College of Cardinals and the Roman Prelature to "take up again the weighty and learned 'tome' of the Second Vatican Council, and with the analyses of a courageous examination of conscience to leaf through the stupendous pages, re-learning and integrating the purposes that the Council infused into the heart of a Church eager for renewal and reconciliation."[17]

No matter how scientifically and technically advanced, and no matter how historically accurate, no approach to interpreting the Council that disregards living faith on the part of the investigator and the one being investigated will suffice. While living faith and the related participation in the *sensus fidei* is required for all theological inquiry, it is even more so with respect to Vatican II. As a pastoral council, its goal is not just to answer the question that other, doctrinal councils have answered, namely: What is the precise way in which the Church understands what God has revealed, and what are the understandings that the Church is

---

13. Cf. Paul VI, *ES*, 37.
14. See the discussion of this in chapter 1.
15. Paul VI, "Address, June 22, 1973."
16. Paul VI, "Address, November 17, 1973."
17. Paul VI, "Address, December 21, 1974."

able to identify as contrary to this true understanding?[18] In contrast to other councils,[19] Vatican II was not focused on addressing "specific heresies or general disorders" in the Church. Rather, its goal was "to infuse fresh spiritual vigor into the Mystical Body of Christ, insofar as it is a visible society, purifying it from the defects of many of its members and stimulating it to new virtue" (ES, 44). As a pastoral council, Vatican II presupposes the entire history of doctrinal clarification and definition, and seeks to respond to the more fundamental question: Why is this revelation relevant to people's search for a fully human and meaningful life? In this way, it seeks to bring about a renewal through conversion, and this conversion must pass by way of the conscience, the "place" where truth and freedom—the fundamental human dynamism defined in relation to the search for fulfillment—interact with one another.[20]

This understanding of the pastoral nature of Vatican II explains why a purely objective, scientific approach to interpreting the Council that divorces knowledge from conscience and therefore from daily life would leave the subject engaged in such an approach devoid of the disposition required to grasp the move from consciousness to renewal through conversion. There would, then, be only one path for the Church to follow, that of a purely speculative quest for a consciousness of faith that cannot produce the fruit of renewal.

On this point, two texts of Joseph Ratzinger on saints are relevant. The first is directly related to the renewal of Vatican II and Pope Paul's concern for a personal appropriation of faith through conversion. In this text, Ratzinger reminds his audience that Christ is the cause of our conversion.[21] With this focus in mind, true reform will only happen if we

---

18. "The ecumenical councils of the past for the most part furnished the answer to a need for exactness in doctrine, and dealt with various important matters that had to do with the *lex credendi* because heresies and errors were attempting to imbed themselves in the ancient Church in the East and in the West" (John XXIII, "Address, November 14, 1960").

19. Paul VI refers to Vatican II's character as a council of renewal and states that "unlike other Councils, it was not directly dogmatic, but doctrinal and pastoral" ("General Audience, August 6, 1975"). A purely doctrinal council, if ever there were such a thing, would still have a pastoral dimension, if only because doctrinal exactness is necessary for the first path of consciousness. On the pastoral dimension of clarifying revealed truth, see Benedict XVI, "Address, February 10, 2006." See also Wojtyła, SR, 17.

20. "Conscience [is] where the decisive and absolutely personal dialogue between grace and human freedom unfolds" (EA, 73).

21. This focus echoes Pope Paul's "Address for the Opening of Session Two of

allow him to increase and ourselves to decrease (cf. John 3:30); that is, only if that reform comes from deep within the person.

> We must always bear in mind that the Church is not ours but his. Hence the "reform," the "renewals," necessary as they may be, cannot exhaust themselves in a zealous activity on our part to erect new, sophisticated structures. ... I mean to say that what we can do is infinitely inferior to him who does. Hence, true "reform" does not mean to take great pains to erect new facades.... Real "reform" is to strive to let what is ours disappear as much as possible so what belongs to Christ may become more visible. It is a truth well known to the saints. Saints, in fact, reformed the Church in depth, not by working up plans for new structures, but by reforming themselves. What the Church needs in order to respond to the needs of man in every age is holiness, not management.[22]

The second text expands on this theme of the saints who "reform the Church in depth." In it, Pope Benedict equates the saints with the moral sense of Scripture and suggests that they become authentic interpreters of Scripture by becoming living books; in the saints one encounters what is contained in the books of Scripture.

> The interpretation of sacred Scripture would remain incomplete were it not to include listening to *those who have truly lived the Word of God: namely, the saints.* Indeed, *"viva lectio est vita bonorum"*[23] (Saint Gregory the Great, *Moralia in Job* XXIV, VIII, 16: PL 76, 295). The most profound interpretation of Scripture comes precisely from those who let themselves be shaped by

---

Vatican II."

22. Ratzinger, *The Ratzinger Report*, 53. Very similar language, in a different context, by Hans Urs von Balthasar: "Saints are needed if the Church's language down through the centuries, in its thousand tongues, is to be uttered to modern ears as something dear and familiar (rather than as an unintelligible muttering), and if the 'personal opinions' practically everyone has and proclaims nowadays are to be broadened to become views of the Church" (*In the Fullness of Faith*, 24). Balthasar's context is significant. Only with reference to the transcendent principle of the Church's unity, which is God himself, can any one member of the Church reflect the whole while remaining only a part (see 14–16).

23. Literally: "The lives of the virtuous are a living text." The text of Scripture comes alive in the saints; in them we discover the true meaning of Scripture. St. Thomas sees this exactly the same way: "However, as Augustine also says, the meaning of Sacred Scripture is gathered from the action of saints" (*Commentary on St. Paul's Letter to the Romans*, Ch. 1, Lect. 5 [Marietti 80]). Thomas is referring to Augustine's *On Lying*, XV, 26.

the Word of God through listening, reading and assiduous meditation.[24]

The meaning of Scripture unfolds in the lives of the saints because the "Holy Spirit who inspired the sacred authors is the same Spirit who impels the saints to offer their lives for the Gospel."[25]

> The saints are the true interpreters of Holy Scripture. The meaning of a given passage of the Bible becomes most intelligible in those human beings who have been totally transfixed by it and have lived it out. . . . Scripture is full of potential for the future, a potential that can only be opened up when someone "lives through" and "suffers through" the sacred text.[26]

This way of understanding the saints in relation to Scripture parallels the way that the second path of *ES* relates to the first path. Because doctrinal awareness is the objective measure of *metanoia*, the Church's life is the best commentary on doctrine. Pope Paul's vision is that through the process of renewal through conversion the Church and her members conform more perfectly (second path) to the revealed truth about the Church that first becomes more deeply known through doctrinal consciousness (first path). This parallel sheds light on the central dimension of Vatican II as a pastoral council. The pastoral intuition of Paul VI, inherited from his predecessor, is that the Church's life at the time might have been an accurate commentary on the doctrine of the Church that had prevailed until the time of Council,[27] but that the new challenges confronting the Church's mission required a discovery of aspects of the mystery of the Church that correspond to those challenges.

The pastoral nature of Vatican II admits of two understandings that correspond, to a certain extent, to the two understandings of "methods"

---

24. Benedict XVI, *VD*, 48.
25. Benedict XVI, *VD*, 49.
26. Ratzinger, *Jesus of Nazareth*, 1:78.
27. On this, see the article of Yves Congar on ecclesiology in gestation at the time of the Council: "Moving Toward a Pilgrim Church" in Stacpoole, *Vatican II Revisited*. The dramatic rejection of the draft schema on the Church and the remarkable contrast between that schema and the text that was finally promulgated, *LG*, confirm the link between the doctrine concerning the Church (ecclesiology) and ecclesial life. By forging a new ecclesiological synthesis the Council Fathers envisioned a renewal that would result in a corresponding change in ecclesial life. The whole theology of reception is, essentially, a matter of ascertaining this correspondence between the documents and ecclesial life.

discussed earlier in this chapter. "Pastoral" can signify the practical, prudential adaptations of disciplines, vocabulary, and ecclesiastical structures, or it can refer to the goal of promoting a more perfect conformity of the Church with the divine plan. In the latter case, "pastoral" is distinguished from "doctrinal." The doctrinal and pastoral are in no way opposed to one another, since the pastoral presupposes the doctrinal precisely as the second path of conversion presupposes the first path of consciousness. In this light, the doctrinal relates to the pastoral as the allegorical sense of Scripture relates to the moral sense. What Pope Benedict says about the saints's lives being living books because they conform to the printed book of Scripture, applies as well to the relation of the second path of renewal through conversion to the first path of doctrinal consciousness. The most profound interpretation of the revealed doctrine on the Church and to the teaching of Vatican II comes precisely from those who let themselves be shaped by that doctrine and teaching.[28]

It might be tempting to conclude from this brief discussion that as a pastoral council Vatican II is more complete than the preceding councils. With a strong focus on clarifying doctrine, these councils can be compared to focusing on the allegorical or Christological doctrinal sense of Scripture, while excluding the moral and anagogical senses. As a pastoral council, Vatican II united these various senses, and in this respect it would appear to express a fullness of teaching in relation to which other councils would seem to be lacking.[29] Understandable as this line of rea-

---

28. Two texts of Cardinal Ratzinger can serve as commentary on this assertion: "Whether or not the Council becomes a positive force in the history of the Church depends only indirectly on texts and organizations; the crucial question is whether there are individuals—saints—who, by their personal willingness, which cannot be forced, are ready to effect something new and living. The ultimate decision about the historical significance of Vatican Council II depends on whether or not there are individuals prepared to experience in themselves the drama of the separation of the wheat from the cockle and thus to give to the whole a singleness of meaning that it cannot gain from words alone. . . . Despite all the good to be found in the texts produced, the last word about the historical value of Vatican Council II has yet to be spoken. If, in the end, it will be numbered among the highlights of Church history depends on those who will transform its words into the life of the Church" (*Principles of Catholic Theology*, 377-78). "Every council, in order really to yield fruit, must be followed by a wave of holiness. Thus it was after Trent, and it achieved its aim of real reform precisely for this reason. . . . Whether Vatican II and its results will be considered a luminous period of Church history will depend upon all the Catholics who are called to give it life" (Ratzinger and Messori, *The Ratzinger Report*, 42).

29. Toward the end of his article on interpreting Vatican II, Thomas Hughson concludes that thinking of Vatican II as a new Pentecost makes it possible to see the

soning is, it is not necessary to draw this conclusion. The reason is that the faithful who are properly disposed should be expected to internalize the doctrine that a council clarifies in the form of the kind of consciousness that leads to a critical judgment and personal renewal through conversion. Further, previous councils were addressed directly to the clergy, who were responsible for preaching and catechesis. These dimensions of the ministry of the word would complement defined doctrine with the necessary pastoral dimension. Through the liturgy, including devotions, as well as personal prayer and a meaningful inculturation of faith in the believing community, all of the conditions for moving from head to heart, from precise knowledge of faith to living all of the implied demands of faith, were in place so long as there was a vibrant community of faith.

Pope John XXIII judged that the cultural situation at the time of Vatican II was quite different and that pastors could no longer presume that the conditions existed for what Pope Paul would call the examination of conscience. Secularism had made its inroads and there was already a crisis of faith. It was a crisis not with respect to clearly defining faith's content, but with respect to what later would be called a meaningful inculturation of faith. He saw that the modern period was so intent on the pursuit of material goods that this was giving rise to "a total neglect or watering down of the supernatural, spiritual principles that characterized the implanting and spread of Christian civilization through the centuries." Pope John continues:

> In this modern period the question is not so much one of some particular point or other of doctrine or of discipline that has to be brought back to the pure fonts of Revelation and of tradition, as it is of restoring the substance of human and Christian thinking and living.[30]

Pope John was convinced that the Church needed to reform herself, so that she could more brightly reflect into the world the light of Christ, which the world so desperately needs. Christ is the hope of a humanity in crisis, and since the Church's mission is to bring him to the world, the crisis of humanity constitutes a great sign of the times and a call to the

---

Council as the paradigm of councils, in light of which prior councils, which focused on defining doctrine, exhibit a certain deficiency. See Hughson, "Interpreting Vatican II," 3–37.

30. John XXIII, "Address, November 14, 1960."

Church to recommit herself to continuing Christ's own mission as light of the world.

The challenge lies not only with an increasingly secular culture that renders men and women indifferent to morality and religion. Within the Church herself, the influence of the secular culture was creating a form of religious formalism, that is, a superficial, exterior adherence to creed and practices without a sufficient interior grasp of their meaning. Pope John's desire to restore "the substance of human and Christian thinking and living" indicates his awareness of an alarming rift between the faith that the faithful still professed and their daily lives. In its turn, the Council would decry this same division, saying: "This split between the faith which many profess and their daily lives deserves to be counted among the more serious errors of our age."[31] Ten years after the Council, Pope Paul comes back to this theme: "The split between the Gospel and culture is without a doubt the drama of our time, just as it was of other times."[32] Addressing this situation is one of the chief concerns of the New Evangelization, which John Paul II tells us began with Vatican II.[33]

Clearly, baptized people with dysfunctional consciences would be incapable of participating in the renewal envisioned by Pope Paul VI because this renewal presupposes and derives from a judgment of conscience that first identifies and then "denounces and rejects" the defects needing correction. Pope Paul reprises this in the Apostolic Constitution in which he decreed a Jubilee following the Council as a means to engrain the teaching and spirit of Vatican II in the minds, hearts, and lives of the faithful.

> We expect of all the faithful the spiritual renewal that can only be obtained in the intimate sanctuary of their consciences: in the exercise of the virtue of penance, to which is added the Sacrament of Confession, in which the faithful, as in a salvific bath, are immersed in the blood of Christ. This conversion can

---

31. Vatican II, *GS*, 43. Immediately following this, *GS* likens the split between faith and life to the situation addressed by the prophets of the Old Testament and Jesus himself, providing references to Isa 58:1–12, Matt 23:3–23, and Mark 7:10–13. A study of these texts would contribute to a deeper understanding of the crisis of faith that Vatican II addresses. Because it would overburden the present study, an examination of the prophet's mission to reawaken the faith-memory of Israel, and its significance for understanding prophecy and its role in reform, will be the subject of a separate investigation.

32. Paul VI, *EN*, 20.

33. See Wojtyła, *Crossing the Threshold of Hope*, 160.

only be obtained through vital and transforming contact with the divine Savior.[34]

Just as personal conversion entails a judgment about sin, so the *aggiornamento* through *metanoia* envisioned by Pope Paul requires a critical judgment that there is a discrepancy, a distance between God's vision for the Church's perfection and the reality of imperfection on the part of the Church's members. This reinforces the point that the first path of doctrinal awareness regarding the mystery, vocation, and mission of the Church is the essential prerequisite for the second path of renewal.

While Pope Paul does not use the term "self-consciousness" (Italian: *autocoscienza*), this term certainly accurately conveys the reality that he has in mind and analyses in *ES*, in which he employs equivalent phrases such as: "consciousness of herself" (*ES*, 9; Italian: "*la coscienza di se stessa*"), and "the awareness that she must have of herself" (*ES*, 18; Italian: "*la coscienza ch'ella deve avere di sé*"). What Pope Paul says about self-consciousness (*autocoscienza*) in one of his general audiences confirms and reinforces that in *ES* the Church's consciousness of herself is more than a doctrinally precise understanding of her own mystery, vocation, and mission. It entails the kind of critical judgment that leads to conversion under discussion here. Speaking of the religious experience of personal encounter with God, he states that because God is light, when we stand before him "the first effect is that, before we see God, we see ourselves." He continues by describing what this knowledge of self entails.

> Immediately we are invaded by confusion and discomfort, because while we perceive the transcendent Majesty of his presence, we see our own lowliness (even Our Lady experienced this metaphysical humility; do you recall her Magnificat, in which Mary proclaims her littleness before the greatness of God—Lk 1:48?). Further, with humility we discover evidence of our unworthiness (cf. Mt 22:12). This moral-spiritual attitude qualifies as a kind of prayer that ... gives us the consciousness of ourselves. We could call it a prayer of self-consciousness, a reflexive prayer regarding our lives, especially regarding our moral condition.[35]

It is precisely this "moral-spiritual attitude" exhibited in a consciousness of one's lowliness in relation to God's Majesty, a recognition of

---

34. Paul VI, *Mirificus eventus*.
35. Paul VI, "General Audience, January 16, 1974."

the divine intention and an awareness of one's inability to realize it, and a humble abandonment of one's entire self to God's grace, that Pope Paul has in mind when developing the second path of renewal in *ES*. He calls Mary's humility "metaphysical," no doubt in order to avoid any implication that her humility infers any reference to sin on her part. Mary's humility is that of the creature before God. Yet, even before Mary proclaims her humility in the Magnificat, she proclaims it through her response to Gabriel's announcement: "How can this be?" (Luke 1:34) She is conscious that the vocation entrusted to her, to be the virgin Mother of God, is absolutely beyond her; she cannot fulfill it by her own power. The word she must have been thinking of is "impossible," since this is the word that Gabriel uses to reassure her: "For with God nothing will be impossible" (Luke 1:37). Mary will have to rely on a new divine intervention in her life. She will have to be renewed in order to fulfill her mission, to become what God wants her to be.

This Marian consideration sheds light on an aspect of Vatican II considered as a New Pentecost. The relation of Mary's being overshadowed by the Holy Spirit and the fulfillment of her vocation and mission to the descent of the Holy Spirit on Pentecost and the fulfillment of the Church's vocation and mission allows us to see that Vatican II is equally a New Annunciation for the Church. Without phrasing it this way, John Paul II brings this out in his meditation on Mary's faith in his encyclical, *Redemptoris Mater*. He tells us that Mary is the perfect realization of the Council's description of faith in *DV*, 5.[36] Since he holds that the implementation of Vatican II essentially consists in the enrichment of faith by which this same description of faith is realized in the lives of the faithful,[37] his analysis of Mary's faith sets forth the ideal that is the goal of the renewal of Vatican II.

The parallel is clear: as God made known to Mary his vision for her life and renewed her through the overshadowing of the Holy Spirit, through Vatican II the Holy Spirit speaks to the Church of our age in order to lead the Church into a deeper understanding of her mystery, vocation, and mission. Pope Paul's mission is to exhort and to guide the Church in responding to be what God has made known he wants her to be. Only in this way will the Church be able to overcome the moral problem "uppermost in the life of the Church":

---

36. See John Paul II, *RMat*, 13.
37. This is the essential thesis of *SR*.

> We are taken up by the desire to see the Church of God become what Christ wants her to be, one, holy, and entirely dedicated to the pursuit of perfection to which she is effectively called. Perfect as she is in the ideal conception of her Divine Founder, the Church should tend towards becoming perfect in the real expression of her earthly existence. This is the great moral problem which is uppermost in the life of the Church, a problem which reveals what she is, stimulates her, accuses her, and sustains her. (*ES*, 41)

Like Mary, the Church stands in need of divine grace in order to live up to her vocation. Also like Mary, with Vatican II the Church enters into a new awareness of her own mystery, and this constitutes a new call to be graced for renewal. In contrast to Mary, whose humility is entirely metaphysical, the Church's humility is also a "great moral problem" because, unlike Mary, the Church's conversion necessitates graces to turn from sin and to turn to God in order to realize her vocation. Thus, for the Church, perfection entails a "moral problem." But, in the very process of striving to attain this holiness, the Church is brought back to the source and cause of this perfection, Christ himself, for only through him, with him, and in him can she "become what she is."

THE GOAL: HOLINESS

There is no doubt that for Pope Paul the immediate goal of renewal through *metanoia* is growth in holiness: "It is precisely this holiness and splendor which we are endeavoring to discover and promote" (*ES*, 47). All the efforts are directed toward "acquiring that sanctity which Christ teaches" (*ES*, 41). The goal of the intra-ecclesial dialogue is "that the holiness and vitality of the Mystical Body of Christ on earth may be increased" (*ES*, 116). The result will be "new expressions of sanctity" (*ES*, 43). Faithfully reflecting the emphasis of *ES* on holiness, Pope Paul incisively and emphatically underscores the centrality of the call to holiness for the renewal of Vatican II in a post-Conciliar apostolic letter of 1969:

> This strong invitation to holiness could be regarded as the most characteristic element in the whole Magisterium of the Council, and so to say, its ultimate purpose.[38]

---

38. Paul VI, "Motu proprio *Sanctitas clarior*," in *AAS* 61 (1969) 149.

If, then, in *ES aggiornamento* is taken to be "the guiding criterion" of the Council (*ES*, 50), this must be understood in relation to holiness. Indeed, for Pope Paul *aggiornamento* chiefly concerns the moral dimension of personal updating through conversion. He roots it within the Church's "perennial vitality" and "youthful agility," that is, the ability to grow and to adapt. Then he underscores the personal rather than institutional priority that this updating entails.[39] The immediate goal of renewal through conversion is conformity to the divine ideal for the Church (second path), and the ultimate goal is revitalized mission through dialogue (third path). Regarding the immediate goal, Pope Paul writes in terms of *Christian perfection*, *holiness* or *sanctity*, and *charity*; it is a question of leading all the faithful to the fullness of life in Christ.

> The Church will rediscover her renewed youthfulness not so much by changing her exterior laws as by interiorly assimilating her true spirit of obedience to Christ and accordingly by observing those laws which the Church prescribes for herself with the intention of following Christ. (*ES*, 51)

---

39. The primacy of personal renewal in faith and holiness over institutional reform is a constant among Paul VI's successors. Before becoming pope, Cardinal Wojtyła put it this way: "When we speak of 'building up the Church as a community' we are thinking not so much of the process of building or the actual structures envisaged by Vatican II, but rather the attitude without which these structures and that process would be suspended in the void" (*SR*, 367). He is consistent with this as pope: "To carry out better your task of proclaiming Christ to the men and women of today and shedding the light of Gospel wisdom on the challenges and problems that beset the Church and society in Latin America at the beginning of the new millennium, the Church needs *many competent evangelizers* who, brimming with faith and hope, will speak 'increasingly of Jesus Christ' (*EAm*, 67) with fresh zeal and a profound ecclesial spirit. These evangelizers—bishops, priests and deacons, men and women religious, faithful lay persons—are, under the guidance of the Holy Spirit, the indispensable primary agents in the task of evangelization in which persons count more than structures, necessary though at times these may be" ("Address, March 27, 2003," 3). For Benedict: "The Church in Germany is superbly organized. But behind the structures, is there also a corresponding spiritual strength, the strength of faith in the living God? We must honestly admit that we have more than enough by way of structure but not enough by way of Spirit. I would add: the real crisis facing the Church in the western world is a crisis of faith. If we do not find a way of genuinely renewing our faith, all structural reform will remain ineffective" (Benedict XVI, "Address, September 24, 2011"). The *General Catechetical Directory* bears witness to the same conviction: "Any pastoral activity for the carrying out of which there are not at hand persons with the right formation and preparation will necessarily come to nothing. The working tools themselves cannot be effective unless used by catechists who have been rightly formed. Hence, the suitable formation of catechists must come before reform in texts and strengthening of the organization for handling catechesis" (108).

This interior assimilation, he says, "is the secret of her renewal, here her *metanoia*, here her exercise of perfection" (*ES*, 51). The duty that the Church embraces at Vatican II is that "of correcting the defects of its own members and of leading them to greater perfection" (*ES*, 11). Christ calls the Church to perfection, and he provides the means necessary to strive for it (*ES*, 41). Responding to this call entails conversion: "This search for perfection fills her with groanings and prayers, with repentance and hope" (*ES*, 41).

While the pursuit of Christian perfection directly derives from the Church's vertical communion with God and the doctrinal consciousness of the truth he has revealed about the Church (first path), it is not isolated from the Church's mission in the world (third path). For Pope Paul, the conditions in which the Church conducts her mission are an impetus to holiness: "In the pursuit of spiritual and moral perfection the Church receives an exterior stimulus from the conditions in which she lives." This is because the Church "cannot remain unaffected by or indifferent to the changes that take place in the world around her" (*ES*, 42). This stimulus derives from the Church's mission, which requires that "Christian life . . . be adapted to the forms of thought and custom which the temporal environment offers and imposes on her, provided they are compatible with the basic exigencies of her religious and moral program." This process of adaptation is by no means an unprincipled conformity to the values, customs, and mentalities of the world. Rather, the Church seeks "to purify them, to ennoble them, to vivify and to sanctify them" (*ES*, 42).

All of this "demands of the Church a perennial examination of her moral vigilance, which our times demand with particular urgency and exceptional seriousness." The Church "must strive to render herself immune from the contagion of error and of evil" that she encounters in her mission (*ES*, 42).

> In fact it [the Council] awakens in pastors as well as in the faithful the desire to preserve and increase in Christian life its character of supernatural authenticity and reminds all of their duty of effectively and deeply imprinting that character in their own personal conduct, thus leading the weak to be good, the good to be better, the better to be generous, and the generous to be holy. It gives rise to new expressions of sanctity, urges love to be genial, and evokes fresh outpourings of virtue and Christian heroism. (*ES*, 43)

To employ a simile, as clothes must fit the person, so a culture must fit the faithful. A culture fits the faith only to the extent that it is a carrier of the true, the good, and the beautiful. These are determinative of the extent to which the Church is able to accommodate herself to culture and to produce new expressions of holiness.

REFORM CANNOT CONCERN WHAT GOD HAS ESTABLISHED

Pope Paul is convinced that the institutional dimension of *aggiornamento* "cannot concern either the essential conception of the Church or its basic structure." The Church has no authority to alter what has been divinely instituted; that would imply that man stands in judgment of God. Or, it would imply that in some essential way the Church had been unfaithful to what has been divinely instituted: "we cannot level the charge of infidelity against God's holy and beloved Church" (*ES*, 46). It cannot be said that anything essential has been lost along the way of the Church's pilgrimage through history.

Notwithstanding such clear assertions, barely four years after the Council's conclusion, Pope Paul found it necessary to address what he called a spirit of "free criticism" precisely because it trespassed the boundaries he had clearly set forth in *ES*. Further, Pope Paul criticizes "free criticism" for being doctrinally and spiritually cheap, lacking "any doctrinal, disciplinary, liturgical, or community commitment." In other words, "free criticism" does not foster personal conversion into a deeper holiness and a more effective dialogue.

> What shall we say? What attitude should our love for the Church take? Above all we will reflect on this word, "structures," with its various meanings, in order to distinguish structures that are constitutional for the Church, to which we must remain firmly attached—and not only by resignation—from structures deriving from the path of historical tradition and from a development from the essential roots of the evangelical and apostolic message. In these structures there can be elements that are not essential to the image and the permanent life of the Church. There can also be some institutions or customs that are abusive or that are no longer capable of fostering the contact of the Church with historic or social situations that have changed. Here, the reform can and in certain cases must innovate. But, to whom falls the

judgment, the authority, and the responsibility of serious and innovative interventions?[40]

Even with this clarification, Pope Paul is attentive to and warns against more than one temptation that would run counter to a genuine institutional reform of the Church. One of these is an archaizing spirit based on "thinking that the edifice of the Church which has now become large and majestic for the glory of God as his magnificent temple, should be reduced to its early minimal proportions as if they alone were true and good." Another is "the desire of renewing the structure of the Church through the charismatic way . . . thus introducing an arbitrary scheme of artificial renewal in the very constitution of the Church" (*ES*, 47).

Pope Paul gives more attention to a third danger, namely "that the reform of the Church should consist primarily in adapting its sentiments and habits to those of the world" (*ES*, 48). This becomes an issue when those who are engaged in mission can no longer distinguish between what is essential and unchanging, on one hand, and what can be adapted because it is historically or culturally conditioned, on the other hand.[41] The challenge to the Church is "to be in the world, and not of the world" (*ES*, 48).

On this third danger, the Holy Father seems especially attentive to the power of the temptation to a form of accommodation to the spirit of the world that would minimize the "price" of Christian faith, thus, again, a free or cheap criticism. A watering down or even omission of certain of the more demanding elements of Christian life, like the "hard saying" (John 6:60), may make it easier for people to come to Christ and his Church. But, without the death-to-self participation in the Paschal Mystery, which is the very meaning of baptism, would this be a genuine conversion? Would such a "conversion" be anything more than a tacit approval of how people are already living?

Even as the Church cannot accommodate herself to the spirit of the world by removing the more demanding elements of the Gospel, so too she must be ready to remove all that makes conversion into Christ and his Church more difficult than it has to be. Pope Paul asserts that an element of the pastoral nature of Vatican II includes "the desire to make the

---

40. Paul VI, "General Audience, May 7, 1969."

41. As a priest serving in the office of the Secretary of State, Fr. Montini would be personally familiar with the challenge of discerning between what is essential and what can be adapted. One such example was the resolution of the "Chinese rites" controversy with Pius XII's Instruction, *Plane compertum est*, in *AAS* 32 (1940) 24–26.

practice of Christian life as easy as possible," but he immediately qualifies this by adding that it must be "in conformity with its supernatural character" (*ES*, 43). And, if reform includes simplifying some of the Church's laws in order to make it less burdensome to observe them, this does not imply antinomianism. Ecclesiastical law with its binding force always has a place (*ES*, 51), and Pope Paul's focus is on its relation to renewal through conversion.

> The Christian life, which the Church interprets and sets down in wise regulations, will always require faithfulness, effort, mortification and sacrifice; it will always bear the mark of the "narrow way" of which Our Lord speaks to us (cf. Matt 7:13–14); it will require not less moral energy of us modern Christians than it did of Christians in the past, but perhaps more. It will call for a prompt obedience, no less binding today than in the past, that will be, perhaps, more difficult, and certainly more meritorious in that it is guided more by supernatural motives than natural ones.
>
> It is not conformity to the spirit of the world, not immunity from the discipline of reasonable asceticism, not indifference to the laxity of modern behavior, not emancipation from the authority of prudent and lawful superiors, not apathy with regard to the contradictory forms of modern thought, that can give vigor to the Church, or make her fit to receive the influence of the gifts of the Holy Spirit, or render her following of Christ more genuine, or give her the anxious yearning of fraternal charity and the ability to communicate her message. These things come from her aptitude to live according to divine grace, her faithfulness to the Gospel of the Lord, her hierarchical and communal unity. The Christian is not soft and cowardly, he is strong and faithful. (*ES*, 51)

Pope Paul is anything but naïve regarding the demands of the renewal through conversion that he envisions. It is a participation in the violence that Christ suffered in order to establish the Kingdom of God.[42] This evangelical *metanoia* makes demands on every one of a person's faculties and stretches them to new levels of perfection, for only in this way can the whole man be renewed in Christ.

By its nature the conversion that begins with baptism is ongoing. An absence of conversion is a worrisome sign of the religious formalism mentioned earlier, when profession and practice of faith no longer

---

42. On the violence of conversion, see Paul VI, *EN*, 10.

reach the interior depths of conscience, where truth, freedom, and responsibility interact with one another to produce a critical judgment and a commitment to self-reform. The Church is the community of men and women living this commitment to self-reform, and this life of continual conversion is a great sign that gives hope to all who encounter within themselves the dynamisms that are fulfilled in self-renewal. With the benefit of twenty-five years of reflection on Vatican II, John Paul II incisively put it this way:

> Certainly, every convert is a gift to the Church and represents a serious responsibility for her, not only because converts have to be prepared for Baptism through the catechumenate and then be guided by religious instruction, but also because—especially in the case of adults—such converts bring with them a kind of new energy, an enthusiasm for the faith, and a desire to see the Gospel lived out in the Church. They would be greatly disappointed if, having entered the ecclesial community, they were to find a life lacking fervor and without signs of renewal! We cannot preach conversion unless we ourselves are converted anew every day.[43]

The second path of renewal through conversion is not a method of man's invention but a dimension of "the logic of things" established by God. The experience of being enriched by God's love becomes an impetus for sharing this transforming love with others. Pope Paul's emphasis is on calling the Church's members to rediscover the primacy of their relationship with God in order more deeply to experience his love. This will reinforce the exercise of responsible fidelity to God while at the same time impelling the faithful to mission. This is the necessary condition for the transition to the third path of missionary dialogue, in which the perspective changes to a concern that the Church exercise a responsible fidelity to man. Fidelity to God necessarily entails fidelity to man.

---

43. John Paul II, *RMiss*, 47.

5

The Third Path: Dialogue

THOUGH "IN VOGUE" AT the time of its use, it should be apparent from the preceding that Pope Paul's understanding of the third path, dialogue, is more complex and richer than the common understanding. Dialogue, as Paul understands the term, refers to "the manner, art, and style that the Church must infuse into her ministerial activity to meet the dissonant, changing, diverse voices of the contemporary world."[1] In short, dialogue is another way to describe the Church's mission, ministry, service, apostolate and pastoral activity. Pope John Paul II confirms this connection to the Church's mission saying:

> The third path is the way of the apostolate. For the ecclesial community, the method of dialogue is becoming the way in which to work to bring the Lord's comforting message of salvation everywhere.[2]

Likewise, it should be evident that the third path naturally arises from the first two paths; it is necessarily the fruit of an encounter with the Lord. Pope Paul explains this necessity saying:

> The very nature of the gifts which Christ has given the Church demands that they be extended to others and shared with others. This must be obvious from the words: "Going, therefore,

---

1. Paul VI, "General Audience, August 5, 1964."
2. John Paul II, "Angelus Address, August 8, 1999," 2.

teach ye all nations" (Matt 28:19), Christ's final command to his apostles. The word apostle implies a mission from which there is no escaping. (*ES*, 64)

Building on the preceding analyses, then, this chapter's focus is on the "logic" underlying the three paths in order to demonstrate why the first two paths are incomplete without the third and why the third depends on the first two. Secondly, this chapter will draw on the *operatio sequitur esse* principle in order to demonstrate how this logical relationship actually articulates a pastoral agent's participation in the person and mission of Christ.

DISTINGUISH IN ORDER TO UNITE

The third part of *ES* on missionary dialogue begins by indicating that the difference between the Church and the world, the difference on which mission is founded, is the consequence of the first path of doctrinal consciousness and the second path of renewal through conversion.

> If the Church acquires an ever-growing awareness of herself, and if the Church tries to model itself on the ideal which Christ proposes to it, the result is that the Church becomes radically different from the human environment in which it, of course, lives or which it approaches. (*ES*, 58)

As the Church conforms more perfectly to God's plan, an inevitable but understandable distance is created from the rest of mankind. Yet, it must be kept firmly in mind, that God's plan of love is a plan for the fullest flourishing of life for men.[3] Vatican II calls this a fully human life, the realization of the happiness to which all aspire. The Church's mission is to be at the service of promoting this fully human life, which is life in Christ, by proclaiming the power of God's truth and love that make man's transformation possible. Through her, God's grace purifies what is opposed to a fully human life in Christ. This is the conversion by which men cooperate with God's graces to receive his transforming love. The "radical difference" between the Church and the world, though inevitable, cannot be an excuse to compromise the message of liberating truth, since this would leave man exactly where he is. The first and foundational service of

---

3. See Paul VI, *ES*, 63.

the Church to mankind is to proclaim the truth in its integrity and then to accompany those who receive it on the path of conversion.

Pope Paul's address for the closing of the Vatican II is his most emphatic development of this theme of the Church being at the service of promoting a fully human life. He states that "all this rich teaching is channeled in one direction, the service of mankind." This is so central to Pope Paul's understanding of Vatican II, that he repeats: "The Church has, so to say, declared herself the servant of humanity . . . the idea of service has been central." The Church accomplishes this service by leading men to God. The Council's "concern is with man and with earth, but it rises to the kingdom of God." He insists on this other-orientedness of the Church, saying "everything has been referred to human usefulness." Through the Council the Catholic Church "declares itself entirely on the side of man and in his service."

> In this way the Catholic religion and human life reaffirm their alliance with one another, the fact that they converge on one single human reality: the Catholic religion is for mankind. In a certain sense it is the life of mankind. It is so by the extremely precise and sublime interpretation that our religion gives of humanity (surely man by himself is a mystery to himself) and gives this interpretation in virtue of its knowledge of God: a knowledge of God is a prerequisite for a knowledge of man as he really is, in all his fullness; . . . The Catholic religion is man's life because it determines life's nature and destiny; it gives life its real meaning, it establishes the supreme law of life and infuses it with that mysterious activity which we may say divinizes it.[4]

The Church's duty in relation to mankind is anything but sentimentality that is incapable of engagement and sacrifice. It is rooted in divine revelation that gives rise to "a precise and sublime interpretation" of who man is and of his condition. The chief indication of this truth becoming effectual commitment to man is the Incarnation. Because in Christ God has become man

> in everyone we can and must recognize the countenance of Christ (cf. Matt 25:40), the Son of Man, especially when tears and sorrows make it plain to see, and if we can and must recognize in Christ's countenance the countenance of our heavenly Father "He who sees me," Our Lord said, "sees also the Father" (John 14:9), our humanism becomes Christianity, our

---

4. Paul VI, "Address, December 7, 1965."

Christianity becomes centered on God; in such sort that we may say, to put it differently: a knowledge of man is a prerequisite for a knowledge of God.

With these ideas in mind, Pope Paul can insist that Vatican II is a council "concentrated principally on man." This should be no surprise, since God has revealed himself to be concentrated on man, solicitous for man's welfare. The Church's solicitude for man derives from her communion with God and participation in his solicitude for man. She knows man by knowing God and his revelation, so that she has a "theocentric and theological concept of man." The movement is from God to man, even as the commandment to love God with one's whole heart, mind, soul, and strength comes first but necessarily leads to love of neighbor. Pope Paul calls this theocentricity the Council's "guiding principle": to seek *first* the Kingdom of God.[5] The desire to give glory and honor to God is fulfilled by the faithful execution of the missionary mandate. As a consequence, the Council's teaching is "to love man in order to love God."[6]

> To love man, we say, not as a means but as the first step toward the final and transcendent goal which is the basis and cause of every love. And so this council can be summed up in its ultimate religious meaning, which is none other than a pressing and friendly invitation to mankind of today to rediscover in fraternal love the God "to turn away from whom is to fall, to turn to whom is to rise again, to remain in whom is to be secure . . . to return to whom is to be born again, in whom to dwell is to live." (St. Augustine, *Solil.* I, 1, 3; PL 32, 870)[7]

---

5. Paul VI, "Address, December 7, 1965."

6. John Paul II gives a concise summary of the correlativity of this theocentricity and anthropocentricity: "In Jesus Christ, every path to man . . . is simultaneously an approach to the Father and his love. The Second Vatican Council has confirmed this truth for our time. The more the Church's mission is centered upon man—the more it is, so to speak, anthropocentric—the more it must be confirmed and actualized theocentrically, that is to say, be directed in Jesus Christ to the Father. While the various currents of human thought both in the past and at the present have tended and still tend to separate theocentrism and anthropocentrism, and even to set them in opposition to each other, the Church, following Christ, seeks to link them up in human history, in a deep and organic way. And this is also one of the basic principles, perhaps the most important one, of the teaching of the last Council" (*DM*, 1).

7. Paul VI, "Address, December 7, 1965." Cardinal Wojtyła incisively sums up the Church's mission: "To 'make human life more human' is the Council's fundamental objective, closely linked to the desire to share in the divine life and in the mission of Christ" (*SR*, 279).

Since all desire to live a fully human life, nothing is more effective for mission than witness to this life. Conscious of having received this life as a gift of grace and of her mission, the Church can proclaim: "I have that for which you search, that which you lack." Men and women speak of and seek "truth, justice, freedom, progress, concord, peace and civilization," and the Church desires to enter into dialogue with them on these subjects, for "these are words whose secret is known to the Church, for Christ has entrusted the secret to its keeping. And so the Church has a message for every category of humanity" (*ES*, 95). Reading the signs of the times, Pope Paul discerns the yearning and dreams of men for justice and progress, but without reference to God. The Church's mission is to make known "the ineradicable need for the Divine Source and End of all things" so that these "great-hearted" and "noble" aspirations may be realized (*ES*, 104).

The Church's members have such noble and authentically human aspirations in common with all men. The difference is that the faithful have received God's revelation in Jesus Christ as the fulfillment of these aspirations. To respond to the call to holiness is to receive the grace to live up the full potential of one's humanity, since "by this holiness as such a more human manner of living is promoted in this earthly society."[8] Understanding that a recognition of the difference between the Church and the world is necessary in order to unite mankind is key to grasping the relationship among the three paths of *ES*.[9] Essentially, Pope Paul sees the first two paths as the necessary conditions for (the two "if" clauses of *ES*, 58, quoted above) effective missionary activity. The first two paths are causes of the third path in as much as the Church cooperates with God's graces in order to become what she in fact is in God's eyes.

---

8. Vatican II, *LG*, 40.

9. To reiterate, the Church becomes different from the world to the degree that she recognizes how much God's vision for her happiness differs from the world's vision. Since this difference is grounded in his vision of happiness for all mankind, a recognition of the difference is necessary to unite men more closely to God and to one other. Recognition of this difference arises from a faith-awareness of who God is, who we are, and what God is for us (first path), and from conversion into all that God intends us to be (second path). The universality of this divine intention is the inspiration for Christ's command to his apostles, "Go, therefore, to all the nations . . ."

THE LOGIC OF THE THREE PATHS

There is no doubt that for Paul VI the third path presupposes the first two and relates to them as their fruit. In the introductory section of *ES*, he states: "Our third thought ... follows from the first two, and concerns the relationships which the Church of today should establish with the world" (*ES*, 12).

The focus of this chapter being on the interrelationships among the three paths, a clarification about the translation of this passage of *ES*, 12 is in order. "Follows from" is not the most felicitous rendering of the Italian and Latin verbs here, *sorgente* and *oritur*, which mean "to spring from or out of, to arise from or out of, to flow from or out of." The Latin especially has the connotation of "having its origin in." The third path not only comes after the first two, but has its origin in them. If "follows from" is taken in the logical sense of a conclusion being contained in premises, then it comes closer to the Italian and Latin.

Msgr. Giuseppe Colombo, a theologian familiar with Pope Paul VI, and this encyclical in particular, confirms that

> Effectively, the three parts of the encyclical are conceived in a rigorously logical succession, such that from the first part (consciousness of the Church) the second (renewal of the Church) "derives" or ought to derive, and these two converge or generate the third part (dialogue) (cf. *ES*, 13).[10]

Based on this "rigorously logical succession," Colombo sees a philosophical axiom at work that lends itself to assigning a certain priority to the final part on dialogue: "In the end, that which is last in execution, is first in intention."[11]

Applying this axiom to *ES* bestows on dialogue and the related mission and service of the Church, not just any kind of priority, but that of the end, the all-embracing goal. Colombo's own review of the archival evidence of notes and drafts of *ES* confirms that this is an accurate reading of the thought of Pope Paul. Drafts of *ES* in Pope Paul's own writing indicate that from the beginning his main focus was on dialogue, since an early draft of the encyclical contained only a treatment of that theme. At a certain point, Colombo remarks, Pope Paul realized that "the treatment

---

10. Colombo, "Genesi," 135–36. We will return to Colombo's analysis in Part III.
11. Colombo, "Genesi," 135–36

of the theme required the development of necessary presuppositions, precisely the consciousness and the renewal of the Church."[12]

There is no difficulty in acknowledging the primacy of dialogical mission, so long as one avoids concluding that consciousness and renewal through conversion are nothing more than means to the end of reinvigorating the Church's mission through dialogue. They are not means but ends in their own right. Only when sought for its own sake does doctrinal consciousness produce renewal through conversion. Similarly, only when *metanoia* is sought for its own sake does it yield the fruit of reinvigorated mission. This, by the way, indicates the difference between the two senses of method and of *aggiornamento* already discussed. Institutional updating is only a means, not an end, while personal renewal through conversion is an end, a good sought for its own sake. As the perfecting of persons, it naturally yields the fruit of a renewed engagement in mission.

We can conclude, then, that the "rigorous and logical succession" regarding the three paths of renewal set forth in *ES* developed as a result of Pope Paul's realization that dialogue cannot be isolated from the renewal and the consciousness upon which it depends. Dialogue being the intended goal, it cannot be attained except as a fruit of consciousness and renewal. Here we have an initial and fundamental guiding principle for the renewal undertaken by Vatican II, for all programs of formation, and for pastoral theology: pastoral action flows naturally out of spiritual renewal and the doctrinal awareness upon which renewal depends. If the pastoral mission of dialogical service is missing, this can only mean that something is defective in doctrinal and spiritual formation. Pastoral action of service stands in relation to doctrinal and spiritual formation as good works stand to faith: "Faith apart from works is dead" (Jas 2:26).

"ACTION FOLLOWS UPON BEING" (*OPERATIO SEQUITUR ESSE*)

The most foundational way to understand the third path of missionary dialogue as the effect or fruit of the first and second paths is in light of the relation between being and action. This relation is conveyed by the adage, "action/operation follows upon being" (*operatio sequitur esse*). Certain characteristic actions or behaviors are associated with each kind of being, so that by knowing what a thing is one also knows how it will act. Dogs

12. Colombo, "Genesi," 136–37.

bark, cats meow, cows moo, and sheep bleat. Christians are known by their love for one another (John 13:5), their readiness to love and to forgive enemies, their living the beatitudes and fruits of the Holy Spirit, their readiness to be martyred, their adhering to the teaching of the apostles, and the breaking of bread (Acts 2:42).

More than one hundred times, Pope Paul tells us, Vatican II insisted on the Christian dignity conferred on Christians by Christ through the Sacrament of Baptism. In doing so, the Council intended to revitalize an awareness of the connection between this baptismal dignity, this being-in-Christ, and life. This new, supernatural being is a participation in the life of Christ, and in his mission. Therefore, "to evangelize and to live are for us [Christians] even one same thing."[13]

> The Ecumenical Council has effectively put this in light. In reality, each son of the Church, it said, is missionary by his baptismal vocation. He should not be able to shirk this duty without neglecting the exigencies of his supernatural life. No one in the Church is so small and poor that he is not able to make, according to his own condition, his own contribution to the building up of the Kingdom of God on earth.[14]

On another occasion, in a general audience during the first week of Easter, when the impressions of the Easter Vigil Mass were still fresh in Pope Paul's mind, he elaborates on the implications of baptism for Christian life in more general terms.[15] It is clear that in the background he has in mind the Council's pastoral concern regarding the split between faith and life. His focus in this audience is to remind his listeners that

> to be baptized, that is, to be Christians, is not a passing moment, but a permanent state. It is not a thing of little value, but an incomparable boon. And, God willing, besides being decisive for the way we conceive our lives and the discernment and execution of our duties, it is decisive for our salvation.[16]

The grace of new life in Christ constitutes a call to conform one's thoughts, words, and actions to God's plan of love. Knowledge of this plan comes through faith in divine revelation, and the concrete direction for daily life based on this revelation comes from "the interior forum of each one's

---

13. Paul VI, "Address, November 23, 1965."
14. Paul VI, "Message for the World Day for Missions, 1966."
15. Paul VI, "General Audience, April 14, 1971."
16. Paul VI, "General Audience, April 14, 1971."

conscience." A Christian conscience dictates: "Be Christian!" Pope Paul's focus is the high moral standard of Christian life, that "our lives must not contradict our Christian character with which baptism has clothed us."

It is clear that this plan reprises the essential lines of thought on the first two paths of *ES*. What Pope Paul adds in this general audience is the observation that this link between Christian being and Christian living is rooted in "the logic of things," and that this logic is conveyed in the axiom of scholastic theologians: *operatio sequitur esse*. Characteristically Christian actions are indisputable signs[17] that God's love has efficaciously changed the human condition. In biblical language, the acts of Christian virtues are the fruits that are produced in the lives of those who, by the graces conferred through the sacraments, become branches of the Vine who is Christ (John 15:1–6). Just as "each tree is known by its own fruit" (Luke 6:44), so Christians can be known by their actions, especially their love: "By this all men will know that you are my disciples, if you have love for one another" (John 13:35).

Although the *operatio sequitur esse* principle remains only implicit in *ES*, it is the key to grasping why the third path of dialogue (mission, ministry, apostolate, and service) comes last and presupposes the first two paths. Pope Paul exhibits profound theological and pastoral wisdom in following this order. Were he to focus exclusively on mission and to isolate it from doctrinal consciousness and spiritual renewal through conversion, there would be nothing to consider other than methodologies and techniques geared to maximum efficacy in the apostolate. Further, this would effectively marginalize the initiatives of the Holy Spirit in the Church's life because the Spirit works most powerfully through those who are most responsive to his inspirations, namely, saints. The great, fruitful missions in the Church's history have originated with saints. Finally, the essential foundation of the Church's dialogue is the witness of

---

17. "Love of neighbor, action taken to care for the poor, and the practice of works of mercy . . . are so many manifestations of Christian life lived to its fullness. After prayer . . . and as the prolongation of prayer, the practice of charity is the clear sign of the fullness of grace in a soul. This is why the Church has always valued employing the best of her resources and to commit her children to the way of a vibrant charity" (Paul VI, "Address, September 10, 1965"). The vocabulary of "manifestation" and "sign" links this with the ecclesiology of *LG* and the Church as sacrament, that is, sign and instrument. One dimension of the Church's reality as sign is the fully human life of those who have been transformed by the love of God. Since all men desire to be fulfilled in their humanity, the sign of new life in Christ has great power to attract people to the Church.

Christian life. The witness of holiness testifies to the transforming power of God's love and the graces that come through the Church. In the virtuous actions of Christians the world perceives the reality that all men cannot avoid seeking, namely, a fully human life.

Pope Paul gives us a most compelling development of this last point about witness:

> Above all the Gospel must be proclaimed by witness. Take a Christian or a handful of Christians who, in the midst of their own community, show their capacity for understanding and acceptance, their sharing of life and destiny with other people, their solidarity with the efforts of all for whatever is noble and good. Let us suppose that, in addition, they radiate in an altogether simple and unaffected way their faith in values that go beyond current values, and their hope in something that is not seen and that one would not dare to imagine. Through this wordless witness these Christians stir up irresistible questions in the hearts of those who see how they live: Why are they like this? Why do they live in this way? What or who is it that inspires them? Why are they in our midst? Such a witness is already a silent proclamation of the Good News and a very powerful and effective one. Here we have an initial act of evangelization. The above questions will perhaps be the first that many non-Christians will ask, whether they are people to whom Christ has never been proclaimed, or baptized people who do not practice, or people who live as nominal Christians but according to principles that are in no way Christian, or people who are seeking, and not without suffering, something or someone whom they sense but cannot name. Other questions will arise, deeper and more demanding ones, questions evoked by this witness which involves presence, sharing, solidarity, and which is an essential element, and generally the first one, in evangelization.[18]

The *operatio sequitur esse* principle is so much in "the logic of things" that St. Paul cannot set forth the doctrine of God's love and the justification of Christians without at the same time elaborating on how this affects the conduct of Christians. This results in those sections of St. Paul's letters called parenetic, that is, comprised of instruction and exhortation regarding the Christian way of life.[19] In these passages, St.

---

18. Paul VI, *EN*, 21.

19. The word "parenetic" (from the Greek *paraenesis*) refers to a form of exhortatory speech. In the writings of St. Paul, his exhortations are rooted in doctrine regarding the new creation that Christians have become. Vatican II displays this parenetic

Paul contrasts the behavior of formerly Jewish Christians with their prior behavior as Jews, or the behavior of formerly Gentile converts with their behavior before they came to faith. The key is to see that he roots this before-and-after in what Christ has revealed about God, his love, and his law. This doctrine recapitulates the meaning of his converts' encounter with Christ in faith and baptism, to which he ascribes being the cause of a change in who they are, in their very being, which is at the root of their change in behavior. Constantly he reminds his converts of the behavior that befits the children of God, those who have been transformed by the gift of the Holy Spirit. He makes himself the prime example. Before being baptized he "persecuted the church of God violently and tried to destroy it" (Gal 1:13[20]), while afterward he proclaimed the Gospel throughout the world in order to build up the Church (Gal 1:23).

DIALOGUE ROOTED IN PARTICIPATION

It should be apparent from the above that a proper understanding of the third path of dialogue yields a deeper understanding of the applicability of the *operatio sequitur esse* principle. The question yet to be addressed is: Exactly what is the nature of the being (*esse*) that is the source of pastoral actions (*operatio*) that constitute participation in the Church's mission? Because it must be a being (*esse*) that is proportionate to the envisioned action, a more precise understanding of the action called "dialogue" or the "new evangelization" will entail a more precise understanding of the being that gives rise to it.

Genuine Christian charitable action is revelatory of the Christian identity of those who exercise charity because it is a participation in the messianic mission of Christ.[21] This is necessary if the Church's mission

---

quality of style in two fundamental ways. First, there are a great many exhortatory passages in the texts of the Council. See, for example, the final exhortations in *AA*, 33, and *PO*, 22. More directly relevant to this study, the Council as a whole can be considered parenetic, since its purpose is not only to clarify doctrine but to do so in a pastoral style ordered to overcoming the split between faith and life so that the light of Christ might shine more brightly in the world.

20. See also 1 Cor 15:9; Phil 3:5–6; 1 Tim 1:13.

21. It should be obvious that, while pastoral activity involves questions of methods and techniques, it cannot be reduced to such questions. This is one of the major points made by Benedict XVI in his first encyclical. See Benedict XVI, *DCE*, 31: "Individuals who care for those in need must first be professionally competent: they should be properly trained in what to do and how to do it, and committed to continuing care.

and pastoral actions are to be elements of the Church's sacramental nature; they must point to the supernatural reality of participation in divine life, which is their source. It is not necessary that this "pointing" be explicit at the very moment of serving someone in need, but it is a fact that many charitable services, like those of religious men and women, are clearly identifiable as "Catholic" either because of explicit indicators (paraphernalia, clothes, signs, etc.) or explicit behavior connected to the service (e.g., prayer, devotions, Mass, etc.). In one way or another, sooner or later, it will become clear that pastoral agents are acting out of their participation in the mission of Christ, who is the model to be imitated. All that he did was revelatory of who he is. His efficacious acts of healing are rooted in his being with the Father and in his love for men. Jesus knows himself as the Son who is one with the Father and who is sent by the Father to bring divine love into the world: "He who sent me is with me; he has not left me alone, for I always do what is pleasing to him" (John 8:29), and "I am not alone, for the Father is with me" (John 16:32). St. John Paul II expressed this reality in terms of communion as the origin of mission, the *esse* from which missionary action proceeds. At the same time, communion is the goal of missionary action; the purpose of dialogical love and service is to draw men into a participation in the communion of the Father, Son, and Holy Spirit.[22]

Yet, while professional competence is a primary, fundamental requirement, it is not of itself sufficient. We are dealing with human beings, and human beings always need something more than technically proper care. They need humanity. They need heartfelt concern. Those who work for the Church's charitable organizations must be distinguished by the fact that they do not merely meet the needs of the moment, but they dedicate themselves to others with heartfelt concern, enabling them to experience the richness of their humanity. Consequently, in addition to their necessary professional training, these charity workers need a 'formation of the heart': they need to be led to that encounter with God in Christ which awakens their love and opens their spirits to others. As a result, love of neighbor will no longer be for them a commandment imposed, so to speak, from without, but a consequence deriving from their faith, a faith which becomes active through love (cf. Gal 5:6)."

22. John Paul II, *CL*, 32: "Communion with Jesus, which gives rise to the communion of Christians among themselves, is an indispensable condition for bearing fruit: 'Apart from me you can do nothing' (John 15:5). And communion with others is the most magnificent fruit that the branches can give: in fact, it is the gift of Christ and his Spirit. At this point *communion begets communion*: essentially it is likened to a *mission on behalf of communion*. In fact, Jesus says to his disciples: 'You did not choose me, but I chose you and *appointed you that you should go and bear fruit* and that your fruit should abide' (John 15:16). Communion and mission are profoundly connected with each other, they interpenetrate and mutually imply each other, to the point that

Similarly, the focus of spiritual formation is this mission-producing-communion with Christ. Communion, and thus holiness and the spiritual formation that fosters it, is the source of mission, while the focus of pastoral formation is this very same communion as it becomes action directed toward drawing others into communion. This shows how the theme of the spirituality of communion, developed most extensively in the final years of the pontificate of Pope John Paul II,[23] embraces the three dimensions of renewal and formation.

The biblical foundation of John Paul's insights concerning communion as source of mission and communion as the goal of mission is the passage on the vine and the branches, which must bear fruit (see John 15:4–8, 16). Pope Benedict based a complementary reflection on another biblical text to show the inner connection of being with action, communion with mission.

> In considering the question—What is the seminary for? What does this time mean?—I am always particularly struck by the account that Saint Mark gives of the birth of the apostolic community in the third chapter of his Gospel. Mark says: "And he appointed twelve." He makes something, he does something, it is a creative act; and he made them, "to be with him, and to be sent out to preach" (Mk 3:14). That is a twofold purpose, which in many respects seems contradictory. "To be with him": they are to be with him, in order to come to know him, to hear what he says, to be formed by him; they are to go with him, to accompany him on his path, surrounding him and following him. But at the same time they are to be envoys who go out, who take with them what they have learnt, who bring it to others who are also on a journey—into the margins, into the wide open spaces, even into places far removed from him. And yet this paradox holds together: if they are truly with him, then they are also always journeying towards others, they are searching for the lost sheep; they go out, they must pass on what they have found, they must make it known, they must become envoys. And conversely, if they want to be good envoys, then they must always be with him. As Saint Bonaventure once said: the angels, wherever they go, however far away, always move within the inner being of God. This is also the case here: as priests we must go out

---

communion represents both the source and the fruit of mission: communion gives rise to mission and mission is accomplished in communion."

23. Though this theme appears several times prior to the Jubilee Year 2000, it becomes prominent with *NMI* and thereafter.

onto the many different streets, where we find people whom we should invite to his wedding feast. But we can only do this if in the process we always remain with him. And learning this: this combination of, on the one hand, going out on mission, and on the other hand being with him, remaining with him, is—I believe—precisely what we have to learn in the seminary. The right way of remaining with him, becoming deeply rooted in him—being more and more with him, knowing him more and more, being more and more inseparable from him—and at the same time going out more and more, bringing the message, passing it on, not keeping it to ourselves, but bringing the word to those who are far away and who nevertheless, as God's creatures and as people loved by Christ, all have a longing for him in their hearts.[24]

Texts such as these of John Paul II and Benedict XVI indicate how profoundly rooted in biblical revelation the three dimensions of renewal and formation are. They also indicate that the spirit of Vatican II should be understood as the spirit of Catholicism engaging in self-renewal based on a return to the sources (*ressourcement*) for the sake of reinvigorating the life and mission of the Church in response to the particular challenges of the day (*aggiornamento*). At Vatican II the Church especially rediscovered and deepened her understanding of her catholicity (doctrinal awareness). This led to a prolonged pastoral discernment of the situation of man in the contemporary world for the purpose of directing the dynamism of her missionary charity with a wisdom that can effectively serve man in his quest to become more fully human (pastoral, missionary dialogue). The first demand that this deeper understanding of her catholicity and desire more effectively to live it places on the Church is to renew herself in Christ, because in humility she knows that this mission is greater than she is ("How shall this be?") and that only in communion with God can she accomplish it ("I can do all things in him who strengthens me" [Phil 4:13]) (spiritual renewal).

Returning now to the relation between being and action, the inner being of Christ is not directly observable. It can only be known on the basis of what he does and says.[25] His actions disclose the inner and

---

24. Benedict XVI, "Address, September 24, 2011."

25. To be complete, it is necessary to include the Father's testimony regarding the Son, at Jesus's baptism and at the transfiguration, the Father's answer to Jesus's prayer at the raising of Lazarus, and especially his own resurrection. Beginning with Pentecost, the Holy Spirit will bear witness to him.

hidden dimension of his being in relation to his mission, which remains hidden until faith can perceive it, to forgive sins. The first contact with Jesus is most often on the level of basic human and physical needs, yet this first contact opens up to a deeper contact that leads to faith in him. Similarly for his disciples, "good works done in a supernatural spirit have the power to draw men to belief and to God."[26] Clearly, such good works of the apostolate are rooted in the Christian being of those who perform them. They are efficacious signs of the transformation of the heart of the pastoral agent, of that agent's participation in the pastoral charity of Christ.[27] As signs of that charity they contribute to the efficacy of the Church as the sacrament of God's love. The spiritual dimension of life in Christ and the doctrine that gives it content shine through the pastoral dimension of service, apostolate, and ministry.

Participating in the divine pedagogy that works through the visible and human to lead to the invisible and divine, the Church engages in her mission and service in such a way that her actions point to her hidden essence as Bride and Body of Christ. In keeping with the summary of the spirituality of Vatican II given by Paul VI, the Church especially shows herself to be the servant of mankind. Christ-like, selfless service is the sign of the times for the nations by which the Church is the "sign on earth of God's holiness and the living gospel for all to hear."[28] This is why Vatican II and post-Conciliar popes put so much emphasis on witness. Witness is the primary mode of the new evangelization. It points beyond itself to the renewal of mind and heart in Christ that is the source of Christian action. As Pope John Paul II affirmed, "the witness of a holy life is the most convincing affirmation of the Gospel."[29]

> Human sanctity brings God into man's presence in a particular way, becomes a living witness to him and confirms the truth of the Gospel. Thus it does more than anything else to attract others to the way of salvation.[30]

---

26. Vatican II, *AA*, 6.

27. John Paul II, *RMiss*, 42: "The evangelical witness which the world finds most appealing is that of concern for people, and of charity toward the poor, the weak and those who suffer. The complete generosity underlying this attitude and these actions stands in marked contrast to human selfishness. It raises precise questions which lead to God and to the Gospel."

28. "Preface of Apostles II" in *The Roman Missal*.

29. John Paul II, "Address, October 29, 1992," 3.

30. Wojtyła, *SR*, 189.

Once this is perceived, it becomes clear that only those who are deeply conformed to Christ, who can say with St. Paul, "it is no longer I who live, but Christ who lives in me" (Gal 2:20), can engage in mission in such a way as to witness to Christ by way of giving compelling evidence to the transformation his grace has worked in their lives.

Just as importantly, witness makes contact with others in a way that respects their free will and constitutes an invitation to consider whether the fullness of life encountered in Christians corresponds to their own desire to live a fully human life.[31] The expression, "a more fully human life" corresponds to the traditional notion of happiness, which, as St. Thomas understood, all desire.[32] This innate dynamism toward human fulfillment is the reality that the Church's members have in common with every human person. It is therefore the fundamental place of encounter between the Church and all men.[33] Christians are those who have discovered, in faith, the correspondence between their desire for happiness and the person, teaching, and mission of Jesus Christ. Witness occurs when this faith-based relationship is made known through actions and words. This is the most fundamental form of evangelization.

> The witness of a Christian life is the first and irreplaceable form of mission . . . The first form of witness is the very life of the missionary, of the Christian family and of the ecclesial community, which reveal a new way of living . . . everyone in the Church,

---

31. In his important synthesis of the teaching of Vatican II, Cardinal Wojtyła identified the mission of making life more fully human as the Council's principal goal: "To 'make human life more human' is the Council's fundamental objective, closely linked to the desire to share in the divine life and in the mission of Christ" (SR, 279).

32. A representative description of happiness in Aquinas is: "Happiness can be considered in two ways. First, according to the general notion of happiness: and thus, of necessity, every man desires happiness. For the general notion of happiness consists in the perfect good, as stated above (articles 3 and 4). But since good is the object of the will, the perfect good of man is that which entirely satisfies his will. Consequently to desire happiness is nothing other than to desire that one's will be satisfied. And this everyone desires. Secondly we may speak of happiness according to its specific notion, as to that in which it consists. And thus all do not know happiness; because they know not in what thing the general notion of happiness is found. And consequently, in this respect, not all desire it" (ST, I-II, q. 5, a. 8; see also ST, I-II q. 1, a. 7).

33. One disciple of St. Thomas has referred to the various aspirations of men that are rooted in the desire for happiness as so many "obediential potencies to the proclamation of the Gospel in the modern world" that can be found in the "questions, aspirations, and anguishes of men." See Chenu, "De commercio," 650.

striving to imitate the divine Master, can and must bear this kind of witness.[34]

The fidelity of the baptized is a primordial condition for the proclamation of the Gospel and for the Church's mission in the world. In order that the message of salvation can show the power of its truth and radiance before men, it must be authenticated by the witness of the life of Christians. "The witness of a Christian life and good works done in a supernatural spirit have great power to draw men to the faith and to God."[35]

It may be presumed that this "great power" is related to bringing about the perception by others that in the fullness of life encountered in the Christian they have come face to face with that which they are seeking, that which will give ultimate and definitive meaning to their lives. It is the power of the good to attract, while not just respecting free will but precisely by appealing to it. *This kind of witness is the fundamental "method" or "technique" of the renewal of Vatican II and of the New Evangelization.* Whenever power is redefined to equate with efficiency in terms of the effectiveness of human techniques and methods, mission is actually deprived of its true and supernatural power.[36] To the extent that pastoral formation is reduced to training in techniques and methods, it is cut off from the spiritual formation that precedes it. It is likewise cut off from the supernatural mission of the Church, with the result is that criteria other than conversion and holiness are utilized for measuring success in apostolate and ministry.

---

34. John Paul II, *RMiss*, 42. See Paul VI, *EN*, 41: "the first means of evangelization is the witness of an authentically Christian life."

35. *CCC*, 2084, quoting Vatican II, *AA*, 6.

36. Modern man thinks primarily in terms of power relating to efficient causality. Vatican II, Paul VI, and John Paul II think in terms of the power of the good to attract and thus of power relating to final and exemplary causality. With profound insight St. Thomas, whose life's work was taken up with theology, that is, with words in their relation to revealed truth, grasped the relatively inferior power of words in comparison to the witness of a life in possession of the true good of man, that is, of what Vatican II called a fully human life: "In human actions examples have a greater influence than words. This is because a person does and chooses what appears as good to that person. Thus, the actual choice of something manifests its goodness or value to a person even more than what that person teaches should be chosen. This explains why when someone says one thing and does another, what he does has a greater influence on others than what he teaches. Therefore, it is of the greatest necessity to give an example" (*Commentary on the Gospel of John*, Ch. 13, Lect. 3 [Marietti 1781]; my translation).

Pope Paul VI understood things in precisely this way.[37] This is why he referred to the final stage of renewal as dialogue. Dialogue occurs by way of what I have called for years the question-answer dynamic. This means that in his search for ultimate meaning man confronts numerous fundamental questions about his origin and end, about suffering and death, about love and justice and truth, etc. Faith is first of all the discovery that in Jesus Christ these questions are definitively answered. This is what makes faith "existential," to use the terminology of Cardinal Wojtyła.[38] Only those who have discovered that in Christ their fundamental questions about the purpose and meaning of life have been answered can witness to him in such a way that this witness can lead to the same discovery by others. Faith means to believe that "only in the mystery of the incarnate Word does the mystery of man take on light," and that "Christ . . . fully reveals man to man himself and makes his supreme calling clear."[39] Only those with this kind of faith can complement the witness of life with the testimony of words and give an account for their hope to those who, moved first by the witness of their lives, seek to know what it is, or who it is, that inspires them and gives this meaning to their lives.

Now it is clear that the passage from doctrinal formation to spiritual renewal through conversion entails an internal dialogue between one's questions in the search for meaning and the doctrine of the faith. A fully accountable faith that can give reasons for the hope for ultimate and definitive fulfillment (see 1 Pet 3:15) is one that sees the correlation between the search for meaning and the faith of the Church. It is a faith that can say not only that God has revealed this meaning, but also that this meaning has been discovered and personally appropriated, that it is being lived. It is, in other words, the fruit of a joint witness of the Holy Spirit, who takes what is Christ's (see John 16:14–15), and one's own spirit (see Rom 8:16). This provides an additional insight into the passage from mere knowledge of the content of faith, which can only be a reductionist understanding of doctrinal formation, and spiritual renewal through conversion for the sake of a full and personal appropriation of that content. And, only those who have come to such a faith are able to play a role

---

37. Paul VI, *EN*, 21. Much of the relevant text is found above in the section entitled "Action Follows upon Being" in this chapter.

38. See Wojtyła, *SR*, 18, 224.

39. Vatican II, *GS*, 22. Throughout his pontificate, John Paul quotes or refers to this text of Vatican II more than any other Conciliar text.

in leading others to it. You cannot give what you have not received. Such pastoral agents will have a profound regard for the dynamism of human nature and for the dynamics of grace working with that nature. They will act in such a way as to provoke these questions in relation to Christ. As the presence of Christ provoked ultimate questions concerning the faith of Israel, so through his disciples "the very presence of the Church recalls these problems to mind."[40] Wise and well-formed disciples who have observed the movement of grace in themselves, provoking questions and leading to the answers in Christ, will not interfere with the joint witness of the Holy Spirit and of the spirit of those whom they serve and evangelize by interjecting artificially contrived methods and techniques, but will be content to play the humble role of witness.

In light of the preceding the emphasis on spiritual formation and the call to holiness becomes understandable. The saints are "our masters of humanity"[41] and the ultimate *apologia* for Christianity.[42] The greatest *apologia* for the Church is saints because they are the most compelling evidence that God's love is efficacious, that the happiness he offers to human beings has become reality. From this perspective, it is quite natural to claim that spiritual formation for acquiring the holiness that is a participation in God's own life should merit priority over the other dimensions of formation. And because God's life and holiness are essentially his charity and charity is the soul of holiness[43] and the soul of the apostolate,[44] a closer look at charity as the motive of missionary dialogue is in order.

THE MOTIVE: CHARITY

As seen above, the third part of *ES* begins with an assertion that as a result of doctrinal consciousness and spiritual renewal the Church becomes conscious—this would be a second derivative consciousness, the first being the consciousness of discrepancies between the divine ideal and the present reality of the Church—of how "radically different" human life within her is in comparison to human life outside of her. She

---

40. Vatican II, *GS*, 41.
41. Ratzinger, "Reform from the Beginnings," 69.
42. Ratzinger and Messori, *Ratzinger Report*, 129.
43. See *CCC*, 826.
44. See Vatican II, *LG*, 33; *AA*, 3.

becomes aware, in other words, of having received the graces of God's transforming love.

For Pope Paul, one must be loved and experience the fullness of life in Christ—which comes about as a result of renewal through conversion—in order to become a herald of that life.

> If... the Church has a true realization of what the Lord wishes it to be, then within the Church there arises a unique sense of fullness and a need for outpouring, together with the clear awareness of a mission which transcends the Church, of a message to be spread. It is the duty of evangelization. It is the missionary mandate. It is the apostolic commission. (*ES*, 64)

The best way to understand this movement from "a unique sense of fullness" to "a need for outpouring" and a "clear awareness of a mission" is in terms of the second law of love: "You shall love your neighbor as yourself" (Matt 22:39),[45] or, in the equivalent phrasing of the Golden Rule: "as you wish that men would do to you, do so to them" (Luke 6:31). A fully conscious faith is aware of how the blessings of God's love have enriched one's life, and gratitude for those blessings indicate that they constitute the content of one's self love. This then becomes the measure of one's love for others. This is the charity that is the animating force of missionary dialogue.

> The dialogue of salvation began with charity, with the divine goodness: "God so loved the world as to give his only-begotten Son" (John 3:16); nothing but fervent and unselfish love should motivate our dialogue. (*ES*, 73)

The movement here is from the experience of God's love *ad intra*, within the Church, to the projection, the outpouring, the effusion of that same love *ad extra*, toward the world. Bringing together the dialogue of salvation between God and myself (*ad intra*) and the extension of that dialogue between myself and others (*ad extra*), Pope Paul concludes: "To this internal drive of charity which tends to become the external gift of charity we will give the name of dialogue (*ES*, 64).[46] He adds that all of the

---

45. See also Rom 13:9; Gal 5:14; Jas 2:8.

46. Ratzinger writes incisively about the dynamic involved in the movement from *ad intra* to *ad extra* in his *Principles of Catholic Theology*: "The concentration on what is Catholic, which seems at first glance to be directed exclusively inward, thus is revealed in its original impulse to be an emphatic orientation toward those today who are searching.... Only when we see this clearly can we rightly understand the purpose

Council's teachings and decrees must be "inflamed by charity" if they are "really to produce in the Church and in the world that renewal . . . which was the very scope of the council."[47] For Pope Paul, "charity has been the principal religious feature of this council" (*ES*, 23).

Pope Paul's address for the opening of the fourth session most amply develops his understanding of the Council as an act of love. "The Council," he asserts, "is a solemn act of charity for humanity." "Nor," he continues, "does it seem difficult to give to our ecumenical council the *character of an act of love*, of a great, threefold act of love: for God, for the Church, and for humanity." In the development that he gives of these three loves, it is clear that love for God corresponds to the first path of doctrinal consciousness, love for the Church corresponds to the second path of renewal through conversion, and love for humanity corresponds to the third path of missionary dialogue.

Not incidentally, these three loves also correspond to the three lights that Pope John spoke of—*Lumen Christi, Lumen ecclesiae, Lumen gentium*—in his radio message of September 11, 1962, just one month prior to the opening of the Council. Pope John explains that both light and love descend from heaven to earth in Jesus Christ, who as God is Light and Love. In him and through the efficacy of his love, men are made participants in the divine light and love, and by this participation they form the Church of Christ. The Church, finally, is entrusted with a mission to bring this light and love to all men.

In his addresses for the opening of sessions two and four, Pope Paul quotes 2 Corinthians 5:14, where St. Paul writes that "the love of Christ impels us" (*caritas Christi urget nos*).[48] In the address for the opening of session four, he elaborates by saying that "we experience a sense of responsibility for all mankind. We are debtors to all (cf. Rom 1:14). The

---

of Vatican Council II, which, in all its comments about the Church . . . was not primarily concerned with how the Church envisaged herself, with the view from within, but with the discovery of the Church as sacrament, as the sign and instrument of unity" (50). "And we come here upon something unexpected; rightly understood, the path that leads men within and the path that draws them together are not in conflict; on the contrary, they need and support one another" (52).

47. Paul VI, "Address for the Closing of Vatican II, December 8, 1965."

48. Paul VI turns to this text on numerous occasions: "Address, September 10, 1965"; "Homily, March 13, 1966"; "Message for World Day for Missions, 1967"; "Letter, October 22, 1972"; "General Audience, February 20, 1974"; "Message for World Day for Missions, 1974"; "Address, May 9, 1974"; "General Audience, December 15, 1976"; "General Audience, August 25, 1978."

Church, in this world, is not an end in itself. It is at the service of all men." Rooted in the very being of every Christian (*esse*), charity produces an interior élan of service (*operatio*), the goal of which is to bring Christ to all men.

Convinced that love is the meaning of Vatican II, he offers assistance to future historians and researchers who will study the Council by pointing out to them that their questions about the Council will be answered when they realize that the Council was essentially a historic act of love for God, for the Church, and for humanity.

> And here our love has already had and will have expressions that characterize this Council for the history of the present and of the future. Such expressions will one day provide an answer to the researcher who will strive to define the Church in this decisive and critical moment of her existence. He will ask: What did the Catholic Church do at that time? The response will be: "She loved!" She loved with a pastoral heart. Everyone knows this, even if it is very difficult to penetrate the depth and richness of this love, a love that Christ caused to gush forth in the repentant and burning heart of Simon Peter. Do you remember? "Jesus said to Simon Peter, 'Simon, son of John, do you love me more than these?' He said to him, 'Yes, Lord; you know that I love you.' He said to him, 'Feed my lambs'" (John 21:15)! And do you remember the mandate, flowing from the love of Christ, the mandate to shepherd his flock? Oh, yes, it continues still and constitutes the meaning of this cathedra, as it extends to and continues still and constitutes the meaning of your individual cathedras, venerable Brothers. And today this is stated with new consciousness and vigor. This is what the Council is saying: the Church is a society founded on love and governed by love! The Church of our Council has loved, it will be said, she loved with a missionary heart. Everyone knows how this sacred Synod has called every good Catholic to be an apostle, and how it has expanded the focus of apostolic zeal to include all men, all races, all nations, all classes: even when it overwhelms the strength of those embrace it or demands total and heroic dedication from them, the universality of love has had and will always have, in this Council, a solemn voice.[49]

This emphasis on love opens up to yet another angle for a re-reading of the three paths of the Church and a deeper understanding of how they

---

49. Paul VI, "Address, September 14, 1965."

relate to one another. God's love is the essence of the Gospel, the kerygma: "So we know and believe the love God has for us" (1 John 4:16). Because by its very nature this love desires what is good for man, it cannot be revealed merely by a disclosure that unveils something previously hidden, as though a curtain were removed so that a previously covered statue can be now seen. God's love is not a reality that one simply observes while remaining only an uninvolved observer from a distance. It is something that is active and brings about a communication of God's own goodness, thus transforming the one who is loved. For this reason, one cannot know this love in the biblical sense of knowing except by encountering and experiencing it. Only when a person can utter the "for us" of Israel[50] and the "for me" of Mary[51] and St. Paul[52] does one truly know God's love. And the nature of this transformation is to effect a communion of man with God so that man participates in God's own life, and thus also in his mission of love. Israel receives the vocation and mission to be light to the world, Mary to bring the Light of God into the world, and St. Paul to proclaim to the nations the truth about God's love fully revealed in Jesus Christ.

All of this aligns with the three paths of *ES*. The truth about God's love enters more deeply into the Church's consciousness through what Pope John XXIII called "doctrinal penetration." This is the first path. As this love is better known, it gives rise to a first derivative consciousness, which is the realization that because of the perfection of God's love he always has more to give and there is more that I can do to open up to his love. This, along with the concrete actions of conversion aimed at removing obstacles to God's love, is the second path. And I enter on the third path by way of a second derivative consciousness by which I become aware that God's transforming love has resulted in a fullness of life in Christ that is also destined for others. As a result, a greater participation in God's own love makes a missionary consciousness and attitude take deeper root within me.

Because it is a participation in God's own love, as the charity of the Church's members becomes more ardent it also becomes more perfectly catholic, that is, universal. Pope Paul develops this under the heading of humanity belonging to the Church.

---

50. "The Lord has done great things for us; we are glad" (Ps 126:3).
51. "He who is mighty has done great things for me" (Luke 1:49).
52. "The life I now live in the flesh I live by faith in the Son of God, who loved me and gave himself for me" (Gal 2:20).

CATHOLICITY OF MISSION: HUMANITY BELONGS TO THE CHURCH

The catholicity or universality of the Church's mission has been sufficiently present in previous texts that here it suffices to show how this aspect of the third path is related to the first and second paths.

Catholicity is an element of the Church's self-consciousness because it is a property of the Church as God has envisioned and established it: "There is no one who is a stranger to its heart, no one in whom its ministry has no interest. It has no enemies, except those who wish to be such. Its name of Catholic is not an idle title. Not in vain has it received the commission to foster in the world unity love and peace" (*ES*, 94). The Church cannot know herself, cannot think of herself according to the full truth about herself, without thinking also of the world. Consequently, a consciousness (the second derivative consciousness) of what it must be like to live without the graces of fullness in Christ accompanies the Church's self-consciousness of what she has become by God's grace. For, the Church knows that God "desires all men to be saved and to come to the knowledge of the truth" (1 Tim 2:4).[53] This becomes one of "the motives which impel the Church toward the dialogue" (*ES*, 66).

The paradigm of the Church's dialogue with the world is divine revelation, which Pope Paul envisions as a dialogue of salvation in which God takes the initiative of love (*ES*, 70). Because the dialogue of revelation is universal, so is the Church's missionary dialogue with the world.

> The dialogue of salvation was made accessible to all; it was destined for all without distinction (cf. Col 3:11); in like manner our own dialogue should be potentially universal, i.e. all-embracing and capable of including all, excepting only one who would either absolutely reject it or insincerely pretend to accept it. (*ES*, 76)

The doctrinal consciousness that corresponds to this missionary disposition is expressed in the assertion that humanity belongs to the Church. This should not be thought of being like the possession of property that one can dispose of as one wishes. Rather, Pope Paul's emphasis is on a sense of responsibility deriving from an awareness of having been entrusted with a mission. It is more like a stewardship resulting from

---

53. Paul VI quotes this passage near the end of his "Address for the Opening of Session Two of Vatican II."

God entrusting humanity to the Church. In order to be faithful to God, then, the Church must be faithful to the mission that comes with this entrusting. And the only fitting way for this mission to be accomplished is by love.

> Humanity belongs to the Church by the right which the Gospel gives her. She likes to repeat to all who make up the human race: "Come to me, all . . ." (Matt 11:28).[54]

From the perspective of human freedom, it is true that humanity must come to the Church. Yet, from another perspective it is the Church that draws close to humanity. There is an initiative-taking quality to the charity that is experienced as giving rise to responsibility for all mankind. This is why Pope Paul could assert that the "figure of the shepherd who seeks, who chases after, who is solicitous to track down the runaway sheep, gave direction to the Council."[55] He develops this in terms of the theme of humanity belonging to the Church, and roots this in the rights of love.

> The awareness that all mankind, depicted with touching simplicity by the lost sheep, belongs to her, belongs to the Church, has filled the spirit of the Council. Yes, mankind belongs to the Church by a universal divine mandate. The Church has understood, yet again, what a tremendous law the name that authentically distinguishes her entails: Catholic. This means that her mission, her responsibility, her heart have no limits. Therefore, the Church must say that mankind belongs to her. Without tiring, she must face every difficulty heroically and simply. Mankind is hers by right of love.[56]

The "tremendous law" of catholicity is internalized as the impetus of charity that extends to all men. It is rooted in the very nature of the divine life that God communicates to the Church by grace: God's life is supremely shareable. St. Augustine incisively describes what it means to be in possession of this supremely shareable good. God is not loved in the truth of who he is, that is, as the supremely shareable good, unless he is being shared. "For a possession which is not diminished by being shared

---

54. Paul VI, "Address for the Opening of Session Two of Vatican II."
55. Paul VI, "Radio Message for Christmas, December 23, 1965."
56. Paul VI, "Radio Message for Christmas, December 23, 1965."

with others," St. Augustine remarks, "if it is possessed and not shared, is not yet possessed as it ought to be possessed."[57]

Pope Paul's reading of the signs of the times within the Church can be articulated according to this principle. If there is an insufficient zeal for mission among the faithful, this must be explained by a corresponding insufficiency regarding participation in the life of Christ. Pope Paul does not call into question the authentically Christian graces of new life in Christ, anymore than St. Paul does in his parenetic passages. Rather, precisely because both Pope Paul and St. Paul presuppose the being-in-Christ of the faithful brought about by baptism, they can appeal to the faithful to become more fully what they already are. It is a question, then, of deepening the faith that is already possessed. While any number of pastoral initiatives—such as liturgical restorations, the creation of new ecclesiastical structures, and new formulations of faith—can assist with this, none of these can obviate the need for conversion into a fuller participation in divine life.

It is to Pope Paul's great credit that he did not succumb to the temptation to think that the necessary renewal could be achieved simply by manipulation of ecclesiastical institutions and an updating of pastoral and catechetical methods and techniques. Without neglecting to encourage prudent efforts to do precisely this, he maintained the primacy of the call to holiness and to the perfection of charity, for which conversion is the necessary path. This is so much the case that Pope Paul can virtually equate the renewal of Vatican II with the call to holiness, which comes through conversion.[58]

NEW FORMULATIONS OF FAITH

It is significant that Pope Paul's warning against the repetition of formulas that have lost their power to speak to modern man comes in the final section *ES* on mission and dialogue. Our interest is to demonstrate its link with the two preceding paths.

> Many, indeed, are the forms that the dialogue of salvation can take. It adapts itself to the needs of a concrete situation, it chooses the appropriate means, it does not bind itself to ineffectual

---

57. Augustine, *De doctrina Christiana*, I.1: "Omnis enim res, quae dando non deficit, dum habetur et non datur, nondum habetur, quomodo habenda est."

58. Cf. Paul VI, "Motu proprio *Sanctitas clarior*," in *AAS* 61 (1969) 149.

theories and does not cling to hard and fast forms when these have lost their power to speak to men and move them. (*ES*, 85)

As God himself condescends to communicate his eternal thought in human language,[59] so the Church adapts her language for the sake of effectively communicating her message. Encountering diverse cultures and situations in which men live requires "forcing our reasoning process out of the worn paths and by obliging it to deepen its research, to find fresh expressions" (*ES*, 83). Either the Church must define pre-evangelization as a course of instruction in the language and categories of thought of ecclesiastical jargon, or she must realize that precisely because her message is destined to all men its fundamental concepts and categories of thought are themselves of a nature as to correspond to fundamental and universal human experience and the concepts and categories of thought in which men reflect on their experience. This claim was lost on, at least, some who thought that one of the primary objectives of Vatican II was the condemnation of contemporary errors, most especially Modernism and Communism. Not only were they fearful that the adaptation of the wording of doctrine would entail a perversion of her doctrine, but they were seemingly indifferent to the necessity of a pre-evangelization to understand that doctrine absent any adaptation. To them, it would be sufficient that clerics be properly trained to understand that doctrine and communicate it to the faithful.[60] The great challenge of dialogue is for the Church to translate her message into the languages, concepts, and categories of thought of those to whom she desires to communicate her message (fidelity to man), all the while maintaining the strictest fidelity to the meaning of revelation determined by God himself (fidelity to God).[61]

---

59. "In Sacred Scripture, therefore, while the truth and holiness of God always remains intact, the marvelous 'condescension' of eternal wisdom is clearly shown, 'that we may learn the gentle kindness of God, which words cannot express, and how far He has gone in adapting his language with thoughtful concern for our weak human nature.'* For the words of God, expressed in human language, have been made like human discourse, just as the Word of the eternal Father, when He took to himself the flesh of human weakness, was in every way made like men" (*DV*, 13). The asterisk indicates a note that accompanies the text at this point: "St. John Chrysostom 'In Genesis'3, 8 (Homily 17, 1): PG 53, 134; 'Attemperatio' [in English 'Suitable adjustment'] in Greek 'synkatabasis.'"

60. See, e.g., Mattei, *The Second Vatican Council*, esp. chapter 1, section 8: "The Reactions to Neo-modernism during the Pontificate of Pius XII."

61. St. Vincent of Lérins bears witness to the Church's constant concern to strike the balance between *adaption of the message* while safeguarding the *integrity of the*

Pope Paul realizes that the reformulation of faith is not an end in itself. It is a means to effective communication. By their very nature, the concepts of "means" and "communication" entail a reference to governing principles. The end governs every means, and in the case of communication this end is communion in knowledge of the truth. Thus, the truth that God has revealed, that the Church believes, and that she seeks to communicate is the primary governing principle of the Church's dialogue with the world, and the reformulation of faith for the sake of effectiveness is a subordinate principle. Pope Paul refers to the primary governing principle as fidelity to God. This is why reformulation cannot be a capitulation to the prevalent ideas in the cultures in which the Church exercises her mission. This, Pope Paul tells us, is what occurred in varying degrees with "the phenomenon of modernism . . . which still crops up in the various attempts at expressing what is foreign to the authentic nature of the Catholic religion." This was an "abuse exercised against the faithful and genuine expression of the doctrine and criterion of the Church of Christ by psychological and cultural forces of the profane world" (*ES*, 26).

Both the primary principle of fidelity to God and the subordinate principle of reformulation for the sake of effective communication (which Pope Paul calls fidelity to man)[62] are quite simply and harmoniously combined in the following text:

> Nowadays a serious effort is required of us to ensure that the teaching of the faith should keep the fullness of its meaning and

---

message: "Let that which formerly was believed, though imperfectly apprehended, as expounded by you be clearly understood. Let posterity welcome, understood through your exposition, what antiquity venerated without understanding. Yet teach still the same truths which you have learned, so that though you speak after a new fashion, what you speak may not be new" (*Commonitorium* 22, 53; my translation). Commenting on St. Paul's second letter to the Corinthians (esp. 2 Cor 4:2), John Paul II offers a more contemporary witness to the same concern: "*We must not tamper with God's word*. We must strive to apply the Good News to the ever-changing conditions of the world but, courageously and at all costs, we must resist the temptation to alter its content, or reinterpret it in order to make it fit the spirit of the present age. The message we preach is not the wisdom of this world (cf. 1 Cor 1:20), but the *words of life* that seem like foolishness to the unspiritual man" ("Address, May 31, 1982," 3). Finally, there is no better example of the Church's support for this balance than John Paul II's encyclical *SA*. In the examples of Cyril and Methodius, John Paul finds witnesses to the Church's concern for adaptation and fidelity as well as the definitive foundation for dialogue in the dynamisms of our common human nature.

62. This theme of dual fidelity to God and to man will be developed in chapters 8 and 9.

force, while expressing itself in a form which allows it to reach the spirit and heart of the people to whom it is addressed.[63]

The reformulation of the faith that Pope Paul calls for presupposes a re-thinking of the faith, not a re-constitution of it. Only God can constitute the faith, and this is called divine revelation. Nor is it a jettisoning of the old formulas of the faith, but a new formulation that grows out of the old and preserves an essential continuity with it. In his encyclical, *Mysterium fidei*, just three months prior to the close of the Council (September 3, 1965), Pope Paul rejects the idea that the dogmatic formulas of the ecumenical councils expressing the Church's faith in the Trinity, the Incarnation, and the Eucharist be considered "as no longer appropriate for men of our times" and that therefore other formulas should "be rashly substituted for them." Responding to the claim that these formulas are embedded in culturally conditioned vocabulary and must therefore be reworked, he wrote:

> For these formulas, like the others which the Church uses to propose the dogmas of faith, express concepts which are not tied to a certain form of human culture, nor to a specific phase of human culture, nor to one or other theological school.
>
> No, these formulas present that part of reality which necessary and universal experience permits the human mind to grasp and to manifest with apt and exact terms taken either from common or polished language. For this reason, these formulas are adapted to men of all times and all places. But the most sacred task of theology is, not the invention of new dogmatic formulas to replace old ones, but rather such a defense and explanation of the formulas adopted by the councils as may demonstrate that divine Revelation is the source of the truths communicated through these expressions.[64]

The reformulation of the faith is neither radical nor wholesale. The traditional formulations are not inadequate in themselves. They need to be preserved in order to coexist with and serve as measures of the new expressions that are needed in the encounter with new cultures. Because the cultural prerequisites for understanding them no longer pertain, and only because those cultural conditions no longer pertain, the Church must adapt her mode of expressing the divinely revealed and perennially relevant truths of the faith.

63. Paul VI, *QIA*, II.
64. Paul VI, "Address, June 22, 1973."

> The methods of another time, corresponding to the necessities of a different sociological context, no longer make an impression in a society and mentality, profoundly changed. Now, the updating [*aggiornamento*] of pastoral methods has been one of the purposes in the Vatican II, and we have not failed continually to recall its necessity in our teaching.[65]

This is why the reformulation of faith is necessary *ad intra* as well as *ad extra*. For the same reason that the Church does not require those she evangelizes to learn Latin as a condition for hearing the Gospel, neither does she require that believers of one era first acquire the ability to think in the cultural categories of other ages as a condition for catechesis.

The task of reformulating the faith cannot be reduced to being a matter of technical theological competence. Once again we return to the connatural love for the Church and the *sensus fidei*, and with this we discover yet another way that the second path of renewal through conversion is related to the third path of dialogue. Pope Benedict XVI incisively spoke about this dimension of conciliar renewal. A reformulation of faith requires a vital relationship with it. It cannot be reduced to a kind of theological methodology, which would be like a computer-generated translation of a text. It springs from a living faith, a connaturalization by which the person has become one with the object of faith, or, the object of faith has permeated his self-consciousness.

> It is clear that this commitment to expressing a specific truth in a new way demands new thinking on this truth and a new and vital relationship with it; it is also clear that new words can only develop if they come from an informed understanding of the truth expressed, and on the other hand, that a reflection on faith also requires that this faith be lived. In this regard, the program that Pope John XXIII proposed was extremely demanding, indeed, just as the synthesis of fidelity and dynamism is demanding.[66]

Responding to a question about a remark made by Cardinal König regarding "an estrangement of the Church and the world," that is, "a growing discrepancy between the state of consciousness of modern man and of Christian teaching," Cardinal Ratzinger stated:

---

65. Paul VI, "Address, June 22, 1973."
66. Benedict XVI, "Address, December 22, 2005."

> For one thing, we can't find the language for expressing ourselves in the contemporary consciousness. We may come back to terms like original sin, redemption, atonement, sin, and so forth. These are all words that express a truth, but in today's language they don't amount to much for most people. To make their meaning communicable again is doubtless a task to which we should be devoting our efforts. However, that can succeed only if we ourselves live these things interiorly. When they become comprehensible again in new ways by being lived, they can also be stated in new ways. I must add that the communication of Christian realities is never merely intellectual communication. It says something that embraces the *whole* man and that I can grasp only when I enter into the pilgrim community. In this sense, there are two requirements: really to live it and so to come to understand it oneself, and then to create new possibilities of expression through a convincing community that, as it were, ratifies it.[67]

Without a "new and vital relationship" with the truth, without "we ourselves liv[ing] these things interiorly," not only is the *sensus fidei* impoverished, so that the interior auto-critical faculty is lacking to the point that there is great risk of falling short of fidelity to God in the construction of new formulations of faith. Without the authentic internalization of faith in the holiness by which believers become living books, living commentaries on what God has revealed, there is also a risk of cultivating a skepticism regarding the power of God's word and grace to bring about the realization of man's aspirations to live a fully human life.[68] Pope Paul is alert to the how such a skepticism undermines the bold confidence to proclaim the Gospel in full fidelity to the meaning that is received from God.

---

67. Ratzinger, *Salt of the Earth*, 170–71.

68. Rephrased in terms of the senses of Scripture, if the literal and allegorical senses of Scripture should not give rise to the spiritual-moral sense of Scripture, according to which the man of faith perceives the significance of biblical revelation for his life, then it can only be truth that is lacking in relevance. A concluding chapter will argue that the movement from the first path of consciousness to the second path of renewal through conversion can be understood in terms of the relation of the literal and allegorical senses to the spiritual-moral sense of Scripture.

POPE PAUL ON SKEPTICISM

The relation of the second to the third path is further elucidated by Pope Paul's insight regarding what he calls "a kind of skepticism about the power and content of the Word of God." The skepticism he has in mind is rooted in "an immoderate desire to make peace and sink differences at all costs." The costs he has in mind are: "watering down or subtracting from the truth"; the weakening of attachment to faith; making "vague compromises about the principles of faith and action." He concludes that "only he who lives his Christian life to the full" can avoid these errors and "remain uncontaminated by the errors with which he comes into contact" (*ES*, 88).

This comes in the third section of *ES* on missionary dialogue, yet it is directly related to the second path of conversion because it is by conversion that a person lives his Christian life to the full. The question to be answered is: How does this conversion into the fullness of Christian life immunize believers from this skepticism?

The answer lies in the concept of connaturalization. Conversion entails a conformity to Christ such that the faithful can say, with St. Paul: "I have been crucified with Christ; it is no longer I who live, but Christ who lives in me" (Gal 2:20). The two have become one, so that the faithful live in Christ and he lives in them.[69] The faithful have put on the mind of Christ (1 Cor 2:16) and are trained in the values of God's Kingdom. This is conformity to Christ, or connaturalization to Christ, the truth he reveals, and the Church. Because this is caused by God's word and grace, the faithful know by personal experience the power of his word and grace to transform their lives. They know that what God has done for them he is both able and desires to do for others.

Without this confidence in the power of God's word and grace, how can one hope that others can attain what is manifestly out of the reach of man's own power? If, then, man is not capable of conversion into the truth of the Gospel, then Christianity must be rethought in a radical manner and the Gospel must be changed in order to make it attractive and possible for others to welcome. In the end, this results in a conversion-free Christianity, which is no Christianity at all. Ultimately—and this is the key point—God's love does not change anything. It is ineffective. Man must take things into his own hands and redefine the Gospel in order to make it possible for men to live it. In this situation, fidelity to man

---

69. See *CCC*, 521.

eclipses fidelity to God, and thereby shows itself to be only a pseudo fidelity to man.

If God's love does not change anything, then there is no longer anything of real substance that constitutes the difference between the Church and the world regarding which the third section of *ES* begins (*ES*, 58). In that case, what does the Church have to offer the world? As soon as doubt takes hold about the transforming power of God's truth and love, mission must be rethought in order to become nothing more than a mutual agreement that in the end all religions are equal and that, for this reason, there is no essential difference between the Church and the world, and the essential condition for mission no longer exists. This is exactly how Cardinal Ratzinger views this form of adaptation.

> The feeling that, in reality, there were no longer any walls between Church and world, that every "dualism": body-soul, Church-world, grace-nature and, in the last analysis, even God-world, was evil—this feeling became more and more a force that gave direction to the whole. In such a rejection of all "dualism," the optimistic mood that seemed actually to have been canonized by the words of *Gaudium et spes* was heightened into the certainty of attaining perfect unity with the present world and so into a transport of adaptation that had sooner or later to be followed by disenchantment.[70]

Those who journey with Christ through the death and resurrection of conversion cannot be fooled into thinking that there are shortcuts, methods, programs or techniques that can, of themselves, bring about the renewal of the Church. Faith is the only way, and all the programs and methods have value only to the extent that they contribute to one of the three paths set forth in *ES*. Faith that has been tested and enriched by conversion knows by experience that the human, institutional realities of the Church are devoid of power to the extent that they are not in one way or another derived from or at the service of the Gospel and the Eucharist. Following Christ in his death and resurrection is the living of Christian life to the full that Pope Paul identifies as the protection against the skepticism that would diminish the necessity of conversion and thereby compromise the centrality of the Paschal Mystery, and thus

---

70. Ratzinger, *Principles of Catholic Theology*, 383.

the Eucharist, in Christian life and replace it with some other center in the Church's mission of evangelization.[71]

ES describes the difference between the Church and the world in terms of two ways of living, one of faith and grace, and the other a world without these. "The Gospel is light, it is newness, it is energy, it is rebirth, it is salvation. Hence, it both creates and defines a type of new life." The contrast is between reliance on the Gospel and God's grace and living as if humanity's "own energies suffice to give man complete, lasting, and beneficent self-expression" (*ES*, 59). Reliance on God as he has revealed himself in Jesus Christ, or reliance on oneself: It is a question of the efficacy of God's love and thus on the holiness that his love imparts to us:

> This distinction between the life of the Christian and the life of the worldling also derives from the reality and from the consequent recognition of the sanctification produced in us by our sharing in the paschal mystery and, above all, in holy baptism, which, as was said above, is and ought to be considered a true rebirth. (*ES*, 60)[72]

Pope Paul emphasizes that while the fullness of life imparted by God's grace results in a distinction between those who are so graced and those who are not, "this distinction is not a separation" (*ES*, 63). Ten years later, as if he were elaborating on these very words, Pope Paul calls upon the faithful to "remember that being different from what we call the world, in the negative sense, does not separate us from the world, in the positive sense, that is, from humanity, even in its inadequate or deplorable aspects, and in need of the great light of truth and the beneficial medicine of charity."[73] Authentic holiness, that is, the perfection of charity, draws holy men and women closer to those who do not know Christ. Pope Paul elaborates on this in his address to the Council Fathers for the opening of the fourth session:

> Neither will it be able to be said that this conciliar gathering . . . was self-content, closed in on itself, uninformed, or indifferent to the interests of others, of the immense multitudes of

---

71. In this light, one can appreciate the insistence on the Eucharist being the heart of the New Evangelization.

72. See Vatican II, *LG*, 40: "The followers of Christ are called by God, not because of their works, but according to his own purpose and grace. They are justified in the Lord Jesus, because in the baptism of faith they truly become sons of God and sharers in the divine nature. In this way they are really made holy."

73. Paul VI, "General Audience, April 30, 1975."

> men who do not have our good fortune of being welcomed (as we are, without our having merit) into this blessed Kingdom of God, which is the Church.
>
> Not so, not so. The love that animates our communion does not cut us off from men, or make us exclusivist or self-absorbed. Indeed, because the love that comes from God educates us in the sense of universality, our truth impels us to charity. Remember the admonition of the Apostle: "*Veritatem facientes autem in caritate*"—we are doing the truth in charity (Eph 4:15). And here, in this assembly, the expression of the law of charity has a sacred and serious name; it merits being called responsibility. Thus, St. Paul would speak of "urgency": "*Caritas Christi urget nos*"—the charity of Christ impels us (2 Cor 5:14). We experience a sense of responsibility for all mankind. We are debtors to all (cf. Rom 1:14). The Church, in this world, is not an end in itself. It is at the service of all men. It must make Christ present to all individuals and peoples, as broadly and as generously as possible. This is her mission. She is a bearer of love, the advocate of real peace, and she repeats with Christ: "*Ignem veni mittere in terram*," I have come to bring fire on the earth (Luke 12:49). The Church needs this awareness, this declaration, and the Council has given her the opportunity.[74]

John Paul II's thought on this is so close to that of Paul VI that he could have had the just quoted text before him when, addressing the bishops of New Zealand, he clarified that while the biblical understanding of holiness entails the notion of separation for service to God, this service entails mission to men.

> The Old Testament makes it clear that Israel is to be holy as God himself is holy (cf. Lev 19:2). This meant that Israel had to be distinct, just as God is infinitely distinct from the world, as the Bible stresses consistently in forging its doctrine of divine transcendence. But this otherness of Israel is not otherness for its own sake; it is neither introverted nor defensive. Just as God can make all things "good" (cf. Gen 1:31) precisely because he is above all things, so Israel is to be distinct for the sake of service. Just as the infinite transcendence of God makes possible the communication of the perfect love which culminates in Christ's Paschal Mystery, so in the Bible's understanding the holiness of God's people involves that critical freedom in relation to

---

74. Paul VI, "Address, September 14, 1965."

surrounding culture and cultures which makes possible real and genuine service of the human family.[75]

Like his predecessor, John Paul also summed up the meaning of Vatican II in terms of holiness:

> The Second Vatican Council has significantly spoken on the universal call to holiness. It is possible to say that this call to holiness is precisely the basic charge entrusted to all the sons and daughters of the Church by a Council which intended to bring a renewal of Christian life based on the Gospel.[76]

We are now in a position to answer the two questions posed at the outset of this section on the third path. The first two paths are incomplete without the third path because the nature of the Church would not be fully realized without the mission that in the contemporary context takes the form of dialogue. "The task of evangelizing all people constitutes the essential mission of the Church.... Evangelizing is in fact the grace and vocation proper to the Church, her deepest identity. She exists in order to evangelize."[77] A vertical relation of communion with God necessarily entails a horizontal relation of mission to all whom the divine intention of salvation embraces.

The third path cannot be cut off from the first two because this would reduce missionary dialogue to being a merely human endeavor. By its nature, the Church's mission must arise out of doctrinal consciousness and conversion as fruit emanates from a tree. To employ a verb the root of which conveys the notion of mission, doctrinal consciousness and conversion emit missionary dialogue.

We have seen that Pope Paul begins his treatment of the third path by insisting on the difference between the Church and the world. This difference is due to the efficacy of God's truth and grace to transform the lives of believers. This is why the primary mode of the Church's mission is witness to the efficacy of God's love. The very lives of the faithful constitute the most compelling evidence of God's love. Without this difference resulting from God's efficacious love, missionary dialogue lacks the backing of evidence regarding its primary subject, namely, the revelation of God's love in Jesus Christ. If God's love is a subject to be proclaimed but not experienced in is transforming power, skepticism and the necessary

---

75. John Paul II, "Address, November 21, 1998," 3.
76. John Paul II, *CL*, 16.
77. Paul VI, *EN*, 14.

auto-critical faculty for discerning between what is compatible and incompatible with the Gospel will be insufficiently developed, conversion will be diminished, and dialogue will lead to an accommodation that is capitulation to the world rather than the transformation of the world.

6

Implications of the Analysis

THE PRECEDING CHAPTER'S ANALYSIS of the relations among the three paths of *ES* gives rise to a number of important implications. Here, the focus is on two general conclusions, the first being a discussion of the principles governing the causal relations that explain the sequential ordering of the three paths, and the second a retrospective on the three paths in terms of three loves, which, as Pope Paul tells us, constitute the very essence of Vatican II.

SEQUENTIAL ORDER OF THE THREE PATHS

The first principle is that put forth by Monsignor Colombo: what is last in execution is first in intention. The third path of apostolic activity depends on the second path of renewal of Christian life, which in turn depends on doctrinal consciousness. Analogous to a coach who needs to elevate the skill level of athletes in order to improve their performance, Paul VI realized that the reinvigoration of the Church's mission presupposes a renewal of Christian life. Zeal for mission is so much a property of Christian life that the lack of such zeal can only be a sign of a deficiency in authentic Christian holiness. By a parallel path of reasoning, Pope Paul realized that holiness presupposes a penetrating understanding of doctrine. Holiness, the perfection of charity, is so dependent on faith that mediocrity in Christian life can only be the sign of mediocrity in the understanding of doctrine. With the cascade of ordered dependencies determined, the obvious starting point for the renewal that he envisioned is a doctrinal consciousness that by its nature should produce a wave of graces of conversion into an ardent life of Christian holiness. Zeal for souls being a property of holiness, which is the perfection of charity, a corresponding zeal for missionary dialogue should characterize the Church that has thus been renewed.

The movement from the first path of doctrinal consciousness to renewal through conversion can be understood in terms of the biblical principle: "Every one to whom much is given, of him will much be required; and of him to whom men commit much they will demand the more" (Luke 12:48). This verse is referenced in *LG*, 14, to support the assertion that the Church's children should consider their incorporation into the Church as a gift of grace and that "if they fail moreover to respond to that grace in thought, word and deed, not only shall they not be saved but they will be the more severely judged." To take up the theme developed earlier—that because God's love and grace effectively transform those who receive it, there is a difference between the Church and the world—this means that consciousness of having been loved by God is not a motive for triumphalism and separation but rather for humility and conversion. This can be put another way: doctrinal consciousness of what God has revealed about the Church, and especially of his love for the Church, penetrates the moral conscience to become the criterion in light of which critical judgments are made in order to identify discrepancies between the divine ideal and current reality. These critical judgments then guide the acts of renewal through conversion.

The passage from doctrinal consciousness to conversion is based on an understanding of the working of the conscience. By their nature, judgments of conscience bear upon the relation between the faith that is professed and the life that is lived. If there is a deplorable split between faith and life (*GS*, 43), this is explained by some insufficiency either on the part of the intellect or the will, or both. Regarding the will, an insufficient commitment to Christian living is a reality that the Church has no power directly to alter. Nevertheless, God reaches the will of man, and he does so through the Church. The pastoral magisterium of Vatican II is the Church's best calculation about what she can do to be a more effective instrument proposing saving truth in a manner that appeals to consciences and fosters conversion. *ES* sketches the framework for this pastoral magisterium, which intends to present doctrine as truth with two poles of reference. The first pole is the reference to God; the formulation of doctrine must faithfully correspond to what God has revealed. The second pole is the reference to man; the formulation of doctrine must correspond to man's innate dynamisms for truth, goodness, and meaning. When united, these two poles produce the principle of fidelity to God and fidelity to man, a theme that Part II will examine.

The kind of doctrinal consciousness that Pope Paul envisions in *ES* as conducive to conversion has two aspects. The first is a reformulation of faith using, always in a manner that is subordinate to being faithful to God, vocabulary and categories of thought that the Church's contemporaries can most readily understand. The second aspect involves a penetration and understanding of doctrine that discovers within that doctrine its spiritual-moral sense. In order for faith to become the light for people's living, they must perceive its "for me" dimension. That is to say, as is evident in the cases of the Blessed Virgin Mary and St. Paul (see Luke 1:49; Gal 2:20), living faith entails the perception that what God has revealed is Good News that transforms and enriches one's life. There is all the difference between a formulation of doctrine that answers the question, "How, precisely, should this revealed truth be properly understood?" and a formulation of doctrine that answers the question, "How is this relevant, meaningful and significant for me?" Obviously, this second question presupposes the answer to the first. A pastoral presentation of doctrine is not less than doctrinal, but more than doctrinal. It is doctrine set forth with the precision of the Church's faith and done so in such a way that people can more readily perceive that it contains an answer to their search for a fully human and meaningful life. This pastoral approach to doctrinal consciousness may be called an apologetics of meaning. It both deepens the convictions of faith of those who believe, and it attracts those who do not yet believe, since everyone, the faithful as well as everyone else, seeks a fully human and meaningful life.

Turning now to the movement from the second to the third path, several principles have elucidating power. The first is the principle "operation follows upon being" (*operatio sequitur esse*). Through conversion, the faithful are more and more conformed to Christ and increasingly responsive to the prompting of the Holy Spirit (second path). As a consequence of this more perfect participation in the mystery of Christ, it is Christ who continues his mission as Prophet, Priest, and King through the Church and her members (third path). The mission of dialogue that *ES* envisions is properly that of Christ and the Holy Spirit; the *Catechism* refers to it as the "joint mission of the Son and the Spirit."[1] The Church and her members participate in this mission, and they do so more perfectly the more fully they are conformed to Christ, and conversion is the means by which this conformity increases.

The second principle governing the movement from the second path to the third path is "the good is diffusive of itself" (*bonum diffusivum sui*). Just as the goodness of Christ attracts people to him, so the presence of his goodness in the lives of those who are in communion with him acts on the Church's contemporaries and draws them close. The impact of the witness of a fully human life in Christ is the occasion, again, for a perception of the "for me" value of Christian life. The difference between the Church and the world that *ES* takes as the condition for missionary dialogue is the difference between the fulfillment of human aspirations in Christ and the state of restlessness in search of that very fulfillment. The Church speaks most loudly and clearly through her saints, whose human goodness, virtue, integrity, and nobility constitute an alluring witness.

Finally, the very nature of this fully human life in Christ demands that it be shared. The more fully it is possessed, which results from renewal through conversion, the more it impels the possessor to communicate it to others. "If it is possessed and not shared," St. Augustine tells us, this can only mean that it "is not yet possessed as it ought to be possessed."[2] The fruit of the second path is precisely this kind of possession-in-view-of-sharing that alone is worthy of the goodness of divine life. Pope Paul's version of the same comes in terms of charity: "To this internal drive of charity which tends to become the external gift of charity we will give the name of dialogue" (*ES*, 64).

John Paul II sees things in precisely the same way when, in his encyclical on the Church's missionary mandate, he asks, "Why mission?" and answers that it is because all men and women are searching for new life in Christ and our participation in this new life makes us responsive to their search. Because of this participation, this conformity to Christ, which is the fruit of the second path, "mission derives not only from the Lord's mandate but also from the profound demands of God's life within us."[3]

---

1. See *CCC*, 689–90.
2. Augustine, *De doctrina Christiana*, I.1.
3. John Paul II, *RMiss*, 11.

THE THREE PATHS IN LIGHT OF THREE LOVES

Popes Paul and John Paul did not place the call to holiness at the center of their understanding of the renewal of Vatican II as a means to the end of a reinvigorated mission. Holiness, that is, participation in divine life in the perfection of charity, is the supreme end of man. Holiness can never be a means. Nevertheless, the examination of the three paths of *ES* leads to the conclusion that a pastoral concern about a lack of missionary zeal among the faithful was the occasion for these popes to realize that the root cause of missionary mediocrity had to be a mediocrity in Christian living. Christ is the light and hope for all humanity, but this light comes to the world by way of reflection from the Church.

ES proceeds from a focus on love of God to a focus on love of the Church to a focus on love of all mankind because there is an order of logical priority among these loves. To work in reverse order, from the third path to the first path, missionary love of neighbor is a participation in God's own love, which is universal. This love of the third path corresponds to the full realization of the Church's catholicity. More perfect participation in God's love is the fruit of the conversion of the second path. This love concerns the full realization of the Church's holiness, the soul of which is charity.[4] It is participation in Christ's love for the Church, his bride, a love by which he gave himself up to make her holy (Eph 5:25–27). By participating more perfectly in his paschal charity, the mystery of the Church is more perfectly realized in the faithful. Finally, the love of the first path is the response to God's initiative of love, which comes first, so that our love for him is our response to his love for us: "We love, because he first loved us" (1 John 4:19).[5] As we come better to know his love, we also know better his plan of love. The ultimate and unifying goal of this plan of love is the Church: "The Church is the goal of all things."[6] The love that is based on this faith in God's plan is the foundation of the Church's unity. The first path of doctrinal penetration regarding God's love for the Church is the foundation for loving the Church as he does, and for all the efforts of renewal ordered to the fullest realization of the mystery of the Church, which is the realization of his love. As we come better to know God's plan for the Church, especially the regard he has for

---

4. See *CCC*, 826.
5. See *CCC*, 142, 2062, and especially 2567 on the divine initiative.
6. *CCC*, 760.

our dignity and his desire that we be his co-workers[7] in bringing Christ's love to the world, the renewal by which we participate more fully in his love entails engagement in mission to bring the Good News of God's love to others.

By their nature, these three loves are inseparable.[8] When, therefore, the signs of a vibrant missionary love are worrisomely lacking, it is likely that the root cause lies in weaknesses in the other two loves. This was the pastoral situation that Pope John XXIII grasped as if by intuition, and that it was Pope Paul's providential role to discern and to analyze more comprehensively. *ES* is the primary fruit of his discernment and analysis, yet as we have seen (and will see even more clearly in Part II), his discernment and analysis are by no means restricted to *ES*. Rather, they pervade his thoughts on Vatican II and the life of the Church in many other documents as well.

The great merit of Paul VI is to have remained steadfastly true to the logic of his analysis. This logic dictates that authentic renewal of the Church is in its essence the deepening of the renewal of man in Christ. If renewal remains superficially focused primarily on tweaking ecclesiastical institutions, it will remain only a pseudo-renewal. Authentic renewal is nothing more and nothing less than entering more fully into the depths of the mystery of Christ. This is why Pope Paul and Pope John Paul II stress the universal call to holiness.[9] They know that authentic holiness cannot fail to produce abundant fruits, among which are the reinvigoration of missionary activity as well as the reconfiguration of those ecclesiastical realities that are subject to updating. By placing the priority on holiness, the prudence exercised in new missionary initiatives and in the renewal of ecclesiastical institutions will be rooted in a supernatural connaturalization that, if it does not carry a guarantee of being impeccable, has its roots in minds and hearts that have been renewed by the truth and the love of Christ.

This understanding of renewal, which places the priority on holiness, is more than a conclusion derived from a theological analysis of abstract concepts. Rather, it is a fundamental law of the Church's very life:

---

7. On the theme of being God's co-workers, see 1 Cor 3:9; 1 Thess 3:2; Col 4:11; and *CCC*, 307.

8. See the insightful analysis of Nicolas, "Amour de soi."

9. Part II will take up the interest in and continuity of the magisterium on the theme of holiness.

"The saints have always been the source and origin of renewal in the most difficult moments in the Church's history" (*CL*, 16). Indeed, "holiness is the hidden source and infallible measure of her apostolic activity and missionary zeal" (*CL*, 17).[10]

---

10. *CCC*, 828.

PART II

Complementary Themes

7

Two Themes of Pope John XXIII on the Renewal of Vatican II

Pope Paul VI's attention to the "logic of renewal" and the "three loves," demonstrated in the previous chapter, anticipates a convergence of ideas in the post-Vatican II papacy that the next three chapters will elucidate. This first chapter will entail a slight step back in history to illustrate the attention that both John XXIII and Paul VI give to the theme of renewal at Vatican II. This attention is already indicated in the "three paths," but it has yet to be seen how the "three paths" are just one expression—though perhaps the best—of this special attention to renewal. In this time of intense discussion about a hermeneutic of continuity or discontinuity, it is enlightening to note the convergence of John XXIII and Paul VI on this theme of renewal.

To point out that the order among the three dimensions of renewal is compatible with the vision of John XXIII for Vatican II is not to say that Pope John explicitly envisioned things this way. At the same time, the fact that his understanding of the renewal of the Council aligns with the outline of *ES* has a twofold significance. First, it shows the continuity between the two popes' understanding of Vatican II. Second, it adds weight to the hypothesis that this way of thinking is so engrained a dimension of the spirit of Catholicism that it surfaces even when it is not fully consciously expounded.

LIGHT OF CHRIST, LIGHT OF THE CHURCH, LIGHT OF THE PEOPLES

The first theme from John XXIII comes from a text that had a tremendous influence on the dawning of the spirit of Vatican II in the minds of the Council Fathers.

> Here it is opportune and felicitous for us to turn and to recall the symbolism of the Paschal candle: at a certain point in the liturgy, behold how his name resounds: *Lumen Christi*. Then, from all the points of the earth, the Church of Jesus responds: *Deo gratias, Deo gratias*, as if to say: "Yes: *lumen Christi: lumen Ecclesiae: lumen gentium*.
>
> What, in fact, is an Ecumenical Council if not the Church's renewal of itself in this encounter with the presence of the risen Jesus, the glorious and immortal king, shining outward from the whole Church, with salvation, with joy, and with splendor, for all mankind?
>
> In the light of this vision we turn for good reason to the ancient Psalm: "Shine upon us the light of your face, O Lord! You have set joy in my heart. "*Extolle super nos lumen vultus tui Domine! Dedisti laetitiam in cor meum*" (cf. Ps 4:7–8). The new Ecumenical Council desires to be the true joy for the Universal Church of Christ.[1]

The movement from the light of Christ (*Lumen Christi*) to the light of the Church (*Lumen ecclesiae*) to the light of the peoples (*Lumen gentium*) perfectly parallels the movement from doctrinal awareness to spiritual renewal to dialogical mission. Like John the Baptist, the Church is not herself the light, but bears witness to the light (John 1:8). She witnesses, not as an uninvolved reporter, but by way of participation in the light. Vatican II's signature text on the Church, *Lumen gentium*, begins with the theme: "Christ is the Light of nations. Because this is so, this Sacred Synod ... desires ... to bring the light of Christ to all men, a light brightly visible on the countenance of the Church."[2] As the moon brings light to the darkness of night, so the Church illumines the path of faith[3] that men must follow during the time of their earthly pilgrimage. Christ, the true Light of the world, shines through the Church.

---

1. John XXIII, "Radio Message, September 11, 1962."
2. Vatican II, *LG*, 1.
3. See Ps 119:105; Sir 50:29.

Everything begins with the initiative of God revealing himself and his plan of love for men. This revelation reaches its fullness and perfection in Jesus Christ, who is the light from heaven.[4] As the Evangelist records, "I am the light of the world; he who follows me will not walk in darkness, but will have the light of life" (John 8:12). To come to know Christ as the light of the world and all that he reveals and that his Church teaches as participating in this Light corresponds to doctrinal awareness. To live by the light of this faith by eschewing all that is darkness corresponds to spiritual renewal. By this renewal the light of Christ does not just reflect off the Church, leaving her unchanged. It penetrates the Church so that the Church is a source of light for men. Jesus does not hesitate to refer to his disciples as being the light and as the light being theirs: "You are the light of the world. . . . Let your light so shine before men" (Matt 5:14, 16). As these words of Jesus make clear, to participate in the light results in the Church shining for men. This corresponds to dialogical mission, which flows from spiritual renewal.

A NEW PENTECOST

Conceiving Vatican II as a new Pentecost for the Church is the second theme of Pope John XXIII in light of which we perceive the continuity between his vision for conciliar renewal and the three dimensions of renewal of Paul VI. Pentecost comes after and presupposes the public ministry of Jesus during which, through his words and actions, he reveals the truth about God and his plan of love. The public ministry of Jesus corresponds to doctrinal awareness. At Pentecost, by the power of the Holy Spirit, the teaching and very life of Jesus become the truth and life of his disciples. This renewal and strengthening of the inner man by the Holy Spirit corresponds to spiritual renewal. Finally, at Pentecost the apostles proclaim the mystery Christ, and they do so in response to the crowd's question provoked by the manifestation of the Holy Spirit. This corresponds to dialogical mission.

This proclamation of Christ on Pentecost is simultaneously divine and human. It fulfills Jesus's words that the Holy Spirit and the apostles will be his witnesses (John 15:26). This witness is simultaneously by words and actions. These words and actions are light to those who come into contact with them. The witness-proclamation is also manifestly

---

4. See Acts 9:33; 22:6; 26:13.

dialogical. The lived experience of the Holy Spirit by the apostles and those with them gives rise to questions on the part of those who observe them. Pentecost is the beginning of the Church's presence provoking questions that lead to faith.[5] The gift of the Holy Spirit is the fulfillment of all promises, those that are grounded in the dynamisms of human nature itself and thus in men's aspirations to be fully human, and those that have their origin in God's covenantal interactions with the people of Israel. On Pentecost the Church enters into and participates in the communion of Jesus Christ, the eternally begotten Son, with the Father and Holy Spirit. And the world learns that this communion is the inheritance of all who become sons in the Son. The fullness of life that God desires for men, first imparted to the Incarnate Son, is communicated to Christ's disciples, and through them to others.

The Church bears witness to this fullness of life first of all by living it. It is clear, then, that there is no distinction between being loved by God and transformed by his grace to live the fullness of life in Christ, on one hand, and the dialogical mission of the New Evangelization, on the other hand. The first form of service that the Church renders to the world is to live the new life in Christ by the power of the Holy Spirit, thereby to show that man is not deceived when he aspires to a fully human life and to communion with God. This life is not a theory or an otherworldly promise, but a historical reality that possesses the power of the good to attract. As a New Pentecost, Vatican II's goal is to intensify anew the Church's experience of Christ in the power of the Holy Spirit, and thereby to rediscover the primacy of the power of witness over methods and techniques and programs. The witness of holiness is the program. This witness is simultaneously the best way to love others and the best way to respect their dignity and freedom. Witness makes this possible, for "the truth is able to convince by the power of its own truth."[6]

---

5. "The very presence of the Church recalls these problems [about the ultimate meaning of life] to his mind" (Vatican II, GS, 41). "Through this wordless witness these Christians stir up irresistible questions in the hearts of those who see how they live" (Paul VI, EN, 21).

6. Vatican II, DH, 1.

CONCLUSION: THE RENEWAL OF VATICAN II AND THE EUCHARIST

The preceding consideration of the renewal of Vatican II as a new Pentecost can be complemented by a reflection of St. John Paul II on the Eucharist. The mystery of the Church is the mystery of the "double rhythm" of the mission of the Son and the mission of the Holy Spirit, and the causal relation of the former in relation to the latter.[7] This double rhythm and this causal relation are actualized in the Eucharist.

> Christ's Eucharistic presence, his sacramental "I am with you," enables the Church to discover ever more deeply her own mystery. As a sacrament, the Church is a development from the Paschal Mystery of Christ's "departure," living by his ever new "coming" by the power of the Holy Spirit, within the same mission of the Paraclete-Spirit of truth. Precisely this is the essential mystery of the Church.... Through the "departure" of the Son, the Holy Spirit came and continues to come as Counselor and Spirit of truth.[8]

In the Eucharist the Church lives a perpetual Pentecost. To view Vatican II as a new Pentecost for the Church entails, then, a rediscovery of the primacy of the Eucharist in the life of the Church. The dialogical mission and service of the Church, that is, the New Evangelization, are the fruit of a revitalization of full, conscious, and active participation in the Eucharist. This is why the Synod on the New Evangelization includes among its final propositions:

> The Eucharist must be the source and summit of the New Evangelization. The Synod Fathers urge all Christ's faithful to renew their understanding and love for the Eucharistic celebration, in which their lives are transformed and joined to Christ's offering

---

7. In *DeV*, John Paul underscores this causal relationship, based on Jesus's words: "If I go, I will send him to you" (John 16:7). See especially article 8: "While all the other promises made in the Upper Room foretold the coming of the Holy Spirit after Christ's departure, the one contained in the text of John 16:7f also includes and clearly emphasizes the relationship of interdependence which could be called causal between the manifestation of each: 'If I go, I will send him to you.' The Holy Spirit will come insofar as Christ will depart through the Cross: he will come not only afterwards, but because of the Redemption accomplished by Christ."

8. John Paul II, *DeV*, 63.

of his own life to the glory of God the Father for the salvation of the whole world.[9]

The Eucharist assures that the Holy Spirit is the primary protagonist of the New Evangelization, working through the collaboration of those who are transformed to participate in the paschal charity of Christ. This participation presupposes the assent of faith and is directly related to the consent of faith, as we have seen, the two together comprising the full, conscious, and active participation envisioned by the liturgical renewal of Vatican II. All that remains is the fruit of proclaiming Christ by the signs of new life in him and by word, as on Pentecost.

The understanding of Vatican II as a new Pentecost for the Church, then, is Eucharistic and it incorporates the three dimensions of renewal as envisioned by Pope Paul VI in *ES*.

---

9. Synod of Bishops, "13th Ordinary General Assembly, *Final Propositions*," Proposition 34.

8

Pope Paul VI on Fidelity to God and Fidelity to Man

THE THEME OF FIDELITY to God and to man is one of several themes that complement and confirm Pope Paul's insistence on renewal and the primacy of doctrinal awareness and conversion into holiness as the precondition for a revitalization of the Church's mission. Pope Paul writes or speaks of fidelity to God and to man, or its equivalent, only several times. These would likely go unnoticed, were it not for three considerations. The first is not at all unique to this theme. Like many theological themes expounded by contemporary popes, the occasions when they occur are often disparate. They may be developed in a homily, an address, a general audience, an apostolic exhortation, or an encyclical, and the instances of development are often separated by months or even years. In terms of magisterial and chronological context, then, each passage may appear as an isolated voice that risks being drowned out by other voices that, for one reason or another, are louder. Unless the listener is attentive to the softer voice of the theme in question, it easily becomes lost. Often, the relevance of a theme may become apparent only when the individual voices are removed from their original context and brought together to form a theological chorus that is able to project the theme more clearly, without having to compete with the voices of other themes. This chapter's purpose is to provide a stage for a performance by the small chorus of texts of Paul VI on the theme of fidelity to God and to man.

The second and third considerations relate to the overall purpose of the present study. Why would someone listening to the theological symphony of Pope Paul VI take notice of this apparently minor theme of fidelity to God and to man, were it not for the fact that it is not only beautiful in itself but also useful for appreciating other themes? Thus, the second reason why this theme does not go unnoticed here is that this study's analysis of *ES* and of the three paths of renewal has made us attentive to it. A more in-depth knowledge of Pope Paul's vision for the *aggiornamento* of Vatican II makes one alert to complementary ways in which he conveys the same program for renewal—among them, the theme of fidelity to God and to man. Third, the theme of fidelity to God and to man in Pope Paul might go unnoticed were it not for the development it receives in the pontificate of John Paul II. Whether John Paul draws from his predecessor in this matter is not clear. What is clear is that the more ample development that the Polish Pope gives to this theme is in exactly the same line of thought of Paul VI. A separate chapter will present the theme of fidelity to God and to man in the pontificate of John Paul II.

The theme of fidelity to God and to man has already been encountered in previous chapters. The introduction to chapter 2 ends on this theme, and it appears in several other places as well. We have seen Pope Paul insist that the Church's mission or apostolate—which constitute fidelity to man—requires being faithful to Christ's teaching.[1] Fidelity to man through mission entails a responsible re-articulation of the Church's faith in order to make it intelligible for the Church's contemporaries, and this responsibility is measured by fidelity to Christ and to the teaching of the Church.[2]

---

1. *ES*, 88, quoted in chapter 2.

2. The inseparability of fidelity to Christ and to the Church is a constant in the magisterium of Paul VI. See, for example, "First, have great love for Jesus Christ; try to know him well, remain united to him, have great Faith and great trust in him. Second, be faithful to the Church, pray with her, love her, make her known, and always be ready, as your Martyrs were, to bear frank witness to her" (Paul VI, "Homily, August 2, 1969"). See also: "May your faithfulness to that resolution enable you to say with Saint Paul at the end of your earthly lives: 'I have kept the faith' (2 Tim 4:7); I have been faithful to God, to Christ, to the Church, faithful to my vocation, to the ministry which has been entrusted to me" (Paul VI, "Address, December 20, 1969"). "We are well aware that in our efforts to achieve renewal within the Catholic Church and sincere dialogue with those who are not in full communion with her, We must remain faithful to the truth which We have received from the Apostles and Fathers of the Church" (Paul VI, "Address, December 3, 1964"). "And as you explore and live the mystery of Christ, you must likewise, in the words of the Second Vatican Council, 'be penetrated

As in all things, Christ is our model.³ His fidelity to his Father is the model of the Church's fidelity. By grace his model is internalized, so that our fidelity is not a knockoff of his, but a participation in it.⁴ In an earlier Christocentric summary of *ES*, we have seen that Christ lives according to this twofold fidelity: first, to his Father, and because of this primary fidelity, he is faithful to the mission the Father entrusts to him.⁵ It could be said that the measure of Christ's fidelity to his Father is his fidelity to the mission he receives from the Father. To adapt a phrase from John Paul II, Christ's mission flows from his communion with the Father; his mission is that communion in action.⁶ Since Christ's mission is to redeem mankind and this constitutes his fidelity to man, it is clear that fidelity to man is contained in and derives from his fidelity to the Father. This is true for the Church's members as well: because God's will is the salvation of the world, fidelity to God and to his will entails fidelity to man through mission.

It is immediately clear that this twofold fidelity correlates to the three paths of renewal of *ES*. It is one thing to know God's plan of love for oneself and for others (first path of doctrinal awareness) and another to give oneself over to that plan and to enter into it in communion with God

---

with the mystery of the Church' (Vatican II, *OT*, 9). Christ is your example, and with him you must love the Church and give yourself up in sacrifice for her. For you, fidelity to Christ will always demand fidelity to the Church—fidelity to her unity and to the message of salvation that she announces 'not in plausible words of wisdom, but in demonstration of the Spirit and power, that your faith might not rest in the wisdom of men but in the power of God' (Cor 2:4–5). Yes, the message that we preach is the seeming folly of the Cross, and it completely supersedes human wisdom. It is to this message, as proclaimed by the Church, that we owe complete fidelity. Fidelity is the virtue of our times, and it is to fidelity that we exhort you today: in particular, fidelity to the Church's Magisterium" ("Address, March 4, 1978"). Faithful to Christ: Addresses of: April 28, 1969; August 7, 1972; November 11, 1972; April 9, 1973; June 10, 1977; June 20, 1977; May 6, 1978; *EN*, 39. Fidelity to the Church: Addresses of: December 20, 1963; February 4, 1971; December 19, 1974; January 11, 1975.

3. See *CCC*, 520.

4. The *CCC* sets down a principle with vast applications regarding Christ as the Model of Christian life: "Christ enables us to live in him all that he himself lived, and he lives it in us" (521).

5. See chapter 2 above.

6. "Communion and mission are profoundly connected with each other, they interpenetrate and mutually imply each other to the point that communion represents both the source and the fruit of mission: communion gives rise to mission and mission is accomplished in communion" (John Paul II, *CL*, 32). For scriptural foundations, see John 5:17, 19; 8:28.

in Christ through conversion (second path of renewal). The objectivity of this conversion is assured by fidelity to the revealed truth that is the content of doctrinal awareness. Once this communion reaches a certain degree of maturity, mission (third path of dialogue) becomes the expression of that communion in missionary charity. The objective content of this mission—which is the essential expression of fidelity to man—is also assured by fidelity to the revealed truth that is the content of doctrinal awareness.

The aim of this chapter, then, is to elucidate the theme of fidelity to God and to man in Pope Paul VI, in order to demonstrate that it serves as a simplification or recapitulation of the tripartite plan for renewal set forth in *ES*. This will result in seeing, first, that for Pope Paul, while fidelity to God corresponds chiefly to the first path of doctrinal awareness, it also embraces the second path of renewal through conversion and the third path of missionary dialogue. Second, it will result in seeing that while fidelity to man corresponds chiefly to the third path of mission through dialogue, it nevertheless embraces the first and second paths as well. The upshot of this is to reinforce the logic described in previous chapters, according to which the three paths are inextricably related. With this logic clarified, the *aggiornamento* of Vatican II can be examined anew to shed further light on fidelity to God and to man.

"FIDELITY TO GOD AND TO MAN" AS A RECAPITULATION OF VATICAN II

Though separated by eight years, two of Pope Paul's discussions of fidelity to God and to man come in the context of reflecting on the implementation of Vatican II. The first appears in an apostolic exhortation expressly dedicated to taking stock of certain challenges encountered in early years following the Council. The second occurs in an address to religious superiors in which the Holy Father takes up the Council's call for the renewal of religious orders.

Apostolic Exhortation *Quinque iam anni*

Five years after Vatican II, Pope Paul VI addressed an apostolic exhortation to the worldwide episcopate. Essentially, it is an encouragement to vigilance in exercising episcopal responsibility for the integrity of the

Catholic faith in the context of disseminating the Council's teachings and carrying out its pastoral directives.[7] Appealing to the bishops' sense of personal responsibility, Pope Paul invites them to join him in an examination of conscience regarding their solicitude in addressing threats to the integrity of the Catholic faith and related potential omissions in exercising their authority in the face of these threats.

As a succinct summary of the objective standard for this examination, Pope Paul quotes from two sources in order to convey what he refers to as the commitment that the bishops made at Vatican II. Neither of these sources is among the sixteen official documents of Vatican II, yet both are intricately part of the Council's history and of fundamental importance for grasping its true spirit, and thus for authentically interpreting it. We turn, then, first to examine the Council's Message to Humanity and second the address of Pope John XXIII for the opening of the Council.

Message to Humanity of Vatican II

The first source that Pope Paul employs in his exhortation comes from the first "document" of Vatican II. The Message to Humanity, issued on October 20, 1962, just nine days after the Council's opening, is nonetheless a text of great importance for ascertaining the authentic spirit of the Council.[8] Pope Paul selects a passage from this Message to make it clear that the vigilance the bishops need to exercise has two points of reference.

> Devoting our attention to reading the signs of the times, we would like, in a fraternal spirit, to make together with you an examination of our fidelity to the commitment we bishops undertook in our Message to Humanity at the beginning of the Council: "We shall take pains so to present to the men of this age God's truth in its integrity and purity that they may understand it and gladly assent to it."[9]

7. This is how John Paul II sums up *QIA* when he refers to it to show the continuity of his pastoral solicitude, in communion with the worldwide episcopate, with his predecessor. See *CT*, 61; "Address, June 23, 1984," 7; *Ecclesia Dei*, 5; "Address, October 26, 1998," 5; "Homily, December 10, 2000," 3.

8. One measure of this is the affinity of the Message to Humanity with the radio address of John XXIII, delivered one month prior to the Council's opening. John XXIII's secretary, Loris Capovilla, asserts that this radio address "stands as perhaps the most complete indication of John's thinking on the direction the Council should take" ("Reflections on the Twentieth Anniversary," in Stacpoole, *Vatican II Revisited*, 119).

9. Vatican II, "Message to Humanity," in *AAS* 54 (1962) 822.

Pope Paul takes this text to indicate that those who participated in Vatican II were conscious that their teaching office entails two relationships, one with God and his truth, and the other with those to whom their teaching is addressed. The relationship with God requires acknowledging that the truth of divine revelation is his; he is its source and he determines the meaning of its content.[10] To be in communion with the God of revelation entails transmitting that revelation "in its integrity and its purity." Put another way, in its teaching the Church must be on guard against any merely human calculation—a calculation deriving from principles other than principles of faith—that would add anything extraneous to divine revelation or omit anything essential to it in order to render the content of revelation more palatable or acceptable to the Church's contemporaries. In relation to the men and women of our time to whom the message is addressed, the commitment is to teach in a manner judged to make the message understandable and to foster assent to it.

There is nothing new in this commitment. In every age the Church exercises her teaching ministry conscious of these three relationships, as Pope Paul acknowledges:

> The Church has always had this duty of handing on the faith in its fullness and in a manner suited to men of their time. That means trying to use a language easily accessible to them, answering their questions, arousing their interest and helping them to discover, through poor human speech, the whole message of salvation brought to us by Jesus Christ.[11]

St. Paul attests to the apostolic origin of fidelity to the content of the Gospel being the measure of to fidelity to God himself. To the Galatians he expresses his dismay over those among them who "are so quickly *deserting him who called you* in the grace of Christ and turning to a different gospel" (Gal 1:6; emphasis added). God takes personally the changing of the content of revelation. The reason is that faith's assent to that content is based on a conviction about his credibility. Because God vouches for everything he has revealed, to alter the content of revelation is to substitute some other authority for God's authority.[12] For St. Paul, a change in the

---

10. The same is true of the Church: It is God's Church—*Ecclesiam Suam*.

11. Paul VI, *QIA*.

12. This is what St. Thomas identifies as the essence of the sin of heresy. See Aquinas, *ST*, I-II, q. 11, a. 1. St. James argues in precisely the same manner, showing that faith has an all-or-nothing quality. See Jas 2:10–11.

essential content of the Gospel means that people have placed their trust in someone else's credibility (2 Cor 11:1–5). This is why he goes to such great lengths to convey that his authority comes from the commission he has received from Christ (Gal 1:11—2:9).

St. Paul is also the model for safeguarding the unchanging integrity of the Gospel against the temptation to adapt its content to make it more appealing. The Galatians' alteration of the content of the Gospel is not only the occasion for him to insist in its inalterability, but also to disclose that his concern to be faithful to God takes priority over and is in fact the condition for his fidelity to men: "Am I now seeking the favor of men or of God? Or am I trying to please men? If I were still pleasing men, I should not be a servant of Christ" (Gal 1:10). For St. Paul, to change the content of the Gospel would be to seek the favor of men rather than of God. He must put God first, and the concrete way he does this is by safeguarding the content of the Gospel. At the same time, we know that this fidelity to God by way of fidelity to the Gospel is not at all incompatible with a certain kind of adaptation or accommodation to men: "I have become all things to all men" (1 Cor 9:22). So, there are three fidelities in St. Paul's apostleship: to God, to the Gospel, and to men.[13] The key is to see that his fidelity to the Gospel is the way in which he remains faithful to God, who is its source, and to men, to whom it is destined to be proclaimed.

These three relationships—with God the Source of the message, with the message, and with those to whom the message is proclaimed—place the Church and those who teach in her name in the position that may be compared to that of an ambassador.[14] The ultimate goal of the ambassador is to unite the speaker with the listener in a communion of thought. The objective reality of this communion depends upon the ambassador's ability to mediate what the speaker says in the language of the listener. Clearly, this requires that the ambassador be an adept translator, having a mastery of both languages, in order to facilitate a communion in thought with both the one for whom he speaks and the listener. In this twofold communion there is temporal and conceptual precedence of communion with the one for whom he speaks, since it is his thoughts

---

13. St. Paul sees himself as the servant of all three: servant of Christ or of God (Rom 1:1; Gal 1:10; Col 4:12; 1 Tim 1:12; Titus 1:1); servant of the Gospel (Rom 15:16; Eph 3:7; Col 1:23); servant of those to whom he is sent (1 Cor 9:19; 2 Cor 4:5).

14. St. Paul provides a biblical foundation for this imagery in 2 Cor 5:20; Eph 6:20; Phil 1:9.

that are communicated, first through his own words, and then through the substantively equivalent words of the translator.

In Christological terms, Jesus Christ is the only mediator between God and man (1 Tim 2:5) because he alone is true God and true man. His words, gestures, and actions infallibly communicate divine truth in humanly accessible revelation.[15] Only the one who is from heaven can bear witness to heavenly, that is, divine things, drawing from what he has seen and heard (John 3:31–32). In ecclesiological terms, vertical communion with God in Christ is the foundation for and cause of the mission of mediation to promote communion among men, both *ad intra*, those who believe in him, and *ad extra*, among those who do not yet believe in him.[16]

Opening Address of Pope John XXIII

The second non-conciliar text from which Pope Paul draws to develop his thought about the two dimensions of the Church's mission-for-communion is the address of Pope John XXIII to open the Council. Prior to quoting it, Pope Paul acknowledges, "in the present circumstances the urgently preeminent task ["of keeping pure and entire the faith entrusted to us and the mission of proclaiming the Gospel unceasingly"] encounters more difficulties than it has known in past centuries." The reason is that between the Church and society there is no longer a homogeneity of culture that can serve as a medium of communication.

> In fact, while the exercise of the episcopal teaching office was relatively easy when the Church lived in close association with

---

15. Jesus "perfected revelation by fulfilling it" (*DV*, 4), and this includes the perfection and fulfillment of the divine condescension involved in revelation (*DV*, 13). "While He was on earth Christ revealed himself as the Perfect Communicator. Through his 'incarnation,' He utterly identified himself with those who were to receive his communication and he gave his message not only in words but in the whole manner of his life. He spoke from within, that is to say, from out of the press of his people. He preached the Divine message without fear or compromise. He adjusted to his people's way of talking and to their patterns of thought. And he spoke out of the predicament of their time. Communication is more than the expression of ideas and the indication of emotion. At its most profound level it is the giving of self in love" (Pontifical Council for Social Communications, *Communio et progressio*, 11).

16. Discussing dialogue as the horizontal dimension of the Church's life, Cardinal Wojtyła underscores that the "horizontal dimension follows the vertical one and not vice versa" (*SR*, 37).

contemporary society, inspiring its culture and sharing its modes of expression, nowadays a serious effort is required of us to insure that the teaching of the faith should keep the fullness of its meaning and scope, while expressing itself in a form which allows it to reach the spirit and the heart of all men, to whom it is addressed.[17]

Six years later, Pope Paul identifies "the split between the Gospel and culture" as "the drama of our time."[18] The great cultural divide between the Church and the societies in which she lives requires that the Church recognize that her ambassadorial authority is not universally recognized, even among those who are baptized. She must, therefore, adopt a new mode of relating to people living in this new cultural order. Pope Paul and Vatican II call this new mode "dialogue."

During the centuries of Christendom and several centuries following it, during which a predominantly Christian culture was the norm, the Church and her contemporaries had many fundamental conceptual points of reference in common. Among the examples that could be adduced, the vocabulary of miracles, grace, the supernatural, virtues, heaven, hell, sin, conscience, sacrament, word of God, Sermon on the Mount. People could presume being understood when they quoted from Scripture as an authority, and when they spoke of prayer, baptism, the Golden Rule, the flood and Noah's ark, bishops and the pope, and the Eucharist.[19] At the time of Vatican II, the Church had become conscious of a disparity between her religious culture and an increasingly secular culture that more and more influenced the thinking and actions of her contemporaries, and even her own members. There being no qualified translator other than the Church herself, since in Christ the Church is the sacrament of mediation between God and men, it is up to the Church to find a way to communicate the unchanging truth of divine revelation in speech that her contemporaries are able to understand.

Pope Paul follows this cultural contextualization—this reading of the signs of the times—by quoting a passage of Pope John's opening address, a passage that has become the go-to text for his successors when they summarize his vision for Vatican II as a pastoral council.[20] Pope Paul

17. Paul VI, *QIA*.
18. Paul VI, *EN*, 20.
19. See Dr. Holly Ordway's comments on this in her interview with Carl Olson in Olson, "The Art of Imaginative Apologetics."
20. Typically, only part of this text is quoted. See Paul VI, "Address for the Opening

introduces it by saying, "No one has better shown the duty laid upon us in this regard than our predecessor, Pope John XXIII."

> In response to the deep desire of all who are sincerely attached to what is Christian, Catholic and apostolic, this teaching must be more widely and more deeply known, and minds must be more fully permeated and shaped by it. While this sure and unchanging teaching must command faithful respect, it should be studied and presented in a way demanded by our age. The deposit of faith itself—that is to say the truths contained in our venerable teaching—is one thing; the way in which these truths are presented is another, although they must keep the same sense and signification. The manner of presentation is to be regarded as of great importance and if necessary patient work must be devoted to perfecting it. In other words there must be introduced methods of presentation more in keeping with a magisterium which is predominantly pastoral in character.[21]

As if he were commenting on this description of the pastoral character of Vatican II, Pope Paul VI includes the following in his closing address:

> But one thing must be noted here, namely, that the teaching authority of the Church, even though not wishing to issue extraordinary dogmatic pronouncements, has made thoroughly known its authoritative teaching on a number of questions which today weigh upon man's conscience and activity, descending, so to speak, into a dialogue with him, but ever preserving its own authority and force; it has spoken with the accommodating friendly voice of pastoral charity; its desire has been to be heard and understood by everyone; it has not merely concentrated on

---

of Session Two of Vatican II"; "General Audience, September 7, 1966"; "Homily, September 29, 1967"; "General Audience, April 3, 1968"; "General Audience, December 4, 1968"; "General Audience, August 12, 1970"; "General Audience, September 30, 1970"; *QIA*; "Address, November 21, 1977." See also John Paul II, *Sapientia Christiana*, III; "General Audience, April 13, 1988," 5; "Address, December 22, 1992," 2; *Veritatis splendor*, 53n100; *Ut unum sint*, 18; *FR*, 92. Also Benedict XVI, "Address, December 22, 2005"; "Address, September 20, 2012"; "Homily, October 11, 2012."

21. Paul VI, *QIA*. The reference given for the original text of John XXIII is *AAS*, 54 (1962) 792. Attention to the difference between the official Latin text and an Italian original, as well as the accuracy of translation, has been the subject of persistent discussion. Those who argue for the primacy of the Latin include: McCarthy, "The Second Vatican Council"; Amerio, *Iota Unum*. On the other hand, Laurentin, *L'Enjeu du Concile*, 15, 104n5, prefers the Italian. Laurentin demonstrates the continuity in Pope John's thought by comparing the opening address to his homily of December 4, 1962.

intellectual understanding but has also sought to express itself in simple, up-to-date, conversational style, derived from actual experience and a cordial approach which make it more vital, attractive and persuasive; it has spoken to modern man as he is.[22]

Pope Paul also gives us an explanation for the need for this pastoral mode of teaching. It is entirely due to the historical changes that have been nothing short of revolutionary in their effect on the Church's relation to society and culture. During the age of Christendom, "the exercise of the episcopal teaching office was relatively easy when the Church lived in close association with contemporary society, inspiring its culture and sharing its modes of expression." In contrast to this, the Church at the time of Vatican II found herself marginalized. With respect to influencing culture, she was more an outsider looking in. In such a situation, "a serious effort is required of us to insure that the teaching of the faith should keep the fullness of its meaning and scope, while expressing itself in a form which allows it to reach the spirit and the heart of all men, to whom it is addressed."[23]

In the preceding, the emphasis is on presentation,[24] that is, the manner or style in which the teaching is formulated in order to increase the likelihood of its being understood and received, or, to remove obstacles to its being understood and received. For Pope John, Pope Paul, and the Council Fathers, the real task of Vatican II was effectively to communicate the deposit of faith. They took up the challenge to present the Church's teaching in a way that it inform the minds and hearts of men for the sake of their salvation in Christ. The mode of presentation is, then, a means to the end of realizing the effective transmission of the message of salvation in Christ.[25]

---

22. Paul VI, "Address, December 7, 1965."

23. Paul VI, *QIA*.

24. In the translation of the passage of Pope John's address for the opening of Vatican II that is quoted in *QIA*, the fourfold occurrence of "presentation" or "be presented" is felicitous because it serves to underscore the main line of thought in this passage. "Presentation" and "be presented" correspond to four more or less equivalent Italian and Latin phrases. Italian: *maniera . . . di formulare; esposta; modo con il quale esse sono annunziate; forma di esposizione*. Latin: *ea ratione pervestigetur et exponatur; tradita accurata illa ratione verba concipiendi et in formam redigendi; modus, quo eaedem enuntiantur; rationes res exponendi*.

25. The importance of presentation for the Council Fathers was not lost on John Paul. He agrees that "the Council's enormously rich body of teaching and *the striking new tone* in the way it presented this content constitute as it were a proclamation of

Since the focus at this juncture of *Quinque iam anni* is on those to whom the message of salvation is addressed, the measure for fashioning this presentation is that it correspond to what is "demanded by our age." This is consistent with what Pope Paul wrote six years earlier in *ES*:

> And was not the Council itself assigned—and justly so—a pastoral function which would be completely focused on the injection of the Christian message into the stream of the thought, of the speech, of the culture, of the customs, of the strivings of man as he lives today and acts in this life? Even before converting the world, nay, in order to convert it, we must meet the world and talk to it. (*ES*, 68)

This text is especially important because it indicates that Pope Paul's understanding of dialogue includes the goal of conversion. Why is this? Because God's dialogue with man through Jesus Christ is the paradigm for the Church's dialogue with the world. The goal of God's dialogue with man, that is, the dialogue of salvation, is communion with God, and this communion necessitates the renewal, the conversion, the transformation of man. Pope Paul recognizes that because dialogue must always respect human free will, the presentation of truth, no matter how effectively adapted to the mentality of those to whom it is directed, does not by itself guarantee conversion. But, it is a necessary condition for the conversion that brings about communion. This is why he also writes:

> If this approach does not aim at effecting the immediate conversion of the interlocutor, inasmuch as it respects both his dignity and his freedom, nevertheless it does aim at helping him and tries to dispose him for a fuller sharing of sentiments and convictions. (*ES*, 79)

In this text, the goal of conversion is communion ("sharing of sentiments and convictions") that admits of degrees ("a fuller sharing"). Whether effected immediately or coming later, conversion is always the means by which people move from partial to full communion. Regardless, the agent of dialogue has a role to play in disposing people to conversion by showing the relevance of the message of the Gospel. This is all an ambassador is able to do. Whether conversion occurs is a matter of a person's submission to the power of the truth that is presented, since truth convinces by the power of its own truth.[26] In light of this, the view

---

new times" (*NMI*, 20).

26. "The truth cannot impose itself except by virtue of its own truth, as it makes its

that spread quickly after the Council, that dialogue excludes the goal of conversion, simply does not represent the thought of Paul VI.[27]

Consistent with this goal of conversion, Pope Paul gives considerable attention to the characteristics of the Church's dialogue with her contemporaries, calling it "a method of accomplishing the apostolic mission" and "an example of the art of spiritual communication" (*ES*, 81). The importance of dialogue derives from the seriousness of the mission, which is salvation. For this reason, Pope Paul calls the dialogue a "dialogue of salvation" and stresses that this translates into an "apostolic care to review every angle of our language to guarantee that it be understandable, acceptable, and well-chosen" (*ES*, 81). He elaborates on this in terms of a pastoral prudence that applies universal and unchanging principles to concrete circumstances and actions.

> Finally, pedagogical prudence, which esteems highly the psychological and moral circumstances of the listener (cf. Matt 7:26), whether he be a child, uneducated, unprepared, diffident, hostile. Prudence strives to learn the sensitivities of the hearer and requires that we adapt ourselves and the manner of our presentation in a reasonable way lest we be displeasing and incomprehensible to him. (*ES*, 81)

> It [the dialogue] adapts itself to the needs of a concrete situation, it chooses the appropriate means, it does not bind itself to ineffectual theories and does not cling to hard and fast forms when these have lost their power to speak to men and move them. (*ES*, 85)

In terms of the formula of fidelity to God and to man, here Pope Paul is emphasizing fidelity to man, though without that precise formula. The actual phrase, "fidelity to God and to man," comes near the end of *Quinque iam anni*, where it clearly serves as a kind of summary of the

---

entrance into the mind at once quietly and with power" (Vatican II, *DH*, 1).

27. Nor does it represent the thought of John Paul II. See, for example, *RP*, 25: "The Church in fact uses the method of dialogue in order the better to lead people—both those who through baptism and the profession of faith acknowledge their membership of the Christian community and also those who are outside—to conversion and repentance, along the path of a profound renewal of their own consciences and lives in the light of the mystery of the redemption and salvation accomplished by Christ and entrusted to the ministry of his Church. Authentic dialogue, therefore, is aimed above all at the rebirth of individuals through interior conversion and repentance, but always with profound respect for consciences and with patience and at the step-by-step pace indispensable for modern conditions."

main theme of this short apostolic exhortation, a theme developed earlier by drawing from the Message to Humanity and Pope John's opening address. Referring to all that precedes, Pope Paul succinctly summarizes the commitment, goal, and spirit of Vatican II:

> In being thus faithful to God and to the men to whom he sends us, we shall then be able, with prudence and tact, but also with clear vision and firmness, to make a correct assessment of opinions.[28]

The goal of Vatican II is to spread the Catholic faith and to do so in a way that reformulates Catholic doctrine in a manner that makes it both intelligible and attractive to the men and women of the time. Efficacy in communication, however, is not the sole criterion for this reformulation or adaptation because the message has an objective content and meaning, which are determined by the God of revelation and clarified and defined by the Church. For this reason, fidelity to God is the necessary condition for being faithful to man. Like a physician who draws on generally applicable principles learned in medical school and does not alter the definition of health to suit particular patients but treats them so that they are healed and changed so as to come closer to the ideal of perfect health (call this biological conversion), the Church receives from Christ the definition of what it means to be fully human and measures her love for men in terms of leading them to Christ, so that by following him they become more fully human.[29]

The twofold fidelity to God and to man concisely summarizes the *aggiornamento* of Vatican II. Fidelity to God assures the enduring identity of the Church, its mission, and the content of the message she proclaims. In the language of Pope Benedict XVI, it is the foundation for the hermeneutic of continuity.[30] At the same time, fulfillment of the mis-

---

28. Paul VI, *QIA*.

29. Cardinal Wojtyła succinctly summarizes the goal of Vatican II in terms of this theme of promoting a more fully human life: "To 'make human life more human' is the Council's fundamental objective, closely linked to the desire to share in the divine life and in the mission of Christ" (*SR*, 279). The Christocentric foundations for this were clearly set down at Vatican II: "The truth is that only in the mystery of the incarnate Word does the mystery of man take on light. . . . Christ, the final Adam, by the revelation of the mystery of the Father and his love, fully reveals man to man himself and makes his supreme calling clear" (*GS*, 22), and "Whoever follows after Christ, the perfect man, becomes himself more of a man" (*GS*, 41).

30. See Benedict XVI, "Address, December 22, 2005."

sion entrusted to the Church by God is the primary objective, and this requires adaptation, not of the content of the message of salvation, but of its mode of expression. This is fidelity to man.

As with any duality, it is necessary to give each term its proper weight in order to avoid an imbalance that occurs when concern for one of the two fidelities risks eclipsing the other. Throughout his pontificate dedicated to promoting the *aggiornamento* of Vatican II, Paul VI indefatigably sought to maintain the correct balance that excludes two extremes: on the one hand, shrinking from the creative initiatives required to proclaim the Gospel in language that the Church's contemporaries can understand because of an exaggerated fear of failing to be faithful to God; on the other hand, paying insufficient attention to fidelity to God in the name of a pastoral solicitude for men that uncritically adopts new means guided by the sole criterion of efficacy in communication.[31]

Address to Superiors of Religious Orders

Pope Paul returns to the theme of fidelity to God and to man in an address to superiors of religious orders.[32] He tells them, in essence, that the "accommodated adaptation" of religious orders called for by Vatican II in the decree *Perfectae caritatis*[33] can be summed up in being faithful to

31. Paul VI's remarks in a General Audience (December 4, 1968) beautifully illustrate the balancing act demanded by the two fidelities. After acknowledging "the marvelous certainty of our faith," he admits a certain "spiritual fear" of not exactly knowing how to communicate that faith to others. He recognizes that our efforts at adapting the revealed Word to the understanding of the listeners can "go beyond the intent that makes it commendable, and beyond the measure of fidelity to the divine message." Yet, this is precisely the challenge of a Conciliar *aggiornamento*. Not only must one remain faithful to the grandeur of the Gospel, and sensitive to the dispositions of an audience, but one must also be aware of one's own limitations as well as the limitations and excesses of one's time. This balancing act is more amply developed in my article, "Pope Paul VI on the Renewal of Vatican II." A brief summary of an exchange between several priests and their bishop may be permitted here. A final meeting was held to bring to term a process of discernment regarding the selection of a program of theological formation for lay leaders in a diocese. Several priests were in favor of a program that emphasized proficiency in methods of communication, while others favored a program that stressed doctrinal theological education. At one point a priest of the latter group stated: "I can see that the first program will produce people who are effective communicators, but shouldn't we be asking: What is the message that they will be effectively communicating?"

32. Paul VI, "Address, April 15, 1978."

33. In the Latin text, the term "*accomodata renovatio*" appears ten times, including

God and faithful to man. Put another way, Pope Paul applies to religious the threefold plan of renewal set forth in *ES*, as this plan is simplified and recapitulated in the formula, "fidelity to God and to man."

In contrast with *Quinque iam anni*, in which "fidelity to God and to man" comes at the end and summarizes the apostolic exhortation's main theme, in the address to superiors it comes immediately after the greeting and establishes the unifying theme of the address.

> At this time in history when so many are striving to rediscover their vocational identity, your welcome presence offers us an appropriate occasion to direct our encouragement to the commitment of fidelity to God and to man of today![34]

Pope Paul develops the first member of the fidelity-duality in a strongly Christocentric manner, stating that this "double and unwavering fidelity" is a hallmark of every Christian who, by reason of baptism, is incorporated into Christ, and there is no "other Jesus" (2 Cor 11:4). Religious have a particular way of being faithful to Jesus. What is distinctive and unchangeable for them as religious is living by vow the three evangelical counsels. Fidelity to the counsels and to the charism of their founder, who incarnates a particular dimension of the life of Christ, is for religious the concrete form of fidelity to God.

Then, taking up fidelity to man, Paul states, "But a special fidelity to humanity is also characteristic of religious." This fidelity, he states, "is not extrinsically added onto the previous fidelity, but derives naturally from it." As Christ was faithful to the Father by fulfilling the mission of salvation entrusted to him, so religious "cannot fail to direct their whole life . . . to the goal of the salvation men, whom therefore it is necessary sufficiently to know and evangelically to love."

The important assertion here is that fidelity to man presupposes and flows from fidelity to God. Christ's sacrifice is the exemplar; he offers himself *to* the Father *for* the sake of men. He lives his communion with the Father by fulfilling the mission the Father ordained for him. His fidelity to the Father comes first, but it does not stand alone. For this reason, his fidelity to man "is not extrinsically added onto the previous fidelity, but derives naturally from it." The two commandments of love, love of God and love of neighbor, are inseparable, yet there is an order between

---

the descriptive title. The English version on the Vatican website translates it as "adaptation and renewal."

34. Paul VI, "Address, April 15, 1978."

them such that love of God has the primacy and it necessarily entails love of neighbor.

A sentence from one of Pope Paul's general audiences sums up this twofold orientation of fidelity to God and to man in language that is reminiscent of *ES*: "The Church has a twofold basic purpose: to be what Christ wills her to be, and to make herself better and better fitted to infuse the energies of faith and grace into the modern world, by the means of her traditional institutes and her spiritual experience."[35]

Significantly, Pope Paul virtually equates fidelity to God and to man with the *aggiornamento* of Vatican II, when he states: "From these considerations derives the duty of a constant and profitable *aggiornamento*."[36] This is significant because, as we will see further on in this chapter, this is not the only instance of the conciliar *aggiornamento* being explicated by the principle of fidelity to God and to man. For religious, the accommodated renewal or *aggiornamento* of religious life "does not aim at anything other than an ever better opportunity for apostolic presence, 'such that their testimony be clear to all and our Father in heaven be glorified' (*PC*, 25)."[37]

The goal of the renewal of religious life is the same as the overall goal of the renewal of the Church initiated by Vatican II. To be what Christ wills the Church to be corresponds to the first two paths of renewal of *ES*. The Church must first deepen her understanding of what Christ wills her to be through doctrinal penetration, then she cooperates with his grace to be transformed into his will through conversion. This gives rise to all the efforts by which the Church strives to adapt her methods for the sake of an effective dialogical mission in the world, the third path of *ES*.

FIDELITY TO GOD'S MESSAGE IS THE WAY TO BE FAITHFUL TO GOD AND TO MAN

Two additional occasions when Pope Paul speaks of fidelity to God and to man can be grouped together by reason of a particular emphasis on a third fidelity that serves to shed further light on the way that fidelity to God and fidelity to man relate to one another. That third fidelity,

---

35. Paul VI, "General Audience, January 14, 1970."
36. Paul VI, "General Audience, January 14, 1970."
37. Paul VI, "Address, April 15, 1978."

discussed earlier, is fidelity to the message of the Gospel, the message that God has revealed for the sake of man's salvation.

Address to Italian Professors of Sacred Scripture[38]

In his address to those who teach Sacred Scripture to seminarians, what Pope Paul has to say about fidelity to God and to man comes after he makes three points. All three points move in the direction of emphasizing that the study of Sacred Scripture cannot be reduced to an inquiry into a message that was relevant in another era and has been preserved in the sacred text in a way that its relevance is irretrievably locked in the past. The Bible certainly preserves this meaning that is linked to a particular period of salvation history, but it is much more than that. It is the word of God for the Church of all times, and the task of exegesis includes the disclosure of this diachronic relevance of Scripture.

Pope Paul develops his thought on this, first by insisting that the task of exegesis is ultimately at the service of and finds fulfillment in preaching. Biblical interpretation "has not completed its task until it has shown how the meaning *of Scripture can refer to this moment of salvation, that is, until it has shown the application in the present circumstances of the Church and the world.*" Second, in the process of interpreting the text, "*the person of the interpreter is not a stranger to the process itself,* but he is involved, is challenged with his whole being"; "Anyone who scrutinizes Scripture is first scrutinized by it."[39] By its very nature, God's word draws the reader into a dialogue with him, a dialogue that is intended to include every human being. Third, the Holy Father reminds his audience of "the *need to find a certain connaturality* of interests and problems, with the subject of the text."[40] By this he means to enter into the text in order to find its "for me" value. This requires a prior connaturality with the Church (*ES*, 37). Since the same Spirit who speaks through the sacred authors is also at work guiding the Church, both in hierarchical gifts and in the gifts and fruits of holiness of the faithful,[41] connaturalization with the Church

---

38. Paul VI, "Address, September 25, 1970."
39. Paul VI, "Address, September 25, 1970."
40. Paul VI, "Address, September 25, 1970."
41. "The Church, which the Spirit guides in way of all truth (cf. John 16:13) and which he unifies in communion and in works of ministry, he both equips and directs with hierarchical and charismatic gifts and adorns with his fruits" (Vatican II, *LG*, 4). This translation corrects the version on the Vatican II website, which has "unified"

entails connaturalization with Scripture. The desire for full communion with the apostolic Church on the part of those Christians whose faith rests solely on Scripture confirms the fact that each connaturalization is but an aspect of one connaturalization with the Holy Spirit. There may be a more pronounced awareness of one or the other aspect of this one connaturalization. For many who seek full communion with the apostolic Church, awareness of connaturalization mediated through the Bible precedes but eventually opens up to awareness of connaturalization mediated through the Church. The point is that connaturality with the subject of the text implies connaturality with the Church, since the Church is the subject of the biblical text.[42] To enter more deeply into the text of the Bible is to enter more deeply into the life of the Church, and vice versa. Exegesis and preaching, therefore, are always necessarily biblical and ecclesial, and for this reason it is always faithful to the Holy Spirit whose past inspiration of the Sacred Scriptures is meant to be discovered as relevant and thus to bear the fruit of faith in and through the ongoing assistance that the same Spirit provides to the apostolic Church.

Following what he writes about preaching, Pope Paul underscores the importance of fidelity to God's word. Jesus Christ, the eternal Word of God, is the original "exegesis" of the Father. He is therefore the fixed norm of all fidelity. Christ's revelation, historically and culturally instantiated as it is, "will always remain the fundamental norm of all that will be said about Christ until the end of time."[43] People of all subsequent historical periods and cultures must faithfully turn to him as he lived in his own time and culture in order to discover the formative, divine truth that is present in him and thus in the historical moment and culture in which he

---

rather than "unifies."

42. This is true for the three ways in which one can understand that the Church is the subject of Scripture. First, the Church is the subject of Scripture in the same sense that Christ is the subject of Scripture. All of Scripture bears witness to the mystery of Christ, and the Church is the full realization of the mystery of Christ, the very purpose of his mission. Second, the Church is the subject of Scripture as its author, that is, the Bible is the product of the conspiracy (breathing together) of the Holy Spirit and the sacred writers with faith in the mystery of Christ (whether as promised and awaited, or as having come). Third, the Church is the subject of Scripture with respect to the particular subjects (events and persons) addressed in particular pericopes, since all of these contribute in one way or another to the disclosure of the mystery of the whole Christ.

43. Paul VI, "Address, September 25, 1970."

lived. Following this, Pope Paul introduces the principle of fidelity to God and to man in order to bring his point of focus into clear view.

> But fidelity to the Incarnate Word also requires, by virtue of the dynamics of the Incarnation, that the message be made present, in its entirety, not to man in general, but to the man of today, to the one to whom the message is announced at the moment. Christ made himself a contemporary of the men of his time and he spoke in their language. Fidelity to him calls for this contemporaneity to continue. This includes all the work of the Church, with her Tradition, the Magisterium, and preaching.
>
> Exegetes should contribute to this task. Fidelity to modern man is demanding and difficult, but it is necessary if you want to be completely faithful to the message. This is neither servility nor mimicry, but courageous preaching of the Cross and Resurrection, with trusting certainty that this message will resonate in the heart of modern man. The Church's history gives us shining examples of this courageous actualization of the Word. Saint Catherine of Siena, whom we will soon have the consolation of proclaiming a doctor of the Church, spoke to the men of her time with heated and incisive language, in absolute fidelity to the Gospel message. Between these two fidelities, that of fidelity to the Incarnate Word and that of fidelity to the man of today, there cannot be nor should there be opposition. The first fidelity contains the absolute and irreplaceable norm, the second suggests the modality of translation and explanation of the message.[44]

Pope Paul introduces a third fidelity here, namely, fidelity to the message. In reality, the message not only has God as its source; it is God himself. It is the truth about God and his plan of love definitively revealed in Jesus Christ. When received in faith, this *message about* God's love becomes a divine *act of* love in the here and now of the believer's life. It is the same divine love that was at work throughout salvation history and fully revealed—fulfilled and perfected, in the words of *Dei Verbum*[45]—in Jesus Christ. Because God is eternal and unchanging, the essence of his love cannot change, even if it adapts the manner in which it acts. Put another way, the content of God's love, the good that by love God desires for all men, is unchanging because he himself is this good. Communion with God in faith, hope, and love is essentially the same throughout salvation

---

44. Paul VI, "Address, September 25, 1970."
45. "Jesus perfected revelation by fulfilling it" (Vatican II, *DV*, 4).

history, as is clear when St. Paul teaches that Abraham is the father-in-faith of Christians, and when the Book of Hebrews exalts his faith and the faith of others as paradigmatic for Christians.[46]

For Pope Paul, the message is as an intermediary between God, its Source, and those to whom it is destined. For this reason, fidelity to this message is the concrete, objective measure of fidelity to God and to man. At the same time, the message's universality, which is rooted in the universality of God's love, contains the principle of adaptation or accommodation in light of differing historical epochs and cultures. As a consequence, the law of fidelity to man is not so much a second law that is added to the law of fidelity to God and to his message as it is an explication of a second fidelity that is contained within a first and primary fidelity. As Pope Paul said to religious superiors, fidelity to man "is not extrinsically added onto the previous fidelity, but derives naturally from it."

Pope Paul's Apostolic Exhortation *Evangelii nuntiandi*

The final text of Paul VI that explicitly evokes the principle of fidelity to God and to man is found in his Post-Synodal Apostolic Exhortation, *Evangelii nuntiandi*, on the tenth anniversary of the close of Vatican II. As in the previously examined text, this one also links fidelity to God and fidelity to man by way of a third fidelity, namely, fidelity to the message that comes *from* God and is *for* man.

> "The conditions of the society in which we live oblige all of us therefore to revise methods, to seek by every means to study how we can bring the Christian message to modern man. For it is only in the Christian message that modern man can find the answer to his questions and the energy for his commitment of human solidarity."[47] And we added that in order to give a valid answer to the demands of the Council which call for our attention, it is absolutely necessary for us to take into account a heritage of faith that the Church has the duty of preserving in its untouchable purity, and of presenting it to the people of

---

46. See Rom 4:11, 16; Heb 11. St. Thomas is profoundly attentive to the bond of faith by which believers of the New Covenant are in communion with believers of the Old Covenant: "Now, though our faith in Christ is the same as that of the fathers of old; yet, since they came before Christ, whereas we come after him, the same faith is expressed in different words, by us and by them" (Aquinas, *ST*, I-II, q. 103, a. 4).

47. Paul VI, "Address, June 22, 1973."

our time, in a way that is as understandable and persuasive as possible.

This fidelity both to a message whose servants we are and to the people to whom we must transmit it living and intact is the central axis of evangelization.[48]

The fidelity-duality could not be put more clearly. Preservation of the "untouchable purity" of Gospel message must be combined with presenting that message in a manner that is calculated to make it "as understandable and persuasive as possible." In this way, the Church is conscious of serving her contemporaries by providing them with the definitive answer to the questions they are asking about the meaning and purpose of life.[49] In carrying out the mission received from Christ, fidelity to the message of salvation is fidelity to man. At the same time, as we have seen, fidelity to the message is fidelity to God.

In writing of preserving the Gospel in its purity and being servants of the Gospel, Pope Paul concisely reproduces St. Paul's threefold fidelity and service, mentioned earlier: to God or Christ; to those to whom God sends him; to the Gospel. Thus, St. Paul's self-consciousness as an apostle entails all three dimensions of fidelity: to God, to man, and to the divinely revealed message that is *from* God and *for* man. Such a threefold fidelity is necessary in order to sustain the kind of "constant and profitable *aggiornamento*"[50] envisioned by Pope Paul.

RENEWAL AS *AGGIORNAMENTO* BASED ON *RESSOURCEMENT*

In *ES*, Pope Paul recognizes that *aggiornamento* is the catchword summing up the vision of Pope John XXIII for the renewal of Vatican II. At the same time, he takes *aggiornamento* as the leitmotif his own pontificate,

---

48. Paul VI, *EN*, 3–4.

49. This sheds light on Pope Paul's statement, discussed earlier, of "the *need* [of interpreters of the Bible] *to find a certain connaturality* of interests and problems, with the subject of the text." The interests and problems of mankind are essentially the same in very epoch because they are rooted in human nature. Biblical texts become relevant to faith when they are perceived as divine answers to man's questions. God's answers are universally relevant because of the essential identity of human nature in all men. The Word of God inspired by the Holy Spirit and the apostolic Church assisted by the Holy Spirit are therefore universal or catholic.

50. Paul VI, *QIA*.

thereby signaling his intention to guide Vatican II to its conclusion and to implement it in continuity with his predecessor.[51] On several occasions when he outlines his understanding of *aggiornamento*, he does so in terms that correspond to the principle of fidelity to God and to man.[52] Authentic *aggiornamento* is a balance of unflinching fidelity to divine revelation and the Catholic Tradition, on one hand, and an ardent pastoral adaptation for the sake of maximum efficacy in mission, on the other hand. What Pope Paul says about *aggiornamento*, then, is another way for him to convey the principle of fidelity to God and to man.

An example of this comes in an address to bishops participating in a refresher course in theology, in which he defines *aggiornamento* in terms of what amounts to the law of fidelity to God and to man. Taking the pastoral letters to Timothy as his foundation, he first recalls to bishops that their first and primary duty is to safeguard the deposit of faith so as to "ensure the continuity and purity of the message entrusted to us, to pass it down with consistency in teaching, in truth, and clarity."[53] He especially emphasizes the quality of clarity, which is necessary "so that the People of God are able clearly to distinguish the truth, which is light and strength, from its vague expressions, according to a fashion that we could call gnostic—and so indeed it is—that would confuse the contours and obscure its integrity." The truth, he goes on to say, "is not susceptible to change in its essence, and we need to be even more faithful in safeguarding it, in this time when all things are open for discussion and subject to being relativized under more or less specious pretexts." Then he repeats something he had stated the previous year:

> "The content of the faith either is or is not Catholic. All of us ... have received the faith from an uninterrupted and constant tradition: Peter and Paul did not disguise it to fit the ancient Jewish, Greek, or Roman world, but were vigilant regarding its authenticity, the truth of the unique message." Consider, therefore, the duty of watching over the deposit, which must be passed down

---

51. See Paul VI, *ES*, 50.

52. For further examples than the one given here, and for the connection between the theme of fidelity to God and man and the theme of *nova et vetera* as keys to Paul VI's understanding of the renewal of Vatican II, see Bushman, "Pope Paul VI on the Renewal of Vatican II," 378–80.

53. Paul VI, "Address, November 14, 1975."

by us, integrally and brightly, just as we have received it down through the centuries.[54]

With fidelity to God firmly established, Pope Paul moves on to consider fidelity to man, though as already stated, using different terminology. His remarks build on the text of 1 Timothy 4:2, on preaching the word in season and out of season.

> This is our mission, and also our daily cross. We must put ourselves in tune with the times in order to understand its language and to interpret its *animus* [spirit], so that we can transmit the immutable truth in a formulation that is adapted for the man of today, what he aspires to and understands.... "There are those who repeat the deposit in its verbal textuality, without making a pedagogical effort regarding language and explanation, thus lacking in incisiveness and power, and making the message of truth appear lifeless."[55]

In Pope Paul's view, the apostle's challenge is to make himself understood by people in the context of their daily lives, to accommodate the manner in which the Gospel is communicated without in any way altering the substance of its content. St. Paul is the model of this: "I have become all things to all men, that I might by all means save some" (1 Cor 9:22). This is a biblical foundation for Pope Paul's understanding of *aggiornamento*:

> Here is the need and purpose of *aggiornamento*: to be able better to understand the specific demands of our time, and to acquire the ability to know them better, to make us better understand them. And if the idea, the content, as we have said, is going to be defended against the urge to relativize everything, then we ought instead to know how to manipulate the language, so that it is clear and clarifying, profound and lucid, modern and personal, and each has his own word to say. Certainly, this is difficult: we always need to return again and again to the school of the Gospel, to learn how Jesus spoke in his illustrious catechesis, which still today has the power to seize and to jolt us; we need to go to the school of Paul, the apologists, the Church Fathers, and the great theologians of the past, who have spoken the right

---

54. Paul VI, "Address, November 14, 1975," 1.

55. Paul VI, "Address, November 14, 1975," 2; here Pope Paul is quoting himself from an earlier "Address, November 4, 1975."

word for their time for us to learn even to say the word that has been entrusted.⁵⁶

This understanding of *aggiornamento* leads us back to what was said earlier about those who engage in mission being ambassadors. They are mediators between God and his message of salvation, on the one hand, and those to whom this message is intended to become an invitation, on the other hand. The *aggiornamento* of Vatican II entails the development of a dynamic and relational understanding of the Church, such that her relations to God, to his message, and to those to whom she is sent constitute her self-consciousness, and the three corresponding fidelities constitute the condition for the efficacy of her mission.

In theological appraisals of Vatican II, *ressourcement* precedes *aggiornamento*. Pope Paul shows that he is familiar with this, for on at least two occasions he discusses *ressourcement* as a theological activity at the service of *aggiornamento*.⁵⁷ These two texts invite us to see a parallel between the principle of fidelity to God and to man, on one hand, and the relation between *ressourcement* and *aggiornamento*, on the other hand.

Ressourcement is a French word that signifies the activity of bishops and theologians who reexamine the sources of the faith, especially Scripture, the Church's liturgical life, the Church Fathers, and the great theologians (doctors). It must be emphasized that this activity is guided by the faith and is therefore inspired by a fidelity to God and to his message. Looked at differently, one could say that a hermeneutic of continuity is the foundational presupposition for *ressourcement*. Even if particular *ressourcement* studies focus on arriving at a precise understanding of the Church's profession, celebration, and living of the faith at a particular historical juncture, their findings are indispensable for guiding the Church's dialogue between faith and reason in the present, if this dialogue is to be in harmony with the Church's tradition.⁵⁸ To the extent that *ressource-*

---

56. Paul VI, "Address, November 14, 1975."

57. Paul VI, "Address, March 14, 1974"; Paul VI, "General Audience, August 7, 1974."

58. Joseph Ratzinger's description of the contribution of the *ressourcement* theologians at Vatican II applies to the Church as the conscious subject undertaking renewal of herself. A fruit of *ressourcement* is a faith-based confidence rooted in discerning the distinction between what is essential versus what is historically and culturally contingent in the Church's life. With such a confidence, the Church could engage in a profound renewal of herself with the assurance that it was essentially "an increase of fidelity to her own calling" (Vatican II, *UR*, 6). Through *ressourcement*, the Church "found the norms for renewal" in "the breadth and depth of what had been handed

ment succeeds in accurately distinguishing between the faith of the Church as such and particular historical formulations, celebrations, and ways of living that faith, it becomes a valuable guide for the formulation, celebration, and living of the faith in the "today" of the Church's life.

Ressourcement, then, taken as a whole, is not a recapturing of particular historical instantiations of the Catholic tradition for their own sake. Rather, it is an important, even indispensable, means at the service of the *aggiornamento* that is a property of the Church's life.[59] *Aggiornamento* and *ressourcement* have the same foundation, namely, that the truth of divine revelation transcends any particular historical articulation of it.[60] *Ressourcement*'s fruit is a more precise grasp of the distinction between what is essential and unchanging in the Catholic tradition, and what is historically, culturally, and theologically contingent. Because this distinction must guide all *aggiornamento*, *ressourcement* provides an indispensable service to *aggiornamento*. As Marcellino D'Ambrosio puts it, "the key to theology's relevance to the present lay in the creative recovery of its past. In other words, . . . the first step to what later came to be known as *aggiornamento* had to be *ressourcement*—a rediscovery of the riches of

---

down in Christian tradition." From this "outlook which came from the intrinsic catholicity of the Church," the Church could engage in self-renewal with the *parrhesia* (boldness) of faith. See Ratzinger, *Theological Highlights of Vatican II*, 171–72.

59. Since every science and every branch of a science is a systematic and self-critical exercise of a power of the soul, a better understanding of the nature of that power will contribute to a better understanding of science. In the case of *ressourcement*, the doctrine of St. Augustine on memory has rich implications, which cannot be developed here. It should be pointed out, however, that for Augustine memory is not merely the capacity to retain impressions of past events. Memory presupposes this capacity but adds a specifically human dimension, namely, an understanding of the very meaning or truth of things. Because meaning or truth transcend historical moments, memory does also. Of its nature, its retrieval of the past is directed to an understanding and living of truth or meaning in the present and can be directed to projections regarding the future.

60. *Ressourcement* is guided by faith in the diachronic catholicity of the Church, that is, a conviction that the Church retains her essential identity throughout the ages. It is accompanied by an awareness that the truth of divine revelation transcends any particular historical articulation of it. The irreducibility of revealed truth with any particular doctrinal formulation, or the incapacity of any formulation of faith to exhaust the intelligibility of the revealed truth that formulation conveys, is recognized by the Congregation for the Doctrine of the Faith in *Mysterium Ecclesiae*. The same document refutes the erroneous conclusion that such non-commensurability or inexhaustibility leads to doubt about the truth of dogmatic formulations.

the Church's two-thousand-year treasury."[61] In *ressourcement* theology, the precise understanding of the various historical and cultural expressions of faith is at the service of a re-appropriation of that same faith in new cultural and historical contexts.

With this in mind, the parallel between fidelity to God and *ressourcement*, on one hand, and between fidelity to man and *aggiornamento*, on the other hand, becomes manifest. Fidelity to God means conformity to all that God has revealed and entrusted to the Church, and *ressourcement* is the theological activity based on the supposition that by the guidance of the Holy Spirit the Church remains essentially faithful to that revelation in her teaching, liturgy, and life. Thus, the Church's authoritative teaching and celebration of the Christian mystery, and her recognition of it being authentically lived by the saints, constitute a living commentary or exegesis of divine revelation. Because by Christ's promise the Church is assured to remain faithful to God, *ressourcement* theology mines the Church's history in order to ascertain the precise expressions and modalities of that fidelity to God. *Aggiornamento* means fidelity to man through adaptation or accommodation for the sake of effective pastoral mission, and the theological activity that corresponds to this is that dialogue between faith and reason as reason manifests itself in the cultures and philosophies that the Church encounters in the present day. *Ressourcement* provides this dialogue with a treasure of theological data regarding the historical realizations of that same essential dialogue and thereby provides *aggiornamento* with guiding principles regarding the distinction between what is essential and what is historically and culturally contingent so that *aggiornamento* may be simultaneously faithful to God and faithful to man.

THE NEXUS OF FIDELITY TO GOD AND TO MAN: THE SECOND PATH

As seen in previous chapters, Pope Paul sets forth his understanding of *aggiornamento* as entailing three paths of renewal: doctrinal awareness, renewal through conversion, and dialogical mission. In the texts examined in this chapter, he explains his understanding of that same *aggiornamento* in terms of the duality of fidelity to God and to man. Fittingly,

---

61. D'Ambrosio, *"Ressourcement,"* 532. For brief indications of the same in recent studies, see Ruddy, *"Ressourcement,"* 186–87; Grumett, "Henri de Lubac," 247.

fidelity to God aligns with doctrinal awareness and fidelity to man with mission. But what about the second path of renewal through conversion? Where does it fit in with respect to the law of fidelity to God and to man?

The answer to this question comes, in part, from observing that in the texts examined in this chapter the path of renewal is present, even if that precise terminology is not. To professors of Sacred Scripture, Pope Paul states that in the process of interpreting the Bible the exegete "is challenged with his whole being." He speaks of a connaturality with the Spirit who inspires Scripture, and asserts: "Anyone who scrutinizes Scripture is first scrutinized by it."[62] Clearly, the teachers of Scripture cannot impart to their students—in this case, seminarians—the ability to make Scripture come alive for others through their preaching if they have not first discovered for themselves the meaning-for-today, that is, the "for me" value, of the biblical text. In other words, the truth of Scripture (first path) resonates within the believer's own heart (second path) before he is able to play a role in making it resonate in the hearts of others (third path).

Similarly, the presence of the second path of renewal is readily verified in Pope Paul's address to religious superiors and in *Quinque iam anni*. In the former, fidelity to man is the fruit of following Christ more closely through living vows of the evangelical counsels, so that "those who follow [Christ] more closely cannot fail to orientate their whole life ... to the goal of the salvation men." In *Quinque iam anni*, Pope Paul asks his brother bishops:

> How in fact shall we be able to proclaim fruitfully the word of God, if it is not familiar to us through being the subject of our daily meditation and prayer? And how can it be received unless it is supported by a life of deep faith, active charity, total obedience, fervent prayer and humble penance? Having insisted, as is our duty, on teaching the doctrine of the faith, we must add that what is often most needed is not so much an abundance of

---

62. On another occasion, Paul VI makes the same point about the Scripture scholar's personal adherence of faith to the revealed mystery: "Great tasks await the exegete in the life and future of the Church. For this, he will commit himself to preserve and to augment in himself every day a living relation to the mystery of the God of love, who sent his Son among us to make us his sons by adoption. This mystery ... is recognized only with difficulty by those who are attached above all to earthly values, no matter how noble in themselves" (Paul VI, "Address, March 14, 1974").

words as speech in harmony with a more evangelical life. Yes, it is the witness of saints that the world needs.[63]

It is clear that the second path of conversion is a prerequisite to "fruitful proclamation" (third path).

It is no different for *Evangelii nuntiandi*. As would be expected of a comprehensive apostolic exhortation on evangelization, Pope Paul emphasizes that the condition for fruitful mission or evangelization by the Church is the "constant conversion and renewal" of the Church.

> The Church is an evangelizer, but she begins by being evangelized herself. She is the community of believers, the community of hope lived and communicated, the community of brotherly love, and she needs to listen unceasingly to what she must believe, to her reasons for hoping, to the new commandment of love. She is the People of God immersed in the world, and often tempted by idols, and she always needs to hear the proclamation of the "mighty works of God" (cf. Acts 2:11; 1 Pet 2:9), which converted her to the Lord; she always needs to be called together afresh by him and reunited. In brief, this means that she has a constant need of being evangelized, if she wishes to retain freshness, vigor and strength in order to proclaim the Gospel. The Second Vatican Council recalled (cf. *Ad gentes* 5, 11–12) and the 1974 Synod vigorously took up again this theme of the Church which is evangelized by constant conversion and renewal, in order to evangelize the world with credibility.[64]

This theme of being evangelized as the precondition for actively evangelizing succinctly conveys the relation of the second path of renewal through conversion to the third path of dialogical mission.

The presence of language corresponding to the second path of renewal in *ES* in the texts examined in this chapter indicates that even when Pope Paul does not explicitly refer to the three dimensions of renewal of *ES*, they remain so fundamental to his thinking about the renewal of Vatican II and they are so intricately related to one another that consideration of any one of them entails some mention of the others. In the texts examined in this chapter, fidelity to God corresponds chiefly to the first path of doctrinal awareness, and fidelity to man corresponds chiefly to the third path of dialogical mission. Still, the inseparability of the three

---

63. Paul VI, *QIA*.
64. Paul VI, *EN*, 15; see also 14 and 71.

paths is confirmed by the presence in the same texts of the second path of renewal through conversion.

Most important is Pope Paul's assertion in his address to religious superiors that fidelity to man is not only inseparable from fidelity to God, but contained in it. Fidelity to man, he states, "is not extrinsically added onto the previous fidelity, but derives naturally from it." Once it is perceived that God is love and that he loves man, communion with God necessarily entails communion in the mission of Christ to serve man with and in him. This is why the second path of renewal through conversion into a deeper communion with Christ is more than a bridge between fidelity to God and fidelity to man. It is, rather, the point at which the two can be seen as two dimensions of the one reality of communion with God in Christ. The very nature of collaborating with God in the fulfillment of his plan of love entails that fidelity to God and fidelity to man should be realized in the same acts.

Similarly, all three paths of renewal are expressions of the one fidelity to God. The first two paths of doctrinal awareness and renewal through conversion into deeper communion with God in Christ may be distinguished on the basis that God is both truth and love. The communion that he desires to have with us begins with a communication of revealed truth, for this is how God acts in accordance with the dignity of our free will. He makes known his love and his desire for communion, and thus our vocation, and this constitutes an invitation that calls to our freedom. The first path of renewal consists in a humble turning to God in order to receive from him a deeper, more precise, and more comprehensive understanding of what he has revealed. It is the first act of being faithful to the God who desires that we enter more deeply into communion with him by knowing more fully in faith what he has revealed.

Because God reveals his plan for our fulfillment in him, that is, our vocation, this first act of fidelity to him necessarily leads to a second act of fidelity. For, as Pope Paul indicates in *ES*, greater knowledge of our vocation cannot but shed light on the ways in which we fall short of living up to that vocation. In his love, God desires to give us the graces of conversion in order to convert more fully into our vocation. Cooperating with him in the process of conversion, that is, consenting to receive his grace, is the second act of fidelity to God, and this corresponds to the second path of *ES*.

Finally, fidelity to God culminates in an active participation in God's love for all men. This takes the form of a renewed commitment to and engagement in mission, the third path of *ES*. This active cooperation with God in loving others is already contained in the communion with him that is the goal of the second path of conversion, and this conversion is already contained in the revelation of God's plan of love that is more fully known as a result of the first path of doctrinal awareness. Each path is an unfolding of what is virtual in the prior path(s). In terms of fidelity to God and to man, fidelity to man is contained in fidelity to God, so much so that a lack of commitment to active participation in mission is perceived as a negative sign of the times within the Church, a situation that can only be explained by an insufficiently developed communion with God.

Pope Paul associates fidelity to man with the Church's mission *ad extra*. Thereby, his emphasis is on the Church's pastoral efforts to adapt the manner in which the Gospel is presented so that those to whom it is proclaimed can most readily perceive its truth and relevance. Fidelity to man is also realized in the Church's own life, the mission *ad intra*. As Pope Paul teaches in *Evangelii nuntiandi*, in order to evangelize the Church must first be evangelized. He could just as well have said that the first and second paths of doctrinal awareness and renewal through conversion—this is mission *ad intra*—are prerequisites to the dialogical mission *ad extra*; or, fidelity to God *ad intra* bears the fruit of fidelity to man *ad extra*. The first beneficiaries of the *aggiornamento* of Vatican II are the Church's own members, for whom the Council is the occasion for a doctrinal, personal, and missionary renewal or *aggiornamento*. The third path of dialogical mission is a form of fidelity to man both *ad intra* and *ad extra*: *ad intra*, participation in Christ's mission fulfills man's vocation to be associates,[65] co-workers[66] with God in mission; *ad extra*, those who are evangelized benefit from the evangelizing activity of the Church's members.[67]

---

65. The *CCC* refers to Moses as God's associate: "God reveals himself in order to save them, though he does not do this alone or despite them: he calls Moses to be his messenger, an associate in his compassion, his work of salvation" (2575).

66. The *CCC* refers to the dignity of creatures being "causes and principles for each other, and thus of co-operating in the accomplishment of [God's] plan" (306). Human beings have the dignity of being "intelligent and free causes" who can "enter deliberately into the divine plan" and "fully become 'God's fellow workers and co-workers for his kingdom'" (307).

67. The clergy sexual abuse scandal in the United States is a stinging negative confirmation of the dependence of apostolate and ministry on mission *ad intra*. In addition, George Weigel's analysis of the scandal confirms the dependence of the second

CONCLUSION

The above analysis illustrates how a theme, though infrequent in magisterial texts, can surprisingly show itself to be rich in meaning. Once identified, as in isolating one voice within a choir, and carefully examined both in itself and in relation to other themes, the theme of fidelity to God and to man in Pope Paul VI appears as a re-articulation of the three paths of renewal in *ES*. Fidelity to God chiefly corresponds to the first path of awareness while fidelity to man chiefly corresponds to the third path of dialogue. When invoking these two fidelities, Pope Paul's main emphasis is that fidelity to God assures that the objective content of the Church's missionary dialogue is safeguarded. It is a question of preserving the essential truth of the faith as the content of the love that motivates the Church's mission of service to man.

The two fidelities are united by a logic that necessarily includes the second path of conversion through renewal. One could say that fidelity to God and fidelity to man intersect precisely in the second path. Correlating to the first path of doctrinal penetration, fidelity to God would be incomplete so long as it remained mere knowledge. Since what God reveals is the truth about his love and man's vocation (which is the vocation of the Church), man can only be fully faithful to God by entering into this love and by embracing his vocation. This is the path of conversion into more and more perfect communion with God in Christ. At the same time, this ongoing conversion within the Church is a form of fidelity to man. It is mission *ad intra*, which is the condition for mission *ad extra*. In terms of fidelity to God and man, fidelity to God and man *ad extra* presupposes and is the fruit of fidelity to God and man *ad intra*. In terms of *aggiornamento*, there must be an *aggiornamento* within the Church— which can only be authentic if it is guided by fidelity to God—if there is to be an *aggiornamento* in the methods of dialogical mission, which must also be guided by fidelity to God.

With the theme fidelity to God and to man, Pope Paul gives us a concrete example of theological *aggiornamento*. In reality, the twofold

---

path of renewal through conversion on the first path of doctrinal awareness. Weigel holds that the clergy sexual abuse scandal is rooted in a profound crisis of clerical identity, rooted in a lack of doctrinal clarity regarding the nature of the episcopate and presbyterate. The solution to the crisis that he proposes is a conversion (second path) into the authentic teaching on the episcopate and presbyterate (first path) as set forth in the Second Vatican Council. See Weigel, *The Courage to Be Catholic*, esp. 22–32, 197–202, 219–31.

fidelity is a reformulation of the two great commandments of love of God and love of neighbor. For the Church, love of neighbor means mission, which takes the concrete form of dialogue. Pope Paul calls this "the art of spiritual communication" (*ES*, 81), because in this way the Church is being faithful to man by respecting the dignity and freedom of those with whom she enters into dialogue, while also adapting to historical and cultural situations. Thus, fidelity to man through dialogical mission has two components: fidelity to all that is essential in human nature and fidelity to the historical and cultural vicissitudes of history that condition man's openness to the Church's message. But this fidelity to man always requires fidelity to God, that is, to the truth about man and his fulfillment that he has established as Creator and restored as Redeemer. In a culture like ours that prizes fidelity, that is, truth, in investments and purchases, medical care, sports, media, scientific research, and personal and international relationships, the basic human need of fidelity is abundantly evident. Only fidelity to something greater than all of these, something that transcends them and can therefore endow them with the qualities of objectivity and stability, can assure that these spheres of human relationships are able to contribute to man's authentic development and fulfillment. Pope Paul recognizes that the basic human desire for fidelity is frustrated when men neglect the fidelity that matters most, namely, fidelity to God. His emphasis is that fidelity to man is only a genuine fidelity if it is based on fidelity to God.

The following chapter will show that, among others, Pope John Paul II heard the voice of Paul VI and recognized the significance of fidelity to God and to man as a key theme, not only for the interpretation and implementation of Vatican II, but for the life of the Church in every age.

9

Pope John Paul II on Fidelity to God and Fidelity to Man

JOHN PAUL II DEVELOPS the theme of fidelity to God and to man more amply than Paul VI does. This chapter investigates the two primary applications that John Paul makes of this principle. First, and consistent with his predecessor, John Paul employs it to convey the balance that must be struck as the Church executes her mission. In the Church's efforts to be faithful to man in serving him, the truth that God has revealed in Jesus Christ must be her constant guide. This is essentially what Pope Benedict calls the hermeneutic of continuity (fidelity to God) and reform (fidelity to man). Second, John Paul engages the principle of fidelity to God and to man in order to make a clarifying synthesis of one of the major pastoral concerns of Vatican II, namely, to refute the charge that faith and religion are alienating for man.

FIDELITY TO GOD AND TO MAN: A LAW OF THE CHURCH'S LIFE

For John Paul II, fidelity to God and to man is a law of the Church's life that he associates with the renewal of Vatican II. He also indicates that this law applies to various groups within the Church precisely because they participate in the Church's life and mission and thus in the *aggiornamento* initiated by the Council.

There is nothing new in John Paul's assertions that Vatican II is essentially an ecclesiological council. In perfect consistency with Pope Paul's first path of doctrinal awareness, the Council marks a new stage in the Church's self-consciousness.[1] It is natural, then, that this step forward in self-consciousness should entail a deeper awareness of an essential law of the Church's life. Awareness of this law of fidelity to God and to man is, according to the Polish Pope, at the very center of the renewal of Vatican II. The Council undertook "the immense work of 'updating' the Church under the banner of a twofold fidelity to God and to man."[2] "Fidelity to God and to man was a leitmotiv of the Second Vatican Council (cf. *Gaudium et Spes*, 21)."[3]

Fidelity to God and man is a major principle guiding Vatican II because it is a law of the Church's life, a property rooted in the Church's very nature and mission, so that a change of this principle would result in an essential change in the being of the Church herself. For this reason, this property of the Church, which John Paul calls a law, can be verified in every age of the Church's earthly pilgrimage. Thus, John Paul contends that all ecumenical councils, beginning with the council of Jerusalem (recounted in Acts 15), bear witness to the principle of fidelity to God and to man. It may be that the consciously pastoral orientation of Vatican II results in the principle being more readily discernible in the most recent council. But, this greater clarity allows us to perceive the principle in past councils.

> The Council fostered the renewal of the family of believers, preparing them for a new evangelization. Through the encounter and dialogue with modern cultures, with the emerging needs of the contemporary world, the Second Vatican Ecumenical Council cast greater light on the twofold need of the Church today: fidelity to the Gospel, which is to be handed on in its integrity; and fidelity to man, whose authentic values are to be recognized and promoted in their truth.[4]

1. See John Paul II, *RH*, 7, 11.
2. John Paul II, "Address, December 22, 1997," 7.
3. John Paul II, "Address, October 7, 1986," 7. *GS*, 21, begins thusly: "The Church, faithfully dedicated both to God and to men . . ." The Latin is: "*Ecclesia, fideliter tum Deo tum hominibus addicta . . .*"
4. John Paul II, "Homily, May 24, 1992," 5.

John Paul follows this with a rephrasing of the principle of fidelity to God (by being faithful to the Gospel) and fidelity to man (through dialogue with cultures) in terms that invite us to correlate the doctrinal dimension of Vatican II to fidelity to God and the pastoral dimension to fidelity to man. Just as fidelity to God and fidelity to man are not only inseparable but mutually interpenetrating, so that each is distorted to the extent that it is not complemented by the other, so the doctrinal and the pastoral are two inextricable aspects of the Church's life, vocation, and mission. Vatican II sought to reunite these two dimensions.[5]

As for Paul VI, for John Paul II the twofold fidelity to God and to man characterizes the Church's entire life: "The Church must show its proper and authentic face in the daily striving for fidelity to God and to men."[6] This essential dimension of the Church's life is rooted in the fact that by her nature the Church is communion with God in life and mission.[7] She must be faithful to God who sends her, and she must be faithful to those to whom she is sent. She accomplishes this by being faithful to what God has revealed.[8] Her deepest essence as communion gives her this relational identity that is marked by the twofold fidelity to God and to man, which necessarily entail a third fidelity, to the Church.

Fidelity to God is neither abstract nor subjective. The concrete way in which the Church's members live out their fidelity to God is by being faithful to the Church, since the Church has a precise place and role in God's plan. Thus, John Paul speaks of a third fidelity, just as Pope Paul does:

> I want to exhort all of you to renew your fidelity to Christ—by knowing him better, loving him still more, and following him unconditionally; your fidelity to the Church, Bride of Christ, who gives his Word and the means of salvation, prompting us to become a people of brotherhood, sons of God; your fidelity

---

5. An indication of the need for this reunification is the debate during the Council about just how the pastoral and doctrinal should be understood and how they relate to one another. This debate has continued since the Council, with many authors juxtaposing the two, as if a Council had to be either doctrinal or pastoral.

6. John Paul II, "Message for the World Day of Prayer for Vocations, August 15, 1995," 4.

7. See Vatican II, *AG*, 2.

8. On these three fidelities—to God, to man, and to the message of salvation—see chapter 8 above.

to man, created in God's image, whose dignity must always be respected and his rights protected.[9]

IN RELATION TO EVANGELIZATION AND INCULTURATION OF FAITH

John Paul enlists the principle of fidelity to God and to man in relation to evangelization and inculturation of faith. Because culture is a property rooted in the social nature of man,[10] fidelity to man entails attention to culture. John Paul rephrases the well-known injunction of St. Peter to be ready to give an explanation for the hope by which we live (1 Pet 3:15): "The guiding principle of Christian proclamation, namely, fidelity to God and fidelity to man, requires constant attention to contemporary culture."[11]

Another example comes in an address to the Roman Rota, in which John Paul situates the Rota's mission within the Church's mission to evangelize cultures. Here, the doctrine that becomes the concrete measure of fidelity to God is that marriage is a natural institution established by God himself. Because cultures inevitably influence how marriage is understood and lived, it is necessary to read of the signs of the times regarding the positive and negative influences of contemporary cultures on marriage. He continues:

> The Church, therefore, although with all due attention to the culture of every people and to the progress of science, should always be attentive so that the people of today are offered the entirety of the gospel message about marriage, as it has matured in her consciousness through centuries of reflection carried out under the guidance of the Spirit.[12]

The Rota upholds and applies the Church's marriage law, which "touches upon elements and protects values which the Church wants to guarantee at the universal level, beyond the variety and changing nature of cultures in which the individual particular churches operate."[13] This

---

9. John Paul II, "Address, December 5, 1988," 2.

10. "Culture is so natural to man that human nature can only be revealed through culture" (Pontifical Council for Culture, *Toward a Pastoral Approach to Culture*, I.2).

11. John Paul II, "Address, May 6, 1995," 3.

12. John Paul II, "Address, January 28, 1991," 7.

13. John Paul II, "Address, January 28, 1991," 7.

emphasis clearly corresponds to fidelity to God, and John Paul confirms that this is precisely what he has in mind in his conclusion, which he sets forth in terms of the twofold fidelity:

> In her fidelity to God and to man, the Church acts like the scribe who, having become a disciple of the kingdom of heaven, "brings out of his treasure what is new and what is old" (Matt 13:51 [sic]). In faithful adherence to the Spirit who enlightens and sustains her, as the people of the new covenant, the Church "speaks in all languages, and in love understands and embraces all languages" (*AG*, 4).[14]

The text of Matthew 13:52 on the wise scribe is an apt biblical passage for understanding the renewal of Vatican II as an application of the law of fidelity to God and to man. It is a biblical foundation for developing his thought on Sacred Tradition and its development.[15] Tradition develops in a way that new things are drawn out of the old, as at Vatican II. The relevant point for the present study is that the old corresponds to fidelity to God and the new corresponds to fidelity to man. Both Paul VI and John Paul II make the point that a factor contributing to the development of doctrine is the Church's contact with men and women in various cultures throughout the centuries. Her mission is the occasion for her to have to understand divine revelation (the old) more penetratingly in order to translate it into the languages that men speak (thus producing the new). This is precisely what happened at Vatican II.[16]

For John Paul, the New Evangelization, which he roots in the renewal of Vatican II and which corresponds to the third path of dialogue of *ES*, is a renewed commitment on the part of the Church to be faithful to man. But, this fidelity to man presupposes and is the fruit of being faithful to God. As an "expert in humanity," the Church contributes the treasures of her spirituality and of classical culture to building up "the

---

14. John Paul II, "Address, January 28, 1991," 8. The reference to Matt 13:51 should be to Matt 13:52.

15. An investigation into the use John Paul makes of Matt 13:52 led me to discover, several years ago, the extensive use that Paul VI makes of the same passage. The fruit of that discovery is the previously mentioned article: Bushman, "Pope Paul VI on the Renewal of Vatican II."

16. One can also recognize here the presence of *ressourcement*, corresponding to the old, and *aggiornamento*, corresponding to the new.

civilization of love in a world that is more attentive to man because it is more faithful to God."[17]

Application to Various Groups within the Church

With an eye to implementing Vatican II, John Paul recognizes that everyone who participates in the Church's life and mission thereby participates in this law, this property of the Church's life, which is to live in the twofold fidelity to God and to man. A few examples suffice to illustrate this.

Catechists

Chronologically, the first instance of the theme of dual fidelity in John Paul's pontificate comes in the Post-Synodal Apostolic Exhortation, *Catechesi tradendae* (October 16, 1979). Acknowledging the necessity of a multiplicity of catechetical methodologies, he goes on to explain why this is justified by referring to the law of fidelity to God and to man.

> The plurality of methods in contemporary catechesis can be a sign of vitality and ingenuity. In any case, the method chosen must ultimately be referred to a law that is fundamental for the whole of the Church's life: the law of fidelity to God and of fidelity to man in a single loving attitude.[18]

The meaning is clear. The goal of catechetical activity is to communicate the integral truth of Catholic faith. The catechist is a mediator whose goal is to bring about conformity in thinking between God (and his Church) and those who are catechized. God's thinking, the truth that he knows and has revealed, is the objective norm of communion with him in faith. Fidelity to this revealed truth is fidelity to God. At the same time, it is fidelity to man, since man's supreme good is communion with God by faith in this truth.[19] But, fidelity to man means something more. It means ingenuity in adapting catechetical methods and even the expression of faith itself to the receptivity of those being catechized.

---

17. John Paul II, "Address, February 16, 1996," 7.
18. John Paul II, *CT*, 55.
19. Benedict XVI puts it this way: "Fidelity to man requires *fidelity to the truth*, which alone is the *guarantee of freedom* (cf. John 8:32) and of *the possibility of integral human development*. For this reason the Church searches for truth, proclaims it tirelessly and recognizes it wherever it is manifested" (*Caritas in veritate*, 9).

A clear example of this is seen in the way catechists take into account the age of those whom they teach. This is particularly important when it is a matter of catechesis regarding God's plan for human love and the virtue of chastity, what is commonly referred to as age-appropriate education in human sexuality.[20]

More generally, the law of fidelity to God and to man guides all catechetical instruction. This applies to making use of the *Catechism of the Catholic Church*.

> In this perspective, it is particularly important to study and to apply the *Catechism of the Catholic Church*, an indispensable *vademecum* (guide book) offered to priests, catechists and all the faithful, to direct catechesis on the paths of authentic fidelity to God and to the people of our time.[21]

John Paul's most significant elaboration on the law of dual fidelity with respect to catechesis is the following:

> However, as in all things regarding the education of persons, in particular the education in the faith, quantity must be matched by quality. To be *a catechist of high quality*: this is what those who perform that important task today must aspire to. To be a catechist of high quality in accordance with the characteristics that the Church authentically proposes. You know these characteristics. The catechist must, first of all, be *a person who affirms gospel certainties with conviction*: "We live in a difficult world in which the anguish of seeing the best creations of man slip away from him and turn against him creates a climate of uncertainty. In this world catechesis should help Christians to be, for their own joy and the service of all, 'light' and 'salt.' Undoubtedly this demands that catechesis should strengthen them in their identity and that it should continually separate itself from the surrounding atmosphere of hesitation, uncertainty and insipidity." (*CT*, 56)

---

20. On this, see the text of the Sacred Congregation for Catholic Education, *Educational Guidance in Human Love*, and the text of the Pontifical Council for the Family, *The Truth and Meaning of Human Sexuality*. "Each child is a unique and unrepeatable person and must receive individualized formation. Since parents know, understand and love each of their children in their uniqueness, they are in the best position to decide what the appropriate time is for providing a variety of information, according to their children's physical and spiritual growth" (*Truth and Meaning of Human Sexuality*, 65).

21. John Paul II, "Address, May 8, 2003," 3. The *GDC* incorporates the law of fidelity to God and to man in articles 145, 149, and 283.

The catechist must also be a faithful servant of the gospel *as it was entrusted to the Church by Jesus* and as the Church has assimilated and transmitted it in her bimillenary tradition. The presentation of the faith is authentic, liberating and fruitful if it clearly shows forth the genuine sense intended by Christ and the witness of the Apostles. It is for this reason that, during these years of my apostolic service, I have spoken repeatedly of the "need for a systematic catechesis" (*Catechesi tradendae*, 21) and for "integrity of content" (*Catechesi tradendae*, 30). It would truly be a grave sin against fidelity to the gospel, but also against culture, if the immense patrimony of the faith contained in and developed from the Bible and made explicit and defended by the Church, under the guidance of the Spirit, for these twenty centuries, were in some way distorted. It is precisely with a view to facilitating the transmission of the incomparable riches of the faith, as they have been authentically re-proposed for our era by the Second Vatican Council, that the Extraordinary Synod of Bishops asked for the composition of a "catechism for the universal Church."

The catechist must also be an expert in humanity[22], that is, deeply attentive to the sensibility and the problems of the persons being catechized; it is of no use to give a beautiful lesson if it does not respond to the questions and the expectations of those to whom it is directed.

Here, along with being systematic and integral, catechesis must be intensely meaningful; it must, that is, prolong the attitude of Jesus who, as he gives the Word of life, meets each person in the reality of his needs, his expectations, and his ability to understand.

Finally, the catechist must suit his teaching to the social context in which those being catechized live. In other words, he must not reduce his service to the Word of God to purely interior forms of adherence and of worship, but must open himself to the great moral and social questions of our day, questions which

---

22. The theme of the Church as "an expert in humanity," comes from Paul VI, "Address, October 4, 1965." See also Paul VI, *Populorum progressio*, articles 4 and 13, referred to by John Paul in *Sollicitudo rei socialis*, 7n10. For John Paul II, see "Address, January 28, 1979," III.3; *Veritatis splendor*, 3; *Ex corde Ecclesiae*, 3; "Letter, May 2, 2002," 4; "Address, March 31, 2000," 3; "Message for 22nd World Communications Day"; "Address, October 23, 1982," 2; "Message for World Migration Day, 1997," 2; "Address, November 26, 2002," 2; "Homily, January 25, 1979," 3; "Address, November 8, 2001," 2; "Angelus, August 2, 1998," 1; "Message for Brazil's Lenten "Campaign of Fraternity 2003'"; "Address, November 22, 1991," 4; "Message to the Young People of Cuba"; *Sollicitudo rei socialis*, 7, 41; *Pastores gregis*, 66.

I have recalled more in the Encyclical *Sollicitudo Rei Socialis*. He proclaims the gospel to the men and women of today, whom he helps to grow according to a strong and intense morality which must be measured against respect for and the elevation of the human person, especially with regard to the poor, throughout the world. He must always join solidarity and freedom (cf. *Sollicitudo Rei Socialis*, 33).

If realized in a consistent way, these characteristics permit the fulfillment of what remains as it were "a law that is fundamental for the whole of the Church's life: the law of fidelity to God and of fidelity to man, in a single loving attitude" (*CT*, 55).[23]

Clearly, according to John Paul, the catechist must be faithful to God by being faithful to his Gospel, and faithful to humanity by making sure that his teaching is suited to the people of today.

In the transitional paragraph, John Paul states, "it is of no use to give a beautiful lesson if it does not respond to the questions and the expectations of those to whom it is directed." In terms of the law of fidelity to God and to man, this means that a lesson that is everything it should be in terms of fidelity to God is of little value if it is not at the same time adapted to the actual disposition(s), openness, or potential for receiving that lesson of those to whom it is addressed. Fidelity to God without fidelity to man may be fidelity on the level of the truth of the *content* of revelation, but it is not fidelity to the *motive* of revelation, that is, God's love and his own manner of adapting revelation to the actual state of those to whom he reveals himself. The mutual interpenetration of the two fidelities is such that the formula could easily be reversed: It is of no use to give a lesson that is well adapted to an audience, that is, faithful to man, if it is not faithful to God by accurately containing the truth of divine revelation.

The underlying vision for catechesis is that it is dialogical by nature. This does not require that there be an actual, verbal back-and-forth between catechist and catechized, though of course this is not in principle proscribed. Rather, catechesis is dialogical because of the correspondence between the "questions, needs, expectations, and ability to understand" of those being catechized and the manner in which these are taken into account and addressed. Catechesis becomes dialogical, not primarily by reason of an outward back-and-forth, but by reason of the perception on the part of those catechized that their aspirations (conscious or

---

23. John Paul II, "Address, April 25, 1988," 3.

otherwise), questions, and preoccupations are being addressed. This assures that the content imparted through catechesis is not mere data that can only be retained by memorization but life-giving, meaning-giving truth that becomes light for one's living because it conveys the "for me" value of revealed truth.

Catechists can only accomplish this kind of concrete fidelity to man if they themselves have discovered the life-giving and meaning-giving qualities of revealed truth. Certainly, instruction in various human sciences—developmental psychology, family systems, sociology, and pedagogy—can be very useful in assisting catechists in acquiring that expertise in humanity that allows them to craft meaningful lessons. Nevertheless, fidelity to man cannot be reduced to following precise and predetermined formulas or guidelines. Nothing can replace the catechist's experience of his own humanity in dynamic interactivity of his own human aspirations and freedom with God's grace and the gift of faith. Without this, the knowledge acquired by anthropological studies can only give rise to pre-conceived methods and techniques. When a catechist's preoccupation with these is overriding, then there is no real fidelity to man and no real dialogue. These are replaced by fidelity to a system.[24] The most effective catechists are those whose expertise in humanity derives also from their own experience, so that their self-consciousness is a participation in the self-consciousness of the Church herself.[25] This then becomes an

---

24. In *QIA*, Pope Paul warns against "a tendency to reconstruct from psychological and sociological data a Christianity cut off from the unbroken Tradition which links it to the faith of the apostles, and a tendency to extol a Christian life deprived of religious elements." He also clarifies that while sociological data, and for that matter the data from all the human sciences, "are useful for better discovering the thought patterns of the people of a particular place, the anxieties and needs of those to whom we proclaim the word of God," nevertheless conclusions drawn from this data "could not of themselves constitute a determining criterion of truth." Vatican II encouraged the use of the human sciences as aids in reading the signs of the times: "On a number of occasions, the Second Vatican Council stressed the positive value of scientific research for a deeper knowledge of the mystery of the human being" (John Paul II, *FR*, 61). A note in *FR* refers to *GS*, 57 and 62. In addition, see *OT*, 2, 20; *AA*, 32; *CD*, 17. These sciences provide precious information about the actual state or condition of the men and women that the Church is called to serve, and this is very helpful when it comes to applying the axiom, that which is received is received according to the mode of the receiver (see below). Nevertheless, reading the signs of the times is ultimately a judgment based on faith.

25. It would be interesting to compare the notion of the Church's self-consciousness to the *sensus fidei*, but that is beyond the scope of this study. Certainly, one way to describe the goal of formation for catechists is to promote a more mature *sensus*

internal, auto-critical principle guiding the concrete application of the law of fidelity to God and to man.

Priests and Religious

In a letter addressed to seminarians, John Paul takes the perfect "Yes" of Christ to the Father as the model of the priest's "Yes" of total self-donation to God, and takes the word "fidelity" as synonymous with this "Yes." The seminary, he writes, "is to be the school of this fidelity," and this fidelity has three dimensions: "*fidelity to Christ, to the Church, and to your own vocation and mission.*"[26] What he says about fidelity to Christ is, in essence, the outline of presbyteral spirituality. It corresponds to the second path of renewal through conversion or transformation into Christ. Fidelity to the Church is not really something distinct from fidelity to Christ. Since Christ lives in the Church, makes himself present in the Church, and in her draws close to all the faithful and is communicated to the world, "fidelity to Christ is thus extended in fidelity to the Church."[27] To be faithful to the Church means to accept it as the mystery of or expression of God's love that it is. This aspect of fidelity to the Church corresponds to the first path of *ES*, the path of doctrinal awareness, which serves as the objective foundation for a life of continual deepening in understanding "the whole truth" and integrating "new lights" that will come throughout a priest's pilgrimage of faith.

The third fidelity is the priestly vocation and mission. By divine institution, this vocation has an objectively determined essence, within which priests will necessarily have to adapt for the sake of pastoral effectiveness as they "take into account the needs of our brethren and our society." As a result, he writes, "Your fidelity to Christ and the Church ... becomes transformed into greater fidelity to man and to the society of

---

fidei in them, so that they can draw on this as an auto-critical principle to guide their selection of vocabulary and examples as they strive to implement the law of fidelity to man. It is possible to see this aspect of the *sensus fidei* as a participation in Christ's own knowledge of what is in men (John 2:25). John Paul II frequently refers to this passage of John's Gospel in order to convey the interior source from which Christ drew in his interactions with men. The principle set forth in *CCC*, 521—"Christ enables *us to live in him* all that he himself lived, and *he lives it is us*."—provides the foundation for reflecting on the catechist's participation in Christ's knowledge of what is in every man.

26. John Paul II, "Message to Seminarians in Spain," 2.
27. John Paul II, "Message to Seminarians in Spain," 4.

our times."²⁸ Here, as elsewhere, fidelity to man corresponds to the third path of mission through dialogue.

The verbs that John Paul uses in this text indicate that it is not so much a question of three distinct fidelities as it is of three dimensions of a single all-embracing fidelity. Fidelity to Christ *extends* to fidelity to the Church because the latter is included in the former. In turn, fidelity to Christ and the Church are *transformed* into fidelity to man because they are not complete without the essential complement of service to man.

Addressing a group of religious, John Paul refers to the prophetic nature of their "following the chaste, poor, and obedient Christ in anticipation of the coming of the Kingdom and stressing the primacy of God over every human concern, no matter how legitimate." Such following of Christ "is *the training ground* of total fidelity to Christ and attentive openness to man." He sums up fidelity to Christ and fidelity to man: "these are the poles of reference to guide you in the search and following of new ways of evangelization and human development, with wide-ranging mission, remembering the words of the Council, which invites you to make every effort to ensure that through you 'the Church, in a striking manner, daily presents Christ to believers and non-believers alike' (*LG*, 46)."²⁹

Eastern Churches

An example that illustrates the extent to which John Paul sees the twofold fidelity as a law of the Church's life comes in an address concerning Eastern Churches. He states that they are "called to maintain a twofold fidelity." The first fidelity is to "the traditions which have been handed down to them" and which "unite them to their own Mother Churches." This assumes that these traditions are historical and cultural realities through which the Holy Spirit has guided these Churches, so that fidelity to God becomes specified by fidelity to these traditions.

Then he proceeds to consider fidelity to man.

> Second is fidelity to the men and women of today with their joys and hopes, their sorrows and pain, their desires and expectations, as they thirst for the truth and the fullness of life that finds its source only in God; this is faithfulness to the continuing search, especially in consumer-oriented societies, for the deeper

---

28. John Paul II, "Message to Seminarians in Spain," 5.
29. John Paul II, "Address, April 28, 1991," 3.

meaning of life. This twofold fidelity is fidelity to God and to his revelation—shining brightly in the many different traditions which come from the Apostles through the Fathers (cf. *Orientalium Ecclesiarum*, 1)—and fidelity to man and to his need of God, in the various ways in which this is expressed.[30]

What is common and constant in fidelity to man is human nature. Every human person experiences the God-given, natural dynamisms that impel him toward truth, fullness of life, and definitive meaning in communion with God. Reading the signs of the times, in this case the influences of a consumer-oriented society, the Church discerns the state of these dynamisms—what threatens them and prevents them from being fulfilled, what is conducive to their fulfillment, and what threatens or is conducive to man's openness to the Gospel—so that her fidelity to man is tailored to the concrete situation of individuals and groups.

Active Members of the Church

The corporal works of mercy and efforts to defend and to promote human dignity through social justice are especially conspicuous indicators that fidelity to God and to man are inseparable. Speaking of "volunteers of proven solidarity and great generosity" who work "for a project of human liberation and of effectively promoting man's dignity," John Paul calls them "true witnesses: *witnesses of fidelity to man and to Christ.*"[31]

The baptismal dignity of every member of the Church entails participation in the Church's life and mission and thus in the law of twofold fidelity. Having become incorporated into Christ and thus having been made participants in his life and mission, the faithful live according to the law of fidelity to God and to man, for "Christ came not to be served, but to serve (cf. Matt 20:28), through fidelity to the Father and fidelity to man."[32] John Paul reiterates this baptismal participation in the law of fidelity to God and to man in a homily in which he calls the faithful of Merida, Venezuela, to a renewal of their faith: "To renew the faith means to deepen the knowledge of Catholic doctrine; to have the vital experience of love for God and for the brethren; it means to announce the

---

30. John Paul II, "Message to the Prefect for the Congregation for Oriental Churches."

31. John Paul II, "Address, February 22, 1997," 3.

32. John Paul II, "Address, May 12, 1982," 2.

Gospel to others."³³ These three dimensions of renewal manifestly align with the three paths of *ES*. Then, he links the renewal of faith to three dimensions of fidelity: "Only this renewed faith will be able to lead to fidelity: fidelity to Jesus Christ, to the Church, to man." Fidelity to Christ, he states, "is inseparable from fidelity to the Gospel," and so is fidelity to the Church: "To be faithful to the Church means not to let yourself be dragged down by doctrines and ideologies contrary to Catholic dogma." Finally, he turns to fidelity to man:

> The same renewed faith must bring along with it fidelity to man. Faith teaches us that man is the image and likeness of God, which means that man is gifted with an immense dignity. This person, a child of God, we must accept, love and help. Fidelity to man requires us to accept and respect his traditions and his culture, to help him advance, to defend his rights and to remind him of his duties. This triple fidelity to Jesus Christ, to the Church and to man must be a true challenge in the face of the future, in order to have the faith of the people of Venezuela grow in depth.³⁴

Saints

As a law of the Church's life, one can expect to find fidelity to God and to man exemplified in the lives of the saints. For example, John Paul tells us that Blessed Ceferino Jiménez Malla did not have to choose between being faithful to God by embracing Christian life to the full and being faithful to all that is true, good, and beautiful that he received and lived in the culture characteristic of Gypsies. "He is a beautiful example of fidelity to the faith for all Christians, and especially for you who are close to him because of your ethnic and cultural ties."³⁵ And he could sum up the life of a holy priest by saying that Blessed Domenico Lentini was "a priest

---

33. John Paul II, "Homily, January 28, 1985," 8. There are striking similarities of this homily with his letter of 1982 to seminarians in Spain (see above) regarding the three fidelities to Christ, to the Church, and to man.

34. John Paul II, "Homily, January 28, 1985," 8.

35. John Paul II, "Address, March 21, 1997," 3. Here John Paul could have quoted from the Decree on Missionary Activity, as he does elsewhere: "As the Second Vatican Council teaches, 'they should acknowledge themselves as members of the group in which they live, and through the various undertakings and affairs of human life they should share in their social and cultural life' (*AG*, 11)" ("Address, February 2, 1988").

with an undivided heart, [who] could combine *fidelity to God with fidelity to man*.³⁶ St. Maximilian Kolbe is a third example:

> The Church ... continues to proclaim the Good News in a world that changes, faithful to the inheritance she has received, but aware that methods and words must be adapted to the mentality of the men of today. St. Maximilian knew how to speak and to make himself understood by his contemporaries. He knew how to be faithful to God and faithful to man in truth and holiness.³⁷

It is to be expected that John Paul should attribute the principle of twofold fidelity to the faith and life of the Blessed Virgin Mary. This expectation is not unfulfilled. In a prayer of entrustment to Mary, John Paul addresses her as "Virgin of the Magnificat, faithful to God and to humanity."³⁸ Because Mary is the perfect model of faith and type of the Church, she is the perfect model of fidelity to God and fidelity to man.

Vatican II Responds to the Charge of Alienation

A final consideration regarding the principle of fidelity to God and man relates to one of the major pastoral concerns of Vatican II, namely, the need to respond to the charge that religion, and Catholicism in particular, is a hindrance to man reaching his true fulfillment. Precisely at a moment in history when the collective consciousness virtually equated being fully human with being engaged in the great, historical, and worldwide struggle for justice, Christianity, so the accusation goes, proposes an otherworldly preoccupation that diminishes people's sense of responsibility for mankind's future. With a vigorous apologetic response, aiming not so much to analyze the errors of the humanisms and philosophies of history in vogue at the time as to expound the way that the Church understands her own humanism and commitment to man and his future, the Council set out to set the record straight. In his address for the closure of Vatican II, Pope Paul could look back at the Council's accomplishment in this domain:

> We call upon those who term themselves modern humanists, and who have renounced the transcendent value of the highest realities, to give the council credit at least for one quality and to

---

36. John Paul II, "Homily, October 12, 1997," 4.
37. John Paul II, "Message, September 18, 2001," 2.
38. John Paul II, "Act of Consecration to the Virgin of the Thirty-Three," 3.

recognize our own new type of humanism: we, too, in fact, we more than any others, honor mankind.[39]

Vatican II sets forth the Church's understanding of her role in the modern world and what it means to promote authentic human development. Not only is faith not an impediment to such promotion, it is the very foundation and motive for engagement in human development that is consonant with the full truth of human dignity. In other words, fidelity to God does not exempt the Church from fidelity to man. Precisely the opposite, fidelity to God is the source, motive, and guiding principle of fidelity to man. Rightly understood, fidelity to man is contained in fidelity to God and is not merely added to it as a distinct, autonomous principle.

To the best of my knowledge, Pope Paul does not directly introduce fidelity to God and to man in his discussion of the Council's response to the accusation that Christianity is detrimental to human development. In his unflagging commitment to implement Vatican II, he addresses this pastoral concern, and on occasion he introduces a term that the Council does not use. That term is alienation. Though it is not found in the Conciliar documents, some Council Father's used it in their interventions.[40] Pope Paul's successor, John Paul II, gives considerable attention to the issue of alienation, not only prior to and during his pontificate, but already during the Council itself. And he invokes the law of fidelity to God and fidelity to man as a summary of his rebuttal to the claim that Christianity is alienating. Because John Paul's treatment of alienation is more frequent and more systematically developed, the following is based primarily on his work.

The Mutual Complementarity of Theocentrism and Anthropocentrism

An incisive text in John Paul II's encyclical on divine mercy, *Dives in misericordia*, serves to show the continuity of thought that unites his understanding of fidelity to God and fidelity to man as a key principle of the renewal of Vatican II, and that of St. Paul VI. The foundation for John Paul's understanding of the complementarity of the two fidelities is profoundly Christological and anthropological. It is Christological: because

---

39. Paul VI, "Address, December 7, 1965."

40. The intervention of Cardinal Silva Henriquez, on a draft of *GS*, is an example. See *AS* III/V, 236.

Jesus Christ is true God and true man, the two fidelities are not only inseparable; they are mutually interpenetrating. By reason of the personal unity of divinity and humanity in Christ, every act of his is simultaneously fidelity to God and to man. It is anthropological: because man is made in God's image, when he acts in conformity to the truth about himself, man is simultaneously faithful to God and faithful to himself.

John Paul introduces his encyclical on God's mercy, *Dives in misericordia*, by situating it in relation to his first encyclical, *Redemptor hominis*, and his commitment to implement Vatican II. Then he announces the theme of the Father's mercy, quoting the text of *Gaudium et spes* that for him recapitulates the teaching of Vatican II in Christocentric terms: "Christ . . . fully reveals man to himself and brings to light his lofty calling," and he does this, John Paul II underscores, "in the very revelation of the mystery of the Father and of his love" (*GS*, 22). With the Christological focus established, he moves on to the anthropological focus to assert "that man cannot be manifested in the full dignity of his nature without reference—not only on the level of concepts but also in an integrally existential way—to God."[41]

His next move is to situate the theme of mercy in relation to contemporary man. The message of God's mercy corresponds to the "sufferings and hopes . . . anxieties and expectations" of contemporary man. Referring to the main theme of his first encyclical and thus to the program of his pontificate, he asserts that man is the path for the Church. The Church exists to serve man, and this means that she "must travel *this way* with every individual *just as Christ traced it out* by revealing in himself the Father and his love." This corresponds to fidelity to man.

Then comes his articulation of the mutual interpenetration of fidelity to man and fidelity to God.

> In Jesus Christ, every path to man . . . is simultaneously an approach to the Father and his love. The Second Vatican Council has confirmed this truth for our time.
>
> The more the Church's mission is centered upon man— the more it is, so to speak, anthropocentric—the more it must be confirmed and actualized theocentrically, that is to say, be directed in Jesus Christ to the Father. While the various currents of human thought both in the past and at the present have tended and still tend to separate theocentrism and anthropocentrism, and even to set them in opposition to each other, the

---

41. John Paul II, *DM*, 1.

Church, following Christ, seeks to link them up in human history, in a deep and organic way. And this is also one of the basic principles, perhaps the most important one, of the teaching of the last Council.[42]

Clearly, anthropocentricty corresponds to fidelity to man, and theocentricity corresponds to fidelity to God. The core of Vatican II's teaching, he tells us, is not just to assert but convincingly to explain that theocentrism is incomplete and eventually falsified if it is not complemented by anthropocentrism, and, conversely, that anthropocentrism is incomplete and eventually distorted if it is not complemented by theocentrism.

The Religious Meaning of Vatican II and of the Church's Humanism

Comparing the above text of John Paul to Pope Paul's closing address, the continuity of thought is striking. The "religious value of this Council," Paul states, derives from the fact that it is an act of the Church, and "the raison d'être of the Church [is] her direct relationship with the living God." This theocentricity is "the guiding principle which was to give direction to the future council." A fair-minded reading of the texts, he is convinced, will suffice to discover that "The council documents . . . leave wide open to view this primary and focal religious intention."

For Pope Paul, the religious or theocentric nature of the Church can be distinguished but not separated from her mission of service to mankind, that is, from what he calls her humanism. It is certainly an indication that this second dimension of humanism—or anthropocentrism, or fidelity to man—is less well understood and even called into question that Pope Paul devotes more words to discuss this than he does the first dimension of being religious—or theocentricism, or fidelity to God. Precisely because of the Church's religious orientation to God, she draws close to man, even as God himself became man in order to draw close to all men.

> But we cannot pass over one important consideration in our analysis of the religious meaning of the council: it has been deeply committed to the study of the modern world. Never before perhaps, so much as on this occasion, has the Church felt the need to know, to draw near to, to understand, to penetrate, serve and evangelize the society in which she lives; and to get to

42. John Paul II, *DM*, 1.

grips with it, almost to run after it, in its rapid and continuous change. This attitude, a response to the distances and divisions we have witnessed over recent centuries, in the last century and in our own especially, between the Church and secular society—this attitude has been strongly and unceasingly at work in the council.[43]

Confirming that the Church's commitment to man is misunderstood, not only *ad extra* but also *ad intra*, Pope Paul goes on to acknowledge that this emphasis on solicitude for man had caused some within the Church to be leery that an "excessive responsiveness to the outside world . . . may have swayed persons and acts of the ecumenical synod, at the expense of the fidelity which is due to tradition, and this to the detriment of the religious orientation of the council itself." Pope Paul does "not believe that this shortcoming should be imputed to it, to its real and deep intentions, to its authentic manifestations." In other words, Vatican II placed fidelity to God and to man in a mutually complementary balance, such that neither was over weighted at the expense of the other.

For Pope Paul, this balance is rooted in the twofold orientation of charity as love of God and of neighbor: "charity has been the principal religious feature of this council. Yes, the Church of the council has been concerned, not just with herself and with her relationship of union with God, but with man." It is true that "the Council's rich teaching is channeled in one direction, the service of mankind" and that "the Church has, so to say, declared herself the servant of humanity." It is also true that the Church understands this service to man in terms of her unique mission to unite men with God.

> Any careful observer of the council's prevailing interest for human and temporal values cannot deny that it is from the pastoral character that the council has virtually made its program, and must recognize that the same interest is never divorced from the most genuine religious interest, whether by reason of charity, its sole inspiration (where charity is, God is!), or the council's constant, explicit attempts to link human and temporal values with those that are specifically spiritual, religious and everlasting; its concern is with man and with earth, but it rises to the kingdom of God.[44]

---

43. Paul VI, "Address, December 7, 1965."
44. Paul VI, "Address, December 7, 1965."

Fidelity to man entails serving him by bringing him into communion with God in Jesus Christ. Since God desires this communion with man, fidelity to man is simultaneously fidelity to God. This shows that the theme of fidelity to God and to man is present in the innumerable texts in which Popes Paul and John Paul discuss the essentially religious orientation of man's being and activity, and of the Church's mission to bring man's religious dynamism to fulfillment in Christ.

Vatican II Responds to the Charge of Alienation

Several texts of Vatican II stand out for directly expressing the Council's concern to rebut the charge of alienation. The Council asserts that Christian holiness promotes a more fully human way of living.[45] It likewise affirms that religious life of profession of the evangelical counsels "does not detract from a genuine development of human persons, but rather by its very nature is most beneficial to that development."[46] The Council warns against concluding from faith's conviction that the world in which we live is passing away (1 Cor 7:39) and our true home is heaven that Christians "may therefor shirk their earthly responsibilities." It immediately adds that "by the faith itself they are more obliged than ever to measure up to these duties."[47] The Church's mission entails working for the fulfillment of the world's purpose in justice, charity, and peace.[48]

It is striking that both Pope Paul and Pope John Paul interpret Vatican II's emphasis on promoting integral human development as the Church's response to the charge of materialist anthropologies and atheism that faith and religion prevent man from being fully human, in a word, that faith and religion are alienating for man.[49] The principle of fidelity to God and to man constitutes the core of Vatican II's refutation of this charge.

Both Popes see the charge of alienation as the context for a passage in the introduction to *Gaudium et spes*, where the Council states that "growing numbers of people are abandoning religion in practice"

45. Vatican II, *LG*, 40.
46. Vatican II, *LG*, 46.
47. Vatican II, *GS*, 43.
48. Vatican II, *GS*, 36.
49. Paul VI speaks of alienation in this sense; see Addresses of April 23, 1965; August 28, 1968; June 21, 1976; January 14, 1978; Homilies of February 11, 1970; March 2, 1975; General Audiences of July 10, 1968; March 24, 1971.

and that "the denial of God or of religion" are "presented as requirements of scientific progress or of a certain new humanism."⁵⁰ Later in the same document, the Council returns to this sign of the time when it addresses systematic atheism, which exalts human freedom to the point that it holds that "this freedom cannot be reconciled with the affirmation of a Lord who is author and purpose of all things, or at least that this freedom makes such an affirmation altogether superfluous." The text goes on to identify forms of atheism that define human liberation "especially through [man's] economic and social emancipation." The Council's concern is that "this form [of atheism] argues that by its nature religion thwarts this liberation by arousing man's hope for a deceptive future life, thereby diverting him from the constructing of the earthly city."⁵¹

Alienation is precisely this, namely, the impeding of man from self-fulfillment. Cardinal Wojtyła takes this up more systematically than Paul VI. The charge of alienation is "the root and epitome of the arguments against religion in general and Christianity in particular."⁵² The charge alleges: "By professing and practicing a religion man deprives himself of his own right to his humanity"⁵³ Thus, "to alienate means . . . to de-humanize."⁵⁴

The Church knows that the true cause of alienation is sin.⁵⁵ "God's alienation from man," John Paul affirms, "is due to man's sin: it is the fruit

50. Vatican II, *GS*, 7, quoted in Pope Paul's General Audience, July 10, 1968.

51. Vatican II, *GS*, 20.

52. Wojtyła, *SR*, 273 (see also 72). This same understanding of alienation occurs in his essay, "The Person: Subject and Community," in *Person and Community*, 256.

53. Wojtyła, *Sign of Contradiction*, 34. In *The Acting Person*, Wojtyła accepts as the definition or description of alienation the "draining or sifting man from his very own humanness, that is, as depriving him of the value that we have here defined as 'personalistic'" (297). More generally, alienation is the "'usurpation' of something that is the property of another" ("General Audience, November 12, 1986," 4).

54. Wojtyła, *Sign of Contradiction*, 34. Peter Simpson follows Wojtyła in a philosophical understanding of alienation as the negation of participation: "Alienation signifies that man is deprived of the personal value of his action. In order to overcome alienation love of neighbor must be at the foundation of all the communities and systems that man develops and establishes at any level . . . man must embrace the true human good and genuine participation with others" (*On Karol Wojtyła*, 45).

55. "Man's freedom is limited and fallible. In fact, man failed. He freely sinned. By refusing God's plan of love, he deceived himself and became a slave to sin. This first alienation engendered a multitude of others" (*CCC*, 1739). See also John Paul II, "General Audience, November 12, 1986." Vatican II recognizes that modern men can be alienated from divine matters by their fascination with and overreliance on science

of his alienation from God."[56] John Paul sees this played out in the drama of the temptation and sin of Adam and Eve, as the serpent's ruse and their sin result in man depriving himself of—alienating himself from— the truth about God as love. Consequently, man also deprives himself of—alienates himself from—the truth about himself, which because he is image of God, is correlative to the truth about God.[57] For John Paul II, the essential terms and dynamics of the drama of the sin of Adam and Eve is repeated throughout history and sheds light on the form of all the ideologies that present God as an enemy of man's authentic fulfillment.[58]

Based on his personal experience and understanding of the human person, John Paul also sees alienation as a state of being that impedes the fulfillment that comes with love. Since man is made in God's image and God is love, man finds fulfillment in the love of mutual self-giving.[59] Thus, "A society is alienated if its forms of social organization, production and consumption make it more difficult to offer this gift of self and to establish this solidarity between people."[60] There is no question that he attributes this line of thought to Vatican II:

> Vatican II perceives in contemporary social processes—those connected with the enormous advance of technological, industrial, and material factors—the *danger of a fundamental alienation of human beings*. People can easily become tools in the system of things, the material system created by their own

and technology (*AG*, 11).

56. John Paul II, "Homily, November 29, 1981," 2.

57. See John Paul II, "General Audience, November 12, 1986," 5, 9. See also John Paul II, *DeV*, 37–39, where it becomes clear that for John Paul the root of all alienation is suspicion or doubt about God's love.

58. In *Octogesima adveniens*, 27, Paul VI states that ideologies that exclude God are the cause of alienation.

59. The text to which John Paul most often refers to support this anthropology of mutual self-giving is *GS*, 24: "This likeness reveals that man, who is the only creature on earth which God willed for itself, cannot fully find himself except through a sincere gift of himself (cf. Lk 17:33)."

60. John Paul II, *Centesimus annus*, 41. This passage is the most elaborate discussion of alienation in the encyclicals of John Paul II. See also his "Address, October 11, 1991," in which he quotes from this passage of *Centesimus annus*, 41. It becomes clear that it is not required that an ideology or culture explicitly deny God in order to be alienating. Alienation is fundamentally an interior condition of man whereby he relies on himself for his future fulfillment rather than on God, because he does not know God as creative and provident love (see n49).

intelligence, and they can become objects of different kinds of social manipulation.[61]

For Vatican II, Paul VI, and John Paul II, alienation constitutes a fundamental and perennial sign of the times. The problem is that when entire cultures that were formally Christian become materialistic and secular, Christians are placed in the position of feeling as if they must choose between two definitions of human happiness, two visions of human fulfillment: on one hand, being a scientifically up-to-date person who is fully committed and engaged in making the world conform more fully to human dignity; on the other hand, being an other worldly oriented person of faith who is not contributing to the great struggle of creating a better future for mankind. In other words, fidelity to God and fidelity to man are fundamentally opposed to one another, and one has to choose: either fidelity to God or fidelity to man.

The message of Vatican II is that because man is made in God's image and finds fulfillment in communion with God, alienation from God is the cause of de-humanization and thus of man's alienation from himself. Since the Church's mission continues the mission of Christ, which is to reconcile men to God through the forgiveness of sins and draw men into communion with God in love, the resounding assertion of Vatican II in response to the charge of alienation is that only in Christ can man fully realize his own humanity. In other words, the Church's humanism takes Christ as the model of human perfection. In him, as we have seen, fidelity to God and to man are not in any way in tension with one another. Rather, they mutually complement and complete one another. To take just a few examples:

> Whoever follows after Christ, the perfect man, becomes himself more of a man.[62]

---

61. Karol Cardinal Wojtyła, "Rodzicielstwo a 'communio personarum'" [Parenthood and the 'Communio Personarum'], quoted in Gregg, *Challenging the Modern World*, 141. As a participant in the Council, Bishop Wojtyła was already thinking in terms of responding to the charge of alienation. See his intervention in *Acta Synodalia* IV/II, 660–63. A translation of the relevant part of this intervention can be found in Williams, *The Mind of John Paul II*, 178–79. On p. 211, Williams gives a helpful summary of Wojtyła's work in *The Acting Person* on alienation being opposed to participation.

62. Vatican II, *GS*, 41. In *GS*, Jesus Christ is called the perfect man three other times (articles 22, 38, 45).

Faith throws a new light on everything, manifests God's design for man's total vocation, and thus directs the mind to solutions which are fully human.[63]

Thus the mission of the Church will show its religious, and by that very fact, its supremely human character.[64]

The Church holds that the recognition of God is in no way hostile to man's dignity, since this dignity is rooted and perfected in God. For man was made an intelligent and free member of society by God who created him, but even more important, he is called as a son to commune with God and share in his happiness. She further teaches that a hope related to the end of time does not diminish the importance of intervening duties but rather undergirds the acquittal of them with fresh incentives. By contrast, when a divine instruction and the hope of life eternal are wanting, man's dignity is most grievously lacerated, as current events often attest; riddles of life and death, of guilt and of grief go unsolved with the frequent result that men succumb to despair.[65]

Pursuing the saving purpose which is proper to her, the Church does not only communicate divine life to men but in some way casts the reflected light of that life over the entire earth, most of all by its healing and elevating impact on the dignity of the person, by the way in which it strengthens the seams of human society and imbues the everyday activity of men with a deeper meaning and importance. Thus through her individual members and her whole community, the Church believes she can contribute greatly toward making the family of man and its history more human.[66]

By this holiness as such a more human manner of living is promoted in this earthly society.[67]

All men should take note that the profession of the evangelical counsels, though entailing the renunciation of certain values which are to be undoubtedly esteemed, does not detract from

---

63. Vatican II, *GS*, 11.
64. Vatican II, *GS*, 11.
65. Vatican II, *GS*, 21.
66. Vatican II, *GS*, 40.
67. Vatican II, *LG*, 40.

> a genuine development of the human person, but rather by its very nature is most beneficial to that development.[68]
>
> To "make human life more human" is the Council's fundamental objective, closely linked to the desire to share in the divine life and in the mission of Christ.[69]

In other words, man is being faithful to the dynamisms of his own nature, he is being faithful to himself, by being faithful to God. Or, to reverse the polarity: by being faithful to God man is at the same time being faithful to himself.

HOLINESS: LIVING WITNESS TO THE LAW OF FIDELITY TO GOD AND FIDELITY TO MAN

For John Paul II, as for Pope Paul VI, fidelity to God and to man is no abstract principle. It is a law that governs virtually every dimension of the Church's life and mission. For this reason, it is to be expected that along with a new consciousness of the Church, which is precisely the focus of the renewal of Vatican II, a new consciousness of this law would emerge. Further, for John Paul II the new consciousness of the Church and the new consciousness of the law of dual fidelity are integral to the New Evangelization, which began with Vatican II.[70] Though John Paul popularized the term, New Evangelization, he credits Pope Paul for minting it,[71] precisely in the apostolic exhortation, *Evangelii nuntiandi*, which is in essence a decennial anniversary reflection on the renewal of Vatican II.[72] Essentially, New Evangelization is the third path of dialogical mission of *ES*. Thus, it is not surprising that the Church's new consciousness of herself and of fidelity to God and to man, which are integral to dialogical mission, should be associated also with the New Evangelization.

---

68. Vatican II, *LG*, 46.
69. Wojtyła, *SR*, 279.
70. See John Paul II, *CTH*, 160.
71. See John Paul II, *CTH*, 114.
72. "We wish to do so [fulfill the papal office "of encouraging our brethren in their mission as evangelizers"] on this tenth anniversary of the closing of the Second Vatican Council, the objectives of which are definitively summed up in this single one: to make the Church of the twentieth-century ever better fitted for proclaiming the Gospel to the people of the twentieth-century" (*EN*, 2).

Earlier in this chapter, we encountered John Paul referring to those who work closely with the poor as "true witnesses: *witnesses of fidelity to man and to Christ*."[73] On another occasion he similarly links the theme of witness (or testimony) to the principle of dual fidelity: "the Church prepares to cross the threshold of the Third Millennium . . . convinced of the fundamental and primary service which she must provide as a testimony to her fidelity to God and to the men and women of the continent."[74] In other words, the Church is making a statement about herself and about her place in God's plan by living according to the law of dual fidelity.

The introduction of the theme of witness leads to a final and pivotally fundamental application of the principle of fidelity to God and to man, namely, that living by this law of dual fidelity is the essential fruit of the renewal of Vatican II. It is both the goal of the renewal *ad intra* and the fundamental strategy for mission *ad extra*, that is, for dialogical mission or New Evangelization. To grasp this entails seeing that life according to the law of dual fidelity is synonymous with holiness, which is the perfection of charity in its twofold orientation of love of God and love of neighbor.

What is witness? Essentially, it is Christian life on display, accompanied by the witness of words to explain that life. It is the life of participation in the holiness of Christ viewed from the angle of its relation to those who observe it. As we have seen, especially in the previous chapter, since Christ is true God and true man, his life is the supreme model of fidelity to God and fidelity to man. He is the pre-eminent witness[75] to this dual fidelity, which is to say that he alone definitively reveals it. In fact, as we have seen in this chapter, for John Paul II this goes to the very heart of revelation, since Christ redeems man by vanquishing the lie of the serpent that God is a threat to man's fulfillment. The Church's members participate in this redemption and thus also in Christ's witness by living according to the law of fidelity to God and to man.

This witness projects to the world the goodness of a fully human life as the fruit of God's love fully revealed in Christ. It demonstrates that God's love is efficacious in changing the human condition. Since all seek

73. John Paul II, "Address, February 22, 1997," 3.
74. John Paul II, *EAm*, 75.
75. "Christ, whose mission we continue, is the 'witness' *par excellence* (Rev 1:5; 3:14) and the model of all Christian witness" (*RMiss*, 42). Since by baptism "Christ enables *us to live in him* all that he himself lives, and *he lives it in us*" (*CCC*, 521), the Church necessarily participates in his mission of witness.

to live a fully human life, this witness is endowed with the power to attract. In precise terms, since the proper effect of the good is to perfect and all desire their own perfection, by making the good that all seek present Christian witness draws people to this fullness of life in Christ. And it does so in the only way that is worthy of human dignity, that is, by respecting people's freedom.

In light of the foregoing, we are in a position to acknowledge the significance for the theme of fidelity to God and to man of statements of Popes Paul and John Paul, which summarize the renewal of Vatican II in terms of holiness and witness.

> This strong invitation to holiness could be regarded as the most characteristic element in the whole Magisterium of the Council, and so to say, its ultimate purpose.[76]
>
> The Second Vatican Council has significantly spoken on the universal call to holiness. It is possible to say that this call to holiness is precisely the basic charge entrusted to all the sons and daughters of the Church by a Council which intended to bring a renewal of Christian life based on the Gospel.[77]

John Paul takes up this theme in his encyclical on the permanence of the Church's missionary mandate:

> The witness of a Christian life is the first and irreplaceable form of mission ... The first form of witness is *the very life of the missionary, of the Christian family*, and *of the ecclesial community*, which reveal a new way of living.[78]

This is the witness of holiness. Holiness is not only the motivating force, the soul of missionary activity. It is the light of Christ himself radiating into the world through the holiness of the Church's members, so that they can be signs of God in the world.[79]

A year before his death, John Paul takes up the theme yet again:

> The Second Vatican Council, as the foundation of its program for the renewal of the Church's witness to Christ before the

---

76. Paul VI, "Motu proprio *Sanctitas clarior*," in *AAS* 61 (1969) 149.
77. John Paul II, *CL*, 16.
78. John Paul II, *RMiss*, 42.
79. See John Paul II, *RMiss*, 90–91.

> world, held out to all the baptized the high ideal of God's *universal call to holiness*.[80]

The continuity of the immediately preceding text with the thought of Paul VI is explicit just a few lines later:

> The great challenge of the new evangelization to which the Church is called in our time requires a credibility born of personal fidelity to the Gospel and the demands of Christian discipleship. In the memorable words of Pope Paul VI, "it is primarily by her conduct and her life that the Church will evangelize the world, namely, by her living witness of fidelity to the Lord Jesus—the witness of poverty and detachment, of freedom in the face of the powers of this world, in short, *by the witness of her holiness*" (EN, 41).[81]

Because of *EN*'s relation to Vatican II, Paul VI's elaboration of this theme of the witness of holiness in *EN* is as a commentary on the renewal of Vatican II. And clearly, John Paul is fully in alignment with his predecessor on this point.

It is significant that John Paul should clarify that holiness does not separate Christians from the rest of the world: "*holiness is not useless to the world*. It does not only build up the Body of Christ, but leaves an indelible mark on the succession of events and in the diversified formation of society itself."[82] For John Paul, man's agency in shaping history and culture is essentially moral in nature. It is thus a function of his conscience.

> So we find ourselves here at a crucial moment, when at every step time and eternity meet at a level which is proper to man. It is the level of the conscience, the level of moral values: the conscience is the most important dimension of time and history. For history is written not only by the events which in a certain sense happen "from outside"; it is written first of all "from within": it is the history of human consciences, of moral victories and defeats.[83]

"Can history ever swim against the tide of conscience?"[84] To ask this question boils down to asking: Can history, which is something created,

---

80. John Paul II, "Address, April 29, 2004," 2.
81. John Paul II, "Address, April 29, 2004," 5.
82. John Paul II, "Homily, September 27, 1997," 3.
83. John Paul II, *Dilecti amici*, 6.
84. Wojtyła, *Memory and Identity*, 74.

escape the providential direction of God, the Creator? Can man and his freedom direct history in such a manner that it is unable to find a place in God's plan? As divine revelation amply demonstrates, even man's offenses against his own conscience (e.g., the hard hearts of Pharaoh and Judas, the judges's suppression of their consciences because of their lust for Susanna[85]) do not escape the plan of God.[86] With faith in Christ, man is called to denounce the perversion of his own conscience and to receive the gift of a purified conscience (Heb 9:9, 14; 10:22; 1 Pet 3:21) so that he can call good and evil by their proper names[87] and thereby cooperate with God in directing history to the fulfillment of his plan. God directs history through those holy men and women whose consciences are purified by the blood, that is, the love of Christ. Holiness and a purified conscience assure the Church's fidelity to God.

Without using the term "fidelity to man," the reality that it signifies is manifestly present when John Paul states, "Genuine holiness is not a turning away from the world and the needs of the human family. Rather, as the Council states: 'By this holiness a more human way of life is promoted even in this earthly society' (*LG*, 40)." Holiness "and commitment to the well-being and progress of the human family are not mutually exclusive. They are both necessary parts of the one Christian discipleship."[88]

Because the holiness of the Church's members is a participation in the holiness of God, John Paul is able to root this emphasis on holiness entailing engagement in service to mankind in God himself. Just as God's holiness defines him as the unique and transcendent God of infinite perfection and this is the very source of his initiative of love in creation and redemption, so for those who are made sharers in divine life of holiness

---

85. Deviating from a more literal translation, the New Revised Standard Version of the Bible (1989) certainly conveys the meaning of Dan 13:9 when it renders the phrase, "they perverted their minds" of other versions as "they suppressed their consciences."

86. For Ratzinger, God's rationality and freedom are so transcendently perfect that they can embrace creatures's irrationality and misuse of freedom. See Ratzinger, *Truth and Tolerance*, 150–54; Ratzinger, *Introduction to Christianity*, 158–61. St. Thomas expresses the same thing when he teaches that nothing can fall outside the order of the universal cause. The example he gives is man's misuse of his freedom (which is always a violation of his conscience—see *ST*, I-II, q. 19, a. 5). "Hence that which seems to depart from the divine will in one order, returns into it in another order; as does the sinner, who by sin falls away from the divine will as much as lies in him, yet falls back into the order of that will, when by its justice he is punished" (*ST*, I, q. 19, a. 6).

87. "A result of an upright conscience is, first of all, *to call good and evil by their proper name*" (John Paul II, *DeV*, 43).

88. John Paul II, "Address, November 23, 1986," 5.

(2 Pet 1:4) are set aside, consecrated for service to God, and this service entails a mission of service to mankind.

> The Old Testament makes it clear that Israel is to be holy as God himself is holy (cf. Lev 19:2). This meant that Israel had to be distinct, just as God is infinitely distinct from the world, as the Bible stresses consistently in forging its doctrine of divine transcendence. But this otherness of Israel is not otherness for its own sake; it is neither introverted nor defensive. Just as God can make all things "good" (cf. Gen 1:31) precisely because he is above all things, so Israel is to be distinct for the sake of service. Just as the infinite transcendence of God makes possible the communication of the perfect love which culminates in Christ's Paschal Mystery, so in the Bible's understanding the holiness of God's people involves that critical freedom in relation to surrounding culture and cultures which makes possible real and genuine service of the human family.[89]

This insistence that holiness entails engagement in active service to man has two pastoral values. First, *ad intra*, it has the value of clarifying an essential element of the Christian vocation. John Paul is engaging in a purification of the concept of holiness. This aligns it with the first path of *ES*, doctrinal awareness or penetration, which we have seen is the necessary starting point for the renewal of Vatican II. Second, *ad extra*, this same teaching has an apologetic value. This looks at the *same teaching* in relation to those who do not profess Christian or Catholic faith, and especially those who subscribe to the Marxist charge that faith—here it is holiness—alienates man from his true vocation to engage in the betterment of the world. For those who are committed to making the world conform more completely to human dignity, not only is the Church's understanding of holiness not an obstacle that should scandalize them. It is actually an affirmation of a common value based on which a certain bond uniting the Church and those committed to human development can be acknowledged. The *same teaching* that is received by the faithful *ad intra* as the objective criterion for fidelity to God in renewal also has value for fidelity to man in witness and dialogue *ad extra*.[90]

---

89. John Paul II, "Address, November 21, 1998," 3.

90. Recall what Paul VI says about the Church's dialogue with the world: "And before speaking, it is necessary to listen, not only to a man's voice, but to his heart. A man must first be understood—and, where he merits it, agreed with" (*ES*, 87).

Even if there have been times when some or even many Catholics have given a counter-witness to authentic holiness by shrinking from engagement in the world, the Church gains credibility *ad extra* not only, first, by reason of her teaching that the authentic meaning of holiness includes existential engagement, and second, by reason of the witness of those whose lives exemplify this teaching, but third also by the fact that she shows herself to be self-corrective in this regard. That this third aspect of credibility *ad extra* is a conscious dimension of John Paul's understanding of the renewal of Vatican II and thus of the New Evangelization, and that witness to the law of dual fidelity contributes to this credibility, is evident in numerous texts, once the equivalence is seen between fidelity to man and commitment and service to man.

> The great challenge of the new evangelization to which the Church is called in our time requires a credibility born of personal fidelity to the Gospel and the demands of Christian discipleship.[91]
>
> This dimension of charity to the poorest and the lowliest is a pledge of credibility of the entire Church: the credibility of her message, but also the credibility of those who, captivated by Christ and having contemplated him, can see him in the faces of those with whom Christ himself wanted to identify and can express his compassion for every human being (cf. *Novo millennio ineunte*, 49).[92]
>
> Your service to the sick enables you with great credibility *to proclaim to the world the demands and values of the Gospel of Jesus Christ*, and to foster hope and renewal of heart.[93]
>
> Therefore care and concern for people close to death is one of the most important signs of ecclesial credibility.[94]
>
> The Synod's debate on the *relevance* and *credibility* of the Church's message in Africa inescapably entailed consideration of the *very credibility of the proclaimers of this message*. The Synod Fathers faced the question directly, with genuine frankness and devoid of any complacency. Pope Paul VI had already addressed this question in memorable words when he stated: "It is often

---

91. John Paul II, "Address, April 29, 2004," 5.
92. John Paul II, "Address, December 18, 2003," 4.
93. John Paul II, "Address, September 14, 1987," 6.
94. John Paul II, "Message, June 21, 1998," 5.

said nowadays that the present century thirsts for authenticity. Especially in regard to young people, it is said that they have a horror of the artificial or false and that they are searching above all for truth and honesty. These *signs of the times* should find us vigilant. Either tacitly or aloud—but always forcefully—we are being asked: Do you really believe what you are proclaiming? Do you live what you believe? Do you really preach what you live? The witness of life has become more than ever an essential condition for real effectiveness in preaching. Precisely because of this we are, to a certain extent, responsible for the progress of the Gospel that we proclaim" (*EN*, 76).

That is why, with reference to the Church's evangelizing mission in the field of justice and peace, I have said: "Today more than ever, the Church is aware that her social doctrine will gain credibility more immediately from *witness of action* than as a result of its internal logic and consistency (*Centesimus annus*, 57)."[95]

Already in *ES*, Paul VI refers to the Church's solicitude for man as this is evident in the social encyclicals. In his view, the Church's dialogue with the world is a reality that Vatican II should more consciously and deliberately engage in, but it is not something new. It began with Pope Leo XIII, who made "the object of his richest instruction the problems of our time considered in the light of the Word of Christ."[96] The social encyclicals are evidence of the Church's track record of solicitude for man. And as *Gaudium et spes* makes clear, the focus of this dialogue is man. The whole theme of reading the signs of the times in light of the Gospel is an effort by the Church to grasp the precise state of man's dynamisms in relation to his true good. It is vital to keep together the two dimensions of the Church's witness, that is, words and deeds. The witness of active service to defend, to heal, and to promote human dignity complements the Church's witness of words that is found in the Church's social teaching. One need only think of Mother Teresa of Calcutta.

"Apologetics of meaning" aptly names the Church's awareness of how her credibility is linked with the witness of holiness, that is, the witness of a fully human life in Christ. "Holiness," John Paul II writes," is "a message that convinces without the need for words."[97] It is important to

---

95. John Paul II, *Ecclesia in Africa*, 21. See also John Paul II, "Address, November 19, 1991."

96. *ES*, 67.

97. John Paul II, *NMI*, 7.

point out that the Church's concern with credibility with her contemporaries does not give rise to actions that are distinct from the Church's fidelity to God. Rather, it is by being faithful to God, which as we have seen is also to be faithful to man, that the Church gains the credibility that she desires solely for the sake that men should accept the message to which she bears witness. The Church's understanding of man, her anthropology and corresponding humanism, hold that it is a property of human nature to seek the meaning of life. Human nature, in its dynamic search for meaning, is the fundamental meeting point between the Church and the world. At Vatican II, the Church describes her mission in terms of bringing to all men the definitive meaning that they seek. This meaning is the truth about what it means to be human, and Jesus Christ has definitively revealed this truth. He is the perfect man who fully reveals man to himself.[98]

Other examples could be adduced to show that Vatican II and the post-Conciliar popes have sought to clarify the Gospel in terms and categories in which her contemporaries think and act, both for the sake of renewal *ad intra*—for the faithful living in the cultures in which these values and modes of thought are prevalent, so that there is need to explain precisely how these are compatible or not compatible with the Gospel—and for the sake of dialogue and the promotion of credibility *ad extra*. What Pope John Paul II does with the notion of solidarity is a prime example.[99]

Another example is what Pope Benedict does to clarify the Church's understanding of charity in *Deus caritas est*, in which he links his pontificate to Vatican II by confronting head on the charge that charity is a form of alienation.[100] Among the errors and objections that he addresses

---

98. See Vatican II, *GS*, 22. John Paul II quotes this text more than any other text of Vatican II. For him, it recapitulates the essential meaning and spirit of Vatican II.

99. In *Centesimus annus*, 10, John Paul shows that the essential positive values of solidarity have been present in the teachings of preceding popes. He combines the positive values into a definition-description of solidarity in *Sollicitudo rei socialis*, 9, 26, 38, and 39.

100. Once it is recalled that in his Address on the Closing of the Council on December 7, 1965, Pope Paul summarized the spirituality of the Council as that of the Good Samaritan, the four mentions of the Good Samaritan in *Deus caritas est* constitute a perhaps more subtle linking of his pontificate with Vatican II. What could be a more compelling counter to the objection that Catholic faith is alienating and disengages believers from active involvement in behalf of the poor than asserting that the Church lives by the motivating charity of the Good Samaritan?

is the charge that by meeting the needs of the poor, Christians in effect condemn them to remain poor. The accusation is that rather than to lift people out of poverty, which is what justice demands, Christian charity serves to safeguard the prerogatives of those who are better off by reinforcing the gap between two classes.[101] John Paul had already shown that the equality that justice seeks often falls short of establishing a genuine order of justice, and that efforts to alleviate poverty exclusively through economic and political systems often perpetuate and exacerbate the distance between classes, and introduce new forms of injustice.[102] The Church's response, then, is that Christian charity and mercy affirm all that is true about justice and bring justice to a perfection that it cannot attain by itself.

A final example brings us back to the objection that religion and faith, and thus God himself, are alienating for man. To reiterate the point of interest this holds for the present study, so long as the misconception persists among the Church's contemporaries that God is man's enemy, she and the Gospel will be a priori shut out. In the name of her mission to serve man, the Church finds herself in the position of having to emphasize the most fundamental of biblical verities, namely, that God is love and that he places his wisdom, love, and power at the service of man. John Paul stresses this divine love on a multitude of occasions, for example, when he interprets the refrain of the Book of Genesis that after each day of creation God so to speak steps back to inspect what he has done and sees that it is good. Since to love is to desire what is good, this means that God's motive for creating and redeeming is love.[103] With regard to man, both John Paul and Benedict depict God's attitude toward man by saying that for him to love man is to say, "It is good that you exist."[104] In his first encyclical, John Paul declares that the Gospel is a great affirmation of man and of his dignity, an act of amazement over man. If man is amazed at himself, this is because God is first to be amazed.[105] It is clear that such emphasis on God's love as affirming the goodness and dignity

---

101. See Benedict XVI, *DCE*, 26. See also Ratzinger, *Dogma and Preaching*, 174–78.

102. See John Paul II, *RH*, 16–17, and John Paul II, *DM*, especially 12 and 14 (also, 2, 4, 7, and 8).

103. See Wojtyła, *Sign of Contradiction*, 20–21, 55–56; John Paul II, *DA*, 7; *DeV*, 37–39.

104. See John Paul II, *CTH*, 20; Ratzinger, *To Look on Christ*, 83.

105. See John Paul II, *RH*, 10.

of man directly refutes the charge that God, and therefore Christian faith and the Church, are alienating for man.

All that the Church teaches, in the name of fidelity to God's revelation, about the human person's rights, duties, conscience, and transcendence, and call to discover the full truth of his humanity in Jesus Christ—in a word, all that the Church holds by faith, and particularly her moral and social teaching—is the foundation for her fidelity to man. The preceding examples, which illustrate the responsiveness of the Council and of the post-Conciliar popes to the charge of alienation in its various forms, are so many specifications of the general principle that Pope Paul VI sets forth in his summation of the spirit and teaching of Vatican II:

> But we call upon those who term themselves modern humanists, and who have renounced the transcendent value of the highest realities, to give the council credit at least for one quality and to recognize our own new type of humanism: we, too, in fact, we more than any others, honor mankind.[106]

With the preceding in mind, it should be clear that whenever the post-Conciliar popes reiterate the centrality of the call to holiness and insist upon witness as the fundamental form of evangelization, the principle of fidelity to God and to man is in play, and with it, the three dimensions of renewal that it serves to summarize. Awareness of this opens readers to immense depths of meaning contained in the abundant number of texts in which the popes take up the call to holiness and to witness, as they continue to promote the interpretation and implementation of Vatican II.

In the following texts, John Paul's emphasis on holiness corresponds to the second path of renewal through conversion as the requirement of fidelity to God, and mission corresponds to the third path of evangelization through dialogue.

> The call to mission derives, of its nature, from the call to holiness. A missionary is really such only if he commits himself to the way of holiness: "Holiness must be called a fundamental presupposition and an irreplaceable condition for everyone in fulfilling the mission of salvation in the Church" (CL, 17).
>
> *The universal call to holiness* is closely linked to the *universal call to mission*. Every member of the faithful is called to holiness and to mission. This was the earnest desire of the Council, which hoped to be able "to enlighten all people with the brightness of

---

106. Paul VI, "Address, December 7, 1965."

Christ, which gleams over the face of the Church, by preaching the Gospel to every creature" (*LG*, 1). The Church's missionary spirituality is a journey toward holiness.[107]

Just as the third path of dialogical mission derives from the second path, so mission derives from holiness. Perhaps more accurately, mission is holiness in action.

In one of the most memorable post-Conciliar texts on witness, Pope Paul shows that it initiates a dialogue by provoking questions in the minds of those who observe how Christians live.

> Above all the Gospel must be proclaimed by witness. Take a Christian or a handful of Christians who, in the midst of their own community, show their capacity for understanding and acceptance, their sharing of life and destiny with other people, their solidarity with the efforts of all for whatever is noble and good. Let us suppose that, in addition, they radiate in an altogether simple and unaffected way their faith in values that go beyond current values, and their hope in something that is not seen and that one would not dare to imagine. Through this wordless witness these Christians stir up irresistible questions in the hearts of those who see how they live: Why are they like this? Why do they live in this way? What or who is it that inspires them? Why are they in our midst? Such a witness is already a silent proclamation of the Good News and a very powerful and effective one. Here we have an initial act of evangelization. The above questions will perhaps be the first that many non-Christians will ask, whether they are people to whom Christ has never been proclaimed, or baptized people who do not practice, or people who live as nominal Christians but according to principles that are in no way Christian, or people who are seeking, and not without suffering, something or someone whom they sense but cannot name. Other questions will arise, deeper and more demanding ones, questions evoked by this witness which involves presence, sharing, solidarity, and which is an essential element, and generally, the first one, in evangelization. All Christians are called to this witness, and in this way they can be real evangelizers.[108]

The silent witness of Christian life is the first element of missionary dialogue. As we have seen, for John Paul holiness is "a message that convinces

---

107. John Paul II, *RMiss*, 90.
108. Paul VI, *EN*, 21.

without the need for words."[109] Its power to evoke the questions mentioned in the above text is rooted in the anthropological presupposition that is not mentioned here, namely, that a dynamism impelling people to aspire to live a fully human life is at work in those who observe the way that Christians live. This dynamism causes them to perceive, perhaps at first only intuitively, that there is something genuinely good and human present in the lives of Christians. The questions that arise in response to Christian witness are not indications of idle curiosity. Rather, they point to the fundamental human dynamism to search for definitive meaning and purpose in life. They are indications of the interest that people are taking, that they are being attracted by the goodness they perceive in Christian life.

John Paul II sees things in precisely the same way when he credits Christian witness with the provocation of questions:

> The evangelical witness which the world finds most appealing is that of concern for people, and of charity toward the poor, the weak and those who suffer. The complete generosity underlying this attitude and these actions stands in marked contrast to human selfishness. It raises precise questions which lead to God and to the Gospel.[110]

This connection between witness and questions indicates that dialogue cannot be reduced to planned techniques and methods. As we have seen, both Pope Paul and Pope John Paul invoke fidelity to God as the objective measure of fidelity to man, that is, of dialogue. Now we are in a position to see that even before this and in a more fundamental way, the first fruit of fidelity to God *ad intra* is renewal through conversion into a fully human life in Christ, and it is the witness of this very life that works to initiate a dialogue. In this light, the second and third paths overlap. They are essentially the same reality viewed from two different perspectives. From the first perspective, communion with Christ is the fruit of the first and second paths, the effect of renewal through conversion. Here the perspective is vertical, as man strives to measure up to his divine vocation. From the second perspective, communion with Christ is a beginning, a catalyst for the conversion of others. Here the perspective is horizontal.

---

109. John Paul II, *NMI*, 7.
110. John Paul II, *RMiss*, 42.

CONCLUSION

The relations among witness, the principle of dual fidelity, and the concern to respond to the charge of alienation allow us to perceive the contribution of several themes of John Paul II and Benedict XVI in relation to the New Evangelization as the fruit of the renewal of Vatican II. Because the New Evangelization is essentially identical with the third path of dialogical mission of *ES*, this results in a more comprehensive understanding of the renewal of Vatican II as outlined in *ES*. A suitable final theme to bring this chapter to a conclusion is that of the witness of joy, a theme especially valued by Pope Benedict XVI.

The renewal of Vatican II—the goal of which can now be described as the revitalization of the Church's mission through witness that gives rise to dialogue—is the context in light of which the theme of joy in Benedict XVI is best understood.[111] Joy is the state of the will when man has come into possession of a desired good.[112] The ultimate source of joy is possession of the highest good, which is God himself. In other words, joy is rooted in that religious dimension of man's nature that Pope Paul tells us is Vatican II's fundamental focus.[113] For Pope Benedict, God's love affirms the goodness of man's humanity.

> Only if God accepts me, and I become convinced of this, do I know definitively: it is good that I exist. It is good to be a human being. If ever man's sense of being accepted and loved by God is lost, then there is no longer any answer to the question whether to be a human being is good at all. Doubt concerning human existence becomes more and more insurmountable. Where doubt over God becomes prevalent, then doubt over humanity follows inevitably. We see today how widely this doubt is spreading. We see it in the joylessness, in the inner sadness, that can be read on so many human faces today. Only faith gives me the conviction: it is good that I exist.[114]

---

111. On this theme in the work of Joseph Ratzinger, see Murphy, *Christ Our Joy*.

112. "Love causes a desire for the absent good and the hope of obtaining it; this movement finds completion in the pleasure and joy of the good possessed" (*CCC*, 1765).

113. See chapter 4 above on the personal appropriation of faith in the documents of Vatican II and in *ES*.

114. Benedict XVI, "Address, December 22, 2011."

Coming to faith in God's love, man comes into possession of the truth about God and the truth about his own humanity. His joy is thus twofold, in the goodness of God and in the goodness of his own humanity.

This joy is not something that man can attain by his own effort. It is a gift that accompanies God's love, which can only received as a gift.

> The source of Christian joy is the certainty of being loved by God, loved personally by our Creator, by the One who holds the entire universe in his hands and loves each one of us and the whole great human family with a passionate and faithful love, a love greater than our infidelities and sins, a love which forgives.[115]

It is fitting that in his final general audience Pope Benedict should disclose in very personal terms his desire, which is essentially the desire that makes the Church missionary: "I want everyone to feel loved by that God who gave his Son for us and who has shown us his infinite love."[116] This is equivalent to saying that he would like everyone to come to faith in Christ, for the essential content of this faith is the love of God. This is evident in the scriptural verse that perhaps best serves as a summary of the Benedictine pontificate: "So we know and believe the love God has for us" (1 John 4:16).

Christian joy is a sign of the presence of that fully human life that all people seek. It is proof that God's love is effective in enriching people's lives. It is proof that men are not deluding themselves in longing for the fullness of life, and that already here on earth there is a happiness that can be realized, even if it is a gift rather than the final product of human striving. As a result, the most effective way to be faithful to man is to evangelize by the witness of a holy life that is the fruit of being open oneself to God's love, so that those who do not yet know his love can be drawn to it through the witness of joy in being loved by him.

---

115. Benedict XVI, "Address, June 5, 2006."
116. Benedict XVI, "General Audience, February 27, 2013."

PART III

Ecclesiam Suam:
A Path for the Church

10

Three Paths of Renewal and Three Dimensions of Formation

DURING A MEETING WITH rectors and students of pontifical colleges, a seminarian from the United States asked Pope Francis: "We have come to Rome above all for an academic formation and to keep faith in this commitment. How do we not neglect an integral priestly formation, either at the personal or community level?" While acknowledging that academic formation is the "main purpose" of the time a future priest spends in the seminary, the Holy Father warns against what happens when academic formation is isolated from three other dimensions of formation.

> It's true that here in Rome emphasis is placed—since this is why you were sent—on intellectual formation; however, the other three pillars must be cultivated, and all four interact among themselves, and I wouldn't understand a priest who comes to get a degree in Rome and does not have a community life. This is not all right. Either he is not taking care of his spiritual life—daily Mass, daily prayer, *lectio divina*, personal prayer with the Lord—or his apostolic life: on the weekend doing something, for a change of air, but also the apostolic air, doing something there . . . It's true that study is an apostolic dimension; but it is important that the other three pillars are also looked after! Academic purism is not beneficial, it is not beneficial.[1]

---

1. Francis, "Address, May 12, 2014." In this same address Francis states that he has referred to the four pillars of formation many times. Addressing the community of

Pope Francis's words are noteworthy for several reasons. First, he identifies four dimensions—he calls them pillars—of priestly formation: intellectual (or academic), spiritual, apostolic (or pastoral), and personal (community life). Second, he emphasizes that all four must be cultivated at the same time. Third, their cultivation is of a nature that they must interact among one another. No one of the dimensions can remain quarantined from the others. Fourth, he confirms the third point by giving an example of a defect that results when one pillar is cut off from the others. He terms this defect academic purism, which becomes a risk when academic formation is not properly complemented by personal, spiritual, and pastoral formation.

Elaborating on what he means by academic purism, Francis says that if academic formation is isolated from the others "there is a danger of

---

the Leonine College ("April 14, 2014"), he also emphasized that the four dimensions need to interact with one another: "Every Seminary, yours too, aims to prepare future ordained ministers in a climate of prayer, study and fraternity. It is this evangelical atmosphere, this life full of the Holy Spirit and of humanity, that allows those who immerse themselves therein to assimilate day by day the mind of Jesus Christ, his love for the Father and for the Church, his unreserved dedication to the People of God. Prayer, study, fraternity and also apostolic life: these are the four pillars of formation, which interact. A strong spiritual life; a deep intellectual life; community life; and lastly, apostolic life; with no order of importance. All four are important. If one of them is missing, formation is not comprehensive. And these four interact. Four pillars, four elements on which a seminary must base its life." He also mentions the four pillars of formation when speaking to seminarians and novices ("Address, July 6, 2013"). In this address, as in others, the Holy Father also speaks of community life. Here it seems to be equivalent to or at least a key element of personal formation. See also: Francis, "Address, May 5, 2014." In an *Ad limina* Address on April 3, 2014 to the bishops of Rwanda, he mentioned the human, intellectual, and spiritual formation of the laity and of priests. This comes in the context of his desire to see a renewal in their hearts of "the faith and courage necessary for your demanding pastoral mission." Speaking about Catholic schools to the bishops of the Netherlands in an *Ad limina* Address of December 2, 2013, he stated that the education [intellectual formation] these schools provide will also "nourish their human and spiritual formation." This should "support their faith [intellectual formation] and lead them to an encounter with Christ [spiritual formation]" in a "spirit of openness" for the spreading of the Gospel [pastoral formation]. He reminded the bishops of Poland ("Address, February 7, 2014") that the high standard of intellectual and pastoral formation that seminarians receive "must always be accompanied by human and spiritual formation." Addressing the Italian bishops ("Address, May 19, 2014") he elaborated on human formation, saying that it is both cultural and affective. In an Angelus Address ("Angelus, February 2, 2014") he mentions that the presence of religious "strengthens and renews . . . commitment to human formation, the spiritual formation of young people, and families." He mentions intellectual, spiritual, and human formation in an address on June 7, 2013.

sliding into ideologies." This "sickens one's conception of the Church" and leads to "a non-Christian hermeneutic, a hermeneutic of an ideological Church." The antidote to such an illness is to experience the Church, to live her own life, and to serve her.

> To understand the Church, one must understand her through study but also through prayer, through community life and through apostolic life . . . To perceive the Church with the eyes of a Christian; to understand the Church with the mind of a Christian; to understand the Church with the heart of a Christian; to understand the Church through Christian works. Otherwise one does not understand the Church, or understands her poorly. Therefore, yes, it is important to emphasize academic study because that is why you were sent here, but do not neglect the other three pillars: the spiritual life, community life and the apostolic life.[2]

The Church is not an abstraction, but the Spouse and Body of Christ, the communion of those who participate in divine life by the gift of the Holy Spirit. The Church is not just an object of knowledge but an object of the love that is a participation in God's own love for the Church.[3] For

---

2. Francis, "Address, May 12, 2014."

3. Paul VI writes something very similar to Pope Francis's emphasis on a lived experience of the Church as the remedy for tendencies to reduce the Church to an object merely to be analyzed: "If we can only stir up this awareness of the Church in ourselves and foster it in the faithful by the noble and pastoral art of education, many of the apparent difficulties which are today exercising the minds of students of ecclesiology will in fact be overcome. I mean such difficulties as how the Church can be at once both visible and spiritual, free and yet subject to discipline, claiming to be communal in character and yet organized on a sacred, hierarchical basis, already holy and yet still striving for holiness, at once both contemplative and active, and so on. All these matters will become clear through our actually living the Church's life. This is the best illustration and confirmation of its teaching" (*ES*, 38). Benedict XVI also addresses this issue, not with respect to ecclesiology alone, but regarding all of theology: "There is actually a theology that wants above all to be academic, to appear scientific and forgets the vital reality, the presence of God, his presence among us, his talking today not just in the past. Even St. Bonaventure distinguished two forms of theology in his time and said: 'There is a theology that comes from the arrogance of reason, that wants to dominate everything, God passes from being the subject to the object of our study, while he should be the subject who speaks and guides us.' There is really this abuse of theology, which is the arrogance of reason and does not nurture faith but overshadows God's presence in the world. Then, there is a theology that wants to know more out of love for the beloved, it is stirred by love and guided by love. It wants to know the beloved more. And this is the true theology that comes from love of God, of Christ, and it wants to enter more deeply into communion with Christ" ("Address, June 10, 2010").

this reason, an integral formation for priests—and, as we shall see, for every member of the Church—must recognize what is unique about the object(s) of faith and about the subject of faith, the person who believes. By its nature, intellectual formation cannot be something abstract or merely conceptual. It must open up to and be complemented by living the faith through the cultivation of a spiritual life (guided by spiritual formation) and through ecclesial service (guided by pastoral formation). Knowing the faith is not enough. The content of faith must permeate a person's entire life, become the content of prayer and spiritual life, and lay claim to a believer's life, time, and energy in the fulfillment of the tasks of his vocation.

It is certainly in harmony with Pope Francis's response to observe that while more time may be given to academic formation than the other dimensions of priestly formation, this does not constitute a reason for thinking that it is the most important dimension. The simple reason is that a priestly vocation presupposes and specifies the universal vocation to holiness of baptism. A seminarian entrusts his vocation to the Church and engages in a rigorous program of academic (or theological) formation because he has discerned a call from God that his path to holiness is by way of priestly ministry. In this light, spiritual formation is prior to theological formation and embraces the totality of a student's life in a way that theological study does not. Everything a seminarian does should be sanctifying.

Emphasis on the various dimensions of formation is not unique to Pope Francis. It is a common theme among the post-Vatican II popes. A noteworthy illustration is the call of Pope Benedict XVI to the lay faithful to "intensify their formative commitment" so that they can more effectively and more fruitfully participate in the Church's life and mission. "To carry out their mission in a responsible and faithful way," he asserts, "the laity need a solid doctrinal, pastoral, and spiritual foundation and appropriate support."[4]

This renewed call for a threefold formation—doctrinal, pastoral, and spiritual—is a stable feature of the teaching of Vatican II and of the popes and curial departments following the Council. The same threefold

---

4. Benedict XVI, "Message to Bishop Luis Collazuol."

formation applies to clergy[5] (priests, seminarians, deacons), religious,[6] laity,[7] and those engaged in apostolates and ecclesial service, for example, catechists,[8] missionaries,[9] and people in associations dedicated to works of charity.[10] The universal application of the threefold formation

    5. See Vatican II, *OT* (Spiritual Training, Ch. IV; Ecclesiastical Studies, Ch. V; Pastoral Training, Ch. VI); Catholic Church, *Code of Canon Law*, cc. 244, 248, 252, 255 (spiritual, doctrinal-theological, pastoral); Congregation for Clergy, *Directory on the Ministry and Life of Priests*, 74–78 (human, spiritual, intellectual, pastoral); Congregation for Catholic Education and Congregation for Clergy, *Basic Norms for the Formation of Permanent Deacons*, 66–88 (human, spiritual, doctrinal, pastoral); *PDV* (Spiritual Life of the Priest, Ch. III; Priestly Vocation and the Church's Pastoral Work, Ch. IV; human, 43–44; spiritual, 45–49; intellectual, 51–56; pastoral, 57–59).

    6. See Vatican II, *PC*, 11, 18 (spiritual training; apostolic formation); Catholic Church, *Code of Canon Law*, cc. 660, 661 (spiritual, doctrinal, apostolic, practical). See also c. 735 on formation for societies of apostolic life (doctrinal, spiritual, apostolic).

    7. See Vatican II, *AA*, 28–29, 32 (human, spiritual, doctrinal, for apostolic or pastoral action). In *CL*, 60, John Paul II writes of spiritual, doctrinal, and human formation. It could be that his special mention of formation in the Church's social teaching corresponds to pastoral formation, since this is especially relevant to "their special task to order and to throw light upon these [secular] affairs in such a way that they may come into being and then continually increase according to Christ to the praise of the Creator and the Redeemer" (Vatican II, *LG*, 31). John Paul also connects "human values" to "the missionary and apostolic activities of the lay faithful," so that here human formation is closely related to pastoral formation or formation for the apostolate. The *Code of Canon Law* affirms that the lay faithful who "permanently or temporarily devote themselves to special service of the Church are obliged to acquire the appropriate formation required to fulfill their function properly and to carry out this function conscientiously, eagerly, and diligently" (c. 231). The most complete description of what that formation should entail is in c. 229 §1: "Lay persons are bound by the obligation and possess the right to acquire knowledge of Christian doctrine appropriate to the capacity and condition of each in order for them to be able to live according to this doctrine, announce it themselves, defend it if necessary, and take their part in exercising the apostolate." Without much difficulty one can align acquiring knowledge of Christian doctrine with theological or doctrinal formation, being able to live according to this doctrine with spiritual formation, and announcing and defending this doctrine, as well as exercising the apostolate, with pastoral formation.

    8. See Vatican II, *AG*, 17 (Catholic doctrine; Christian character, piety, and sanctity of life; catechetical method and pastoral practice); *CD*, 14 (doctrine of the Church, theoretical and practical knowledge of laws of psychology and of pedagogical methods); Congregation for Clergy, *GCD*, 112–15 (theological-doctrinal, anthropological, methodological) and *GDC*, 238–47 (being, knowing, savoir-faire; human, Christian, apostolic).

    9. See Vatican II, *AG*, 25–26 (spiritual and moral training; doctrinal training/missiological studies; apostolic training).

    10. For example, in an address of February 29, 2008 to the Pontifical Council *Cor Unum*, Pope Benedict calls for a formation of those involved in works of charity "on

underscores the importance of an accurate understanding of each of these dimensions and how they interact with one another.

This importance becomes all the more pronounced when an implicit postulate is made explicit: there is a correlation between the quality of formation of those who promote the Church's mission and the quality of the mission itself. Illustrative of the Church's conviction regarding this correlation is the unequivocal assertion:

> Any pastoral activity for the carrying out of which there are not at hand persons with the right formation and preparation will necessarily come to nothing.[11]

The better the formation of those engaged in pastoral activity—that is, mission, service, ministry, apostolate—the more fruit that can be expected from their activity.

It is crucially important to see that the fruit of which it is a question here is the salvation of souls, building up the Body of Christ by bringing the life of Christ to those who do not have it (this is the mission *ad gentes*) and by enriching that life for those who have already been baptized (this is pastoral care for those receptive to it, and New Evangelization for those baptized who are distant from the Church).[12] This clearly indicates that mission, ministry, apostolate, and service presuppose what has traditionally been called a zeal for souls, that is, an ardent charity. For those who participate in the pastoral office of Jesus Christ through Holy Orders, Vatican II calls this pastoral charity.[13] For all of the faithful, the Council refers to charity as the soul of the apostolate.[14] This emphasis on charity shows that spiritual formation necessarily has a certain priority in relation to pastoral formation. This should not be construed as implying a temporal precedence, as though spiritual formation had to be completed before one could begin pastoral formation. Formal and systematic spiritual formation and pastoral formation can and perhaps should take place simultaneously.

While ecclesial documents and practice consistently identify four dimensions of formation—human, theological or doctrinal, spiritual,

---

both the human and professional, as well as the theological-spiritual and pastoral level."

11. *GCD*, 108.
12. On the three spheres of missionary activity, see John Paul II, *RMiss*, 33–34.
13. See *LG*, 41; *PO*, 14–17.
14. See *LG*, 33; *AA*, 3.

and pastoral[15]—for merely practical reasons, human formation will not be considered in this study. Omitting it should in no way be taken as a devaluation of its importance. In fact, properly understood, it should be thought of as a prerequisite to the other dimensions, even if during intensive programs of formation, like a seminary, it can also accompany them. What John Paul II writes about the relation of human formation to spiritual formation contains a principle that is applicable to its relation to the other dimensions or pillars of formation: "Human formation, when it is carried out in the context of an anthropology which is open to the full truth regarding the human person, leads to and finds its completion in spiritual formation."[16] A number of texts of Vatican II on human formation indicate that it is understood as the development of a person's natural, human aptitudes, both personal as well as cultural or national.[17] Once the supernatural life in Christ is described as making people more fully human,[18] the case could be made that all dimensions of formation contribute to human formation. One can see here an application of the principle: grace builds on, heals or purifies, perfects, ennobles, and elevates what is true, good, and beautiful in individuals and cultures.[19] This is precisely what the most recent Norms for Priestly Formation states:

---

15. Those who are called to form pastoral agents according to this threefold plan must themselves be formed accordingly. As if attentive to the principle that the agent must be proportioned to the effect, Vatican II stresses the qualities of the faculty of seminaries: "Administrators and teachers of seminaries are to be selected from the best men, and are to be carefully prepared in sound doctrine, suitable pastoral experience and special spiritual and pedagogical training" (*OT*, 5). This applies to all who are involved as teachers, guides, and mentors for those being formed.

16. John Paul II, *PDV*, 45.

17. See Vatican II, *AA*, 29; *AG*, 16; *GE*, 1, 2, 7, 8; *OT*, 3, 11.

18. See *GS*, 11; "To 'make human life more human' is the Council's fundamental objective, closely linked to the desire to share in the divine life and in the mission of Christ" (Wojtyła, *SR*, 279).

19. In the documents of Vatican II, the verbs vary to some extent. See *LG*, 13 (purifies, strengthens, elevates, and ennobles); *GS*, 40 (healing and elevating); *GS*, 49 (ennobling, healing, perfecting and exalting); *GS*, 58 ("The Gospel of Christ constantly renews the life and culture of fallen man, it combats and removes the errors and evils resulting from the permanent allurement of sin. It never ceases to purify and elevate the morality of peoples. By riches coming from above, it makes fruitful, as it were from within, the spiritual qualities and traditions of every people and of every age. It strengthens, perfects and restores them in Christ. Thus the Church, in the very fulfillment of her own function, stimulates and advances human and civic culture"); *GS*, 76 (foster and elevate).

> A correct and harmonious spirituality demands a well-structured humanity; indeed, as St. Thomas Aquinas reminds us, "grace builds upon nature" (*ST* I, Q. 2, a. 2, ad. 1), it does not supplant nature, but perfects it (cf. *ST* I, Q. 1, a. 8, ad. 2).[20]

Not only do the documents of Vatican II and the post-Conciliar popes consistently propose the three dimensions or pillars of formation, but this threefold blueprint also constitutes the very structure and essence of the renewal of Vatican II. The goal of the Council's renewal is the reinvigoration of the Church's mission of service to mankind in the circumstances of contemporary secularism, materialism, and relativism. This revitalization of mission is envisioned, not as a specific activity that in some manner could be conceived as something in addition to Christian life as such. Rather, it is understood as emanating from Christian life, as its fruit. Mission, and all terms associated with it—dialogue, ministry, apostolate, service, and the New Evangelization—is so much a part of Christian life itself that if the judgment is made that mission is lacking or insufficiently engaged this can only mean that Christian life itself is deficient.

The remedy, therefore, can only be a deepening, an enriching, a maturing of Christian life. Such renewal on the part of the Church's members results in a full, conscious, and active participation by all in the Church's life and a new and more effective mission of evangelization.[21] The personal deepening or renewal of Christian life, in turn, presupposes a clear understanding of the doctrine that provides the content of the faith-vision that is the objective measure of renewal. And with this the trilogy of formation, now seen as reproducing the theological format for the renewal of Vatican II, as set forth in *ES* and examined in Part I, is complete. The Church participates more fully in Christ's mission to the extent that she: (1) understands more fully the mystery of Christ and her own role in God's plan; (2) opens herself more fully to the transforming grace of God in order more fully to participate in Christ's life and conform more fully to her vocation; (3) recommits herself to the mission

---

20. Congregation for Clergy, *The Gift of the Priestly Vocation*, 93.

21. This extends to the entire life of the Church what Vatican II identified as the key goal of the liturgical renewal: "Mother Church earnestly desires that all the faithful should be led to that fully conscious, and active participation in liturgical celebrations which is demanded by the very nature of the liturgy. . . . In the restoration and promotion of the sacred liturgy, this full and active participation by all the people is the aim to be considered before all else" (*SC*, 14).

God entrusted to her in order to produce the fruit of salvation for all the world.

With realities so fundamental as the renewal of Vatican II, the programmatic outline of *ES*, and formation for effective fulfillment of vocations and mission in play, the value of a fresh look at the three dimensions of formation is warranted. An inquiry into what is proper to each of the three dimensions and how they are related can result in new insights that can in turn guide the wide range of formational programs and activities upon which the efficacy of the New Evangelization depends. The business of Part III of this study is to search for insights and guiding principles that can be gleaned from Pope Paul VI's understanding of the renewal of Vatican II, as set forth in *ES*. What emerges from this inquiry is the organic unity of the three dimensions of formation, and the foundations of their interrelatedness.

For reasons that will become clear, when the three dimensions of formation are listed, doctrinal formation nearly always comes first. One may provisionally conclude that spiritual formation and pastoral formation depend upon it in some fundamental way. For this reason, if doctrinal formation is not adequate, spiritual formation and pastoral formation will be defective. Consequently, it is futile to hope that any one of these alone, or any combination of only two, can bear the weight of the hopes of the renewal of Vatican II and the kind of formation envisioned by the Church. In fact, even if all three are robustly developed yet treated as autonomous, self-contained dimensions of renewal and formation, the hopes associated with the renewal of Vatican II evaporate. To grasp something of the nature of each of these three dimensions of formation and renewal and their organic unity is to possess a key to a more effective promotion of the Church's renewal and mission.

Depending on a number of factors, it can be tempting to assign priority to one or another of these dimensions. Because spiritual formation and pastoral formation depend on doctrinal formation, one can readily assign the latter a certain priority. On the other hand, if one can assume a solid doctrinal formation, that is, an accurate understanding of the faith in its integrity and of one's vocation, it would be possible to give spiritual formation pride of place. For Paul VI and John Paul II, such an emphasis is at the heart of the understanding of Vatican II as a pastoral council. The Council's goal was not so much to arrive at greater doctrinal precision, though that did occur, as to promote a more thorough personal assimilation of the faith, thereby overcoming the alarming situation described as a "split between faith . . . and daily life."[22] In other words, the goal was to foster a genuine spirituality that is in reality nothing other than a life given direction and meaning by the faith that one professes. Assigning a priority to spiritual formation would, then, reflect the disposition of the Church at the time of Vatican II. What the Church teaches and how this should be understood was considered a given; the perceived challenge was that this patrimony of revealed truth be personally appropriated and lived in such a way that it permeate every aspect of the faithful's lives. It is in this light that one should understand Paul VI and John Paul II when they summarize the purpose of the Council in terms of the call to holiness.[23] The privileged place of spiritual formation is reinforced by the consideration that pastoral formation presupposes holiness and the spiritual formation that is most directly associated with it.

Holiness and spiritual formation give rise to mission and pastoral formation as naturally as faith and doctrinal formation give rise to holiness and spiritual formation. For Cardinal Wojtyła, the future Pope and Saint, John Paul II, at the heart of it all is what he called "existential faith,"[24] that is, a faith that is accompanied by a range of attitudes that render a person ready to engage in the actions corresponding to one's vocation.[25] Because pastoral formation is the dimension of renewal most proximate to the daily living of faith and the revitalized mission that Vatican II envisioned, one could for good reason assign it a certain priority. Yet, without spiritual formation it would be soulless and unable to realize its own proper goals. This is because Christians are called not only to accomplish, as efficaciously as possible, all the actions that their vocations entail, but to perform them in a certain manner.[26] That manner is, in the

22. Vatican II, *GS*, 43.
23. See above chapter 4, n39, and chapter 9, nn76–77.
24. See Wojtyła, *SR*, 15–18, 224.
25. See Wojtyła, *SR*, "Part III: The Formation of Attitudes." An attitude results from the content of faith defining who a person is. Wojtyła calls it one's self-consciousness. Since a person cannot fail to project his very being into action, how he understands his being, his self-consciousness, necessarily becomes projected into action. Traditional Thomistic philosophy gets at this in terms of first act and second act. For Wojtyła, whose fascination was with the human person and especially human freedom, the acting person cannot fail to seek his own fulfillment in his actions. The substance or content of this happiness will always correspond, concretely, to a person's understanding of himself, that is, to his self-consciousness.
26. In *SR*, Cardinal Wojtyła developed this manner of fulfilling Christian duties in terms of consciousness and attitude. This places the emphasis on the interior

final analysis, the motive of charity, "the soul of the apostolate,"[27] which is cultivated through spiritual formation.

The integral formation that the Church envisions requires that all three dimensions develop together. This does not necessarily mean that each be allotted the same amount of time, so that a lack of balance among them would be determined by quantifiable comparisons. The ratio of time allotted to each will be determined by numerous factors, especially the vocation envisioned and what a person or group brings to the program of formation.

Spiritual formation, presupposing doctrinal formation and completed by pastoral formation, has perhaps received the greatest theological emphasis by the post-Conciliar popes. This is evident, for example, in the following remarks of Pope John Paul II:

> As places which accept and train those called to the priesthood, seminaries must prepare the future ministers of the Church to live "a solid spirituality of communion with Christ the Shepherd and of openness to the workings of the Spirit, that will make them specially able to discern the needs of God's People and their various charisms, and to work together." Therefore, in seminaries "there should be special insistence upon specifically spiritual formation, so that through constant conversion, the spirit of prayer, the practice of the Sacraments of the Eucharist and Penance, the candidates may learn to be close to the Lord and learn to commit themselves generously to pastoral work."[28]

---

dimension of self-determination or virtue, thereby showing the inseparable connection between spiritual formation and pastoral action.

27. See Vatican II, *LG*, 33; *AA*, 3.

28. John Paul II, *EAm*, 40. The words that are quoted are from propositions 51 and 52, from the Special Assembly for America of the Synod of Bishops, November 12 through December 12, 1997. It is noteworthy that the outline of *EAm* mirrors that of *ES*. At the outset of *EAm*, John Paul states that the commemoration of the fifth centenary of the evangelization of America has "made all American Catholics more deeply aware of Christ's desire to meet the inhabitants of the so-called New World so that, gathering them into his Church, he might be present in the continent's history. The evangelization of America is not only a gift from the Lord; it is also a source of new responsibilities" (*EAm*, 1). *EAm* proposes that the Church in America experience a "fresh encounter with Jesus Christ [that] will make all the members of the Church in America aware that they are called to continue the Redeemer's mission in their lands." Such an encounter, "if it is genuine ... will also bring a renewal of the Church," and this "will strengthen the bonds of cooperation and solidarity in order that the saving work of Christ may continue in the history of America with ever greater effect." Encountering Christ is "'the path to conversion, communion and solidarity.' To the extent that

A profound, personal participation in the mystery of Christ, that is, communion with him, is the source of the pastoral discernment that is critical to the ministry of priests. This communion with Christ is the goal of spiritual formation, which is deserving of "special insistence" because a priest's generous commitment to his ministry is rooted in his conversion into deep communion with Christ. For priests, a generous commitment to ministry *is* their communion with Christ translated into action.

An indication of the inseparability and mutual interpenetration of the three dimensions of formation is that different texts can place a particular emphasis on one or the other. Because it is foundational for spiritual formation and because of a growing awareness of deficiencies in doctrinal formation, it has also received considerable emphasis. Notwithstanding this, when the specific groups within the Church (clergy, religious, laity) and their various ministries, apostolates, and services in the Church are considered, in some texts the predominant stress is on pastoral formation. It would seem that emphasis or even prioritization of one or another of the three dimensions is the result of perspective or of a perceived need to address particular concerns, and should not be taken as an endorsement of an essential priority of one dimension of formation over the others.

In texts that take up the subject of formation and its three dimensions, one not infrequently finds some general indications regarding the interrelationships among the three dimensions, or, in the language of Pope Francis, how they interact with one another. For example, Vatican II exhorts: "The spiritual training [of seminarians] should be closely connected with the doctrinal and pastoral. . ."[29] John Paul II reflects at some length on the interrelations among these dimensions in the spiritual formation of priests, which has three elements: "The decree *Optatam totius* would seem to indicate a triple path to be covered: a faithful meditation on the word of God, active participation in the Church's holy mysteries, and the service of charity to the 'little ones.'"[30] While meditation on the word of God is not exactly the same as theological study, these three dimensions of priestly spirituality closely parallel the three dimensions of

---

these goals are reached, there will emerge an ever-increasing dedication to the new evangelization of America" (*EAm*, 7). New evangelization is the fruit of the profound communion resulting from renewal through conversion, and this renewal is rooted in a deepened awareness of the mystery of Christ and of the Church.

29. Vatican II, *OT*, 8.
30. John Paul II, *PDV*, 46.

formation. For John Paul, prayerful meditation on God's word is linked to conversion and fulfillment of the mission entrusted by God.[31] The section on intellectual formation begins with a statement about its connection with human and spiritual formation.[32]

Clearly, the insistence that the three dimensions are related in a way that integral formation would be lacking without all three, and that each is in a way dependent on the others and contributes to their vigor, gives rise to the question why this is the case, and this question can only be answered by determining more precisely how they are related.

The purpose of this study is to propose an answer to this question about how the three dimensions of formation are related and why they are nearly always set forth with doctrinal (or theological) formation coming first, spiritual formation second, and pastoral formation third. The answer has already been suggested in our analysis of the vision of Pope Paul VI for the renewal of the Church that he proposed to the Fathers of Vatican II. It will be seen that the three dimensions of formation correspond precisely to the tripartite structure of his first encyclical, *ES*. This should not be surprising, since the goal of formation for ministry, religious life, and the lay apostolate, and the goal of the renewal of Vatican II, are the same: to foster an effective participation in the mission of Christ and the Church rooted in a deepening of communion with him, on the foundation of the faith in what he has revealed about God, about man, and about man's place the fulfillment of God's plan for the Church.

It is rightly expected that the quality of formation for those actively participating in the Church's mission will translate into a proportionate quality of that mission. This is the foundation for the vital importance of arriving at a principled understanding of the order among the three dimensions of formation. Such an understanding gives direction to decisions regarding programs for the formation of agents of ministerial, apostolic, and pastoral activity, while it also provides principles to shape an integrated curriculum in pastoral theology. Thoughtfully constructed curricula and programs of formation for priests, deacons, religious, the laity, catechists, and indeed all who turn to the Church for their formation, equips them responsibly to embrace the duties and tasks associated with their vocation.

---

31. See John Paul II, *PDV*, 46.
32. See John Paul II, *PDV*, 51.

The demonstration of the relevance of *ES* for shedding light on how the three dimensions that are common to the ecclesial renewal of Vatican II, formation, and pastoral theology, and how these three elements interact with one another, proceeds as follows. First, it will be proposed that the Encyclical's movement from consciousness, to renewal, to dialogue can be understood in light of: (a) principles of Christian anthropology; (b) the development of faith recorded in Sacred Scripture and illustrated by Mary's faith at the Annunciation, Jesus's encounter with the Samaritan woman, and the origin of the Church's mission through Peter and the apostles on Pentecost; (c) the progression in the Mass from Liturgy of the Word, to Liturgy of the Eucharist, to the dismissal. This will lead to a closer look at the Church's mission as understood by Vatican II and the post-Conciliar popes, for it is ultimately in light of this mission that the fittingness of the three dimensions of formation becomes evident. The penultimate consideration will show the continuity between the three dimensions of renewal as understood by Paul VI and two themes that his predecessor associated with the renewal of Vatican II. Finally, some indications of the preceding for developing an integrated curriculum in pastoral theology will be given. This will include some conclusions about the foundational importance of sound doctrine for renewal, formation, and pastoral theology, and about the importance of spiritual formation.

11

How Are the Three Dimensions of Renewal/Formation Related?

THE MOVEMENT IN *ES* from awareness to renewal to dialogue already sheds significant light on the three dimensions—doctrinal, spiritual, and pastoral—of formation. Doctrine informs us of God's plan for the Church. Following this doctrinal penetration, and assuming the presence of a love for the Church and humility, the perception of a lack of conformity to God's plan is the impetus for spiritual renewal, that is, for conversion into a deepening communion or participation in the mystery of Christ. Spiritual formation, then, presupposes and flows from doctrinal formation, which gives renewal or conversion its divinely established objectivity. This greater conformity to Christ in turn yields the fruit of Christ-like service, the dialogue that takes the form of ministry, apostolate, and pastoral action of all kinds. To take up again the language of Vatican II, we can say that participation in the Church's life and mission becomes conscious through doctrinal awareness and formation, that it then becomes more fully realized through the renewal of conversion and spiritual formation, and it becomes active through the many forms of dialogical service and the corresponding pastoral formation.

Paul VI did not elaborate further how he understood the order among awareness, renewal, and dialogical mission-service. *ES* gives the impression that the movement from one to the other is natural, even spontaneous. Is there anything more that can be said about the structure of *ES* that might yield further insight into how the three dimensions are related, thereby providing principles that can lead to a deeper understanding of the interrelatedness of the three dimensions of formation?

As previously examined,[1] one of Pope Paul's close associates, Msgr. Giuseppe Colombo, addresses this question. First, he remarks that "the three parts of the encyclical are thought in rigorous and logical succession, so that from the first part (consciousness of the Church) 'derives' or should derive the second (renewal of the Church), and these two converge to engender the third part (dialogue) (cf. *ES*, 13)." Then he identifies a philosophical axiom that lends itself to assigning a certain priority to the final part on dialogue. "The end, which comes last in execution, is first in intention."[2] This implies that the unifying goal of the Council is a reinvigorated missionary outreach of service to mankind, or dialogue with the world, and this is consistent with what we know about the pastoral purpose of Vatican II. It might also be taken to imply that doctrinal awareness and spiritual renewal are in some way subordinate to mission (ministry, apostolate, service). Depending on how one understands "subordinate to" here, this may or may not be true.

When the relation of doctrinal awareness and spiritual renewal to pastoral mission is not properly understood there is cause for serious concern over the potential of losing sight of or even inverting fundamental theological values. If they are understood as subordinate in the way that means derive their value from an end, then there is a risk of seeing doctrinal awareness and spiritual renewal as contingent and reconfigurable based on a calculation of what one might think is most expedient for the dialogue of mission and service. In this case the effectiveness of pastoral activity becomes primary and there is a danger of relativizing doctrinal awareness and spiritual renewal through conversion. In terms developed earlier, this would amount to the concern to be faithful to man trumping the concern to be faithful to God. Yet, this kind of relativizing of doctrinal and spiritual formation has consternated many, leading them to charge that Vatican II in effect reversed the traditional priorities of Catholicism. What could be higher in importance than liturgical worship? Didn't the Council itself recognize the liturgy as source and summit of the Church's life, and the supreme manifestation of the mystery of the

---

1. See chapter 5 above.
2. Colombo, "Genesi," 135–36.

Church? And how can divinely revealed truth and contemplation of that truth be in any way subordinated to the activity of pastoral action?

Questions like this could be multiplied, but one that should not be omitted here concerns the conversion that is at the heart of spiritual renewal. With a genuine concern for efficacy of pastoral action, rooted in the dynamism of pastoral charity, agents of pastoral activity can be tempted to look for techniques, programs, or methods, and lose sight of the primacy of conformity with Christ in the Paschal Mystery. The primacy of the Paschal Mystery as the summit of the divine pedagogy, which is God's pastoral theology, is a postulate of the divine logic of love. Only the gift of mature faith can safeguard its primacy as the soul of the apostolate and depository of the principles that must guide pastoral activity, and even mature faith can be put to the test on these points.

Throughout his distinguished theological service to the Church, Joseph Ratzinger has been as attentive as anyone to an emphasis on pastoral action and service to the point of neglecting the place of doctrinal awareness and spiritual renewal. Though the vocabulary of *ES* is not found explicitly in his insightful analyses, the reality of the three paths of the renewal of Vatican II certainly are present in his work. His concern has been with the risk of exaggerating the Council's intention to reinvigorate the Church's pastoral mission and to equate this with the so-called spirit of Vatican II in a way that diminishes the importance of doctrinal awareness, sometimes even to the point of pitting doctrine against pastoral charity, as if truth were a hindrance to love. He has been especially attentive to the diminished emphasis on conversion and the corresponding centrality of the Paschal Mystery and the Eucharistic. Responding to this alarming sign of the times, his warning against relativism and the inversion of the priority of orthodoxy with respect to orthopraxis goes to the very heart of how doctrinal awareness and pastoral mission are related. His comments about the saints pointing the way to true reform and about the incontestable fruit of their missions confirm the irreplaceable role of spiritual renewal or conversion in relation to mission. His related cautions about an activist ecclesiology are in essence warnings about the danger of cutting pastoral mission off from doctrinal awareness and spiritual renewal.[3]

---

3. The reader desiring to consult actual texts of Ratzinger on these themes can find them in Ratzinger and Messori, *The Ratzinger Report*; Ratzinger, "Reform from the Beginning"; Ratzinger, "The New Questions That Arose in the Nineties: The Position of Faith and Theology Today" in Ratzinger, *Truth and Tolerance*, 115–37; Ratzinger,

At the same time, Ratzinger-Benedict XVI does not overreact to create a disequilibrium of another kind, by neglecting or diminishing the importance of pastoral mission and service. This is clear in his encyclical, *Deus caritas est* (*DCE*), which masterfully maintains the balance of the three dimensions in perfect alignment with the schema of *ES*. There is a clear emphasis on Christ-like service and the witness of agape that is essential to the Church's life. With its clarifying teaching on agape and eros, *DCE* contributes to a doctrinal formation or awareness of the Church's vocation that leads to a deeper understanding of what the Church prays when asking the Lord to bring her to the fullness of charity.[4] The theme of purification of concepts[5] and the clarification of the nature of Christian love set forth the doctrinal foundation for the mission of mercy. The four times that *DCE* mentions the Good Samaritan[6] may even be a subtle indication of a conscious desire on the part of Benedict XVI to connect his first encyclical with the renewal of Vatican II, since in his closing speech at the Council Pope Paul VI stated that the spirituality of Vatican II is that of the Good Samaritan.[7] Finally, the encyclical insists that the Church is

---

Principles of Catholic Theology, 367–93. More recently, as Pope, he has reiterated these themes. For example, addressing the Church's response to the "absence of God from our society," he warns against "the pressure of secularization" that would lead to "becom[ing] modern by diluting the faith," and continues: "Of course, the faith has to be thought out and especially lived out today in a way which is new, in order to become something which belongs to the present. But it is not the dilution of the faith which helps us here, but only living the faith fully in our world of today. . . . Tactical changes will not save us, will not save Christianity, but only a faith which is thought out and lived out anew, by means of which Christ and with him the living God may enter into this world of ours" ("Address, September 23, 2011"). On another occasion, he addressed the question of reform that is needed to remedy stagnation in Church attendance and priestly vocations, and the increase of skepticism and unbelief. While "many things need to be done," he said, "doing on its own does not solve the problem. The core of the crisis of the Church in Europe is the crisis of faith. If we do not find a response to that problem, if faith is not re-vitalized to the point where it becomes a matter of profound conviction and a real source of strength thanks to the encounter with Jesus Christ, all the other reforms will remain ineffective" ("Address, December 22, 2011").

4. "Remember, Lord, your Church, spread throughout the world, and bring her to the fullness of charity, together with N. our Pope and N. our Bishop and all the clergy" (Eucharistic Prayer II).

5. See Benedict XVI, *DCE*, 4, 5, 6, 8, 10, 17, 28, 29. Related to this are the themes of healing (*DCE*, 5, 9, and 31), and liberation (*DCE*, 6 and 31).

6. See Benedict XVI, *DCE*, 15, 25, 31 (twice).

7. "We prefer to point out how charity has been the principal religious feature of this council. Now, no one can reprove as want of religion or infidelity to the Gospel

not just one institution of social service among others, but that its acts in behalf of the poor are rooted in Christian charity, so that participation in God's own love, which comes through conversion,[8] (spiritual renewal), is the presupposition of the Church's mission (dialogical service).[9]

---

such a basic orientation, when we recall that it is Christ himself who taught us that love for our brothers is the distinctive mark of his disciples (cf. John 13:35); when we listen to the words of the apostle: 'If he is to offer service pure and unblemished in the sight of God, who is our Father, he must take care of orphans and widows in their need, and keep himself untainted by the world' (Jas 1:27) and again: 'He has seen his brother, and has no love for him; what love can he have for the God he has never seen?' (1 John 4:20).''

"The old story of the Samaritan has been the model of the spirituality of the council. A feeling of boundless sympathy has permeated the whole of it. The attention of our council has been absorbed by the discovery of human needs."

"The Church has, so to say, declared herself the servant of humanity" (Paul VI, "Address, December 7, 1965").

8. *DCE* does not employ the vocabulary of "conversion," but conveys the same reality by the vocabulary of "transformation" (see *DCE*, 19, 39, 40) and "renewal" (of man's love as a response to God's love) (*DCE*, 2, 18, 42).

9. Among the numerous remarks throughout Ratzinger's theological work that underscore the presupposition of holiness as the font of mission and pastoral action, the following are representative. After quoting Eph 5:2, that Christ loved and gave himself up for us all, he quotes St. Paul in Gal 2:20, where the apostle applies this most personally to himself: "The Son of God . . . loved me and have himself [up] for me." Ratzinger comments: "Each one of us can and may apply to himself the dramatic personalization that Paul accomplishes in these words. Every man may say: The Son of God love *me* and have himself up for *me*. Only with this statement does Christological catechesis become gospel in the full sense of the word. We are not an indistinct mass before God. Christ does not and did not treat us as such. In all truth, Christ walked his path for me. This certainty is a grace given to accompany me in all the stages of my life, in my successes and failures, in my hopes and my suffering. He did all that he did for me and for every man who crosses my path in life: Jesus loved him, too, and gave himself up for him, just as he loved and loves me still. When we have learned to believe this again, when we are able to announce it to others as the message of truth, evangelization takes place. Then we know that the kingdom of God is near. And this knowledge gives us the strength to live and act out of this nearness" (Ratzinger, *Gospel, Catechesis, Catechism*, 71). Authentic catechesis and evangelization cannot be reduced to passing on a formulaic truth about God and his love. That would be to leave behind the second part of Gal 2:20. Authentic catechesis and evangelization certainly do communicate this general truth about God, but in addition they require that the catechist and evangelist have been transformed by this love. In terms of the three dimensions of renewal, this means that one cannot pass immediately from doctrinal awareness to catechesis and evangelization. The intermediate step is personal appropriation of the doctrine through personal conversion. In light of this, Ratzinger's comments can be seen to confirm what the *GCD* (1971) and the *GDC* (1997) say about the role of witness in catechesis, and what they say about witness can be seen as confirming the place

Returning now to *ES*, answers to questions about the ways in which the three dimensions of renewal are related have serious consequences for the way we understand the Church. The reason is that these answers depend upon the way the Church is understood (doctrine). Here, two remarks are in order. The first is to recall the teaching of St. Thomas Aquinas on the mixed life, contemplative and active, as that which most perfectly reflects the life of Christ.[10] Contemplation and active service, truth and active love, are not and cannot be opposed. Second, when ministry, apostolate, and service are treated primarily as a programmatic implementation of strategies, methods, and techniques for efficiency in mission, without sufficient regard for doctrinal and spiritual formation, one can legitimately ask whether there is anything distinctively Christian about the Church's pastoral activity. Pastoral prudence, which gives final, concrete guidance to pastoral actions, reasons from principles of faith (imparted through doctrinal formation) that precede and give direction to naturally known principles that may be taken from human sciences. This pastoral-prudential reasoning is at the service of pastoral charity, and thus presupposes it. Pastoral prudence (or pastoral theology) goes beyond doctrine (or doctrinal theology) in the way that prudence goes beyond universal moral principles. The concern of pastoral prudence is to fulfill the mission received from God in concrete acts of love of neighbor. The ultimate goal of all pastoral activity is to communicate to others a participation in saving truth through faith, or to foster growth in this participation. This is a supernatural task that requires the proportionate supernatural motive of charity, which in turn presupposes the doctrine known by faith.[11]

To return to Colombo's remarks on *ES*, we must reflect on an implication of the axiom, that which is last in execution is first in intention. This would appear to bestow on dialogue and the related mission and service of the Church, not just any kind of priority, but that of the end, the all-embracing goal. Confirmation of this as an accurate reading of the thought of Pope Paul is supported by Colombo's own review of the archival evidence of notes and drafts of *ES*. These provided him with

---

of spiritual formation as a bridge between doctrinal formation and pastoral formation.

10. See Aquinas, *ST*, II-II, qq. 179–82.

11. Benedict XVI devotes an important paragraph of *DCE* to identify what is specific to Christian acts of love for the poor. To be effective, this love requires certain human competencies that Christians will have in common with others who are also serving the poor. See chapter 5, n22 above.

the information to conclude that from the beginning Pope Paul's main focus was on dialogue, since an early draft of the encyclical contained only a treatment of that theme. At a certain point, Colombo remarks, "Pope Paul realized that the treatment of the theme required the development of the inseparable presuppositions, precisely the consciousness and the renewal of the Church."[12] There is no difficulty in acknowledging the primacy of dialogical mission, so long as one keeps in mind the distinction between the practical and speculative orders and how they are related. The practical order cannot be separated from the ontological order, which governs the practical order and is presupposed by it. The practical order of love calls for the virtue of prudence to deliberate about means, and the practical truth of these means derives from their relation to ends that are objective because rooted in human nature and human fulfillment in communion with God. The truth about this is supplied by faith in what God has revealed about man and his plan of love for man (doctrinal awareness).

We can conclude, then, that the "rigorous and logical succession" regarding the three paths of renewal set forth in ES developed as a result of Pope Paul's realization that dialogue cannot be isolated from the spiritual renewal and the doctrinal consciousness upon which it depends. Being the intended goal, dialogue cannot be attained except as a fruit of consciousness and renewal. Here we have an initial and fundamental guiding principle for the renewal undertaken by Vatican II, for all programs of formation, and for pastoral theology: pastoral action flows naturally out of spiritual renewal and the doctrinal awareness upon which renewal depends. If the pastoral mission of dialogical service is inadequate, this can only mean that something is defective in doctrinal and spiritual formation. Pastoral action of service stands in relation to doctrinal and spiritual formation as good works stand to faith: "Faith apart from works is dead" (Jas 2:26). *Pastoral action is doctrine and spiritual life in action of service to others.* To cut pastoral formation off from doctrinal and spiritual formation is to deprive it of its objective content (doctrine) and soul (spirituality). At the same time, we have seen that Pope Paul's presentation in ES showed that doctrinal awareness leads logically to and is completed in a way by spiritual renewal. Similarly, renewal leads to and is completed by dialogue.

---

12. Colombo, "Genesi," 136–37.

However the relations among these three is understood, it seems that reducing doctrinal formation and spiritual formation to being means to the end of pastoral activity does not correspond to the thought of Pope Paul. If doctrinal awareness and renewal through conversion are not means to the end of dialogue, what precisely is their relation to dialogue?

Certainly it would be helpful for all who are involved in establishing and implementing programs of formation if we could expand our understanding of these relationships. While recognizing that the following considerations are not taken from Pope Paul himself or recognized authorities on his teaching, they can be offered to shed further light on the fundamental structure of *ES*. The goal is to explain the order of *ES*. This requires vigilance to avoid imposing upon this datum to be explained a preconceived pattern or principle that would in any way contort Pope Paul's message. Since Pope Paul wrote from within the Catholic Tradition, and indeed from within that period of heightened awareness of that Tradition at the time of Vatican II, the most solid hope for further light will come from principles found in that same Tradition.

IN LIGHT OF ANTHROPOLOGICAL TRUTHS

The correlation of three fundamental truths about the human person to the three dimensions of renewal and formation shows that there is nothing at all accidental about the progression from awareness to renewal to dialogue. The anthropological principles that underpin *ES* are treated first because they are most fundamental, and for this reason they account for the other considerations that shed some light on the relations among the three dimensions of formation.

All that God accomplishes in the economy of salvation is motivated by his love for man and is guided by his wisdom. A variety of phrases combine these two attributes of divine love and wisdom. For example, Vatican II employs "goodness and wisdom"[13] and the *CCC* speaks of God's

---

13. God's love (or goodness) and wisdom are the absolute starting point for all of divine revelation. This is why all reflection on faith must be labeled "theology," that is, discourse about God. It is understandable, then, why after their respective introductions, both *Lumen gentium* and *Dei Verbum* begin by referring to God's love and wisdom: "The eternal Father, by a free and hidden plan of his own wisdom and goodness, created the whole world" (*LG*, 2). "In his goodness and wisdom God chose to reveal himself and to make known to us the hidden purpose of his will" (*DV*, 2).

"plan of loving goodness" and "plan of loving kindness."[14] "Logic of love" is especially frequent in John Paul II and Cardinal Ratzinger. Because he loves us, God desires to give what is good, especially the goodness of participation in his own life. Because he is wise, he takes all things related to the communication of his life into account. He loves us according to a plan, which creates a discernible order in divine revelation, and this is called the economy of salvation. The wisdom that guides it is the divine pedagogy, by which God condescends to speak to man in a manner that is intelligible to him.[15] By the logic of love God adapts or accommodates his interactions with man, knowing that his love must be received knowingly and freely. The divine pedagogy operates according to the axiom, that which is received is received according to the mode of the receiver.[16]

The three dimensions of renewal and formation take their place in this divine pedagogy or plan of love. The sequence begins with theological or doctrinal formation because of the place of knowledge in every free human act, whether it be an act of receiving God's gifts or one that puts those gifts into action. Throughout the entire process of formation, renewal, and active participation in Christ's mission, God desires our free cooperation, and knowledge is the condition for this. God first calls, makes known his will, and invites us to respond. In this light, the

14. *CCC*, 50, 51, 2617, 2807.

15. See Vatican II, *DV*, 13 and 15.

16. No doubt *The Book of Pastoral Rule* of St. Gregory the Great is the outstanding patristic development of this principle. Book III develops the myriad ways of adaptation or accommodation of the pastor's ministry to the mode of reception of those he serves. St. Gregory acknowledges that he took the principle, "one and the same exhortation does not suit all," from St. Gregory Nazianzen. In Gregory's own words: "according to the quality of the hearers ought the discourse of teachers to be fashioned, so as to suit all and each for their several needs, and yet never deviate from the art of common edification" (*Pastoral Rule*, III, Prologue). This does not lead Gregory to lose sight of the essential unity of the Church. Conscious of the Church's catholic unity, Gregory asserts the uniqueness of each individual without detriment to what he calls the "common edification." This respect for the diversity-in-unity that constitutes the Catholic Church is expressed as follows: "Every teacher, in order to edify all in the one virtue of charity, must touch the hearts of his hearers by using one and the same doctrine, but not by giving to all one and the same exhortation" (*Pastoral Rule*, III, Prologue). This can be understood as a continuation in the Church of St. Paul's guiding principle: "I have become all things to all men, that I might by all means save some" (1 Cor 9:22). St. Thomas often made use of the principle. See Aquinas, *Commentary on Aristotle's "De Anima"* (Marietti, 377); *ST*, I, q. 84, a. 1; I, q. 89, a. 4; II-II, q. 172, a. 3 obj. 1; III, q. 11, a. 5; q. 62, a. 4, obj. 1; Suppl. q. 52, a. 4; q. 70, a. 3, obj. 4; q. 85, a. 1; q. 92, aa. 1, 2.

renewal of Vatican II and ongoing formation reproduce the structure of evangelization and initiation. Just as the Church's missionaries's first contact with people is by way of witness of life and words, which makes known the Gospel of Jesus Christ and constitutes an appeal to their free will, so ongoing doctrinal formation is a kind of re-evangelization, a fresh proposal of the saving truth of the Gospel as it comes to us in Scripture and through Tradition. The difference between the first evangelization and the evangelization that takes place in ongoing formation is that the latter presupposes the fundamental entrustment of oneself to God that is the foundation for adherence to what he reveals.[17] The dynamic of conversion that typifies authentic catechesis is operative in all authentic doctrinal formation.[18]

This is the occasion to remark that doctrinal formation is not a means to the end of renewal or dialogue. It is, rather, an end in itself, a good to be pursued for its own sake and not merely for the sake of something else. Doctrinal formation is a deepening of communion with God in the truth known by faith. Out of love for him, a person of faith should desire more fully to know God and his plan of love. In reality, "it is intrinsic to faith that a believer desires to know better the One in whom he has put his faith, and to understand better what he has revealed; a more penetrating knowledge will in turn call forth a greater faith, increasingly set afire by love."[19] The initial gift of faith is a grace, but it is the pledge of future graces aimed at deepening the initial understanding of faith.[20]

This doctrinal penetration or enrichment of faith is a participation in the mystery of the Church, in which there is growth or development in understanding divine revelation. The faithful prayerfully reflect upon and study what God has revealed, forging a synthesis between faith and life. In this they are aided by the preaching of the apostles's successors and their collaborators.[21] At Vatican II, perhaps more than at any other ecumeni-

17. "'The obedience of faith' (Rom 13:26; see 1:5; 2 Cor 10:5–6) is to be given to God who reveals, an obedience by which man commits his whole self freely to God, offering 'the full submission of intellect and will to God who reveals' (*Dei Filius*, Ch. 3), and freely assenting to the truth revealed by him" (*DV*, 5).

18. On the dynamic of conversion in catechesis, see *GDC*, 53–57.

19. *CCC*, 158.

20. "To bring about an ever deeper understanding of revelation the same Holy Spirit constantly brings faith to completion by his gifts" (*DV*, 5).

21. "This tradition which comes from the Apostles develops in the Church with the help of the Holy Spirit. For there is a growth in the understanding of the realities and the words which have been handed down. This happens through the contemplation

cal council, the Church was conscious of this process of development in the understanding of the apostolic deposit of faith.²² It is understandable, then, that a fruit of the Council should be the kind of consistent emphasis on doctrinal formation as the first element of formation, which leads to a full, conscious, and active participation in the Church's life and mission.

The passage from awareness (doctrinal formation) to renewal (spiritual formation) through conversion is based on the Gospel principle that from whom much is given, much will be required (see Luke 12:48).²³ Man naturally experiences an internal sense of responsibility once he perceives the connection between what he knows and what he considers doing. Such connections register in the conscience, and its judgments lead to efforts to conform action to truth. If we focus on the message of God's love in Christ, the passage from doctrinal formation to spiritual formation is the movement from learning about God's love revealed in Christ to encountering that love, especially but not exclusively in the

---

and study made by believers, who treasure these things in their hearts (see Lk 2:19, 51) through a penetrating understanding of the spiritual realities which they experience, and through the preaching of those who have received through episcopal succession the sure gift of truth. For as the centuries succeed one another, the Church constantly moves forward toward the fullness of divine truth until the words of God reach their complete fulfillment in her" (*DV*, 8).

22. Fr. John Courtney Murray, SJ, perceived that "the issue of development of doctrine ... is the issue underlying all issues at the Council" (Murray, "This Matter of Religious Freedom," 43). Elsewhere he wrote: "The problem of the development of doctrine was in reality the fundamental problem underlying all the other problems treated by the Council. The Council itself showed, perhaps as never before in history, that the Church itself does not accept the error of archaism, which consists in the desire to halt the Church's growth in her understanding at any level of evolution—scriptural, patristic, medieval, modern, contemporary—and to refuse the possibility of new growth. No other conciliar text challenges this error as directly as *Dignitatis humanae*. No doubt this is the reason why it encountered so much opposition. This is certainly also its ultimate theological significance. And perhaps in this significance one finds implicitly contained the significance of the entire Council, which bears witness in multiple ways to the growth of the Church: growth in its historical consciousness, in its human consciousness of human dignity, in its ecumenical consciousness of its ministry of reconciliation, and above all in its evangelical consciousness that the Church has of herself and of the word that was entrusted to her by God—a word that is not only the 'word of truth' (Jas 1:18), but also and identically the word of freedom" ("Vers une intelligence du développement de la doctrine de l'Église sur la liberté religieuse," in Hamer and Congar, *Vatican II*, 147).

23. Vatican II, *LG*, 14 refers to the text of Luke 12:48 to support the assertion that awareness of belonging to the Church is a gift of grace that entails a serious responsibility and should be the occasion for humility (rather than a spirit of triumphalism).

sacraments. The truth that God is love is complemented by the truth that his love is offered in and through the Church's teaching, worship, and life. To assent to the truth that God loves all men entails that he loves me and that he invites me to receive that love through the Church. The truth that Christ is the model of human perfection in love entails that he is the norm for my use of freedom. All the efforts to conform one's life to the truth known by faith fall under the heading of renewal through conversion. Since conversion requires cooperation with God's grace, this includes guidance about how to dispose oneself to be receptive to God's love as it comes to us through the sources of grace (Scripture, liturgy, prayer, penance, evangelical counsels, fidelity to the duties of one's vocation, charisms). Spiritual formation is the instruction and guidance given for the sake of fully responding to God's approach of love.

The following movement, from renewal to dialogical mission and service, is based on the principle that action follows upon being (*operatio sequitur esse*). It is basically the argument that underpins St. Paul's moral exhortations. By baptism those to whom he writes have died to their old, sinful way of life and have risen to new life in Christ. Now that they are incorporated into Christ and are God's adopted children, they should act accordingly. The spiritual renewal of conversion brings about greater conformity to Christ, so that the life of Christ in the faithful (see Gal 2:20; *CCC*, 521) becomes an internal principle of action. As Vatican II taught, the Church is a sacrament through which Christ continues his mission as Prophet, Priest, and King. Christ the Servant, the Good Samaritan, and the Physician continues to exercise his merciful love in behalf of all those in need, and he does this through those whose hearts are conformed to his, having become participants in his paschal charity.[24] As Jesus was led by the Holy Spirit (see Luke 4:1), so those who are responsive to the Spirit's promptings are best able to realize in their own lives the mystery of the Church and discern the signs of the times in order to fulfill the Father's will of mercy toward all in need of being loved.

Another biblical text that sheds light on the progression from awareness to renewal to dialogue or mission comes to mind as a person envisions the actions of reaching out to others in service and dialogue. Having come to a greater awareness of the Church's vocation and mission, and of one's personal vocation and the specific form of service to which one is called, a person may immediately think of engaging in those

---

24. Paschal charity is the soul of the apostolate. See Vatican II, *LG*, 33; *AA*, 3.

actions corresponding to this awareness. Yet, when it comes to serving others, Jesus advises: "Why do you see the speck that is in your brother's eye, but do not notice the log that is in your own eye? Or how can you say to your brother, 'Brother, let me take out the speck that is in your eye,' when you yourself do not see the log that is in your own eye? You hypocrite, first take the log out of your own eye, and then you will see clearly to take out the speck that is in your brother's eye" (Luke 6:41–42). Most importantly, by going through the process of renewal through conversion, a person learns the ways of God's grace and patience, and becomes humble. How can a person play a role in the apostolate of accompaniment without these dispositions, which cannot be acquired by study alone, but only by the experience of being accompanied by the Lord himself?

In a complementary way, the movement from doctrinal formation to spiritual formation, and then from spiritual formation to pastoral formation, can be understood in terms of the dynamics and metaphysics of love. Because it is impossible to love something one does not know, various forms of the ministry of the word (evangelization, catechesis, theology, doctrinal formation) must precede spiritual formation. Spiritual formation aims at the perfection of charity, and charity presupposes faith precisely because the object of the will is the good *as known*.[25] For the movement from spiritual formation (or renewal through conversion) to pastoral formation (or dialogue), it suffices to recall Pope Paul's incisive assertion, "the internal drive of charity . . . seeks expression in the external gift of charity."[26] Put another way, the love of neighbor that gives rise to mission presupposes the love of self and love of God that are the catalyst for spiritual renewal: "You shall love the Lord your God with all your heart, and with all your soul, and with all your mind. This is the great and first commandment. And a second is like it, You shall love your neighbor as yourself" (Matt 22:37–39). The good that one clings to out of self-love becomes the norm of authentic love for others. The Golden Rule possesses a missionary dynamism.

25. Thomas Aquinas teaches: "The will follows the apprehension of the reason or intellect" (*ST*, I-II, q. 19, a. 10); "Since the object of the will is the apprehended good, we must judge of the object of the will according as it is apprehended" (*ST*, I-II, q. 13, a. 5, ad. 2); "Things that are in the intellect are the principles of those which are in the appetite, in so far as the apprehended good moves the appetite" (*ST*, II-II, q. 7, a. 2, ad. 1). Accordingly, Mary must first apprehend by faith the good she is being offered—to be the Lord's unique associate in the fulfillment of his plan of love—before she can consent to receiving the grace that makes this possible.

26. Paul VI, *ES*, 64.

Pastoral formation, which envisions effective ministry, apostolate, and service, is in essence a formation for communicating the good of divine life to others. Just as charisms are subordinate to charity and their exercise is motivated by charity, so pastoral formation is subordinate to spiritual formation, the latter being the soul of all mission, service, and dialogue. In fact, pastoral formation may be understood as instruction and training for the effective exercise of charisms.[27] Since charisms are directed to the good of others for the sake of building up the Church, they presuppose love of God and love of self, which logically precede love of neighbor, and thus they presuppose spiritual formation.[28]

Pastoral formation is nearly always listed after doctrinal or theological formation and spiritual formation. The reason is that of the three dimensions of formation, it alone is a means. Pastoral formation is concerned with practical matters related to efficacious pastoral action. Ecclesiologically, it is a formation directed to the effective exercise of charisms for the sake of building up the Church. As gratuitous graces, charisms render those who exercise them proportionate to the end of a successful communication of grace to others. In the theology of St. Thomas Aquinas, charisms are instruments through which God works to build up the Church.[29]

St. Paul's teaching on charisms and charity emphasizes that charity has a primacy over charisms. But it does not suggest that charity can exist without charisms. That would leave a person with charity in a state

---

27. The ecclesiology of Vatican II includes a latent theology of charisms. See Albert Vanhoye, "The Biblical Question of 'Charisms' after Vatican II," in Latourelle, *Vatican II*, 439–68; Schurmann, "Les Charismes Spirituels." A charism is a gift of God for the sake of serving others in order to build up the Body of Christ. "Every 'living' Christian has a specific task (and in this sense a 'charism') 'for the building up of the body of Christ'" (Congregation for the Doctrine of Faith, "Letter to Bishops," 25). Charisms, then, are defined in terms of personal vocation inasmuch as they concern one's function in the Body of Christ. Thus, pastoral formation is at the service of directing the exercise of charisms. While general principles derived from doctrine and spirituality apply to all, specific pastoral elements pertain to each function within the Church. For example, the exercise of the charism of the word in preaching for deacons, priests, and laity; the charism of living the evangelical counsels for the consecrated; the charisms of parenting and of work for the laity.

28. It is not possible to develop the dynamic of love further here. The metaphysical foundations for the movement from love of self to love of God to love of neighbor, developing the thought of St. Thomas Aquinas, are set forth in Nicolas, "Amour de soi," 5–42.

29. See Aquinas, *ST*, II-II, q. 173, a. 4; q. 177. a. 1; q. 177, a. 1, ad. 1; q. 178, a. 1.

of frustration, desiring the supernatural good for others but lacking the ability, the power, actually to impart that supernatural good.

Charisms and thus pastoral action presuppose a mature love of neighbor. This love is on the order of the end, for charity is participation in God's own life of love. For this reason, spiritual formation pertains to the end. Similarly, doctrinal formation pertains to the end, since its goal is a deeper penetration into revealed truth. This is a perfection of the theological virtue of faith, which is clearly an end because it is participation in God's own truth.

Truth and Love

An insight of St. Thomas Aquinas regarding the relation between the interior mystery of the Trinitarian processions and the economic mystery of the missions of the Son and Holy Spirit sheds additional light on our subject. It provides a Trinitarian foundation for the anthropological foundation just discussed.

> The Son is the Word, not any sort of word, but one who breathes forth Love. Hence Augustine says (*De Trin* IX, 10): "The Word we speak of is knowledge with love." Thus the Son is sent not in accordance with every and any kind of intellectual perfection, but according to the intellectual illumination, which breaks forth into the affection of love, as is said (John 6:45): "Everyone that has heard from the Father and has learned, comes to Me," and (Ps 39:3): "In my meditation a fire shall flame forth." Thus Augustine plainly says (*De Trin* IV, 20): "The Son is sent, whenever he is known and perceived by anyone." Now perception implies a certain experimental knowledge, and this is properly called wisdom (*sapientia*), as it were, a sweet knowledge (*sapida scientia*).[30]

As the interior mystery of the Trinity is not complete with the first procession of the Word, but only with the procession of the Holy Spirit, so the revelation of God is not complete with the mission of the Word. The mission of the Holy Spirit fittingly complements the mission of the Word. For St. Thomas, both of these missions are rooted in the spiritual nature of God, that is, divine intellect and will, as well as the order between them, such that the procession and mission of the Word fittingly precedes

---

30. Aquinas, *ST*, I, q. 43, a. 5, ad. 2.

the procession and mission of the Holy Spirit because "nothing can be loved by the will unless it is conceived in the intellect."[31] Because we are made in God's image, we are by nature made for a synthesis of truth and love.[32] This is raised to a supernatural level by God's grace, which imparts a participation in the Trinitarian life of the processions, relations, and missions. To elucidate the thought of St. Thomas on the precise nature of the mission of the Son as entailing love, Fr. H.-F. Dondaine, OP, invokes the distinction between speculative and experiential knowledge. "Experiential" is used here in place of the usual translation of "experimental" in order to avoid confusion that could result from the common understanding of "experimental" as relating to scientific experiments or some untested product or procedure (e.g., an experimental prototype).

Before reproducing Dondaine's comments, it is important to clarify this distinction between speculative and experiential knowledge. St. Thomas draws on this distinction in his comments on Jesus's words to the Jews: "But you have not known him; I know him" (John 8:55). Thomas is attentive to the fact that the Jews prided themselves on possessing knowledge of the true God. He quotes Psalm 76:1 and Psalm 147:20 to alert the reader to the fact that he is aware that Jesus's words might seem to contradict something that is divinely revealed. In order to safeguard the authority of the Old Testament, he affirms that the Jews with whom Jesus was contesting possessed knowledge of God, but of a certain, defective kind. He holds that they "have not known him *with affection.*" The sign of this lack of affection is the failure to keep God's commandments. On this point, St. Thomas quotes the Letter to Titus: "They profess to know God; but they deny him by their deeds" (Tit 1:16).[33]

In contrast, Jesus knows the Father both with speculative knowledge and with affective knowledge, and the sign of the latter is that he keeps the Father's word.[34] Acting on what one knows of God is an indication of a union of wills. For, the motive for any act is to obtain some good, in

---

31. See Aquinas, *ST*, I, q. 27, a. 3, ad. 3.

32. What can be known is either practical or speculative. Both engender love, in different ways. Practical truth presupposes the end that is willed, and its goodness derives from the perception of its relation to the realization of the willed end. Speculative truth is sought for its own sake. Because it is a common good, it is not possessed qua common unless it is willed for others.

33. Aquinas, *Commentary on the Gospel of John*, Ch. 8, Lect. 8 (Marietti 1282); emphasis added.

34. Aquinas, *Commentary on the Gospel of John*, Ch. 8, Lect. 8 (Marietti 1286).

this case, the good of the fulfillment of the Father's will. Therefore, action speaks more loudly about what a person values, that is, holds as true concerning his good, than a merely notional, verbal declaration. This is why

> in human actions examples have a greater influence than words. This is because a person does and chooses what appears as good to that person. Thus, the actual choice of something manifests its goodness or value to a person even more than what that person teaches should be chosen. This explains why when someone says one thing and does another, what he does has a greater influence on others than what he teaches. Therefore, it is of the greatest necessity to give an example.[35]

For St. Thomas, it is possible to possess faith without charity. "For faith is a knowledge of the word of God ... which word is not perfectly possessed or perfectly known unless the love which it hopes for is possessed."[36] Faith is dead and cannot produce good works (Jas 2:17, 20, 26) when it is not informed by charity, by which a person loves himself as God loves him.[37] We can say that faith that is not brought to perfection by charity holds to knowledge about God, but it does not result in knowing God in the biblical sense of experiencing his goodness.[38]

With the preceding as background, the commentary of Fr. Dondaine can now be reproduced:

> St. Thomas distinguishes and opposes *experiential* knowledge and *speculative* knowledge. To know by simple speculative knowledge that the Son is born of the Father (as the catechism or theology makes known to us) does not suffice for a mission of the Son. It is necessary to have a knowledge of this Person that is "in a certain way experiential" (I Sent., d. 15, *exp. textus*),

---

35. Aquinas, *Commentary on the Gospel of John*, Ch. 13, Lect. 3 (Marietti 1781). This reminds one of the famous words of St. Francis of Assisi: "Let us preach always, and [only] when necessary, let us use words."

36. Aquinas, *Commentary on St. Paul's Letter to the Galatians*, Ch. 5, Lect. 2 (Marietti 286).

37. Aquinas, *ST*, II-II, q. 178, a. 2, ad. 2. See also, *Commentary on the Gospel of John*, Ch. 4, Lect. 2 (Marietti 577); Ch. 5, Lect. 5 (Marietti 793); *Commentary on St. Paul's Letter to the Romans*, Ch. 1, Lect. 15 (Marietti 302); Ch. 8, Lect. 2 (Marietti 1162).

38. On the experiential nature of the biblical notion of knowing, see Vanhoye and Corbon, "Connaître," 199. The same emphasis on experience appears in the related entries found in Hartman, *Encyclopedic Dictionary of the Bible*, 1290, and in Bauer, *Encyclopedia of Biblical Theology*, 474.

that is, a knowledge the medium of which is not an idea that is transmitted but *something lived by the subject*, a gift of grace received in the soul and representing the Person. What, then? It is a practical valuation [Fr.: appréciation] of the Goodness of God, God efficaciously tasted as good, in himself and *for me*, as *the Good that I love and to which I order my entire life* (I Sent., d. 15, q. 4, a. 1, ad. 3; a. 2, ad. 4). Briefly, "a knowledge of God such that love proceeds from it suffices to verify a mission of the Son ... any love of charity suffices for a mission of the Holy Spirit" (I Sent., d. 15, q. 5, a. 1, qa. 2). The least act of living faith, that is, faith working in charity, corresponds to this description.[39]

Something is lived by the subject because it is perceived as the promise of personal enrichment, as the fulfillment of the acting subject's love of self. Throughout the Bible, faith in God is faith in what he has done *for* his people. This means that God's acts of love correspond to his people's self-love, the way a shepherd's solicitude and corresponding acts of protecting his flock and guiding them to verdant pastures and water are good for his sheep.[40]

This provides an anthropological insight into the prophet's denunciation of Israel for forgetting the Lord.[41] The great sign of having forgotten the Lord is that the people no longer observe the Lord's precepts. Such a failure, such disobedience, can only mean that they have lost sight of the value of these precepts, that they no longer perceive them as good for them. And this can only be explained by the fact that the precepts of the Lord have become disconnected from his mighty works of liberation. Once settled in the land of milk and honey, Israel is tempted to take freedom and the bounty of the land for granted, forgetting that it is a gift of God's mercy, that were it not for his intervention, they would still be slaves in Egypt. Thus, for Israel, the key to keeping the laws set down by Moses is to recall that they were once slaves in Egypt (Deut 16:12; see Deut 26:6–10). In other words, the key is to call to mind that the precepts of the Lord are inseparable from his merciful love and thus inseparable from Israel's own self-love.[42] This is why the disobedience of sin is always

---

39. Dondaine, *Saint Thomas d'Aquin*, 377; emphasis added.

40. On the biblical theology of the theme of God as shepherd and his people his flock, see the article by Lesquivit and Léon-Dufour, "Pasteur et Troupeau," and Guillet's "La typologie de l'Exode dans l'ancien et nouveau Testament."

41. See Jer 2:32; see also Jer 13:25; 18:15; Ezek 22:12; 23:35; Hos 13:6.

42. In this way, the people's sin of disobedience is in reality an act of self-destruction. For, the purpose of the law is to preserve the twofold freedom—from tyranny at

a suicidal act.[43] As the *CCC* explains, the commandments always come in the second place and must be understood in the context of God's liberating intervention.[44] Once they are disconnected from his liberating love, they lose their "for me" value.

Perhaps the movement from head to heart, from speculative knowledge about God to experiential knowledge of God, is equivalent to Cardinal Wojtyła's understanding of the relation of consciousness to attitudes.

> Man responds to God's self-revelation by offering himself wholly to him (cf. DV, 5). This response is the fruit of faith, and it is thus clear that the essence of faith consists of more than a purely intellectual assent to the truth revealed by God, or a kind of reflection of that truth in man's consciousness. "Self-abandonment to God" as a response to revelation bears witness also to the fact that faith expresses itself through man's attitude: this attitude belongs to the very essence of faith, since it corresponds to the full reality of revelation. This is not merely a fact or set of facts to be accepted by the mind: it is God's action in unfolding himself to man through Jesus Christ and becoming part of his life and destiny. We might say, weighing our words carefully, that revelation expresses an "attitude" on God's part towards man, and consequently the response to it must be expressed in man's attitude towards God.[45]

Wojtyła's understanding of self-consciousness and attitude are at the heart of his anthropology. For a truth to penetrate our self-consciousness means that it becomes an element of our identity, our self-definition. It means that it contributes to the elaboration of the very meaning of our

---

the hands of a foreign power, and from exploitation within the chosen people—that is first a pure gift resulting from God's mighty works. "The ten commandments, like the whole Law which is their commentary, have no other aim in view than to preserve Israel from a twofold slavery into which both ancient and modern civilizations have fallen and continue to fall. On one side there is an *exterior* slavery which would supplant the people's exclusive dependence on the Almighty. On the other side there is the whole master-slave relationship which would put each individual in danger of being no longer immediately dependent on the Almighty, since one or the other of his brothers would blot out that dependence by usurped authority" (Barthélemy, *God and His Image*, 62).

43. "As a rupture with God, sin is an act of disobedience by a creature who rejects, at least implicitly, the very one from whom he came and who sustains him in life. It is therefore a suicidal act" (John Paul II, *RP*, 15).

44. See *CCC*, 2056–63.

45. Wojtyła, *SR*, 204.

life. It follows from this that it cannot fail to produce a corresponding attitude, which Wojtyła defines as a readiness to act. And, as we have seen, at work in every act is the desire for self-fulfillment, that is, love of self.[46] The logic here is that of the relation of first act to second act, being to action. According to the principle, *operatio sequitur esse*, a being has no choice but to act in conformity to its being, its nature. Man's nature being rational, the being upon which he acts is conscious. Thus, man's functioning definition of happiness crystallizes his being and it is this being that manifests itself in action. Once man perceives a necessary relation between a potential action and his functioning definition of happiness, he experiences an interior necessity to perform that action. This is the judgment of conscience, in which the movement from is to ought is formulated, a movement from "this is who I am" to "this is what I must do based on who I am." In other words, the promptitude to act that constitutes the essence of attitude is rooted in the conviction that certain actions are good because they are realizations of one's self-consciousness, because they correspond to one's functioning definition of happiness.

Regarding the three dimensions of renewal and formation, the insight into the Trinitarian processions and missions has two applications. First, it provides the definitive foundation for the relation of truth (doctrinal penetration and formation) to love (spiritual conversion and formation), rooting that relation in the life of the Trinity. Because man is made in God's image, the precedence of truth in relation to love is a feature of his own being. Second, grace brings about a supernatural participation in Trinitarian life and thus also in the missions of the Son and the Holy Spirit. The same precedence of truth in relation to love that characterizes the divine missions is a constitutive feature of the Church's mission as well.

This second application is very important for those involved in mission, which is everyone. Many experience a kind of frustration regarding the limits of their efforts to draw others into the mystery of Christ. Catechists, parents, and pastors can find themselves wondering if they could not and should not do more. Dismayed by how long it often takes for the knowledge they impart to move, as they say, from the head to the heart, they sometimes assume that this delay is due to something lacking in

---

46. Wojtyła calls the acting subject the "primary and principal object" of human action and willing (*The Acting Person*, 150). What he means by this is that man cannot fail to love himself and thereby to seek his own fulfillment. Rocco Buttiglione has a helpful discussion of this in *Karol Wojtyła*, 142.

their parenting, catechizing, or preaching. They are certainly right to look for every possible way to promote this movement from head to heart, but they must recognize that this is ultimately a matter of grace and of God's regard for man's free will. Only God can act on the human will directly and assure that its dignity and freedom are not compromised.

The dismaying delay between the moment of imparting truth and the moment when it is fully internalized is a feature of Jesus's own mission. Since the Church's mission is a participation in his mission, it is to be expected that this should also be a feature of our efforts to evangelize. No greater an art of teaching can be imagined than that displayed by the eternal Word of God. Yet, rejection by the majority of the Jews, including the doctors of the Law, Peter's denial, the dispersion of the apostles when Jesus is arrested, and the mock trial conducted by the religious leaders indicate that even for him something more than teaching is required for people fully to internalize the message of God's love. That "something" is the encounter with his love, the experience of having been loved by him and thus enriched in one's being.[47] We see this vividly conveyed in the story of the Penitent Woman (Luke 7:36–50) and the healing of the blind man (John 9). In both cases, the one who is healed by Jesus's love comes to know his identity, while those for whom he is only a theological riddle do not discover who he is.

The universal act of love of Jesus is his priestly sacrifice. This is the act of love that addresses the universal need for forgiveness of sins. Because the gift of the Holy Spirit is the fruit of his sacrifice, this means that the remission of sins comes with the gift of the Holy Spirit. We see this clearly on Pentecost: "Repent, and be baptized every one of you in the name of Jesus Christ for the forgiveness of your sins; and you shall receive the gift of the Holy Spirit" (Acts 2:38). The mission of the Word prepares

---

47. For Benedict XVI, "knowing that one has been loved by God" is the very essence of faith ("Message for Lent, 2013"). "This is faith: being loved by God and letting oneself be loved by God in Jesus Christ" (Benedict XVI, "General Audience, February 16, 2011"). For Benedict, the key biblical text for this is 1 John 4:16: "we know and believe the love God has for us."

for[48] and causes[49] the mission of the Holy Spirit. Even for the Incarnate Word of God, the Sacred Scriptures witness to a kind of delay between the ministry of teaching and the full internalization of the content of that teaching, a delay between the act of love on Good Friday and the Gift of that very love on Pentecost. The liturgy of the Mass reflects this relationship, as it moves from the Liturgy of the Word to the Liturgy of the Eucharist.[50] Finally, this relation between the mission of the Word and the mission of the Holy Spirit points to the relation of the prophetic office to the priestly office, which is yet another important consideration regarding the relation between the first and second dimensions of renewal and formation.

The evangelists's passing observation that when Jesus was arrested Peter followed him "at a distance" (Matt 26:58; Mark 14:54; Luke 22:54) points to the fundamental explanation for the delay being discussed, namely, the process of conversion by which a disordered love of self is gradually overcome. The fact that Peter followed Jesus shows that he is attached to him, that there is genuine love for Jesus. That he followed at a distance shows that there is also a measure of love of self in Peter that has not yet been purified. His self-consciousness, his definition of happiness, and his love are not yet fully identified with following Jesus. Peter is "split within himself,"[51] torn between love of self to the point of contempt for God and love of God to the point of contempt for self (St. Augustine). This same split and tension between two loves is evident in the fear of the Jews that kept Peter and the apostles shut away in a room (John 20:19, 26). This was their state until they received the Gift, the Holy Spirit. With

---

48. It should be noted that the nature of this preparation is precisely the apostles's realization that they were unable to follow Jesus "now" (John 13:36), that is, prior to his death, resurrection, ascension, and sending of the Holy Spirit. In the divine pedagogy, the apostles experience the "gap" between speculative knowledge of Christ and the experiential knowledge that comes with the gift of the Holy Spirit. St. Paul also experienced this gap between knowledge of God's Law and performance (Rom 7), and the corresponding experiential love of God that comes with the gift of the Holy Spirit (Rom 8).

49. To demonstrate this causal relation is the thrust of St. Peter's discourse on Pentecost. See Acts 2:22–36.

50. The Liturgy of the Word confronts us (CCC, 2706) with the word of God to which we know from experience we cannot, on our own, conform ourselves. Thus, it invites us to enter into the profound humility of the apostles between the time of their denial and dispersion and the outpouring of the Holy Spirit on Pentecost.

51. Vatican II, GS, 13.

this Gift the interior split and tension caused by a disordered love of self is finally and definitively overcome.[52]

The problem of overcoming disordered love of self (sin) in order to forge a personal synthesis of truth and love is compounded by a culture that narrows the range of reason to the domain of scientifically verifiable phenomenon. This is a major theme of the reading of the signs of the times of Joseph Ratzinger/Benedict XVI. Vatican II was alert to it, as is clear in the distinction it makes between genuine human wisdom and science (without in any way diminishing the value of science).[53] Not all objects of knowledge should be expected to be of value for the human heart in the way that revelation of God's love in Christ and all that is related to it is. This is why a culture that is long on the quantification of the relationships that constitute the universe and on the technological utility of knowledge and short on the moral dimension of human reality places obstacles to the natural move from the first to the second dimension of renewal and formation.

As is to be expected, the primacy of what can be called impersonal activities of the mind[54] did not suddenly erupt. We know that volcanic eruptions and earthquakes are preceded by lesser seismic events that are precursors to them. So, too, for the Church. As an example, we can take the observation of a Trappist monk, more than a decade before Vatican II. Thomas Merton insightfully realized:

> The "problem of unbelief" in modern times is clearly not a problem of faithlessness but of irrationality . . . It is because men are not able to think for themselves that they are so often incapable either of belief or of unbelief . . . The first step in bringing men

---

52. The fear of "the circumcision party" that Peter exhibited in Antioch (Gal 2:12) is different in nature from the fear that he experienced prior to Pentecost. St. Thomas, following the Gloss, holds that Peter's fear is not merely human or worldly, but "a fear inspired by charity" (Aquinas, *Commentary on St. Paul's Epistle to the Galatians*, Ch. 2, Lect. 3 [Marietti 80]). Accordingly, Peter's love for the unity of the Church causes him to fear a potential threat to that unity.

53. See Vatican II, *GS*, 15.

54. There is no intention here to deny that science has great potential for serving the human person. There are many aspects of science and of scientific research that are ordered, either directly or indirectly, to improving the human condition. This is to be applauded. At the same time, it should be obvious that the human needs that can be met by science are such that they cannot meet man's most fundamental needs, to know how to live (moral dimension) and to be loved—and to be loved precisely when he encounters in himself the ground for his un-lovability when he sees that he has misused his freedom to reject the only Love that can fulfill his need for love.

to faith is taken on the level not of theology but of philosophy. It is not a matter of faith but of reason.[55]

The problems of unbelief and of irrationality are not without implications for understanding the pastoral magisterium of Vatican II. An astute participant in the Council weighed in on the fundamental question regarding the Council's authority and how its pastoral nature should be understood. He saw that there was a divide among the Council Fathers and that one of the points of division concerned the understanding of how the Magisterium should express itself. Some wanted to limit it to defining the intelligible content of divine revelation, while others desired to present that same saving truth in a manner that would be conducive to conveying not just its truth with precision, but also the relevance, significance, value, and meaning of that truth for a person's life. In other words, a pastoral magisterium sets forth revealed truth in a manner that is calculated to make it more likely that people will perceive its "for me" value, that is, how it corresponds to their love of self.

> This Council is pastoral in its fusion of truth and love, "doctrine" and pastoral solicitude; it wished to reach beyond the dichotomy between pragmatism and doctrinalism, back to the biblical unity in which practice and doctrine are one, a unity grounded in Christ.[56]

As Ratzinger would write years later, the theological questions regarding God's being presuppose the encounter with him through his acts of love for man. "Faith in an *actio Dei*," he declared, "is antecedent to all other declarations of faith."[57] The Scriptural foundations for the precedence of the *actio Dei* are too numerous to attempt to identify them all. In the Gospels, this is evident when Jesus's acts of forgiving sins give rise to the question about who he is (Luke 5:21; 7:49), and how he answers the Baptist's question about his identity by recounting the good works and signs he has performed (Matt 11:2–6; Luke 7:19–23). The various covenants that comprise Scripture as a whole, understood as a history of salvation, bear witness to the precedence of the *actio Dei*. Each covenant begins with a totally gratuitous initiative of God's love in behalf of his people, an initiative that results in a dramatic change in his people's

---

55. Merton, *The Ascent to Truth*, 36.
56. Ratzinger, "Announcements and Prefatory Notes of Explanation," in Vorgrimler, *Commentary on the Documents of Vatican II*, 1:299.
57. See Ratzinger, *Principles of Catholic Theology*, 185.

condition, so that they know that indeed they have been loved by God. Only after this liberating encounter does God fully reveal himself and make known the conditions for his people to remain living in the gift of his love. Presenting the evidence for and analyzing this structure of the covenants in depth being beyond the scope of the present study, we turn now to consider several biblical passages that illustrate the pattern of three dimensions that are involved in the encounter with God.

IN LIGHT OF SACRED SCRIPTURE

The precedence of the *actio Dei*, the anthropological principles described above, and the internal structure of the three paths and three dimensions of formation are confirmed in the faith of Mary at the Annunciation, in the encounter between Jesus and the Samaritan woman at the well, the account of Jesus meeting the disciples from Emmaus, and in the events surrounding Pentecost.[58]

Mary's Faith at the Annunciation

Just as Mary was recognized by the Fathers of Vatican II to be the type and exemplar of the Church and the model of all Christian virtue,[59] one might expect that she also would be seen as the model of the renewal undertaken by the Council. A chapter on Mary crowns the Council's central document, *LG*, while in *DV*, 8 she is implicitly referenced as a model of growth in understanding what God has revealed.[60] In *RMat*, John Paul II meditated on her faith as model of the Church's faith and set forth his

---

58. One aspect of the pastoral style of Vatican II is the effort to reunite the metaphysical and definitional distillations of the content of divine revelation with the historical, action, narrative dimension. More generally, the Council can be seen as a concerted effort to unite the allegorical (Christocentrically doctrinal) sense of Scripture with the moral sense, with the latter being understood in the most fundamental manner as a concern to show that what God has revealed is his answer to man's deepest aspirations and most vexing questions. For more on the Council's emphasis on the economy of salvation as a key to understanding its pastoral character, see Congar, *Le Concile de Vatican II*, 27, 64.

59. See Vatican II, *LG*, 53, 65.

60. "For there is a growth in the understanding of the realities and the words which have been handed down. This happens through the contemplation and study made by believers, who treasure these things in their hearts (see Lk 2:19, 51) through a penetrating understanding of the spiritual realities which they experience" (*DV*, 8).

teaching based on the description of faith in *DV*, 5, which, he said, is perfectly realized in her.[61]

Church documents that teach about Mary consistently use three words when discussing her faith—assent, consent, and obedience.[62] It can easily be demonstrated that these words correspond to the three paths of renewal and the three dimensions of formation. Thus, at the Annunciation Mary's faith exhibits the same fundamental movement from awareness, to renewal, to dialogical mission and service. The Annunciation begins with the Archangel Gabriel revealing God's plan to Mary, that the hope in his promises that had been kept alive for centuries and in which she lived is now to be definitively fulfilled in and through her.[63] The divine promises are ages old, but the way in which and the time at which they will be fulfilled are made known to Mary as a new revelation that can only be apprehended by faith. This newness of the message conveyed by Gabriel's words is reinforced by the Angel's abrupt and unexpected intervention. Suddenly, Mary comes to a new awareness of her faith, and this entails a new awareness of her vocation. A revelatory, doctrinal penetration occurs as her faith *assents* to the new and final things God is accomplishing. She is not just informed about God's plan, as if he wished merely to notify her of events that she would only observe. She is made aware of her place in that plan, how it depends on her, in a word, she is made aware of her vocation.[64] To all of this she gives the *assent* of faith,

---

61. "As the Council teaches, '"The obedience of faith" (Rom 16:26; cf. Rom 1:5; 2 Cor 10:5–6) must be given to God who reveals, an obedience by which man entrusts his whole self freely to God' (*DV*, 5). This description of faith found perfect realization in Mary" (John Paul II, *RMat*, 13).

62. Vatican II speaks only of the *consent* of Mary in chapter 8 of *LG*. The assent of faith is considered especially in *DV*, 5 (without any reference to Mary), while obedience is found in both. All three are found in John Paul II (especially in *RMat*), and in the *CCC*.

63. These two prepositional phrases, that the mystery of God's love is fulfilled *in* Mary and *through* Mary, is yet another confirmation of the movement from awareness to renewal to service and mission. Because Mary is free and the mystery is one of love, God begins by informing her of his plan. Mary is the first beneficiary of the Incarnation, the first to have faith in God's becoming man, the first to be in communion with him in faith, thus the plan of love of fulfilled in her. Then she is called to bring Christ into the world for the salvation of men, thereby becoming the unique associate in the realization of the Lord's plan of salvation in Christ.

64. That faith includes, besides assent to the truth about God and his plan that he has revealed, coming to an awareness of one's place in his plan, that is, one's vocation, is often repeated by John Paul II. In this he sees an important element of the renewal of Vatican II and its pastoral goal of overcoming the split between faith and life. "Man's

that is, she holds it as true because its origin is in God. As John Paul traces Mary's pilgrimage of faith, he uses two expressions to convey the essential continuity of the content of her faith: confirmation and new light. With every event following the Annunciation, what Mary assented to will be confirmed while at the same time she understands it more fully because new light is cast upon it.[65] Mary is the model of an ever-deepening understanding of the mystery of God and his plan of salvation. All of this corresponds to doctrinal penetration and doctrinal formation. Cardinal Wojtyła calls this the enrichment of faith in the objective sense, that is, with respect to the understanding of faith's content.[66]

---

proper response to God's self-revelation consists in self-abandonment to God. This is the true dimension of faith, in which man does not simply accept a particular set of propositions, but accepts his own vocation and the sense of his existence" (*SR*, 20). "In accepting this revelation men are not only confronted with a reality which is God in himself, but at the same time find that they have been led into the depth of this mysterious, supernatural reality and thus that their vocation is to be united with God" (*SR*, 55).

65. Already, at the Annunciation, the theme of confirmation and new light is present: "And when the Virgin, disturbed by that extraordinary greeting, asks: 'How shall this be, since I have no husband?' she receives from the angel the confirmation and explanation of the preceding words. Gabriel says to her: 'The Holy Spirit will come upon you, and the power of the Most High will overshadow you; therefore the child to be born will be called holy, the Son of God' (Luke 1:35)" (*RMat*, 9). In *RMat*, 16, John Paul sees the same pattern present in the Presentation. Simeon's words to Mary first "confirm the truth of the Annunciation," but they also "cast new light on the announcement which Mary had heard from the angel." At the Annunciation, Mary's question, "How shall this be?" is the bridge between a first assent and a doctrinal penetration to a deeper understanding. Though it remains implicit at the Presentation, this question accompanies her pilgrimage of faith and keeps her heart open to every confirmation and new light. The crucifixion of Jesus is the definitive confirmation of Simeon's prophetic words about Christ, while at the same time it answers the question of how precisely he will be a sign of contradiction (see *RMat*, 18). This pattern can be perceived in the Resurrection and the gift of the Holy Spirit on Pentecost, which confirm what Gabriel said about a kingdom without end, while shedding a definitive light on the nature of that kingdom. Once again, "How shall this be?" is the bridge. One can easily imagine Mary living in the most intense way the spirituality of "How shall this be?" while accompanying Jesus on the way of the Cross and witnessing his death. Believing in all that God had revealed through Gabriel, that all the promises made to Israel and the unending kingdom are to be fulfilled in Jesus, the definitive dark night of faith occurs when the King dies. "And now, standing at the foot of the Cross, Mary is the witness, humanly speaking, of the complete negation of these words [of Gabriel]" (*RMat*, 18). The Resurrection and Pentecost are God's answer to the "How shall this be?" of Mary's faith occasioned by Jesus's death.

66. See Wojtyła, *SR*, 18.

At the Annunciation the immediate effect of Gabriel's words is to make Mary acutely conscious of a disproportion between her current state and the vocation that has just been set before her. What God expects of her is beyond her, and so she asks: "How shall this be?" She knows that by herself she cannot bring to fulfillment what God is proposing. She is confronted by an apparent impossibility. And, apparently, Gabriel picks up on this and responds by saying, in effect, that she is not alone. God does not expect her to fulfill her vocation by herself. He wanted her to express her humility by confessing her powerlessness. God himself will supply for her need and bridge the gap between her place in God's plan, her vocation, and her lowliness, for "with God nothing will be impossible" (Luke 1:37). This removes the apparent contradiction, and in faith Mary is able to see that by the overshadowing of the Holy Spirit the plan can be accomplished. Only by God's grace can his word be fulfilled in and through her. Only by God's grace can she live up to the demands of and fulfill the mission entrusted to her. By faith Mary first embraces the vocation to which she had given her *assent* of faith as the truth and meaning-giving reality of her life. Now, in a second moment of faith, she *consents* to being renewed by grace by being overshadowed by the Holy Spirit in order to fulfill that vocation. Taking up a Patristic theme, Pope John Paul II puts it this way: Mary conceived the Word of God in her mind by faith (by the *assent* of faith) before conceiving him in her womb (by the *consent* of faith).[67]

God clearly desires Mary's cooperation, including her question, "How shall this be?" He desires, first, that she desire what he desires. For this to happen, he first makes known his plan and her place in it. For, as we have seen, man can only desire that which he knows. To the plan that God reveals Mary gives the *assent* of faith. As a result, she and God are one in this knowledge. Mary now knows and desires what is for her the next major stage in her pilgrimage of faith, namely, to be the mother of the Messiah and Son of God. For this she desires a transformation that only God can bring about, and when Gabriel makes known that this will happen by her being overshadowed by the Holy Spirit, Mary responds with the *consent* of faith. Mary's transformation by the power of the Holy Spirit is the model for the renewal that follows upon doctrinal awareness. This analysis of Mary's faith shows us that the passage from awareness

---

67. See John Paul II, *RMat*, 13.

to renewal is the humility expressed in "How shall this be?" followed by consent to be transformed by the power of God's grace.

It should be noted, here, how much renewal depends upon God's grace. Though our cooperation is required, renewal cannot be reduced to our efforts alone. Therefore, renewal will always have a sacramental dimension, with the Eucharist at its center.

Finally, Mary commits herself to "walk unhesitatingly according to her own personal gifts and duties in the path of living faith."[68] That is, her faith shapes her entire life as she sets herself to fulfill all that the mission the Lord has entrusted to her implies. She defines herself in terms of communion with God in the fulfillment of his plan. The content of her love of self corresponds in all things to the content of God's love for her. There is no distance in her following her Lord. Recognizing her subordinate role, she knows herself as the Lord's handmaid. Her whole life is defined in terms of being at the service of Jesus's mission. She is his closest associate in loving those he is sent to save. She lives her entire life in the perfect *obedience* of faith, submitting herself to enact every detail and duty of her vocation. By taking her place in God's plan, Mary's essential service, the fruit of her being overshadowed by the Holy Spirit, is to bring Christ into the world and to cooperate in his mission through intercession (as seen at Cana). As Mediatrix of all graces, Mary is the supreme realization of God's will that those he has made in his image come to the perfection of participating in his life by being his co-workers in redemption, thereby exercising a genuine though participatory or instrumental causality in communicating divine life to others.[69]

To summarize: Mary first *assents* in faith to the word of God made known by Gabriel. This means that her initial response is to hold what these words signify as true because they come from God, through his messenger. This revelation sheds new light on what Mary had known by faith and awaited in hope. Her response of faith is an intense moment of doctrinal awareness, of growth in understanding God's plan. She becomes more fully aware of the divine wisdom and of her place in God's plan. God makes these known to her because he desires her free cooperation. At the same time, because this cooperation is beyond her, she *consents* to be acted upon by God so that his word may be effective in her. The free cooperation that God desires, because this is in keeping

---

68. Vatican II, *LG*, 41.
69. See *CCC*, 307.

with her dignity as image of God, requires that she first understand God's intention. She understands what God intends to do, and this makes her consent to being overshadowed by the Holy Spirit in a free act of communion with God, an engagement of her liberty that assures she is truly God's associate or co-worker. In this way we see that the consent of faith and personal transformation by the power of God's grace presuppose the assent of faith.[70]

Mary's consent to be loved by God brings about a real change in her. She is now the Mother of the Redeemer, and her vocation and mission are defined in reference to the mission of the Son. To be the Lord's handmaid means to be at the service of Jesus's mission. She *obeys* God in all she does, conforming her actions to his will. This obedience of faith, this faith-in-action, presupposes the consent of faith, which presupposes the assent of faith. The assent of faith is the condition for the consent of faith, and consent of faith is the condition for and leads to a life of obedience of faith. Mary's faith is the model of awareness leading to renewal, and renewal leading to mission.

The Samaritan Woman

The three aspects of formation and the structure of the three dimensions of renewal, as outlined by Pope Paul VI in his first encyclical, *ES*, are also on display in the account of the Samaritan woman's encounter with Jesus at the well of Jacob (John 4:1–42). After John sets the scene (vv. 1–7), this passage unfolds as a dialogue in which Jesus slowly brings this woman to understand that he is the promised Messiah (v. 26), who fulfills the promises of God by giving the water of the Holy Spirit that wells up to eternal life (v. 14), so that people can worship God in spirit and in truth (v. 23).

> *Jesus ... discusses the most profound mysteries of God with her.* He speaks to her of God's infinite gift of love, which is like a "spring of water welling up to eternal life" (John 4:14). He speaks to her about God who is Spirit, and about the true adoration which the Father has a right to receive in spirit and truth (cf. John 4:24). Finally he reveals to her that he is the Messiah promised to Israel (cf. John 4:26).[71]

---

70. Similarly, the sacraments presuppose the assent of faith. See *CCC*, 1123. God wants us to know the nature of his love, and especially how it is more perfectly realized in the Eucharist, so that we can desire what he desires to accomplish in the sacraments.

71. John Paul II, *Mulieris dignitatem*, 15.

Jesus's conversation with the woman corresponds to the first path of renewal, the path of doctrinal penetration (John XXIII) or awareness (Paul VI). What Christ reveals to her simultaneously adds to, purifies, and deepens the knowledge that she already possesses. She knows that the well at which she met Jesus is the well of Jacob, and she senses that what Jesus is saying about himself implies that he is greater than Jacob (v. 12). By his knowledge of her life, she concludes that Jesus is a prophet (v. 19). She is aware, at least generally, of the historical and theological difference between Samaritans and Jews (v. 20). She is aware of the promise of a Messiah, who will make all things known concerning God (v. 25). Precisely at this point, when the woman professes her knowledge of a promised Messiah, Jesus reveals that he is this promised Messiah (v. 26).

As the dialogue unfolds, Jesus presents himself as wanting to make a gift to her (v. 10). Since giving a gift is the act of love, this total stranger, Jesus, is saying: "I want to love you. Will you open yourself to my love?" She cannot do this on her own. She is in need of God's grace, and bestowing this grace is at the center of Jesus's mission as Messiah. It is the grace of humility and repentance. For, "God opposes the proud, but gives grace to the humble" (Jas 4:6; 1 Pet 5:5). Jesus graces this woman by leading her into a confrontation between God's will and her life, so that she can freely make her own the truth of the words that he speaks.[72]

This makes it clear that what Jesus reveals about himself is inseparable from revealing this woman to herself. His words are not just truth to be taken in as mere information, which would reduce faith to a simple assent. In "discussing the most profound mysteries of God *with* her" and disclosing them *to* her, Jesus informs this woman's intellect with the truth about God's love *for* her. He is calling her to believe in him as the Messiah and offering her the water of eternal life, the gift of worshipping God in spirit and in truth. With this, Jesus offers her the gift that fulfills the deepest aspirations of every human heart: to be in communion with God.[73] But how is it possible for a woman who is living outside the law of God to receive such a gift?

---

72. See *CCC*, 2706, 2723. The pericope of the Samaritan woman's encounter with Jesus exemplifies the movement from *lectio* to *meditatio*, which is another duality in the Catholic tradition that can shed light on the movement from awareness to renewal. *Lectio* is an attentive taking in, and is followed by *meditatio*, which the *CCC* describes in terms of confrontation in order to make the content of what is read one's own. This happens through *conversio*, which bears the fruit of *oratio* and *contemplatio*, and finally, according to St. Francis de Sales, *resolutio*.

73. See *CCC*, 2560.

Acceptance in faith of Jesus's gift necessarily entails a renunciation of all that is opposed to this gift, all that presents an obstacle to its reception. In other words, a "Yes" to be loved by God in Christ is the undoing of a life of refusal to be loved by God in Christ. This woman must come to see her former way of life as shutting out God's love, making decisions without consulting God, living as if God does not exist. This is what Jesus intends by leading her into a new awareness of her sins. And the context in which this confrontation takes place is all-important. It is the context of God's offer of love, the fulfillment of her deepest aspirations, which only God can fulfill. Perhaps she had given up on such hope, resigning herself to her situation and to her weakness. By his love, Jesus, who is the resurrection (John 11:25), gives new life to her long dormant hope. And it is this newly resurrected hope that opens her to the gift that Jesus offers. The power of this gift of love unleashes in her the power to reform her life, symbolized by her leaving behind the bucket she had brought to the well.

In anticipation of the next section, it is worth pointing out an important similarity between the Samaritan woman's discovery of Jesus as Messiah and St. Peter's profession of faith in Jesus as Messiah (Matt 16:16–28). In both cases, there is a purification of the concept of Messiah. St. Peter is certainly correct when he declares that he believes Jesus is the Messiah. But it becomes clear that Peter's notion of Messiah did not include the suffering and death that Jesus foretold immediately after his profession of faith. Peter has to become humbled by confronting his own limited understanding in order to arrive at a deeper and more accurate understanding of God's definition of what it means for Jesus to be Messiah. Peter has to undergo a doctrinal penetration that is also a doctrinal purification. It further becomes clear that what Jesus discloses about how he will fulfill his mission as Messiah cannot remain a merely objective truth for Peter to know and to hold in his memory as mere data. In reality, Jesus's way of fulfilling his mission as Messiah entails a life-and-death reality for Peter and the apostles. In a similar way, the Samaritan woman discovers that she is involved in Jesus's mission as Messiah. He cannot reveal to her what it means to worship God in spirit and in truth without revealing at the same time how her life deviates from this worship. It cannot be otherwise, since he defines his mission in terms of love and communion with him. By leading her into a confrontation with her sin, Jesus is leading her into the death-event of his paschal mystery. She must

HOW ARE THE DIMENSIONS OF RENEWAL/FORMATION RELATED? 255

die to her sins in order to drink the water that will flow from his pierced side for the forgiveness of sins.

Returning now to the Samaritan woman, according to the logic of men, it is not possible that a woman who is living with her sixth husband could come close to God, could be worthy to receive his gift of grace. Rather, she deserves to be stoned for adultery—five times over! No wonder she slinked to the well at the hottest time of the day, when no one would be there. As in their shame Adam and Eve tried to hide from God, this woman's fear of confronting her neighbors, who knew full well of her situation, controls her life. With his offer of God's love, Jesus puts an end to her hiding and makes her conversion possible. "When he crosses a person's life, Christ disquiets his conscience and reads his heart, as happened with the Samaritan woman when he told her 'all that she ever did' (cf. John 4: 29). Above all, he moves her to repentance and love."[74]

The woman's conversion (the second path of renewal) bears the fruit of a profound change in her behavior, and this change corresponds to the third path of renewal. Interiorly transformed by Jesus's merciful love, she immediately becomes "an associate in his compassion, his work of salvation" (*CCC*, 2575), a collaborator in his mission (*CCC*, 307), as she runs through town to invite her neighbors to come and to meet Jesus (vv. 28–30). Rightly, the Synod on the New Evangelization observes, "Whoever receives new life from encountering Jesus cannot but proclaim truth and hope to others. The sinner who was converted becomes a messenger of salvation and leads the whole city to Jesus."[75] Prior to meeting Jesus, this woman feared encountering her neighbors. After her encounter, she seeks them out. Her fearlessness, her *parrhesia*, is the fruit of her love. "Perfect love casts out fear" (1 John 4:18). Her conversion is not only about her. It is also about those whom Jesus wishes to encounter through her.

The Samaritan woman's evangelizing is a participation in what Pope Paul VI calls the dialogue of divine revelation, God's own dialogue of salvation with the world. The wonder is that God calls us to participate in this dialogue, first as recipients, and then as agents who cooperate with him in heralding the Good News to our neighbors. This woman from Samaria, who in the Gospel remains unnamed,[76] takes her place alongside

---

74. John Paul II, "General Audience, August 9, 2000," 3.

75. Synod of Bishops, "Message to the People of God, October 7–28, 2012," 1.

76. In the tradition of the Eastern Churches, she is known as St. Photina (the one who was enlightened) and is held to have been martyred during the persecution of Nero.

the Blessed Virgin Mary, who by her very presence proclaimed the Good News of God's love to her kinswoman, Elizabeth, and Mary Magdalene, who hurried to inform the apostles that the Lord had risen. On account of the Samaritan woman's testimony to her encounter with Christ, her neighbors go to meet him, and eventually believe in him (vv. 39–42).

The Preface for third Sunday of Lent incisively expresses the transformation that Jesus worked in the Samaritan woman's life. "For when he asked the Samaritan woman for water to drink, he had already created the gift of faith within her and so ardently did he thirst for her faith, that he kindled in her the fire of divine love." The dynamic of the Samaritan woman's encounter with Jesus serves as a key for interpreting the renewal of Vatican II, the Church's daily life, the New Evangelization, and pastoral theology: conversion into the mystery of Christ, based on the truth that he reveals, bearing fruit for a revitalized mission.

The Disciples' Encounter with Jesus on the Road to Emmaus (Luke 24:14–35)

These were disciples who had accompanied Jesus on his final pilgrimage to Jerusalem. They knew his teachings, and they knew all that had happened to him during his final days. But they did not understand the full meaning of his teachings and especially of the final events of his life. They exemplify St. Mark's observation about the disciples's inability to understand Jesus's words about the Son of man being delivered over to men and killed, only to rise after three days (Mark 9:31–32). And so, the hope that they had placed in Jesus, the hope that he had invited them to place in him, has died. "We had hoped that he was the one to redeem Israel" (Luke 24:21). Their hope died with Jesus, but it would rise to new life with his resurrection.

Jesus's mission is to bring hope back to life. Hope is love that is sustained by a reasonable expectation that fulfillment will come. Jesus is the fulfillment of all hope that is based on a properly ordered love of self. But this resurrection of hope is rooted in a new understanding of God's plan. The hearts of the disciples from Emmaus could burn precisely because as Jesus explained the Scriptures to them they could hope in their fulfillment. Hope must be preceded by faith.[77] And what is the precise

---

77. "Absolutely speaking, faith precedes hope. For the object of hope is a future good, arduous but possible to obtain. In order, therefore, that we may hope, it is

content of his exposition of the Scriptures? It concerns the place of the death of the Messiah in God's plan: "'Was it not necessary that the Christ should suffer these things and enter into his glory?' And beginning with Moses and all the prophets, he interpreted to them in all the scriptures the things concerning himself" (Luke 24:26-27).

For the disciples from Emmaus, this is the essential content of their doctrinal penetration. It is clear that Jesus intended all along to reveal himself to them in the breaking of the bread. It is just as clear that prior to this, as a necessary preparation for it, he brought them to the fullness of faith about his paschal mystery, and with this new faith to new hope. The transformation that Jesus brings about in them is from "We had hoped . . ." to "Did not our hearts burn within us?" (Luke 24:32). Having brought their hope to life, Jesus fulfills this resurrected hope in the breaking of the bread. All that remains for them is to enter on to the third path of mission. "And they rose that same hour and returned to Jerusalem. . . Then they told what had happened on the road, and how he was known to them in the breaking of the bread" (Luke 24:33-35). Their mission is to do for others what Jesus had done for them: to bring hope to life!

Is not bringing hope to life the essential mission of the Church? Certainly, an affirmative response to this question is one way in which the Church understands her mission. The Church is conscious that by proclaiming the truth about God's love, which has been fully revealed in Jesus Christ, she is responding to the deepest needs of man: "man needs God, otherwise he remains without hope."[78] In the certitude of faith in this revelation, "with frank confidence [the Church] stands upon the path of history and says to men: 'I have that for which you search, that which you lack'" (*ES*, 95). From her own saving encounter with God's love in Christ, "the Church knows that her message is in harmony with the most secret desires of the human heart when she champions the dignity of the human vocation, restoring hope to those who have already despaired of anything higher than their present lot."[79]

---

necessary for the object of hope to be proposed to us as possible. Now the object of hope is, in one way, eternal happiness, and in another way, the Divine assistance, as explained above: and both of these are proposed to us by faith, whereby we come to know that we are able to obtain eternal life, and that for this purpose the Divine assistance is ready for us, according to Hebrews 11:6: 'He that cometh to God, must believe that he is, and is a rewarder to them that seek him.' Therefore it is evident that faith precedes hope" (Aquinas, *ST*, II-II, q. 17, a. 7).

78. Benedict XVI, *SS*, 23.
79. Vatican II, *GS*, 21.

Continuing the mission of Christ himself, the Church walks alongside her contemporaries and engages them in a dialogue about the events concerning their hopes. Like Jesus accompanying the disciples from Emmaus, she often remains anonymous during much of the journey. She appears as just another traveller along the way. But in the questions she asks she knows that she is leading her contemporaries into a conversation about their deepest hopes and the corresponding deepest despairs, in keeping with the paradox of death being the prelude to life: "unless a grain of wheat falls into the earth and dies, it remains alone; but if it dies, it bears much fruit" (John 12:24). Only when all other hopes have died by proving themselves impotent can birth be given to a new hope in what God alone is able to fulfill by making a gift of himself to man. The final act of this hope-fulfilling love is the gift of the Holy Spirit.

> By thus giving witness to the truth, we will share with others the mystery of the heavenly Father's love. As a consequence, men throughout the world will be aroused to a lively hope—the gift of the Holy Spirit—that some day at last they will be caught up in peace and utter happiness in that fatherland radiant with the glory of the Lord.[80]

This gift of the Spirit is perpetuated in the celebration of the Eucharist,[81] where faith is able to recognize the risen Lord, in the very act of self-donation to the Father for the sake of man's salvation. As Jesus prepared the disciples from Emmaus for this transforming encounter in the Eucharist with a doctrinal penetration and this bore the fruit of their mission to proclaim his resurrection, so the Church's life continues according to the rhythm of the three dimensions of renewal. Doctrinal penetration into the full meaning of the inspired word of God leads to the Eucharistic encounter that renews and deepens participation in the mystery of Christ, and this participation bears the fruit of the mission of bearing witness to this same mystery of Christ.

St. Peter and the Apostles on Pentecost

St. Luke's account of Pentecost marks a profound transition in the apostle's lives. On Pentecost, Christ's word's about the joint witness of the apostles and the Holy Spirit (John 15:26–27) are fulfilled in the outpouring of the

---

80. Vatican II, *GS*, 93.
81. See John Paul II, *DeV*, 61–65.

Holy Spirit and the apostles's witness to Jesus being the Christ. The dramatic nature of the apostles's transformation becomes evident by considering their condition prior to the descent of the Holy Spirit. In contrast to the boldness[82] of their proclamation of the mystery of Christ after having received the Holy Spirit, prior to Pentecost they are seized with a fear that prevents them from proclaiming his mystery. "For fear of the Jews" (John 20:19),[83] the apostles cling to what little security closed doors can offer. This is their condition prior to receiving the gift of the Holy Spirit.

In these circumstances, there is no hope for a mission to the ends of the world. The apostles are closed in on themselves. There is still the kind of predominance of self-love that caused St. Peter to follow Jesus, after his arrest, "at a distance" (Matt 26:58). He is following because he is attached to Jesus, because he loves him. Yet, he follows "at a distance" because his love for the Lord is not yet strong enough fully to purify his love of self by subordinating it to love of God. Shortly before Jesus's arrest he declares that he is ready to go to prison with Jesus and even to die with him (Luke 22:33). While this shows Peter's devotion to and love for Jesus, these are not deep enough or intense enough for him to follow through—*at that time*. For, Jesus knows that *eventually* Peter would go to prison and die for him: "Where I am going you cannot follow me *now*; but you *shall* follow afterward" (John 13:36; 21:18–19). Peter will follow Jesus afterward, that is, after the Lord's passion, death, resurrection, and ascension, and after and in the power of the gift of the Holy Spirit.

To acquire the depth and intensity of love that would allow him to follow Jesus to the end, Peter requires purification of his love. Regarding the apostles's interior state when they are locked away out of fear, St. Catherine of Sienna comments: "They remained barred in through fear, because the soul always fears until it arrives at true love."[84] Elaborating on this, Fr. Garrigou-Lagrange indicates that the need for the second conversion is rooted in a self-love that is not yet purified: "It is a strange but not uncommon mixture of sincere love of God with an inordinate love of

---

82. On boldness as a quality of witness to Christ in the Holy Spirit, see Acts 2:29; 4:13, 29, 31; 28:31.

83. John makes the "fear of the Jews" something of a theme: "Yet for fear of the Jews no one spoke openly of him" (John 7:13). "Openly" here translates the same Greek word, *parrhesia*, that is translated as "boldly" or "with boldness" in the verses identified in the previous note. Similarly, Joseph of Arimathea conceals that he is a disciple of Jesus "for fear of the Jews" (John 19:38).

84. As quoted in Garrigou-Lagrange, *The Three Ways*, 35.

self."[85] An inordinate love of self does not extinguish love of God and love of neighbor, but it does prevent these two loves from arriving at a point of perfection that makes sacrifice, precisely self-sacrifice, a component of the logic of love.[86]

The scene of the apostles locking themselves in a room in order to be safe depicts Christ's Church in a state of gestation. They have left everything to follow Jesus, but now that he is no longer there to lead them as he had, they are unable to lead themselves into the mission that Jesus entrusts to them. Jesus would lead them, but according to a new mode of leading. He would lead them from his place at the right hand of the Father, through the guiding light of the Holy Spirit, but for them to cooperate with this new form of leadership, they have to be renewed.

The Church Cannot Close in on Herself

To the extent that the Church on the eve of Vatican II could be likened to the apostles being closed in on themselves, a new outpouring of the Holy Spirit, a New Pentecost, becomes an imperative. The popes of Vatican II are certainly not reticent about calling for the Church to overcome any tendency to close in on herself, since this is contrary to her missionary mandate and her catholicity. Pope Paul VI compares the Holy Year of 1975 to a time of plowing the earth. Its goal is to revive the fertility of the field of the Church. The plow being used by the Farmer and his associates is none other than the Second Vatican Council, understood as a culture of love not only for the Church but also for all humanity. For, "the Church is not an institution closed in itself; rather, she is destined for all mankind. She is potentially universal, for the salvation of the world."[87]

---

85. Garrigou-Lagrange, *The Three Ways*, 37; see also 42–43. The third conversion is also necessary because of an imperfection of love that remains after the second conversion. See Garrigou-Lagrange, *The Three Ways*, 48–65.

86. On sacrifice as a component of the logic of love, see the section "The Sacrifice of Self to God" in Nicolas, "Amour de soi," 33–34. While Nicolas analyzes the movement from love of self to love of God from a metaphysical perspective, he describes this movement in biblical and spiritual terms, as a sacrifice.

87. Paul VI, "General Audience, April 30, 1975." The text continues: "The Holy year is not a purely devotional time. As we said on another occasion, is an awakening, and first of all, an awakening from an interior slumber, which causes many people to be somnolent and lazy, who appear to be awake and alive yet sleeping inside. It is an awakening especially of moral and spiritual consciousness."

Pope Paul takes up this theme in the apostolic exhortation, *Evangelii nuntiandi*, which would become the Magna Charta for the systematization of Vatican II's renewal of the Church's missionary awareness.

> And it is above all his mission and his condition of being an evangelizer that she is called upon to continue (cf. *LG*, 8; *AG*, 5). For the Christian community is never closed in upon itself. The intimate life of this community—the life of listening to the Word and the apostles's teaching, charity lived in a fraternal way, the sharing of bread (cf. Acts 2:42–46; 4:32–35; 5:12–16)—this intimate life only acquires its full meaning when it becomes a witness, when it evokes admiration and conversion, and when it becomes the preaching and proclamation of the Good News. Thus it is the whole Church that receives the mission to evangelize, and the work of each individual member is important for the whole.[88]

The three dimensions of renewal of *ES* are evident in this text. The first sentence is a summary of the doctrine regarding the Church's mystery and vocation.[89] The second sentence is the moral imperative based on this doctrine. The Church must fight against any temptation to close in on herself if she is to live in conformity with the truth about her missionary nature. By its very nature, her interior life is not only one of unity and holiness in the bond of apostolic faith. It is also catholic, as it shines forth in the world through witness and proclamation.

Chronologically more proximate to the Council, Pope Paul stresses that the Church's mission is to bring Christ into history as she strains towards her eschatological encounter with him. The glorified Lord

---

88. Paul VI, *EN*, 15.

89. A somewhat more elaborate doctrinal elaboration precedes this sentence. It is significant that Pope Paul precedes this passage with a summary of what revelation makes known about the Church's origins. The New Testament bears witness that the Church "is linked to evangelization in her most intimate being." The first link is that the Church is the fruit of evangelization: "the Church is born of the evangelizing activity of Jesus and the Twelve." She owes her very existence to the initiative-taking love of Christ, in which he makes the apostles participants. The second link is that the Church receives the mission to continue the evangelizing mission of Christ and the apostles: "Having been born consequently out of being sent, the Church in her turn is sent by Jesus." Pope Paul sums up this revealed doctrine on the Church's origins in terms of the Conciliar ecclesiology of the Church being the sacrament of Christ and of his mission of love. Until the Second Coming of Christ, the Church remains in the world as a sacrament or sign of Jesus's presence and of the continuation of his mission by the collaboration of his disciples with the Holy Spirit.

accompanies his Church along her pilgrimage of faith, during which her mission is to bear witness to him. For this reason

> The Church is not an institution closed in on itself, concerned only with defending and preserving itself. The Church is born to bear witness: The Lord said to the apostles before leaving them, "you will be my witnesses ... to the ends of the earth" (Acts 1:8). The Church is meant to cover the earth, is established for all mankind; she is universal, that is catholic.[90]

Through the Council, the Holy Spirit guides the Church into a rediscovery of her catholicity[91] and thus into a deepened consciousness of her missionary nature.

For John Paul II as well, for the Church to close in on herself is to betray her missionary mandate. The Council's rediscovery of the missionary implications of the Church's catholicity means that "In continuing the great task of implementing the Second Vatican Council, in which we can rightly see a new phase of the self-realization of the Church ... the Church herself must be constantly guided by the full consciousness that in this work it is not permissible for her, for any reason, to withdraw into herself."[92]

> Through the Council the Church did not want in any way to close within itself, to refer to itself (the so-called ecclesiocentrism of the Church), but, on the contrary, it wanted to open itself more widely. We continually make this our goal, which is also our duty; and by implementing it we deepen more the mystery of the Church (cf. *LG*, II); this is in fact the source of openness and of mission (in the mission of the Son and Spirit).[93]

"Openness to the world" is the counter-attitude to the Church being closed in on herself. Very importantly, openness to the world (which can be called horizontal openness) presupposes and derives from a prior openness to divinely revealed truth (which can be called vertical openness):[94]

---

90. Paul VI, "General Audience, July 27, 1966."

91. The rediscovery of the Church's catholicity is the meaning that M.-D. Chenu, OP, attributes to the Council's Message to Humanity (October 20, 1962). See his article "Le Message," 192. See also Tillard, "L'Église relit sa catholicité."

92. John Paul II, *DM*, 15.

93. John Paul II, "Address, December 7, 1985," 10.

94. Similarly, for John Paul II the exhortation, "Be not afraid!" has both a vertical

> Truth, in fact, cannot be confined. Truth is for one and for all. And if this truth comes about through love (cf. Eph 4:15), then it becomes even more universal. This was the style of the Second Vatican Council and the spirit in which it took place.[95]

The precedence of vertical openness in relation to horizontal openness is yet another mirroring of the relation of the first two paths of renewal to the third path. For John Paul II, Vatican II's openness to truth means that the Church turned to God with the expectation of receiving a deeper understanding of her own mystery, vocation, and mission. She was not afraid to embrace the path of development in understanding the apostolic deposit of faith. Nor did she fear embracing a full responsibility for that deeper understanding, insofar as this calls for a renewal through conversion. The fruit of this twofold openness, to a growth in understanding revealed truth and a corresponding growth in conforming to this truth, bears the fruit of a third openness, namely, missionary openness to the world.

There is nothing naïve about fully embracing the Church's vocation of openness to the world.

> The Church is not afraid to live in the world, even though she readily sees the brokenness and sinfulness which abound. When, in the light of Christ, she sees violence and oppression for what they are, when she encounters injustices of any kind, she does not withdraw within herself and try to hide behind the safety of church walls; she does not abandon her mission of evangelization and service. The Church reaches out with compassion to the homeless and refugees; she hears the cry of the poor and the oppressed. The Church knows well that she is a pilgrim community of faith called to serve the human family with evangelical openness and authentic love.[96]

---

and a horizontal application. Vertically, it means overcoming any fear to accepting and following Christ ("Homily, October 22, 1978," 5; "Homily, January 13, 1995," 4–6). At other times, it applies to mission ("Address, April 17, 1999," 2; "Address, October 9, 2003," 5). On other occasions, the two are linked: the exhortation not to be afraid with regard to mission is based on the confidence that Christ is with us ("Homily, May 9, 1999," 4; "Address, February 3, 2001," 5–6).

95. Wojtyla, *Crossing the Threshold of Hope*, 162. The most extensive consideration of the Council's vertical openness to divine truth in the work of Cardinal Wojtyła/John Paul II is his article, "Le problème de l'ouverture au Concile" in *En Esprit et en Vérité*, 231–40.

96. John Paul II, "Homily, November 27, 1986," 5.

The twin foundations of the Church's missionary openness are truth and love. Divinely revealed truth is the objective good that is destined for the liberation of all mankind. It is the supremely shareable common good that is only possessed for what it is when it is being shared. Complementing this is the subjective foundation, that is, participation in the paschal charity of Christ. Together, these two foundations are the remedy to the disease of fear that results in the Church turning in on herself.

Even when it is not a question of a paralyzing fear, John Paul points out there is a kind of introversion that can cripple mission: "All renewal in the Church must have mission as its goal if it is not to fall prey to a kind of ecclesial introversion."[97]

> We must not forget that the intention of the Second Vatican Council was to unleash new evangelizing forces within the Church, in the wake of the devastation caused by the two World Wars and looking to the prospects of the new millennium. A new kind of missionary commitment was required, a new evangelization, and the Council, through the grace of the Holy Spirit, became the means of setting that dynamism in motion. This has been the overriding purpose of every new provision for the life of the Church resulting from the Council. Therefore, we must carefully avoid any form of ecclesial introversion that would be unfaithful to the Council's intention, since it would diminish rather than increase the missionary thrust needed to meet the needs of the new century.[98]

To say that every updating of the Church's life has been at the service of promoting a new evangelization must not be understood narrowly. Since, as we have seen, the third path of dialogical mission presupposes the first two paths of doctrinal penetration and personal conversion, the adjustments in ecclesiastical structures and organizations must simultaneously promote all three paths. A case in point is the consistent insistence on the three dimensions of formation.

Pope Benedict XVI is in perfect harmony with Vatican II and his predecessors. This is evident in one text in which he quotes from Vatican II, Paul VI, and John Paul II:

> The proclamation of the Gospel is intended for all peoples. The Church is "by her very nature missionary since, according to the

---

97. John Paul II, *EO*, 19. For Ratzinger, see *Dogma and Preaching*, 214–15.
98. John Paul II, "Address, September 25, 1999," 6.

plan of the Father, she has her origin in the mission of the Son and the Holy Spirit" (*AG*, 2).

This is "the grace and vocation proper to the Church, her deepest identity. She exists in order to evangelize" (Pope Paul VI, *EN*, 14). Consequently she can never be closed in on herself. She is rooted in specific places in order to go beyond them. Her action, in adherence to Christ's word and under the influence of his grace and his charity, is fully and currently present to all people and all peoples, to lead them to faith in Christ (cf. *AG*, 5).

This task has lost none of its urgency. Indeed "The mission of Christ the Redeemer, which is entrusted to the Church, is still very far from completion . . . an overall view of the human race shows that this mission is still only beginning and that we must commit ourselves wholeheartedly to its service" (Pope John Paul II, *RMiss*, 1). We cannot reconcile ourselves to the thought that after 2,000 years there are still people who do not know Christ and have never heard his Message of salvation.[99]

The three paths of renewal shed light on this text and the preceding texts. Doctrinal awareness includes the truth about the Church's catholicity and missionary character. Therefore, examination of conscience and *metanoia* of the second path bear upon the integral truth of the Church as missionary. A Church that could somehow become self-referential, self-satisfied, or closed in on herself, independent of measuring up to her missionary mandate, would be a disfigured Church.

First and Second Conversions

Let us resume the implications for the three dimensions of renewal in the case of St. Peter and the apostles. In doing so, the privileged place of spiritual renewal through *metanoia*, already observed, even more clearly emerges.

"But with God all things are possible" (Matt 19:26). Who would have thought that a Samaritan woman, who also closed herself off from the world, could be transformed and become a herald of Christ to her neighbors? She, like Peter, is in a state of following God at a distance (Matt 26:58). She knows something of her faith and faith-tradition, but it does not break through to become a force strong enough to motivate her to order her life according to God's will. Like Peter and the apostles,

---

99. Benedict XVI, "Message for World Mission Sunday."

she is in need of a divine intervention. She is in need of the living water of the Holy Spirit that Jesus speaks of, and which she encounters in him and receives from him.

Peter's faith and relation to Jesus is more clearly in evidence. He has left home and family in order to follow Jesus and to live with him. He has received Jesus's teachings. He has professed his faith in Jesus as Messiah, and has had what was erroneous in his understanding of this corrected. He has had his insight about being prepared to forgive seven times expanded by Jesus's formula, seven times seventy. As good and holy as all this is, and as much as it is all the working of grace, God has more to give, and Peter's denials make it clear to him that he stands in need of that something more,[100] if he is to love Jesus as Jesus has loved him, that is, "to the end." In God's plan, the stage of Peter's discipleship and his fall are preparatory, making him ready to receive the gift of the Holy Spirit.

With this gift of the Spirit, Peter's second conversion reaches a summit.[101] The great fruit of this second conversion is that he no longer has a life of his own. The two have become so completely one that St. Paul's words apply: "it is no longer I who live, but Christ who lives in me; and the life I now live in the flesh I live by faith in the Son of God, who loved me and gave himself for me" (Gal 2:20). There is no longer any distance, which is such a crucifixion for love. Peter is definitively liberated from the gripping fear of disordered love of self, and the two great manifestations of this in his life are his fearless proclamation of the mystery of Christ, both by word and by his martyrdom. In keeping with the Dominican

---

100. Drawing on the witness of St. Catherine of Sienna, Fr. Garrigou-Lagrange, OP, discusses the humility that comes with self-knowledge, that is, knowledge of one's sin and imperfections, as the necessary disposition for the graces of the second conversion (see Garrigou-Lagrange, *The Three Ways*, 38–41, 44). Actually, the humility of self-knowledge is already a grace that indicates the transition from the first to the second conversion. For, a greater awareness of one's sin and lowliness is the fruit of a clearer grasp of the call to perfection. This is precisely what St. Paul VI teaches in *ES*: "From this enlightened and effective realization there arises the spontaneous desire to compare the ideal image of the Church just as Christ sees it, wills it, and loves it as his holy and immaculate spouse, with the actual image which the Church projects today.... But the actual image of the Church is never as perfect, as lovely, as holy or as brilliant as that formative Divine Idea would wish it to be. Hence there arises the unselfish and almost impatient need for renewal, for correction of the defects which this conscience denounces and rejects, as if, standing before a mirror, we were to examine interiorly the Image of Christ which he has left us" (*ES*, 10–11).

101. On the second conversion, see *CCC*, 1428–29. Peter's second conversion begins with his tears of repentance, which manifest the humility that is the necessary disposition to receive the gift of the Holy Spirit.

ideal that links contemplation to preaching, as its fruit, Fr. Garrigou-Lagrange gives the following description of the impact of the gift of the Holy Spirit:

> The Apostles received a much greater enlightenment from the Holy Spirit regarding the price of the Blood of the Savior, regarding the mystery of Redemption, foretold in the Old Testament and fulfilled in the New. They received the fullness of the contemplation of this mystery which they were now to preach to humanity for the salvation of men. St. Thomas says that "the preaching of the word of God must proceed from the fullness of contemplation" (*ST* II-II, Q. 188, a. 6). This was most fully verified at that time, as we may see from the first sermons of St. Peter related in the Acts and from that of St. Stephen before his martyrdom. These words of St. Peter and St. Stephen recall the saying of the Psalmist: "Thy word is exceedingly refined and thy servant hath loved it" (Ps 118:140 DRA).[102]

This text brings home an important truth about three paths of renewal. A superficial understanding might lead one to think that a clearer perception of the truths of faith takes place in the first path of doctrinal penetration and then left behind, with the second path of renewal through conversion being restricted to the moral dimension of conversion into a more perfect conformity to doctrine. In reality, the three paths interpenetrate, with each path having a predominant feature. Doctrinal penetration continues throughout the second path of renewal through conversion, as well as in the third path of mission. Similarly, the second path of conversion is not left behind but accompanies the third path of apostolic action. Fr. Garrigou-Lagrange notes how saints well-known for the zeal for souls suffered over the awareness of how far they fell short of the apostolic ideal.[103]

With the gift of the Holy Spirit, Peter's whole life is a witness to Jesus, as Jesus's whole life is witness to the Father. It is clear that for Jesus,

---

102. Garrigou-Lagrange, *The Three Ways*, 52.

103. "The soul now has a sort of living knowledge, an experimental perception, of the supernatural world, a new outlook upon it. And by contrast the soul becomes more conscious of its own poverty. The chief suffering of a St. Paul of the Cross, of a Curé d'Ars, at this stage, was to feel themselves so distant from the ideal of the priesthood, which loomed now so great before them in the dark night of faith; while at the same time they understood better the great needs of those many souls that had recourse to them, imploring their prayers and their help" (Garrigou-Lagrange, *The Three Ways*, 62).

forgiveness of Peter's sin and reconciliation of Peter with himself is not complete until the two are one in mission.[104] Now that the two have become one, Jesus is loving the world through Peter. He continues his mission of love through, with, and in Peter. Peter's entire life is a witness to Christ: first, in the form of his profession of love for the Lord (John 21:15–17); second, in the form of proclamation (Acts 2:14–40); third, in the form of safeguarding the Church's unity, based on purity of revealed truth (Acts 15:1–29; Gal 2:11–14); fourth, in the form of martyrdom (John 21:18–19). These four dimensions of Peter's witness to God's love fully revealed in Jesus Christ correspond to the third path of renewal. This life of witness presupposes the profound transformation that comes to completion with the gift of the Holy Spirit, and this corresponds to the second path of renewal. And this second path presupposes the first path, that period of continually deepening understanding of the mystery that Christ is and that he reveals. For, as we have seen, there comes a point at which Jesus has no more to say. Having fulfilled his mission of revelation, it remains only for Peter and the apostles to understand it more fully[105] and to conform their lives to it so as fully to participate in the mystery of Christ.

The language of first and second conversion is well suited to shed light on the constant movement from the first to the second path of renewal. "Christ's call to conversion continues to resound in the lives of Christians. This second conversion is an uninterrupted task for the whole Church" (*CCC*, 1428). Spiritual theology associates the second conversion with the passive night of the senses and the beginning of the illuminative way.[106] Though it is intended to ground his theory of both a second and a third conversion, Garrigou-Lagrange's proposal to see three stages in the spiritual itinerary of the apostles can be seen to correspond to the three dimensions of renewal.[107] The first period covers the time from their

---

104. The same is true of St. Paul. His baptism for the forgiveness of his sins and the gift of the Holy Spirit is inseparable from the mission that the risen Lord entrusts to him. It is clear that for Jesus, reconciliation is not complete until the repentant sinner is one with him in mission.

105. Coming after the descent of the Holy Spirit on Pentecost, the account of Peter's vision regarding what is clean and unclean, what he learned from this regarding God showing no partiality, and the conclusion he draws from witnessing the Holy Spirit descend upon the house of Cornelius (Acts 10), indicate that revelatory doctrinal penetration continues after receiving the gift of the Spirit on Pentecost.

106. See Garrigou-Lagrange, *The Three Ages*, 1:14, 20, 24, 106.

107. See Garrigou-Lagrange, *The Three Ages*, 1:229. Here Garrigou-Lagrange

call to follow Jesus to the passion. This is the time of intense doctrinal penetration: "To you it has been given to know the secrets of the kingdom of heaven" (Matt 13:11). The second period extends from the passion to Pentecost. This period may be characterized by the exchange between the risen Lord and Peter on the shore of the Sea of Tiberias. In the prior period, Jesus's focus is on Peter's faith: "Who do you say that I am?" In this second period, Jesus asks Peter if he loves him (John 21:15–17). Love is the motive for conversion, and perfect love is the fruit of conversion. For Peter to profess his love for Jesus is for him to participate in the life of the Trinity, for, "the Father loves the Son" (John 3:35; 5:20), and in return, the Son loves the Father. Pentecost inaugurates the third period, which "greatly strengthened their wills to preach everywhere Christ crucified."[108] Having been conformed to Christ and made participants in the life of the Trinity, the apostles are also participants in his mission.

The relation of the second path of renewal through conversion to the third path of mission is evident in Fr. Marie-Eugene's classic study of the spirituality of St. Teresa of Avila.[109] The more a person is conformed to Christ the more the dynamics of his mystery prevail in that person's life. The highest degree of conformity to Christ—or uniformity, as St. Alphonsus de Liguori prefers[110]—is necessarily the highest degree of participation in his mission. Commenting on a text in which St. Teresa recounts the grace of spiritual marriage, Fr. Marie-Eugene is attentive to the way in which her testimony makes it clear that her mission on earth is not only inseparable from her nuptial union with Christ—it *is* that union in missionary mode. The key line of Teresa's account contains the words that the Lord spoke to her: "Behold this nail. It is a sign that from to-day onward thou shalt be My Bride." Fr. Marie-Eugene expounds:

> On carrying her away with him into the bosom of God, the incarnate Word vows her to the service of his honor here below, like a true bride. The wedding ring is replaced by a nail that attaches her to the cross.... The Christ who unites her perfectly to himself is Christ Jesus, triumphant in Heaven and militant

---

points us to an ampler development of the second and third conversions of the apostles in his much shorter work, *The Three Ways*, from which the above is drawn.

108. Garrigou-Lagrange, *The Three Ages*, 1:230.
109. Marie-Eugene, *I Want to See God; I Am a Daughter of the Church*.
110. See Liguori, *Uniformity with God's Will*.

and suffering on earth. It is rather this latter Christ that she is to live and prolong while she is on earth.[111]

The mystery of divine love is revealed in its going out from itself and toward men in the missions of the Son and of the Holy Spirit. But this going forth, this *exitus* of love, has as its goal the transformation of those whom God loves so that their lives become a *reditus* of love, a return to God.

St. Thérèse of Lisieux expresses the same thing in words that are at first startling because she does not see heavenly union with God as rest from her mission. Rather, in heaven the mission that God entrusts to her reaches its perfection because the love that is this mission's soul comes to perfection. Her charity has become so much an intense participation in God's own love that her mission cannot be fulfilled on earth—even as Jesus's mission is fulfilled in the sending of the Holy Spirit after his Ascension. Her charity is as bound by chains so long as her union with God has not been consummated in heavenly glory. Thus, she understands the beatitude of heaven: "Oh, it is love! To love and to be loved and to return to earth to make Love to be loved!" Fr. Marie-Eugene comments:

> Love imprisoned Thérèse of the Child Jesus and forged chains that held her bound. The next life was to give her love full liberty to display all its power and exercise all its virtualities. Thérèse returns to aid all apostles. . . . What attracts her to heaven is the certitude of being able to fulfill this mission until the end of time.
>
> This movement of love descending to conquer by loving and then carrying its prey to the heights is the synthesis of the two-fold movement of love; it is the action of the perfect apostolate because in accord with the movement and action of Jesus himself.[112]

There is no such thing as communion with God in Christ apart from communion in his mission. If the second path of renewal envisions communion with God, as it were, in itself and for its own sake, it needs to be completed by the third path of communion-in-mission.

Taking the third path as communion-in-mission does not mean that there is no mission prior to reaching the heights of mystical union. This is not the meaning of the testimony of Sts. Teresa and Thérèse. Rather, as love becomes more perfect, so too do all the virtues and actions

---

111. Marie-Eugene, *I Am a Daughter of the Church*, 617–18.
112. Marie-Eugene, *I Am a Daughter of the Church*, 622.

it commands, and this includes the apostolic dimension of everyone's vocation. The fact that the third path of active participation in Christ's mission comes last is because it presupposes conformity to Christ that comes through conversion, and conversion presupposes knowledge of God's will and thus of one's vocation.

IN LIGHT OF THE LITURGY

The Mass exhibits the same three dimensions of awareness, renewal, and mission, and the movement from one to another aligns with the movement in Mary's faith from assent, to consent, and to obedience, as demonstrated above. In the Liturgy of the Word, God's revealed truth is proclaimed anew to the Church. It is the same word that the Church and the faithful have already received, but it can always be understood more precisely and more profoundly.[113] This should not be understood primarily as theological insight in a technical sense, though that is by no means excluded. Rather, each time the faithful assemble to celebrate the Lord's redeeming love they should bring with them the vertical openness of faith that Cardinal Wojtyła identifies as foundational to the spirit of Vatican II. It is foundational to the spirit of Vatican II because it is a constitutive quality, a property, of the Church's faith. In reality, the spirit of Vatican II is the spirit of Catholicism as that spirit manifested itself at that time in history and with a pastoral goal of renewal in mind.

For those who seek him, God is ever expanding their capacity to receive his love, for he always has more to give.[114] The life of obedience

---

113. "To bring about an ever deeper understanding of revelation the same Holy Spirit constantly brings faith to completion by his gifts" (*DV*, 5). "For there is a growth in the understanding of the realities and the words which have been handed down.... For as the centuries succeed one another, the Church constantly moves forward toward the fullness of divine truth until the words of God reach their complete fulfillment in her" (*DV*, 8).

114. St. Augustine put it this way: "By delaying [his gift], God strengthens our desire; through desire he enlarges our soul and by expanding it he increases its capacity [for receiving him]" (as quoted in Benedict XVI, *SS*, 33). Similarly, John of the Cross: "The loving soul, however great her conformity to the Beloved, cannot cease longing for the wages of her love, for which she serves the Beloved. Otherwise there would not be true love, because the payment for love is nothing else—neither can the soul desire anything else—than more love, until the perfection of love is reached. Love is paid only with love itself" (John of the Cross, *The Collected Works*, 444). Finally, St. Thomas: "Charity does not actually increase by any act of charity whatever. But any act of charity disposes for an increase of charity, so far as by an act of charity a man becomes

of faith is itself the school of faith. To live it fervently is to be disposed to receive the grace that brings faith to perfection. The call to holiness and to collaborate in the fulfillment of God's will gives rise to the question, "How shall this be?" As it was for Mary, faith grows through a constant process of confirmation and new light, and new light gives rise anew to the question, "How shall this be?" The person of faith who asks this question will, like Mary, be overshadowed by the Holy Spirit, who "to bring about an ever deeper understanding of revelation . . . constantly brings faith to completion by his gifts."[115] In this way the faithful bring to the liturgy an ever-increasing depth of faith and an openness that disposes them to receive God's word anew with the *assent* of faith, which then leads to the *consent* of faith.

In the Liturgy of the Word Christ seems to repeat again and again: "for all that I have heard from my Father, I have made known to you" (John 15:15), and "To you it has been given to know the secrets of the kingdom of heaven" (Matt 13:11). His grace makes us able to bear now what formerly we were unable to bear (John 16:12). By this grace we move from drinking the milk of infants to eating the solid food of more mature faith (1 Cor 3:2; Heb 5:12). In the Liturgy of the Word God especially makes known the place of the Paschal Mystery in his plan of love and the establishment of his kingdom. He repeats the invitation that we become one with him in Christ's ultimate act of love. In the Liturgy of the Word the Church places herself anew before divine revelation in expectation of perceiving God's word with greater understanding and the corresponding challenge of living that word. Jesus knows that his mission of teaching will lead to the Paschal Mystery, and he desires that we know this and that we follow him. In the Liturgy of the Word, he asks, in effect: "Have you understood all this?" (Matt 13:51). Are you at that point that he identifies as "later" in revealing Peter, who overestimates his ability to follow Jesus to jail and to death, to himself (Luke 22:33; John 13:36–37)?

We know that Peter could not follow Jesus "then," but that "later," transformed by the gift of the Holy Spirit on Pentecost, he would follow Jesus and in his turn love "to the end" (John 13:1). Living with God's Word by listening to his words places us constantly in the same position as Peter. We can only follow Jesus when "clothed with the power from

---

more prompt to continue working through charity, and as this disposition increases, the man breaks forth in a more fervent act of charity through which he strives to grow in charity, and then charity is actually increased" (Aquinas, *ST*, II-II, q. 24, a. 6).

115. Vatican II, *DV*, 5.

on high" (Luke 24:49), that is, the power of his love, the gift of the Holy Spirit. "I can do all things in him who strengthens me" (Phil 4:13). To make our own the words of Mary, in response to the proclamation of God's word, which makes known to us God's will and our vocation, we can only say: "How shall this be?" And the answer is always the same: "The Holy Spirit will come upon you, and the power of the Most High will overshadow you" (Luke 1:35).

In this way the Liturgy of the Word leads to the Liturgy of the Eucharist. The Eucharist is the permanent answer to the questions that arise from receiving God's word: "Lord, why cannot I follow you now?," and "How shall this be?" It is the bridge between the "now," which is always the fruit of grace and the pledge of future graces, and the "later," when those pledged future graces become a new "now" of grace. This passage from a "now" of grace to a "later" grace of which the present grace is a pledge, is echoed in Jesus's question, put to his disciples after his teaching on the Eucharist: "Will you also go away?" (John 6:67). This question is "a loving invitation to discover that only he has 'the words of eternal life' (John 6:68) and that to receive in faith the gift of his Eucharist is to receive the Lord himself."[116]

The Eucharist is the source and summit of Catholic spirituality, but it presupposes the correct understanding of revelation (doctrinal formation) so that one can be fully in communion with Christ in this sacrament. So much so that when there is a misunderstanding of the nature of the Kingdom of God that is definitively ushered in by the Paschal Mystery, it is necessary that the Lord bring correction. Thus, to James and John, who ask to sit on either side of him in his Kingdom, Jesus tersely responds: "You do not know what you are asking" (Matt 20:22). Then he shows them that in reality their request regarding their place in his Kingdom is a request to participate in the Paschal Mystery, since it is by the Paschal Mystery that the Kingdom is established. Similarly, in the case of Peter's initial refusal to accept that Jesus's way of fulfilling the mission of the Messiah is by rejection, torture, and death, there is need for a purification of concepts (Matt 16:16–25).

Such purified faith is the fruit of authentic doctrinal formation, and it should be the fruit of every encounter with the word of God. Once purified, faith leads to the Liturgy of the Eucharist, even as Jesus's teaching ministry culminates in the Paschal Mystery. In the Eucharist, God's

---

116. *CCC*, 1336.

word of love made known in the Liturgy of the Word is fully actualized in our presence. God's word becomes active and effective. In the Liturgy of the Word, God tells us that he loves us, and in the Liturgy of the Eucharist he actually loves us. Here we have the most sublime perpetuation of the law that governs divine revelation, which "is realized by deeds and words having in inner unity: the deeds wrought by God in the history of salvation manifest and confirm the teaching and realities signified by the words, while the words proclaim the deeds and clarify the mystery contained in them."[117] In the Eucharist, God's definitive act of love confirms all that God has revealed about love through words, while the words of love proclaim and clarify the Paschal Mystery to which they refer.

In the presence of this perfect love and its implications for those to whom it is addressed, the only appropriate response is humbly to entrust oneself to that word and deed of love: "Lord, I am not worthy that You should enter under my roof. But only say the word and my soul shall be healed." Who is worthy to receive this love? This is the liturgical equivalent of Mary's "How shall this be?" The Prodigal Son, observing his father's lavish exhibition of joy, which is rooted in his love for his son, could have likewise said, "How shall this be?" How is it that my father continues to love me, and to rejoice in my return, even after I have treated him so shabbily? Like Peter responding to the Lord's thrice repeated question whether he loves him, at the moment of being transformed into what we consume we are more confident in God's word, in what God knows. This is why, immediately after confessing our unworthiness, we ask Jesus to pronounce his word of saving love. Peter's response is not an assertion of love as if this could have any substance of its own. "Lord, you know that I love you" and the final intensification of this confidence in what Jesus knows, "Lord, *you know* everything; *you know* that I love you" (John 21:17). In Holy Communion we become one with God's consubstantial Word of love. Full communion with Christ in this sacrament presupposes full communion with him in the assent of faith. The *assent* of faith in the "Amen" that concludes the profession of faith is completed and fulfilled by the Eucharistic *consent* of faith to be loved by God, expressed in the "Amen" before receiving Holy Communion.

In the Mass, there remains only the Concluding Rite and dismissal, with the exhortation to take Christ into the world and to proclaim his mystery by word and action. This is the essential mission of love and

---

117. Vatican II, *DV*, 2.

service entrusted to the Church. To "be with" Christ in the Eucharist is inseparable from "being sent" by him (Mark 3:14). Communion with God is the source of mission. "Go and announce the Gospel of the Lord"; "Go in peace, glorifying the Lord by your life." Pope John Paul II repeatedly emphasizes this essential relationship between communion and mission in his apostolic exhortation on the lay faithful:

> Communion leads to *mission*, and mission itself to communion...
>
> Engrafted to the vine and brought to life, the branches are expected to bear fruit: "He who abides in me, and I in him, he it is that bears much fruit" (John 15:5). Bearing fruit is an essential demand of life in Christ and life in the Church. The person who does not bear fruit does not remain in communion: "Each branch of mine that bears no fruit, he (my Father) takes away" (John 15: 2).
>
> Communion with Jesus . . . is an indispensable condition for bearing fruit: "Apart from me you can do nothing" (John 15:5). And communion with others is the most magnificent fruit that the branches can give: in fact, it is the gift of Christ and his Spirit.
>
> At this point *communion begets communion*: essentially it is likened to a *mission on behalf of communion*. . . .
>
> Communion and mission are profoundly connected with each other, they interpenetrate and mutually imply each other, to the point that *communion represents both the source and the fruit of mission: communion gives rise to mission and mission is accomplished in communion*.[118]

To live out our Eucharistic communion with Christ by carrying him into the world by bearing witness to the life of God within us—to proclaim that we have been loved by God—and by participating in his mission as Prophet, Priest, and King—this is our Eucharistic *obedience* of faith. It is the fruit of the Eucharistic *consent* of faith in Holy Communion, which presupposes a Eucharistic *assent* of faith in the Liturgy of the Word. In a remarkable way then, the Church experiences the three dimensions common to the renewal of Vatican II and to formation for ministry and apostolate in the central liturgical action by which Christ fulfills his promise to be with his Church until the end of time (Matt 28:20).

---

118. John Paul II, *CL*, 31–32.

One might conjecture that it is above all this movement from Liturgy of the Word to Liturgy of the Eucharist to dismissal for mission and service that influenced Pope Paul's reflections on awareness, renewal, and dialogue, even if he was not fully conscious of it. Regardless, the potential of the liturgy to illuminate the three paths complements the potential already illustrated in the principles of Christian anthropology and certain events of Scripture.

12

Cardinal Wojtyła/Pope John Paul II on Faith

COMPLEMENTING THE TEXTS IN which Wojtyła/John Paul explicitly takes up the three dimensions of formation, this chapter looks into his theology of faith in order to show three things: first, that it harmonizes with the anthropological foundation for the logic of *ES* (proposed in chapter 11); second, that this theology of faith is a hermeneutical principle for interpreting the Council drawn from the Council itself; and third, that it can be seen as an elaboration of what remains implicit in *ES*. In this way, this chapter reinforces the continuity between John Paul II and his predecessor regarding the logic of *ES* emerging from essential truths of revelation and Christian life.

John Paul's theology of faith is a foundational element of his understanding and implementation of Vatican II. Since he takes *ES* as the guide for understanding and implementing the Council, it is to be expected that his theology of faith envelops and develops the logic of renewal of Pope Paul in *ES*. For John Paul, faith entails three dimensions, which relate to one another according to the logic of *ES*, just as the three dimensions of formation do.

Four considerations will serve to bring all of this out. The first analyzes John Paul's theology of faith in order to show that the enrichment of faith, which he takes to be the essential goal of Vatican II, consists in a consciousness of the content of faith that gives rise to various attitudes of faith, which are the proximate source of living the faith. The second shows that for John Paul II holiness or spirituality is the hinge that connects doctrine and active participation in the Church's mission. It also shows that holiness-spirituality is not a means to connect doctrine and actively lived faith but rather the very reality of the goal of the renewal of Vatican II. The whole point of Conciliar renewal is to bring about a full, conscious, and active participation in the Church's mission on the part of all the faithful. Since the acts of such participation are rooted in the being of the faithful, John Paul's focus is on the cultivation of that being. The third examines John Paul's understanding of missionary attitude and missionary spirituality. Finally, an inspection of John Paul's vision for the preparation, celebration, and living out of the Jubilee Year 2000 serves to confirm the consistency with which he thinks in terms of the logic of *ES*.

AN INTEGRAL UNDERSTANDING OF THE NATURE OF FAITH

John Paul is consistent with Paul VI's conviction that Vatican II is essentially a council about faith.[1] Paul VI is content to show that while some previous councils take up faith in itself, Vatican II is similar to the majority of councils that pronounced on various subjects of faith. John Paul certainly does this too, but in contrast, he also engages in an analysis of faith, based on the key text of *Dei Verbum*, 5, and with an anthropological slant, in order to show that the implementation of Vatican II consists in nothing more and nothing less than maturation of faith, which he calls the enrichment of faith. His focus on faith is especially evident in his pre-papal synthesis of the Council, *Sources of Renewal*, the unifying idea of which is: "The Council outlined the type of faith which corresponds to the life of the modern Christian, and the implementation of the Council consists first and foremost in enriching that faith."[2] Because the implementation of Vatican II is realized above all by the enrichment of faith, and because he dedicates his entire pontificate to the implementation of the Council, nothing could be more important for understanding John Paul's pontificate than to grasp his understanding of the nature of faith.

1. See Paul VI, "General Audience, March 8, 1967." It is curious that among the specific passages that Pope Paul refers to in order to support his assertion that Vatican II is a council about faith, he omits the text that for John Paul II is the most important text of all, namely, *DV*, 5.

2. Wojtyła, *SR*, 420.

And since he takes both faith itself and Pope Paul's three paths of renewal as hermeneutical keys to Vatican II, it is reasonable to anticipate that his theology of faith represents his own, personal development of Pope Paul's three paths.

Prior to and throughout his pontificate, John Paul insists on correcting an inadequate understanding of faith, namely, that faith is nothing more than an intellectual assent to what God has revealed. In fact, the frequency with which Wojtyła/John Paul II and Ratzinger-Benedict XVI assert that faith cannot be so reduced[3] is evidence of their understanding that one of the main goals of Vatican II as a pastoral council is to correct this anomalous understanding of faith. Presumably, they target this misunderstanding because they judge that it is at the root of the great pastoral crisis that the Council addresses, namely, the split between faith and life.[4] If faith does not give direction to the exercise of human freedom, if there is no difference between the conduct of believers and non-believers, if secular values imbedded in culture influence believers to the same degree that they influence non-believers, if increasing numbers of those who are baptized live "as if God did not exist"—these can only be explained by a defect of faith.

The foundation for a correct understanding of faith is to see that it concerns all of a person's life. The reason for this is that faith is correlative to revelation.[5] Most fundamentally, faith is man's response to revelation.[6] Because revelation is not just the disclosure of truths to be known but actions and words of God by which he makes a gift of himself to man and invites man to communion with himself,[7] the response of faith must be the acceptance of this gift and invitation. For this acceptance to be consistent with human dignity, it must be free, and in order for it to be

---

3. See, for example, Wojtyła, *SR*, 53–54, 140; John Paul II, "Homily, October, 15, 1979," 3; *VS*, 88; "Angelus, November 5, 1995," 1; "General Audience, March 18, 1998," 3; "Homily, October 15, 1999," 2; Ratzinger, "Revelation Itself," in Vorgrimler, *Commentary on the Documents of Vatican II*, 3:172; Benedict XVI, "General Audience, October 24, 2012"; Francis, *Lumen fidei*, 45 (acknowledged by Francis as written by Benedict XVI). In *Ratzinger's Faith* (48–50), Rowland traces the understanding of revelation and faith that Vatican II, Wojtyła, Ratzinger, and others are intent to correct to Francesco Suarez, SJ (1548–1617).

4. See Vatican II, *GS*, 43.

5. See the discussion in Lubac, "Commentaire du préambule du chapitre I," 244–45.

6. See Wojtyła, *SR*, 19–20, 27, 28, 46, 53, 57, 62, 204–5, 207, 216, 330, 422; John Paul II, "General Audience, March 27, 1985"; *FR*, 13.

7. See Vatican II, *DV*, 2.

free faith first must know and assent to what God has revealed about that gift, that is, his love and his plan for men. Consent to receive the gift follows. And because the gift transforms man into a friend of Christ and a collaborator in his mission, the believer naturally lives out all that this entails by obediently fulfilling all of the responsibilities that communion with God entails.

The following passage from *Veritatis splendor* is representative of John Paul's theology of faith:

> It is urgent to rediscover and to set forth once more the authentic reality of the Christian faith, which is not simply a set of propositions to be accepted with intellectual assent. Rather, faith is a lived knowledge of Christ, a living remembrance of his commandments, and a truth to be lived out. A word, in any event, is not truly received until it passes into action, until it is put into practice. Faith is a decision involving one's whole existence. It is an encounter, a dialogue, a communion of love and of life between the believer and Jesus Christ, the Way, and the Truth, and the Life (cf. John 14:6). It entails an act of trusting abandonment to Christ, which enables us to live as he lived (cf. Gal 2:20), in profound love of God and of our brothers and sisters.[8]

This concern to convey the comprehensive nature of faith, and especially its being lived out, runs throughout the writings of Wojtyła/John Paul II. It appears earliest in his first great synthesis of the Council's teaching and spirit while still Archbishop of Krakow;[9] it reappears at the beginning of his papacy;[10] it takes center stage in his extended catecheses on the Creed;[11] and it figures significantly in the encyclicals, *Veritatis splendor*, just quoted, and *Fides et ratio*.

---

8. John Paul II, *VS*, 88.

9. "Man's proper response to God's self-revelation consists in self-abandonment to God. This is the true dimension of faith, in which man does not simply accept a particular set of propositions, but accepts his own vocation and the sense of his existence" (Wojtyła, *SR*, 20).

10. "Revelation consists in the initiative of God, who personally came to meet man, in order to open with him a dialogue of salvation.... But the answer that God expects from man is not reduced to a cold intellectual evaluation of an abstract content of ideas" (John Paul II, "Homily, October 15, 1979," 3).

11. See his general audiences of March 13, 1985 through June 26, 1985. These can be found in the first volume of his collected general audiences on the Creed: John Paul II, *A Catechesis on the Creed*, 1:29–94.

Just as for Paul VI doctrinal awareness is the presupposition for renewal through conversion, so throughout the pontificate of John Paul II the ubiquitous theme of conversion serves as a bridge that connects faith-as-content, known and professed, on one hand, and faith that is lived because it gives meaning to every event of life, on the other hand.[12] Not content simply to clarify the content of faith, he points out its implications for the way believers live. In this way, the pastoral style of John Paul's magisterium mirrors the pastoral style of Vatican II by being invitatory and by exhorting to conversion in order to live what faith professes.[13] Living in a state of conversion, based on the conviction of faith about God's mercy,[14] is the great sign of a living faith, which is able to make a critical judgment regarding the discrepancies between what God has revealed and man's current state.[15] With this the primacy of the doctrine of God's mercy becomes evident.[16] Only if God is merciful is there any hope that an examination of conscience can be the beginning of a restoration to living one's vocation. Through conversion, faith as assent becomes faith that is lived.

It is precisely this concern that faith be lived that leads Wojtyła to refer to the enriched faith that Vatican II strives to foster as existential faith.[17] For him, faith can be considered in terms of its content—its objective dimension—or in terms of its personal, existential dimension. The objective-content dimension answers the questions: What has God revealed? And, how should I understand what he has revealed? The personal-existential dimension answers the question: How does God's

---

12. "It is faith that gives meaning to human existence" (Wojtyła, SR, 24).

13. John O'Malley is widely credited with first having drawn attention to the style of Vatican II. He first writes of styles of reform and styles of historical thinking ("Reform, Historical Consciousness, and Vatican II's *Aggiornamento*"). Later, he studies the literary or rhetorical style of the Council. See O'Malley, "Developments, Reforms, and Two Great Reformations"; "The Style of Vatican II"; "Trent and Vatican II." O'Malley's influence is evident in Famerée's collection of essays, *Vatican II comme style*.

14. See John Paul II, *DM*, 13.

15. John Paul II links this critical judgment with the renewal of Vatican II in his first encyclical. See *RH*, 4.

16. "Some theologians affirm that mercy is the greatest of the attributes and perfections of God, and the Bible, Tradition and the whole faith life of the People of God provide particular proofs of this" (John Paul II, *DM*, 13). It should be pointed out that mercy is God's chief attribute *in relation to man*. It is precisely the truth about God that man as sinner needs to know if he is to have hope of being reconciled with God.

17. See Wojtyła, SR, 20, 24, 27, 28, 140, 203, 207, 211, 224.

revelation answer the questions about the meaning of life?[18] While Vatican II concerns itself with both dimensions of faith, what characterizes it as a pastoral council is its focus on the personal, subjective, existential dimension:

> The enrichment of faith which we regard as the fundamental pre-requisite for the realization of Vatican II is to be understood in two ways: as an enrichment of the content of faith in accordance with the Council's teaching, but also, originating from that content, an enrichment of the whole existence of the believing member of the Church. This enrichment of faith in the objective sense, constituting a new stage in the Church's advance towards the "fullness of divine truth," is at the same time an enrichment in the subjective, human, existential sense, and it is from the latter that the realization of the Council has opened a new chapter of the Church's pastoral activity, interpreting that phase in its widest sense.[19]

The order between these two dimensions of faith mirrors the three paths of renewal of *ES* and the three dimensions of renewal. The enrichment of faith in the objective sense corresponds to the doctrinal penetration of the first path. This in turn gives rise to the conversion by which faith becomes enriched in the subjective, existential sense.

Faith is existential when it adheres to what God has revealed as his answers to man's questions about the purpose and meaning of his existence, his life.[20] If the truths of faith are not seen as God's answer to these questions, its content can only be stored data, information without life-giving relevance. Such faith is incapable of becoming existential and overcoming the split between faith (in the objective sense of content) and life. For, the questions about the purpose and meaning of life are essential questions about what constitutes man's happiness, and it is precisely the perception that the content of faith corresponds to man's striving for happiness that motivates him to act in accordance with this content. This is why John Paul persistently calls on people to reflect on the meaning

---

18. See Wojtyła, *SR*, 18, 24, 95, 140, 225. See also John Paul II, "General Audience, June 5, 1985"; "Address, September 24, 2001"; *RMiss*, 28.

19. Wojtyła, *SR*, 15–18.

20. Theme of man's search for definitive meaning runs throughout John Paul II's pontificate and reaches its summit in his two encyclicals, *Veritatis splendor* and *Fides et ratio*.

of life.[21] Just as the rich young man's search for what he must do to inherit eternal life leads him to Jesus, so John Paul encourages all men and women to take their questions about the meaning of life to Jesus, whose mission is to bring abundant life to all.[22]

This way of looking at faith corresponds to the logic of *ES*. Everything begins with a greater penetration into what God has revealed about man's fulfillment being participation in the life and mission of Christ and of the Church. This then becomes the objective measure for an examination of conscience, which gives rise to conversion. As a result of this conversion, the split between faith in the objective sense of content and faith as lived is overcome. Through conversion, faith as knowledge of what God has revealed becomes existential faith.

> Conversion, therefore, fosters a new life, in which there is no separation between faith and works in our daily response to the universal call to holiness. In order to speak of conversion, the gap between faith and life must be bridged. Where this gap exists, Christians are such only in name.[23]

For Wojtyła/John Paul II, then, the enrichment of faith that is the goal of the renewal of Vatican II is precisely faith that he qualifies as existential. Faith is mature when the doctrine to which it adheres is meaningful for the whole of life and orders all of life to God, and it becomes meaningful when it is perceived as God's answers to man's questions about the purpose and meaning of life.

As said above, because he defines the implementation of Vatican II as the enrichment of faith, and because he dedicates his pontificate to implementing the Council, nothing could be more important for understanding the pontificate of John Paul II than to grasp his understanding of the nature of faith. No text is more significant for his understanding of faith than the following lines from *Dei Verbum*, to which he constantly refers in his reflections on faith.

---

21. See, for example, John Paul II, *Dilecti amici*; "Message to the Youth of Curaçao"; *Veritatis splendor*, Ch. 1. Reading these texts and others, it becomes clear that the encounter between the rich young man and Jesus is John Paul's favorite biblical text for developing the theme of the search for the definitive meaning of life.

22. "I came that they may have life, and have it abundantly" (John 10:10).

23. John Paul II, *EAm*, 12.

> "The obedience of faith" (Rom 16:26; see 1:5; 2 Cor 10:5–6) must be given to God who reveals, an obedience by which man entrusts his whole self freely to God, offering "the full submission of intellect and will to God who reveals" (Vatican I, *Dei Filius*, Chap. 3), and freely assenting to the truth revealed by him.[24]

By faith a person surrenders or entrusts his entire self to God. This rephrases the traditional understanding of faith as man's submission to God of his two highest faculties, intellect and will.[25] By these two faculties, intended by the Creator to give direction to one's freedom and thus to one's entire life, man knows and directs himself to his final end, his happiness. This self-direction, which John Paul calls self-determination, constitutes man's dignity and unifies his entire life.[26] Thus, the submission of intellect and will in faith is a profoundly personal act of self-entrustment to God, and its highly personal nature is seen in the fact that the person of faith receives from God the very definition of his happiness or fulfillment. Nothing is more fundamental, all-embracing, and directive for human freedom and life than the definition of happiness. To turn to God and to allow him to shape one's vision for fulfillment, indeed, to receive this knowledge of his fulfillment and the desire for it as a gift of grace, is the most profound way for a person to place his life in God's hands, the way for human clay to be molded by the divine potter.[27]

But faith cannot remain a response of pure assent to the word of God that is heard. It must project itself into action. The description of faith in *Dei Verbum* indicates that faith "manifests itself as obedience."[28] Those with faith both "hear the word of God and do it" (Luke 8:21).[29] The first trait of Abraham's faith is that he obeyed God's instruction to leave for an unknown land and thus for an unknown future.[30] Christian obedience is

---

24. Vatican II, *DV*, 5.

25. On the necessity of man's intellect and will being perfected by faith, hope, and charity if man is to move himself to the eternal life revealed by God, see Aquinas, *ST*, I-II, q. 62, aa. 3–4.

26. On self-determination, see especially the chapter "The Personal Structure of Self-Determination" in Wojtyła, *Person and Community*. This is a translation of a paper presented by Cardinal Wojtyła in 1974.

27. On the clay and potter imagery, see Isa 29:16; 45:9; 64:8; Jer 18:4–6; Rom 9:21.

28. Fitzmyer, *Romans*, 237.

29. See Luke 11:28; Acts 6:7; Matt 13:23.

30. See Heb 11:8, on which Spicq comments: "The present participle, καλούμενος, emphasizes the perfect synchronicity [of Abraham's obedience] with the interior act of

so perfectly a property of faith[31] that in some texts of the New Testament "faith and obedience are interchangeable."[32] Faith is called obedience antonomastically.[33] As seen earlier, faith entails three acts: assent, consent, and obedience. Because obedience presupposes assent and consent and these are perfected in obedience, faith may be called obedience.

In light of the preceding, it is not a surprise that John Paul should take the text of *Dei Verbum*—with its biblical emphasis on faith giving direction to the whole of life through obedience to what God has revealed—as the Conciliar text on faith as the foundation for his understanding of the implementation of Vatican II. The Council's pastoral concern is to overcome the split between faith and life, especially with respect to mission. Once faith perceives that mission is God's will for every baptized person, it remains only to set out on that mission in the obedience of faith, as Abraham set out for an unknown land and as St. Paul set out on his mission to the Gentiles. Furthermore, faith that obediently embraces the call to mission corresponds perfectly to the dialogue of *ES*, presupposing as it does the first path of doctrinal penetration regarding the vocation to mission and a conversion based on a self-criticism that takes this doctrinal penetration as its measure.

God's Love for Man and Man's Vocation to Love, the Essential Truth of Divine Revelation and the Essential Content of Faith

For John Paul, God's love is the apex, summit, and central truth of revelation.[34] This corresponds to Vatican II.

---

immediate consent" (*L'Épitre aux Hébreux*, II, 347).

31. According to Augustine Bea, *Dei Verbum* takes "obedience of faith" to mean "that particular form of obedience which is the property of faith" (*The Word of God and Mankind*, 104).

32. Käsemann, *Commentary on Romans*, 14.

33. Antonomasia entails "the substitution of a title or epithet for a proper name such as his highness," or as St. Thomas asserts: "that which is applicable to many things in common is ascribed antonomastically to that to which it is applicable by way of excellence" (Aquinas, *ST*, II-II, q. 186, a. 1).

34. "The revelation of divine love [is] the ultimate source of the meaning of everything that exists" (John Paul II, *Salvifici doloris*, 13). "For a Christian, to live is to love and to love is to live" (John Paul II, "Homily, February 20, 1981," 3); "Jesus wished for us to inherit from him nothing less than love of every single human being.... For what else does man seek except to be loved? What else gives human existence its fundamental meaning?" (Wojtyła, *Sign of Contradiction*, 99–100); "The Church's faith reaches its

Since faith is correlative to revelation—that is, defined most generally as man's response to revelation—love is correspondingly the fundamental truth to which faith adheres. Love of God, love of self, and love of others for God's sake gives meaning to every action of life. Put another way, as image of God man is made for love, which means that he is made to define his happiness in terms of relationships—with God, with self, with others. This is the essential meaning of the mystery of redemption in Christ.[35] Love is the essential meaning of human life and the reason why faith can be existential. Further, it is always possible to live with this meaning that faith brings, for, as St. Paul assures, nothing is able to separate us from the love of God revealed in Jesus Christ.[36] For John Paul, Vatican II takes the revelation of God's love for man and the fulfillment of man's vocation to love in Christ as the very center of its pastoral, i.e., anthropocentric, exposition of faith.[37]

That love is the essential content or meaning of revelation explains why faith cannot be reduced to being an intellectual assent. To believe in God's love means to encounter that love and to be enriched by it, not just to know about it. At the same time, knowledge about God's love is required in order to receive it, since the nature of the gift of love is that it must be both freely given and freely received, and knowledge is the condition of freedom. And this relation between knowledge of God's

---

peak in this supreme truth: God is love!... The truth that God is Love constitutes as it were the apex of all that has been revealed.... This truth illumines the whole content of divine revelation" (John Paul II, "General Audience, October 2, 1985," 2). See also: John Paul II, *RH*, 10; *Dilecti amici*, 7; "Message for World Day of Vocations, May 6, 2001," 1–2.

35. See John Paul II, *RH*, 8–10.

36. See Rom 8:38–39.

37. "The true personalistic interpretation of the commandment of love is found in the words of the Council" (Wojtyła, *Crossing the Threshold of Hope*, 201). The Conciliar text he has in mind is *Gaudium et spes*, 24. See also *DeV*, 59: "These words of the Pastoral Constitution of the Council [*GS*, 24] can be said to sum up the whole of Christian anthropology." Wojtyła develops his thoughts on *Gaudium et spes*, 24, as the summary of theological anthropology in his 1974 article, "The Family as a Community of Persons," reproduced in Wojtyła, *Person and Community*, 315–27. Regarding *Gaudium et spes*, 22, the first paragraph of which for John Paul II virtually recapitulates Vatican II, John Paul is attentive to the fact that it is "by the revelation of the mystery of the Father and his love" that Jesus Christ "fully reveals man to man himself and makes his supreme calling clear." Prior to the Council, Wojtyła defines man's fundamental vocation as love, and shows that every particular or personal vocation is in essence some form of specification of love (see Wojtyła, "The Problem of Vocation," in *Love and Responsibility*, 241–44).

love and the experience of actually being loved corresponds to the relation between the first two paths of renewal, doctrinal penetration and transformative renewal. In this way, taking love as the essential content of faith sheds further light on the three dimensions of renewal and the corresponding three dimensions of formation.

John Paul's insistence that participation in God's own charity is the fully human meaning of every moment of life corresponds to the teaching of the Common Doctor that charity informs all other virtues.[38] It also corresponds to Aquinas's teaching that love is not given and received merely by being known. Though knowledge of love is the precondition for receiving it, knowledge only makes the form of the object known exist intentionally, but not really, in the knower. This intentional presence then gives rise to a love of desire really to be united with the object known.[39] This desire is the bridge between doctrinal penetration and renewal through conversion.

Personal Vocation

In order for the meaning of life, fully revealed in the mystery of Christ, to permeate the entirety of a person's life, the universal vocation to holiness and participation in the Church's mission needs to be specified, concretized for each person. For John Paul, this specification of the total entrustment of self to God in faith as response to God's invitation to love is each one's personal vocation.[40]

---

38. See Aquinas, *ST*, II-II, q. 23, a. 8. In his commentary on this article, Marie-Michel Labourdette explains that, while there are several virtues that inform others, only charity is able to inform *all* the virtues because charity alone has God as man's final end as its proper object. This corresponds to St. Thomas's teaching in another work: "But the theologian considers as the final good that which is beyond the capacity of nature, namely, everlasting life, as has been said. Thus, he does not consider the good in human acts without qualification, because he puts the end not in the acts themselves, but in the disposition to that good which he makes the end. He says that only that act is completely good which has a proximate relation to the final good, that is, an act which merits eternal life. He says that every such act is an act of virtue, and every habit properly eliciting such an act he calls a virtue" (Aquinas, *Disputed Questions*, q. 14, a. 3).

39. See Aquinas, *ST*, II-II, q. 23, a. 6, ad. 1.

40. John Paul II speaks and writes of personal vocation frequently. See, for example, *CL*, 58; Messages for the 37th, 38th, and 41st for World Day of Prayer for Vocations (2000, 1; 2001, 1; 2004, 4). On this subject, see Grisez and Shaw, *Personal Vocation*.

> Man's proper response to God's self-revelation consists in self-abandonment to God. This is the true dimension of faith, in which man does not simply accept a particular set of propositions, but accepts his own vocation and the sense of his existence.[41]

To arrive at a faith-based awareness of one's personal vocation, that is, one's place in God's plan of love, rectifies the reductionist conception of faith as intellectual assent to revealed propositions. Here, again, because faith is defined in terms of revelation, this existential understanding of faith derives from the understanding of revelation, which precedes faith. Revelation "is not only the manifestation of the mystery of God, but is also an invitation, by accepting which man participates in the work of salvation."[42] Faith that entails a personal vocation makes it possible to perceive every event, circumstance, and action as a manifestation of God's will.[43]

A believer's personal vocation cannot, properly speaking, be the object of faith because it is not divinely revealed (as are the vocations of Mary, Peter, Paul, and other biblical figures). Nevertheless, what faith assents to as contained in divine revelation provides the principles that guide the discernment of God's will and eventual choice of a vocation. To discover one's personal vocation within the universal vocation to holiness and participation in the Church's mission is to discover one's precise manner of cooperating with Divine Providence.

This integral understanding of faith as entailing personal vocation is doubtless the reason why John Paul so deliberately addresses the faithful in their various states, conditions, and circumstances. It is to inculcate a faith-based sense of vocation that he speaks and writes to bishops, priests,

---

41. Wojtyła, *SR*, 20. He speaks similarly at the outset of his papacy: "Revelation consists in the initiative of God, who personally came to meet man, in order to open with him a dialogue of salvation.... But the answer that God expects from man is not reduced to a cold intellectual evaluation of an abstract content of ideas" (John Paul II, "Homily, October 15, 1979," 3).

42. Wojtyła, *SR*, 53–55. Also, he refers to the vocation-aspect of faith as having "its foundation in the very manner in which the divine Trinity revealed itself" (*SR*, 58).

43. See Vatican II, *LG*, 34 on making a spiritual sacrifice or one's entire life, and *LG*, 41 on fulfilling the call to holiness through all the "conditions, duties, and circumstances" of life. The conditional clause in each text is key. *If* all things are "carried out in the Spirit" and *if* the faithful "receive all things with faith from the hand of their heavenly Father and *if* they cooperate with the divine will," then all of these activities "become 'spiritual sacrifices acceptable to God through Jesus Christ'" and the faithful "will daily increase in holiness."

deacons, religious, consecrated, laity, families, women, workers, youth, elderly, artists, suffering, intellectuals, politicians, theologians, scientists, teachers, migrants, etc.

The question can be asked whether, in light of the preceding, Christoph Theobald might rescind or moderate his complaint that the post-Synodal apostolic exhortations that focus on various states or groups within the Church lack a unifying coherence.[44] Theobald's project of looking for an internal principle within the Conciliar corpus overlooks the unity that John Paul II proposes, namely, enrichment of faith as full, conscious, and active participation in the Church's life and mission, with a particular emphasis on holiness.[45] These themes, which are fundamental for the renewal, interpretation, and implementation of Vatican II, have a differentiated realization among the various states and vocations in the Church. This is why the Council itself produced separate documents for clergy, laity, and religious.[46] The same logic holds for the continental synods leading to the Jubilee Year 2000. The one, holy, and catholic Church subsists in local and particular Churches.[47] As a result, the full appropriation and realization of the teaching and spirit of Vatican II will vary, not essentially, but culturally and circumstantially, among the Churches.

John Paul's principle for interpreting Vatican II is based on the Council's own declared goals, and this unifies the Conciliar corpus with the unity of the final cause. Theobald's proposal to take the "pastorality of doctrine" as the Council's unifying principle leads him to focus on questions of fundamental theology in his effort to interpret Vatican II, especially the relation of the Church today to Sacred Scripture. While Vatican II is certainly the occasion for raising questions of fundamental theology, and of the development of doctrine in particular, there is a risk in taking this "issue underlying all issues at the Council"[48] as a hermeneutical key to the Council. The risk is to devalue what the Council Fathers clearly intended to assert at that time. The merit of John Paul's focus on faith,

---

44. See Theobald, "The Theological Options of Vatican II."

45. On the unifying theme of holiness, see Bushman, "General Introduction," xv–xix.

46. An example of the Council's awareness of this differentiated realization is *LG*, 41, where the essential elements of holiness are shown to be realized in the different vocations within the Church.

47. See Vatican II, *LG*, 13, 23.

48. The phrase is from John Courtney Murray. See Bushman, "Pope Paul VI on the Renewal of Vatican II," 368n59.

the call to holiness, and renewed mission is, first, that these are themes found within the Conciliar corpus, and, second, that they correspond to the explicitly stated goals of the Council.

Anthropological Foundations of Existential Faith: Faith-consciousness and Faith-attitude

Wojtyła/John Paul II's theology of the enrichment of faith is a synthesis of biblical and anthropological terms. It is inseparable from his understanding of Vatican II as a pastoral council.

> The question "What does it mean to be a believing member of the Church?" is indeed difficult and complex, because it not only presupposes the truth of faith and pure doctrine, but also calls for that truth to be situated in the human consciousness and calls for a definition of the attitude, or rather the many attitudes, that go to make the individual a believing member of the Church. This would seem to be the main respect in which the Conciliar magisterium has a pastoral character, corresponding to the pastoral purpose for which it was called. A "purely" doctrinal Council would have concentrated on defining the precise meaning of the truths of faith, whereas a pastoral Council proclaims, recalls or clarifies truths for the primary purpose of giving Christians a life-style, a way of thinking and acting. In our efforts to put the Council into practice, this is the style we must keep before our minds. In the present study, designed to help towards the realization of Vatican II, we shall concentrate on the consciousness of Christians and the attitudes they should acquire. These attitudes, springing from a well-formed Christian consciousness, can in a sense be regarded as true proof of the realization of the Council. This is the direction which should be followed by all pastoral action, the lay apostolate and the whole of the Church's activity.[49]

In order to show in detail how the grace of faith perfects human nature and becomes existential, Wojtyła/John Paul II analyzes how faith-consciousness precedes and is completed by faith-attitude. The former corresponds to the way that faith perfects the intellect and the latter to the corresponding perfection of the will. Faith is enriched and existential (that is, "fully human") when what God has revealed—faith as content, or

---

49. Wojtyła, *SR*, 17–18.

doctrine—permeates man's self-consciousness and his attitudes, thereby perfecting man's two highest powers, intellect and will.[50] He defines both self-consciousness and attitudes in terms of man's fundamental, God-given dynamism to seek his own fulfillment by the development of virtue. He calls this self-determination. The axis of his synthesis, then, is rooted in the relation of intellect to will, but with a phenomenological accent that underscores the unity of object known and knowing subject, and of object willed and willing subject. For John Paul, the existential faith that is the goal of the renewal of Vatican II is realized when the content of faith is fully appropriated or assimilated by informing believers's consciousness and attitudes.

For Wojtyła/John Paul II, the principle that underpins the relation between consciousness and attitude also governs his development of the anthropology of Vatican II. It is the *operari sequitur esse* principle.[51] Vatican II's goal of revitalizing the Church's missionary activity (*operari*) requires a renewal of the mission's agents (*esse*), and the renewal of their Christian being consists precisely in the formation of consciousness and attitude. The essential content of this formation, as we have seen, is love. In this way the dignity of Christians as image of God, that is, as free causes,[52] comes to perfection through participation in God's own love. For, according to St. Thomas, "Each thing is perfect when it can generate things like itself."[53] From this it follows that if the characteristic act

50. Since it is man's dignity to move himself to his end (see Aquinas, *Commentary on St. Paul's Letter to the Romans*, Ch. 2, lect. 3, Marietti, 217), and since he does this through intellect and will, St. Thomas argues that faith, hope, and charity are necessary for man to move himself to his supernatural end. See Aquinas, *ST*, I-II q. 62, aa. 3–4.

51. "In its basic conception the whole of *The Acting Person* is grounded on the premise that *operari sequitur esse*" (Wojtyła, *Person and Community*, 260n6). This is easily reconciled with another statement, "that the personal structure of self-determination, lies at the very heart of my study *The Acting Person*" (188). What a person experiences in self-determination is precisely that concrete being (*esse*), that is, oneself as personal subject, who is the efficient cause of a free act (*operari*) (see 189). The *operari* principle corresponds to St. Thomas's distinction between first and second act. On first and second act, see Aquinas, *ST*, I, q. 48, a. 5. Regarding this, it is significant that St. Thomas, following Cicero, considers virtue as a "second nature" (see *ST*, I-II, q. 58, a. 1), since nature is the principle of operation (*ST*, I-II, q. 49, a. 3; q. 50, a. 2, ad. 3).

52. On free causes collaborating with God, see *CCC*, 306–7. On the dignity of being causes, see Aquinas, *ST*, I, q. 22, a. 3; I, q. 23, a. 8, ad. 2; Aquinas, *Disputed Questions*, q. 11; Aquinas, *De magistro*, a. 1, in *Disputed Questions*.

53. Aquinas, *Disputed Questions*, q. 11, a. 1, fifth *sed contra*. Similarly: "For the natural order requires that a thing should be first perfected in itself, and that afterwards it should communicate of its perfection to others: and this is also the order of charity

of witnessing to the mystery of Christ (*operari*), which is the essence of mission and love, is absent or defective, it must be due to an inadequate formation of consciousness and attitude (*esse*).

The *operari sequitur esse* principle is so fundamental to experience and to the way we think that it is not surprising to discover that Paul VI similarly views Vatican II in its light. The Council is an act of the Church, conscious of "the need to conform our conduct [*operari*] to the dignity of our nature [*esse*]." "Each one should say in the interior forum of his own conscience: 'Christian, be Christian!'"[54] This is the most concise summary of *ES* and of the renewal of Vatican II. The Council reminds us who we are, of our Christian dignity and being, with a focus on the mystery of the Church and our participation in its life and mission. It is replete with exhortations to live out what it teaches about the nature, vocation, and mission of the Church, and the dignity of every baptized to participate in her life and mission.

"Christian, be Christian," is a non-technical translation of the *operari sequitur esse* principle, as is John Paul's "Become what you are."[55] This is the essential meaning of the Council's renewal, which can be understood in light of its goal of promoting "full, conscious, and active participation in the liturgy, which is demanded by the very nature of the liturgy."[56] The renewal of Vatican II is, most generally, ordered to promoting a full, conscious, and active participation in the Church' life and mission, a participation that is demanded by the very nature of the Church.

To realize this goal, the Council adopts a pastoral style of teaching that mimics the relation between the doctrinal and parenetic passages of St. Paul, in which, as Scripture scholars acknowledge, Paul expounds the moral implications of Christians's new being in Christ.[57] This explains

---

which perfects nature" (*ST*, III, q. 64, a. 1); "Since every agent intends to introduce its likeness into its effect, in the measure that its effect can receive it, the agent does this the more perfectly as it is the more perfect itself" (*SCG*, II, 45). Conversely, "all effects are most perfect when they are most like their efficient causes" (*SCG*, II, 46).

54. Paul VI, "General Audience, April 14, 1971."

55. John Paul's exhortation to families is best known: "Family, become what you are" (*FC*, 17).

56. Vatican II, *SC*, 14.

57. Prat explicitly enlists the *operatio sequitur esse* principle in his discussion of Paul's parenetic passages (see *The Theology of St. Paul*, 2:318–19). Spicq writes of "a new moral life that conforms to the exigencies of [the Christian's] new being" (*Théologie morale du Nouveau Testament*, 1:61–62). See also Sensing, "Towards a Definition of Paraenesis."

the numerous exhortations in the Conciliar corpus, whether they take the form of incorporating biblical exhortations[58] or exhortations in the Council's own words.[59] The relevance of this for the interpretation of Vatican II is that as a pastoral council aiming to renew Christian life,[60] it is rooted in doctrine, most especially, according to Paul VI and the witness of those who participated in the Council, the doctrine of the Church. And it is this relation between the doctrine of the Church and life according to that doctrine, which is realized through conversion, that corresponds to the logic of *ES*.

Thus, the relation of doctrine to parenesis in St. Paul emerges as the biblical and anthropological underpinning of Conciliar renewal as expounded by Paul VI in *ES*. And, as we have just seen, the relation of parenesis to doctrine correlates to the *operari sequitur esse* principle. Doctrine corresponds to the truth about Christian *esse*, and parenesis corresponds to doctrine as lived. That is, parenesis aims at the existential faith that John Paul II takes as the realization of Vatican II's renewal. It remains to point out that for John Paul, the *operari sequitur esse* principle is recapitulated in or condensed into the "become what you are" exhortation. For, in explaining the significance of his reference to the "Know Yourself" engraved on the Delphic temple at the beginning of his encyclical, *Fides et ratio*, he states: "Because of what he knows about the world and about himself [call this doctrine regarding *esse*], man can respond to another command passed on to us by Greek thought: *become what you are* [call this *operari*]."[61] Responding to divine revelation by faith, man comes to know the truth about God, himself, and the world, and this truth forms his consciousness and attitudes, whereby his faith becomes existential.

A final anthropological foundation emerges in light of the affinity between St. Paul's parenesis and Vatican II as a pastoral council, on one hand, and the logic of *ES*, on the other. This concerns the role of conscience, which in *ES* is the bridge between doctrinal consciousness and renewal through conversion. To repeat Pope Paul's most concise phrasing, which in context is an explanation of the *operari sequitur esse*

---

58. See for example: Matt 6:6 and 1 Thess 5:17 in *SC*, 12; 2 Thess 5:17 in *SC*, 86; 1 Cor 7:3–6 and Eph 5:25–33 in *GS*, 49; Luke 12:48 in *LG*, 14; 1 Cor 7:31 in *LG*, 42.

59. See for example: *AA*, 6, 33; *AG*, 11; *DH*, 15; *PO*, 16, 22; *OT*, 21.

60. The Council's first goal is "to impart an ever increasing vigor to the Christian life of the faithful" (*SC*, 1).

61. John Paul II, "Address, October 31, 1998," 2.

principle: "Each one should say in the interior forum of his own conscience: 'Christian, be Christian!'"[62] Clearly, the exhortation presupposes knowledge of what it means to be Christian, and thus the doctrine of what God has revealed in Christ, the perfect man, whom Christians not only imitate but in whose life they participate. "Be Christian!" is, then, the all-embracing moral norm. Conscience is the primordial, interior form of parenesis, which accompanies all Christian moral norms and is the predisposition for adhering to external exhortation.[63] To know the truth of the good entails an obligation to act on this knowledge when a person perceives a necessary relation between that truth and his own fulfillment.[64] This is to say that the movement from awareness of the truth about the Church to conversion into that truth presupposes not only a speculative grasp of this truth but also a love of the Church, that connaturalization of which Pope Paul writes.[65] The doctrine of the Church can only be translated into a moral imperative by the conscience on the supposition that a person defines himself, and his happiness, in terms of participating in the Church's life and mission.

The *operari sequitur esse* principle is inseparable from another, *bonum diffusivum sui*, which is manifested in God's acts of creation and redemption.[66] John Paul puts this in personalistic terms: "The supreme Good wants to give himself and to make all who seek him with a sincere heart resemble him."[67] This is what it means for God to love. As image of God, man is called to participate in the divine love that constitutes the Trinity "an eternal exchange of love,"[68] and by which God makes a gift

---

62. Paul VI, "General Audience, April 14, 1971."

63. On this, see Gaffney, "On Parenesis and Fundamental Moral Theology," esp. 31, where he quotes Bruno Schüller, "The Debate on the Specific Character of a Christian Ethic: Some Remarks."

64. Wojtyła/John Paul develops this fundamental anthropology by showing that one's self-determination is "the primary and principal object of the will" (*The Acting Person*, 142; see also 150).

65. Though this text appears above (Ch. 3, especially n8) it bears repeating: "The mystery of the Church is not a mere object of theological knowledge; it is something to be lived, something that the faithful soul can have a kind of connatural experience of, even before arriving at a clear notion of it" (Paul VI, *ES*, 37).

66. See John Paul II, "General Audience, December 18, 1985," 2; "General Audience, May 7, 1986," 2; *DeV*, 37. He frequently quotes Aquinas (*ST*, I, q. 5, a. 4, ad. 2) as the source for the *bonum diffusivum sui* (or *bonum est diffusivum sui*) principle.

67. John Paul II, "Homily, October 12, 1997," 8.

68. *CCC*, 221.

of himself to men in Christ. This participation is the goal of the Church's mission, that is, the dialogue of *ES*, which after Vatican II is called the New Evangelization. The primary mode of this mission is the witness of a holy life, for holiness communicates "a message that convinces without the need for words."[69] Saints are the embodiment of the fully human life that all seek. They make present the divine goodness in which they participate, and they bear witness to the fulfillment of self-determination that is "the primary and principal object of the will." Through the witness of their actions (*operari*) people perceive something of their divine being (*esse*) and freely move themselves to this good, in which they perceive the fulfillment of their fundamental mission of self-determination.

All of this indicates that the absolute foundation for the Church's dialogue with the world is human nature and its dynamism toward self-fulfillment, self-determination. The various concentric circles of the dialogue correspond to the degree to which those with whom the Church is in dialogue share the same convictions about the actual content of self-determination. Based on her faith that "Christ fully reveals man to man himself and makes his supreme calling clear"[70] and that "whoever follows after Christ, the perfect man, becomes himself more of a man,"[71] the Church "with frank confidence stands upon the path of history and says to men: 'I have that for which you search, that which you lack.'"[72]

The goal of the Church's mission, carried out in dialogue, is precisely that of St. Paul: "to bring about the obedience of faith" (Rom 16:26). Man can only come to faith and adhere to faith in a manner that is consistent with his dignity by choosing to believe.[73] And in order to make this choice, he has to perceive that faith is good for him, that he will be enriched by believing, that it corresponds to his fundamental vocation and responsibility of self-determination.[74] This is the reason for the adoption of dialogue as the mode of the Church's mission. The Church's dialogue

---

69. John Paul II, *NMI*, 7. See also Paul VI, *EN*, 21, where he writes of Christians's "wordless witness."

70. Vatican II, *GS*, 22.

71. Vatican II, *GS*, 41.

72. Paul VI, *ES*, 95.

73. Vatican II treats this in its Decree on Religious Liberty, *Dignitatis humanae*.

74. In a theology of faith based on the teaching of St. Thomas Aquinas, this pertains to the role of the will in the act of faith. Theology brings out "the value for salvation" to be found in revealed truth, since all that God has done is "for us men and for our salvation."

is her participation in God's dialogue of salvation, a key characteristic of which that it constrains no one.[75]

For Wojtyła/John Paul II, dialogue is the properly human way of coming to know the truth.[76] It correlates to man's social nature regarding the search for truth. "In its most general and simple sense of an exchange of ideas," dialogue is the way in which people "help one another in the search for truth."[77] Here, Wojtyła defines dialogue by drawing from *Dignitatis humanae*.[78] Nearly a quarter of a century later, as Pope, he indicates again how central *Dignitatis humanae* is to his understanding of dialogue.

> As I have often stated, the Second Vatican Council constituted an extraordinary grace for the Church, and a decisive moment of her recent history. *Dignitatis Humanae* is undoubtedly one of the Council's most innovative texts. It has the specific and important merit of having cleared the way for that remarkable and fruitful dialogue between the Church and the world, so ardently proposed and encouraged by that other great Council document, the Pastoral Constitution *Gaudium et Spes*.[79]

Faith informs self-consciousness when divine revelation is perceived as corresponding to "the primary and principal object of the will," that is, as corresponding to a person's natural dynamism to self-determination. Then faith becomes the essence of one's identity, one's self-definition. It is

---

75. See *ES*, 75, referred to in Vatican II, *DH*, 8.

76. "The transcendent character of the person, together with man's responsibility to the truth, not only constitutes the basis of the dialogue . . ." (Wojtyła, *SR*, 36).

77. Wojtyła, *SR*, 27.

78. "Truth, however, is to be sought after in a manner proper to the dignity of the human person and his social nature. The inquiry is to be free, carried on with the aid of teaching or instruction, communication and dialogue, in the course of which men explain to one another the truth they have discovered, or think they have discovered, in order thus to assist one another in the quest for truth" (Vatican II, *DH*, 3). Bernard Pottier insightfully draws attention to the prominent place of *Dignitatis humanae* in *Sources of Renewal* and in John Paul's understanding of Vatican II. "The orientation of Vatican II is due in part to the modernity of this thesis of *Dignitatis humanae*, which renews the way in which the Church's mission is understood in today's world, in large part atheist or unbelieving. It is important to avoid severe condemnations and to be prepared for dialogue. This is why witness is one of the major themes of Vatican II" (Pottier, "Vatican II," 366).

79. John Paul II, *DH*, 2. Already, in a published letter written during the Council, Wojtyła refers to *DH* as "a reference text for many other documents" (*En Esprit et en Vérité*, 234).

not just information or data that is retained. Rather, it is knowledge that gives definitive meaning and purpose to life because it concerns above all man's final end, and for this reason it integrates all of life into a simple unity of participating in the mystery of Christ. Man cannot fail to seek his own fulfillment, he cannot fail to love himself. As St. Thomas puts it, "the first thing that occurs to a man to think about is to deliberate about himself," especially about his "due end."[80] This explains the role of the will in the act of faith,[81] so that faith-informed self-consciousness is not just information taken in about man's happiness, as if man could be neutral in relation to it. By its very nature, faith-consciousness gives rise to actions that are ordered to the realization of man's happiness. And this is the reason why consciousness engenders various attitudes on the part of the will.

The human person is a meaning-seeking being[82] in the double sense that corresponds to the traditional office of the wise man: to know order (both about God, creation, and himself) and to produce order (both within himself and outside of himself). Faith is the gift by which man knows what God knows about himself, creation, and man, and by which he participates in God's ordering activity. Essentially this means building up the Church, a civilization of love, since God is love and man, made in his image, is made for love. Existential faith—faith that informs consciousness and attitudes—allows man to know the truth about love and to order his life accordingly, seeing every event and action of his life in terms of love, since "divine love [is] the ultimate source of the meaning of everything that exists."[83]

Such existential faith is the goal of Vatican II as a pastoral council ordered to overcoming the "split between faith and life."[84] It is the fruit of the renewal *ad intra* through conversion, which produces the spirituality of living with the meaning that derives from what God has revealed in Christ, who "fully reveals man to man himself and makes his supreme calling clear."[85] For Wojtyła/John Paul II, it is by reason of the very na-

---

80. Aquinas, *ST*, I–II, q. 89, a. 6.

81. On the relation of intellect and will in St. Thomas, see *ST*, I-II, q. 9, a. 1; q. 16, a. 4, ad. 1; q. 17, a. 1. Faith provides the first principles that man needs in order to direct himself to his supernatural end. See Aquinas, *ST*, I–II, q. 62, a. 3.

82. See John Paul II, *FR*.

83. John Paul II, *SD*, 13.

84. Vatican II, *GS*, 43.

85. Vatican II, *GS*, 22.

ture of faith that the "fact of knowing them better [the truths studied in catechesis] should make them even more challenging and decisive for one's life."[86] Doctrinal awareness or consciousness leads to spiritual renewal based on a fundamental attitude of being ready to conform one's thoughts, words, and actions to the vocation that God reveals to man and that is condensed in doctrine.

The fruit of spiritual renewal based on doctrinal consciousness is what Wojtyła calls attitudes, which correlate to the various truths of doctrine. The subjective appropriation of the faith by consciousness calls for all those actions by which a person's response to revelation becomes concrete by embracing his vocation. The general attitude of faith by which a person is ready to perform any good work directed by God—the "obedience of faith"—becomes specified by the implications for action deriving from specific truths of the faith. Thus, consciousness gives rise to various attitudes, which are so many dispositions of readiness to engage in those actions that are called forth by the commitment of faith. Like Mary, a person stands ever ready as the Lord's handmaid. Consciousness is the assimilation by the believing subject of the content of faith, while attitude is the assimilation by the subject of the moral implications of his new being in Christ.

When Wojtyła/John Paul II states that the implementation of Vatican II consists in the enrichment of faith thus understood, he is in effect following the three-dimensional program of renewal of Paul VI in *ES* and developing it from the perspective of a theology of faith and its anthropological foundations.

SPIRITUALITY AND MARIAN SPIRITUALITY IN PARTICULAR

In the corpus of John Paul's writings, addresses, and homilies, the one word, "spirituality," conveys the reality of existential faith. For John Paul, spirituality is a synthesis of three dimensions of renewal and of formation. While it is not only possible, but for the sake of theological analysis necessary, to distinguish faith as content and faith as lived, the very nature of faith requires that the two always be joined. Spirituality is the full assimilation in consciousness and attitudes of what God has revealed and what man adheres to by faith. This is the transformation of human

---

86. John Paul II, *CT*, 25.

being into Christian being, which manifests itself in the actions that correspond to this being (*operari sequitur esse*).

The prime example of a lived spirituality of faith is the Blessed Virgin Mary. Following Vatican II, John Paul proposes Mary and her obedience of faith as the model that all Christians should imitate. Faith, then, is not just knowing about Mary. It is a participation in the mystery of God's love as it is revealed in the efficacious transformation the Mother of God, manifest in her obedience of faith. Faith in what God has revealed about Mary means to take her as the model of all Christian virtues and to reproduce that model in one's life. What God has revealed about Mary cannot be reduced to the defined dogmas about Mary, even if these do convey important aspects of the mystery of her place in God's plan. This is why, in his encyclical on Mary, John Paul meditates[87] on her pilgrimage of faith. In this way he expounds on the Mariology of Vatican II by presenting the revealed truth about Mary in a manner that mirrors St. Thomas Aquinas's treatise on the life of Christ.[88]

According to Wojtyła, in contrast to a doctrinal council, which "concentrate[s] on defining the precise meaning of the truths of faith . . . a pastoral council proclaims, recalls or clarifies truths for the primary purpose of giving Christians a life-style, a way of thinking and acting."[89] The great Marian dogmas had been defined prior to Vatican II. The pastoral challenge that the Council addresses is that of presenting what God has revealed about Mary in a way that attracts the faithful to her because they discover in her life a reflection of the mystery of Christ, who "fully reveals man to man himself."[90] It is precisely the perception of the relation of the truth about Mary (or any divinely revealed truth) and one's

---

87. It is significant that John Paul describes what he writes about Mary as a "reflection" (*RMat*, 1) and as an invitation to "meditate together" (*RMat*, 8) rather than as an authoritative teaching. This is especially fitting for an encyclical on Mary, since it corresponds to her own faith, which Scripture describes as a pondering in her heart of what God has revealed (see Luke 2:19, 51). John Paul is exercising his Petrine magisterium *with* the all the faithful, leading "those who treasure these things in their hearts" in "contemplation and study" (*DV*, 8) of what God has revealed about Mary.

88. The title of chapter 8 of *LG* prolongs this salvation history-based approach to the mystery of the Church. The impact of this dimension of the pastoral nature of Vatican II is seen in the emphasis on the economy of salvation in the *CCC*, especially its incorporation of a long section on *The Mysteries of Christ's Life* (see Schönborn, *Introduction to the Catechism*, 72–73; "The Divine Economy," 75–84). Another indication of its impact is evident in Benedict XVI's "Foreword" to *Jesus of Nazareth*, 1:xvi–xxiv.

89. Wojtyła, *SR*, 18.

90. Vatican II, *GS*, 22, quoted in *RMat*, 4, 46.

aspiration to live a fully human life that endows Marian doctrine with its power to become light for believers's living. In other words, when people perceive that revealed truth corresponds to their desire for fulfillment or happiness, faith becomes a spirituality.

The emphasis of Wojtyła/John Paul II on Marian spirituality corresponds perfectly to the Council's own assertion that "true devotion [to Mary] . . . proceeds from true faith, by which we are led to know the excellence of the Mother of God, and we are moved to a filial love toward our mother and to the imitation of her virtues."[91] Marian doctrine is not meant to remain at the level of knowledge that informs the intellect and does not affect how a person lives. It is meant to be believed and to become an element of one's self-consciousness, a constituent element of one's definition of happiness, and thus a reference point for the engagement of one's freedom in daily life. This is what it means for faith in what God has revealed about Mary to become a genuine Marian spirituality. John Paul sums this up:

> The Marian Year is meant to promote a new and more careful reading of what the Council said about the Blessed Virgin Mary, Mother of God, in the mystery of Christ and of the Church. . . . Here we speak not only of the doctrine of the faith but also of the life of faith, and thus of authentic Marian spirituality, seen in the light of Tradition, and especially the spirituality to which the Council exhorts us.[92]

With this, the significance of *Redemptoris Mater* in John Paul's pontificate becomes clear. He dedicates his pontificate to the reception of Vatican II, and defines this reception-implementation in terms of faith. The Council is so fundamentally about the enrichment of faith that its teaching on faith in *Dei Verbum*, 5 "is at the very center of the teaching of Vatican II and contains in a certain manner all that the Council wished to say about the Church, mankind and the world."[93] The actual subject of this assertion is man's participation in the priesthood of Christ. This is what is at the center of the Council's teaching. However, Wojtyła identifies the baptismal priesthood of self-offering to God with the self-commitment to God and obedience of faith of *Dei Verbum*, 5.

91. Vatican II, *LG*, 67.
92. John Paul II, *RMat*, 48.
93. Wojtyła, *SR*, 225.

> This commitment, contained in the very essence of faith, is realized most fully in the attitude which derives from sharing in the priesthood of Christ. This attitude, in fact, seems to endow the acts of Christian faith with their fullest existential dimension.[94]

By faith and baptism one's entire life becomes a spiritual sacrifice,[95] that is a liturgy, a service to God.

What the Council teaches about faith and the spiritual sacrifice of the baptismal priesthood is anything but an abstract dogmatic formula, removed from life. The Mother of God is the perfect realization of such existential faith described in article five of *Dei Verbum*.[96] She is the perfect model of the obedience of faith, of existential faith. For this reason, the reception-implementation of Vatican II as a pastoral council for the enrichment of faith consists in cultivating an authentic Marian devotion. With faith that takes Mary as the model of Christian life, the Church can fulfill her vocation and mission as mother.[97] With this, the Council's doctrinal penetration into what God has revealed about the Church's vocation, identity, and mission becomes the spirituality it is meant to be. This is the foundation for the claim that *Redemptoris Mater* has a unique place in John Paul's commitment to guide the implementation-reception of Vatican II.

In fact, John Paul invites us to interpret the development of doctrine that took place at Vatican II in light of Mary's pilgrimage of faith, which personifies "the history of the whole People of God."[98] Specifically, John Paul conveys the reality of the hermeneutic of continuity in his reflections on Mary's pilgrimage of faith in terms of confirmation and new light. Thus, for example, the words of Simeon at the Presentation confirm the words of Gabriel at the Annunciation while at the same time they shed further light on them.[99] Similarly, Vatican II both confirms the Church's faith regarding Mary and sheds new light on that faith. "Linking itself with Tradition, the Second Vatican Council brought new light to bear on the role of the Mother of Christ in the life of the Church."[100] All that the

---

94. Wojtyła, *SR*, 224.
95. See *LG*, 10, 34.
96. See John Paul II, *RMat*, 13.
97. For John Paul, the Church fulfills her call to be the sacrament of Christ through her motherhood. See *RMat*, 43.
98. John Paul II, *RMat*, 5.
99. John Paul II, *RMat*, 16.
100. John Paul II, *RMat*, 42.

Council teaches is governed by this Marian experience of growth in faith through continual confirmation of what the Church has always believed and new light being shed upon it.[101]

The pastoral intention of Vatican II's teaching on Mary is to promote the enrichment of faith, that existential faith by which the content of faith permeates believers's consciousness and attitudes. Faith that is enriched makes what God has revealed about Mary become light for life, that is, a true spirituality.

> In effect, the term spirituality means a mode or form of life in keeping with Christian demands. Spirituality is "life in Christ" and "in the Spirit," which is accepted in faith, expressed in love and inspired by hope, and so becomes the daily life of the Church community. In this sense, by spirituality, which is the goal of conversion, we mean "not a part of life, but the whole of life guided by the Holy Spirit."[102]

Reading the above text from *Ecclesia in America* side by side with the earlier text of *Redemptoris Mater*, 48, the three paths of renewal and three dimensions of formation fully appear. In *Redemptoris Mater*, John Paul links doctrine to spirituality; this corresponds to the movement from doctrinal formation to spiritual formation. In *Ecclesia in America*, the movement is from spirituality (conversion) to "the whole of life guided by the Holy Spirit"; this corresponds to the movement from spiritual formation to pastoral formation. The obedience of faith, or, the spiritual sacrifice of one's entire life, is the active participation in Christ's life and mission, of which Mary is the perfect realization, that the Council seeks to promotes. It is the fruit of a *metanoia* that takes doctrine as objective criterion.

A word is in order here regarding a potential misunderstanding. A narrow understanding of the emphasis on the obedience of faith that gives direction to all of life could result in a devaluation of the contemplative, or immanent dimension of life. To reprise the language of Vatican

---

101. The Council conveys its awareness of this characteristic of its teaching by referring to what Jesus teaches about the wise scribe who, like the master of a household, "brings out of his treasure what is new and what is old" (Matt 13:52). On this, see Bushman, "Pope Paul VI on the Renewal of Vatican II," 385–86.

102. John Paul II, *EAm*, 29. Similarly, John Paul II, *Vita consecrata*, 94 defines spirituality as "a concrete program of relations with God and one's surroundings, marked by specific spiritual emphases and choices of apostolate, which accentuate and re-present one or another aspect of the one mystery of Christ."

II used earlier, a full, conscious, and active participation in the Church's mission is susceptible to the same misapprehension of which full, conscious, and active participation in the liturgy is susceptible. Active participation does not mean that the faithful must constantly be engaged in some kind of exterior action. The active participation in the liturgy that the Council promotes not only includes but prioritizes the immanent acts of faith, hope, and charity, by which the meaning of the liturgy is "elaborated within."[103] Similarly, with regard to active participation in the Church's life and mission, contemplation is part of that mission. Faith calls for all the truth to which it adheres to be projected into action, and this includes contemplation. Faith adheres to the truths that furnish the principles for the active life and that captivate the mind in contemplation. Together, these two dimensions, contemplative and active, constitute a lived spirituality.

THE CALL TO MISSIONARY SPIRITUALITY

A particular emphasis of the renewal of Vatican II is on the revitalization of mission. By following Paul VI in calling Mary the Star of the New Evangelization,[104] John Paul draws attention to this missionary focus of the Council. The New Evangelization, which begins with Vatican II, can be understood, through a spiritual reading of Scripture, as the Church's way of living out the missionary dynamism of Mary's faith. John Paul can thus refer to the evangelization of America and to the New Evangelization as a "new visitation."[105] More broadly and more commonly, he writes of a missionary spirituality.

---

103. This phrase comes from an address of John Paul to workers (see Wojtyla, *The Way to Christ*, 27).

104. Paul VI refers to Mary as "the Star of the evangelization ever renewed which the Church, docile to her Lord's command, must promote and accomplish, especially in these times which are difficult but full of hope!" (*EN*, 82). In the context, Pope Paul links this with the tenth anniversary of Vatican II (*Evangelii nuntiandi* is dated December 8, 1975) and with the anticipated beginning of the third millennium. These are two essential themes of John Paul's theology of the New Evangelization.

105. See John Paul II, "Homily, October 11, 1984," 4; "General Audience, October 17, 1984," 5; "Homily, December 12, 1997," 1.

Wojtyła goes so far as to say that the missionary attitude[106] is the primary attitude deriving from faith in Christ.[107] The relevant point for this discussion is that his understanding of missionary spirituality-attitude reflects the threefold structure of the renewal of Vatican II and of programs of formation.[108] For John Paul II, a missionary attitude presupposes a missionary consciousness, based on ecclesiological doctrine. And with this, the primary anthropological foundation for the three paths of renewal, namely, the relation of intellect and will, reappears in full light: consciousness is the intellect informed by faith when the content of faith is perceived to correspond to man's first and primary dynamism of self-determination, and attitude is the will in a state of promptitude to project that consciousness into action.[109]

---

106. If there is a distinction between missionary attitude and missionary spirituality, it is extremely subtle.

107. "We can indeed to a certain extent equate the fundamental attitude of self-commitment to God with the missionary attitude: man commits himself to God by taking whole-heartedly on himself the divine mission in which Revelation becomes a reality. He accepts the mission in this way, both in himself and in the community" (SR, 207). The foundation of this near identity of missionary attitude with faith is that faith is man's response to revelation, and that while "Revelation is not identical with Mission, [it] is realized in it. The Christian believer who responds to God's self-revelation must find himself within the sphere of that divine mission" (SR, 207).

108. On missionary attitude, see John Paul II, RH, 12; "Homily, September 9, 1984," 6; "Address, May 3, 1988," 2; "Homily, July 16, 1989," 3; "Address, August 19, 1991," 5; "Address, February 20, 1996," 5; "Homily, October 22, 2000," 3 (quoting RH, 12); "Message to the Bishop of Mantua," 2. The expression, "missionary spirituality," appears more often in John Paul's pontificate. See especially RMiss, 87–89. The expression appears once in Vatican II, in AG, 28.

109. An astute reader of Wojtyła summarizes the anthropological dynamics this way: "The philosophical work, *The Acting Person* (1969), and the theological work, *Sources of Renewal* (1972) bear a strong resemblance. Both are ordered by a series of similar concepts: awakening of consciousness, emergence of attitude, and participation. Indeed, Wojtyła situates the first encounter of man with his own human or religious being at the level of intellect; this is the awakening of consciousness. This leads to global mobilization of intentionality with him. Having come to consciousness, man prepares himself interiorly to act. This reflective attitude remains only an indeterminate pre-formation of an action, but it is necessary and decisive for any action that is intended to be coherent. The participation of men among themselves is the normal way for performing action. Great accomplishments as well as the great failures are always lived in solidarity. This outline, common to both works, not only indicates the philosophical unity of Wojtyła's thought, but also his connaturality to the major themes of Vatican II, in every sphere" (Pottier, "Vatican II," 362). See SR, 155–200, where Wojtyła develops the Church's consciousness of mission under the heading of historical and eschatological consciousness. The Church's consciousness of mission is

Missionary spirituality-attitude is the fruit of the Council's renewed awareness of the Church's catholicity,[110] that is, of her missionary nature. This is the first path of doctrinal penetration.[111] This ecclesiological doctrine enters into the Church's consciousness as a result of the realization that it is truth about *her* identity, and precisely because it is *her* identity, this consciousness becomes the occasion for renewal through conversion in the moral sense,[112] a conversion that is based on a critical judgment as a result of comparing the divine ideal of catholicity to the actual state of the Church. The fruit of this conversion is a missionary attitude, which is a readiness to perform the actions corresponding to the missionary consciousness in view of the Church's self-determination.[113] The result of missionary consciousness and missionary spirituality is the complete harmony of being (*esse*) and action (*operari*).

"Missionary activity," John Paul insists, "demands a specific spirituality, which applies in particular to all those whom God has called to be missionaries."[114] For John Paul II, the vocation of missionaries called

---

rooted in her participation in the divine missions of redemption (see also 59–60). He expounds his understanding of the Church's missionary attitude in Part II, chapter 1 ("Mission and Testimony as the Basis of the Enrichment of Faith) and chapter 2 ("Analysis of the Attitude of Participation").

110. As mentioned above, awareness of the Church's catholicity is the meaning that Chenu attributes to the Council's Message to Humanity (October 20, 1962). See his article "Le Message," 192. See also Tillard, "L'Église relit sa catholicité."

111. "The Church's missionary activity is based on deep-seated theological premises, on an understanding of the very essence of the Church, and on its universality and catholicity, corresponding to the eternal design that all should be saved by God's action and redeemed through Christ. In the light of this truth of faith, 'The Church, which has been sent by Christ to reveal and communicate the love of God to all men and to all peoples, is aware that for her a tremendous missionary work still remains to be done'" (Wojtyła, *SR*, 400).

112. These two conversions, intellectual and moral, correspond to the two meanings of the Italian word, *coscienza*, which can mean consciousness or moral conscience. Paul VI employs *coscienza* in both senses in *ES*, and he indicates both consciousness as self-awareness and moral conscience should mature in unison (see *ES*, 21). Of course, there is an order between these two, such that consciousness precedes conscience.

113. Biblically, ecclesial self-determination corresponds to St. Paul's building up the Church (see Matt 16:18; 1 Cor 14:12; Eph 4:12). Alert to the fact that speaking of the Church in terms of self-determination is an application to the Church of Wojtyła's fundamental anthropological principle, Peter Simpson draws the inference that this is to consider the Church as "The Acting People of God" (*On Karol Wojtyła*, 71; see chapter 1, n20 above).

114. John Paul II, *RMiss*, 87. For more on spirituality as the source of evangelization, see also his Post-Synodal Exhortation *Ecclesia in Asia*, 23.

to bring the Gospel to peoples and lands that have not been evangelized (the mission *ad gentes*) is a specification of the baptismal call to participate in the mission of Christ and the Church. All are called to advance the mission of the Church while some do so in a manner that makes it the defining reality of their personal vocation and charism. This kind of vocational concentration or specialization is a constant in the Church's life. All are called to prayer, yet the contemplative life is for those who are called to prayer as their personal vocation and particular service to the Church. Similarly, while all are called to integrate poverty, chastity, and obedience into their lives because this is required for the perfection of charity to which all are called, religious live the evangelical counsels as a consecrated state. The same principle applies to martyrs. Though not all are called to give this supreme witness to the perfection of charity, all are called to love God with their whole heart, soul, mind and strength, and to be prepared to confess their faith before men regardless of the cost.[115] As a final example, while all are called to love the poor by exercising the spiritual and corporal works of mercy, some, like St. Teresa of Calcutta, evidence a charism for caring for the poor.

The principle at work in the preceding examples applies to the call to mission. "The Church is 'missionary' by virtue of its own nature as the instrument of the divine Mission, and this fact must be expressed in the attitude of every member of the People of God whether or not he or she is connected in any way with 'missions' in the institutional sense."[116] All are called to be missionaries, that is, actively to participate in the Church's mission, since everyone is called to bear witness to Christ.[117]

> *The universal call to holiness* is closely linked to the *universal call to mission*. Every member of the faithful is called to holiness and to mission. This was the earnest desire of the Council, which

---

115. "By martyrdom a disciple is transformed into an image of his Master by freely accepting death for the salvation of the world—as well as his conformity to Christ in the shedding of his blood. Though few are presented such an opportunity, nevertheless all must be prepared to confess Christ before men. They must be prepared to make this profession of faith even in the midst of persecutions, which will never be lacking to the Church, in following the way of the cross" (*LG*, 42).

116. Wojtyła, *SR*, 211.

117. "The first form of witness is *the very life of the missionary, of the Christian family*, and *of the ecclesial community*, which reveal a new way of living.... But everyone in the Church, striving to imitate the Divine Master, can and must bear this kind of witness; in many cases it is the only possible way of being a missionary" (John Paul II, *RMiss*, 42).

hoped to be able "to enlighten all people with the brightness of Christ, which gleams over the face of the Church, by preaching the Gospel to every creature" (*Lumen gentium*, 1). The Church's missionary spirituality is a journey toward holiness.[118]

The mission to which all are called is the multi-level dialogue of *ES* and the New Evangelization, which are at the heart of John Paul's pontificate because of their relation to Vatican II. The New Evangelization, the primary, new method of which is dialogue, is the ardently desired fruit of the renewal of Council,[119] flowing from doctrinal consciousness of the Church's mission and the corresponding missionary attitude.

The preceding considerations alert us to the fact that when John Paul emphasizes the universal call to holiness (spirituality), to the point of saying that it is the basic goal of Vatican II,[120] it cannot be separated from the doctrine that it presupposes and the mission that is its fruit. Because it is the nexus of the other two, spirituality or holiness can serve as his focal point, yet without losing sight of doctrinal and pastoral formation. One might also consider that holiness has the advantage of being one of the four creedal notes of the Church. In a way it can be considered the foundational note, first because God is holy and his holiness is irreducible, and second because the communion of participation in God's holiness in charity is the very essence of the Church and the source of her catholic unity. Furthermore, the other two dimensions of renewal and formation neatly align with other notes of the Church. The foundation of the Church's unity being the oneness of faith, doctrinal awareness and formation align with unity. Since mission serves to propagate the faith, mission and pastoral formation align with catholicity. Here, then, a

---

118. John Paul II, *RMiss*, 90.

119. See John Paul II, *RH*, 4, 6, 11, 16.

120. "The Second Vatican Council has significantly spoken on the universal call to holiness. It is possible to say that this call to holiness is precisely the basic charge entrusted to all the sons and daughters of the Church by a Council which intended to bring a renewal of Christian life based on the Gospel. This charge is . . . an undeniable requirement arising from the mystery of the Church. . . . It is ever more urgent that today all Christians take up again the way of the gospel renewal welcoming in a spirit of generosity the invitation expressed by the Apostle Peter 'to be holy in all conduct' (1 Pet 1:15). The 1985 Extraordinary Synod, twenty years after the Council, opportunely insisted on this urgency: 'Since the Church in Christ is a mystery, she ought to be considered the sign and instrument of holiness. . . . Men and women saints have always been the source and origin of renewal in the most difficult circumstances in the Church's history. Today we have the greatest need of saints whom we must assiduously beg God to raise up'" (John Paul II, *CL*, 16).

new light is shed on the three dimensions of renewal and formation: the movement from doctrinal formation to spiritual formation to pastoral formation parallels the sequence in the Church's profession of faith from unity, to holiness, to catholicity.[121]

The call for a missionary spirituality is a salient point of continuity between Pope Francis and his predecessors.[122] Like his predecessors, the related expression, "missionary commitment" appears with significant frequency.[123] For Francis, both missionary spirituality and missionary commitment are the goal and fruit of a missionary transformation,[124] which is the guiding criteria for the pastoral conversion to which he repeatedly exhorts the Church's members. Francis is not deliberate in linking missionary spirituality, attitude, and commitment to Vatican II, as his predecessors do. But he is insistent in exhorting the Church's members to a "pastoral conversion" that corresponds to institutional reformation and personal *metanoia* so that the Church might fulfill her missionary vocation.[125] The following passage on pastoral conversion in his first apostolic exhortation is programmatic for his pontificate:

> I dream of a "missionary option," that is, a missionary impulse capable of transforming everything, so that the Church's

---

121. One can discern the presence of three of the four notes of the Church in the opening sentence of *Sacrosanctum Concilium*, which sets forth the main goals of Vatican II: "This sacred Council has several aims in view: it desires to impart an ever increasing vigor to the Christian life of the faithful [holiness]; to adapt more suitably to the needs of our own times those institutions which are subject to change; to foster whatever can promote union among all who believe in Christ [unity]; to strengthen whatever can help to call the whole of mankind into the household of the Church [catholicity]."

122. See Francis, *Evangelii gaudium*, 78–80; Francis, "Message for World Mission Day 2017," 9.

123. Francis: nearly forty times; John Paul II: nearly six hundred times; Benedict XVI: nearly one hundred times.

124. See Francis, *Evangelii gaudium*, chapter 1: "The Church's Missionary Transformation." Francis takes up the expression, "missionary transformation," on several occasions: "Address, February 13, 2014"; "Address, September 20, 2014"; *Summa familia cura*; "Letter, October 22, 2017"; *Veritatis gaudium*, 3; "Address, May 10, 2018"; "Address, February 9, 2019"; "Address, May 20, 2019"; "Address, September 30, 2019"; *Antiquum Ministerium*, 5.

125. John Paul may be more intentional in stressing that the personal conversion to cultivate a missionary attitude has a certain priority in relation to the institutional, structural dimension of mission. For one reason, every member of the Church must have a missionary attitude and bear witness to the mystery of Christ, while only some are called directly to be involved in missionary structures. See Wojtyła, *SR*, 398.

customs, ways of doing things, times and schedules, language and structures can be suitably channeled for the evangelization of today's world rather than for her self-preservation. The renewal of structures demanded by pastoral conversion can only be understood in this light: as part of an effort to make them more mission-oriented, to make ordinary pastoral activity on every level more inclusive and open, to inspire in pastoral workers a constant desire to go forth and in this way to elicit a positive response from all those whom Jesus summons to friendship with himself. As John Paul II once said to the Bishops of Oceania: "All renewal in the Church must have mission as its goal if it is not to fall prey to a kind of ecclesial introversion" (*Ecclesia in Oceania*, 19).[126]

For a Church that is on pilgrimage toward an ever more perfect realization of her catholicity, pastoral conversion is the intermediate path that must be traveled so that the doctrine of faith regarding catholicity and mission might become a lived missionary spirituality.

It is highly significant that Francis turns to *ES*[127] to elaborate on the "programmatic significance and important consequences"[128] of his emphasis on conversion as the necessary path the Church must take in order to live "permanently in a state of conversion."[129] What this study calls the logic of the three paths of renewal is, then, the conceptual foundation for the very program of his pontificate.[130] In this way, Francis continues the post-Conciliar papal tradition of taking *ES* as the hermeneutical key to unlocking the meaning of the renewal of the Church initiated by Vatican II, which "essentially consists in an increase of fidelity to her [the Church's] own calling,"[131] that is, to the doctrine that condenses what God has revealed about Christ's Church. Francis especially underscores that the Church's calling is to continue the mission of Christ to the poor.[132]

---

126. Francis, *Evangelii gaudium*, 27.

127. Francis, *Evangelii gaudium*, 26.

128. Francis, *Evangelii gaudium*, 25.

129. Francis, *Evangelii gaudium*, 25.

130. Francis refers to *Evangelii gaudium* as the program of his pontificate in his "Letter, June 29, 2017."

131. Francis, *Evangelii gaudium*, 26, quoting Vatican II, *UR*, 6.

132. Francis links the theme of the poor to his selection of the name, Francis, which he takes as "the inspirational idea" of his pontificate (see his "Letter, April 16, 2017"). He first discloses this link three days following his election (see "Address, March 16, 2013").

In relation to this, he is tireless in calling for "a serious examination of conscience, to see if we are truly capable of hearing the cry of the poor."[133] For, an examination of conscience, in light of the truth of vocation in God's plan, is always the first step in the process of conversion,[134] which yields the fruit of fervor for missionary activity. And with this, the three paths of conversion and the three dimensions of formation appear with the full force of the logic by which they are bound: knowledge of God's will is the objective content of conversion that begins with an examination of conscience, and revitalized mission through fidelity to vocation is the fruit of that conversion.

THE JUBILEE OF THE YEAR 2000

Together, John Paul's unified theology of faith, rooted in Vatican II, his promotion of the New Evangelization, also rooted in Vatican II, and his constant incorporation of the three dimensions of renewal, rooted in *ES*, constitute the key to understanding his pastoral purpose in leading the Church across the threshold from the second to the third millennium. There is no doubt that for John Paul, the Jubilee of the Year 2000 was a pastoral opportunity for continuing his commitment to implement Vatican II, which, reduced to its essentials, is a grand ecclesial renewal for the sake of reinvigorating the Church's mission.

> From the beginning of my Pontificate, my thoughts had been on this Holy Year 2000 as an important appointment. I thought of its celebration as a providential opportunity during which the Church, thirty-five years after the Second Vatican Ecumenical Council, would examine how far she had renewed herself, in order to be able to take up her evangelizing mission with fresh enthusiasm.[135]

---

133. Francis, "Message for the Second World Day of the Poor." In "Message for the First World Day of the Poor," he explains that this new institution "should become a powerful appeal to our consciences as believers, allowing us to grow in the conviction that sharing with the poor enables us to understand the deepest truth of the Gospel." See also Francis, "Morning Meditation, March 7, 2014"; "General Audience, November 19, 2014"; "Morning Meditation, March 16, 2017"; "Angelus, July 29, 2018."

134. See Francis, "Message for the World Day of Prayer for the Care of Creation," 3, in which an examination of conscience is the first step in developing a sense of responsibility for the environment.

135. John Paul II, *NMI*, 2.

John Paul makes the Jubilee an occasion to repeat, yet again, "What a treasure there is . . . in the guidelines offered to us by the Second Vatican Council!" Because all of God's gifts, once received, call for man's responsible custodianship, the real question for the Church is whether she has been a good steward of what the Holy Spirit has spoken to the Church through the Council. "For this reason I asked the Church, as a way of preparing for the Great Jubilee, to *examine herself on the reception given to the Council (TMA, 36)*."¹³⁶

Among his final words, looking back at the Jubilee, he emphasizes the providential value of the teachings of Vatican II as guidelines from heaven for the Church's pilgrimage of faith:

> With the passing of the years, *the Council documents have lost nothing of their value or brilliance.* They need to be read correctly, to be widely known and taken to heart as important and normative texts of the Magisterium, within the Church's Tradition. Now that the Jubilee has ended, I feel more than ever in duty bound to point to the Council as *the great grace bestowed on the Church in the twentieth-century:* there we find a sure compass by which to take our bearings in the century now beginning.¹³⁷

Because John Paul fully assimilates Pope Paul's hermeneutical schema for grasping the Council's spirit of renewal for the sake of a reinvigoration of mission, it is to be expected that this hermeneutical schema, set forth in the three paths of *ES*, would be present in John Paul's renewed call, occasioned by the Jubilee of the Year 2000, that the Church fully embrace the teaching of Vatican II. The evidence for this is incontrovertible.

As set forth in *Tertio millennio adveniente*, John Paul proposes for the immediate preparation for the Jubilee Year 2000 to reflect anew on the Church's faith, and this corresponds to doctrinal formation. He expressly encourages the prayerful study of Scripture, Vatican II, and the *Catechism of the Catholic Church*, and recommends specific themes for each of the three years, 1997, 1998, and 1999. Even the choice of subjects for these three years reflects the links between doctrinal awareness, renewal through conversion (or spirituality), and the mission of witness and service, as each year focuses on one of the three divine persons (doctrine), one of the sacraments (renewal), and one of the three theological virtues (life participating in Christ's communion with the Father and love

---

136. John Paul II, *NMI*, 57.
137. John Paul II, *NMI*, 57.

for man).[138] With all of this, he is initiating a period of profound doctrinal penetration, of a deep formation of the Church's consciousness.

As in *ES*, a doctrinal penetration is the catalyst for a critical judgment. John Paul strongly emphasizes that this period of preparation should be accompanied by an examination of conscience.[139] There is no better way for the Church to prepare herself for the bimillennial renewal of her encounter with her Lord than by cultivating that humility that comes from an awareness of the ways in which God's call remains an unfinished task, the ways in which her members fall short of measuring up to the demands of their vocation. The goal of this is to place the Church in the position of Mary, who at the Annunciation becomes aware that she has been entrusted with a mission that she cannot fulfill without a new grace, so that she can only say: "How shall this be?" In the face of the demands of the New Evangelization, realized through the renewal of Vatican II, the Church can do no better than to make these words of the Blessed Virgin her own.

The Jubilee Year 2000 itself falls under the heading of renewal, corresponding to spiritual formation. Just as Mary's humility in faith is preparation for being overshadowed by the Holy Spirit, so the Church's humility before the immensity of the challenge of the New Evangelization is the disposition for being open to the graces of a New Pentecost. In John Paul's vision, the Jubilee is a year of intense encounter that brings the joy of conversion. The time of emphasis on active preparation gives way to a time of active reception of the paschal graces that are God's answer to the question, "How shall this be?"—graces that bring about the desired renewal of man in Christ. In the language of the spiritual tradition of meditation, remote and proximate preparation for prayer blossom into the heart-to-heart colloquy of contemplation.[140] The culmination of the Jubilee Year of intense interpersonal exchange between the Bride and the Bridegroom is a Eucharistic Congress, the summit of all encounters on earth, and the source of the graces by which the Church is empowered to

---

138. This synthesis of a divine Person, a sacrament, and a theological virtue for each of the years of immediate preparation for the Jubilee, as set forth in *TMA*, parallels the efforts of the *CCC* to show how doctrine (Part One), liturgy (Part Two), and life in Christ (Part Three) interact with one another to create a symphony of faith.

139. Even as Montini/Paul VI understands Vatican II as an examination of conscience. See chapter 4, "Second Path: Renewal," above.

140. This is based on the acts of prayer as set forth by St. Ignatius of Loyola and modified somewhat by St. Francis de Sales.

live up to her vocation. Thus, with this Eucharistic Congress, the Jubilee concludes with a renewal of the two great impulses of charity: the first, an eschatological straining for the consummation of all things in the Kingdom of heaven; the second, the missionary impulse of pastoral charity to bring all men to Christ, in other words, the New Evangelization. The consciousness of mission now becomes a missionary attitude.

Immediately following the Jubilee, with *Novo millennio ineunte* John Paul leads the Church through the final steps of the Jubilee encounter of the Church with Christ. With the celebration completed, one might wonder what more could be said or needs to be said. In the mind of John Paul, every encounter with the Lord, every renewal through conversion and deepening of Christian life must bear fruit. God's love is effective. It changes or deepens our being in Christ, as Mary was transformed into her mission at the Annunciation, and as the apostles were transformed into their mission on Pentecost—*operari sequitur esse*. In the first part of *Novo millennio ineunte* John Paul presents the Church with the equivalent of an Ignatian review of the meditation that occurred throughout the Jubilee Year of encounter with the Lord. In the second part he guides the Church in making a transition from the graces of encounter to the graces of fulfilling the duties of vocation. He gives direction to the missionary attitude. The deepened communion with the Lord needs to permeate all of life by becoming a spirituality of communion. Since this communion is dynamic and intended to include everyone, the spirituality of communion embraces the goals of Vatican II: increased vigor of Christian life; ecumenism; mission *ad gentes*; a renewed mission to the older Christian regions where the faith is waning due to the influence of secularism and relativism. In a word, the fruit of the Jubilee is precisely the same as the fruit of Vatican II: a new missionary impulse; an ardent dialogue of salvation; a New Evangelization. Thus, the fruit of the Jubilee Year 2000 is a renewed resolution[141] by the Church to live the graces of vocation she has received in the Jubilee encounter with her Lord. And with this, the logic of the Jubilee is nothing other than a reproduction of the logic of the three dimensions of renewal of Vatican II, as set forth in *ES*.

---

141. For St. Francis de Sales, resolution constitutes the transition from meditative prayer to daily life. See especially chapters 6 and 7 of part two of de Sales, *Introduction to the Devout Life*.

CONCLUSION

Part III makes the case for the actuality of an in-depth study of *ES* more than fifty years after its promulgation. Not only is it relevant as a contribution to the ongoing discussions about the interpretation of Vatican II. It is also relevant for a principled understanding of the three dimensions of all programs of formation in light of a fundamental theology of faith. Thus, Part III presents the compelling parallel between the three paths of renewal of *ES* and the three dimensions of formation (chapter 10), then probes into the foundation(s) of Pope Paul's inspiration for articulating the event of Vatican II in terms of three paths (chapter 11), and finally demonstrates that John Paul's theology of faith is a primary contribution to the Church's task of interpreting and implementing the Council by taking the three dimensions of renewal of *ES* as the fundamental guide (chapter 12).

For John Paul II, the realization of the renewal of Vatican II has several names: the enrichment of faith; existential faith; a missionary spirituality or attitude; the New Evangelization, realized through witness and dialogue. While the first three focus on the renewal of the being (*esse*) of the agents of the Church's mission, the latter names that mission itself (*operari*). The New Evangelization is the activity of those who have been renewed in faith based on the renewal of Vatican II. It is simply the apostolic mission that began on Pentecost as this mission is conducted by those who been renewed based on the teaching and in the spirit of Vatican II. The underlying principle for this understanding of Vatican II as ordered to a New Evangelization is the same as that which underpins the logic of *ES*: *operari sequitur esse*. This is the definitive explanation for why the Church underscores the primacy of the formation of those who promote the Church's pastoral activity: "Any pastoral activity for the carrying out of which there are not at hand persons with the right formation and preparation will necessarily come to nothing."[142] Wojtyła puts it this way:

> When we speak of "building up the Church as a community" we are thinking not so much of the process of building up the actual structures envisaged by Vatican II, but rather the attitude without which these structures and that process would be suspended in the void.[143]

---

142. *GCD*, 108.
143. Wojtyła, *SR*, 367.

To cultivate this attitude, which is essentially the obedience of faith that entails a missionary spirituality, the Church unvaryingly proposes a comprehensive formation that entails three dimensions: doctrinal, spiritual, and pastoral. This study propounds these three dimensions of renewal are governed by the same logic that governs the three dimensions of renewal set forth by Paul VI in *ES*. The examination of this chapter identifies the contribution of Wojtyła/John Paul II to understanding the anthropological foundations of this logic that is common to the renewal of Vatican II and its continuation through programs of formation.

The structure of a human act entails an interaction between intellect and will that is at the center of John Paul's theology of faith. Everything begins with faith-consciousness. In his address for the opening of the Council, John XXIII makes "doctrinal penetration and a formation of consciousness in faithful and perfect conformity to the authentic doctrine" the Council's goal.[144] It is the merit of Pope Paul to insert this into a comprehensive synthesis that incorporates two other emphases of Pope John, namely, *aggiornamento* through personal conversion for the sake of a renewed influence of the Church in the modern world. John Paul's contribution is to develop a theology of faith that is the foundation for the logic of Conciliar renewal. Faith as consciousness is something richer than faith as knowledge of the content of what God has revealed because this content is perceived as corresponding in an essential and necessary way to man's primary dynamism of self-determination. For this reason, faith-consciousness becomes faith-attitude, for man cannot fail to act for his own self-determination.

A corollary of capital importance derives from John Paul's equation of the goal of Vatican II with the enrichment of faith. It is that his focus is on the renewal of individual believers through personal conversion. His Conciliar hermeneutical principle is that of the final cause, which he variously calls the enrichment of faith, existential faith, missionary spirituality, or holiness, which are the source of the New Evangelization. In this way, he is consistent with his predecessors in their likening of Vatican II to a New Pentecost. For, the Holy Spirit is the principal agent of the New Evangelization. At the same time, it is people of mature faith, saints, who are most attentive to his prompting. Just as the Council itself is an event of cooperation between the Holy Spirit and the Council Fathers, so is its implementation. The Spirit of truth, who continues to bear witness

---

144. John XXIII, "Address, October 11, 1962," 5.

to Christ to inform the consciousness of believers, is also the Spirit of holiness, who enlightens the consciences of believers and guides them in conversion, and this same Spirit imparts his various gifts for the sake of building up the Church through the numerous facets of her mission.

In light of the preceding and so much more that could be adduced to show John Paul's unflinching dedication to interpreting and implementing Vatican II, it is stupefying that someone claiming to be theologically informed could level the charge that he failed to implement Vatican II,[145] and that another, claiming to be an adept historiographer, could accuse him and his successor of a theological overreach that impedes the authentic interpretation of Vatican II.[146] In both cases, it would be more accurate simply to acknowledge there is a difference of interpretations of the Council, with John Paul II and Benedict XVI seeing it primarily as calling for a profound spiritual renewal while others focus on the renewal of ecclesiastical structures, the issue of authority, and other aspects of renewal that are related to spiritual renewal as means to an end. It is difficult to disagree with Lamb and Levering when they state that much of the controversy seems to focus on questions of power or authority in the Church.[147] The emphasis on authority by many Vatican II scholars is all the more surprising, given that the Council itself greatly underscored the subordinate, ministerial (diaconal) nature of apostolic authority. The latter is a means to the former; the ministerial priesthood has the nature of a means while the baptismal priesthood (holiness) is the end.[148] Thus, the final chapter of *Lumen gentium* on Mary, as the model of Christian virtues and of cooperation in the fulfillment of God's plan, is the final word of the Council's ecclesiology and the explanation for the importance of *Redemptoris Mater* in the John Paul's project to implement the Council.

---

145. See Kaplan, "Vatican II," 6.

146. Faggioli, *A Council for the Global Church*, 94.

147. When Lamb and Levering write, "It is as though a squabble over papal power were the real issue" (*The Reception of Vatican II*, 10), it is in the context of commenting on Faggioli's claim that John Paul and Benedict XVI "outvoiced" the bishops of Vatican II. This identification of power or authority being a major underlying issue seems to be characteristic of much of the literature on the reception and interpretation of the Council, since questions regarding the status of the local Church and episcopal conferences in relation to the universal Church and the papal magisterium very often predominate.

148. See the *relatio* accompanying the revised text of *Lumen gentium* (AS III/I, 210).

Evidence superabounds that the interpretation and implementation of the Council is the program of John Paul's pontificate. This study presents the evidence that he takes the three paths of *ES* as the normative interpretative framework for his implementation. This places the call to holiness in the position of primacy. And this is an act of faith in the Holy Spirit, who guides the Church through those who are most attentive and responsive to his prompting. His conviction is unambiguous:

> The Second Vatican Council has significantly spoken on the universal call to holiness. It is possible to say that this call to holiness is precisely the basic charge entrusted to all the sons and daughters of the Church by a Council which intended to bring a renewal of Christian life based on the Gospel.... "Men and women saints have always been the source and origin of renewal in the most difficult circumstances in the Church's history."[149]

John Paul's successor sees clearly his predecessor's conviction that revitalization of mission *ad extra* depends upon spiritual renewal *ad intra*:

> The Venerable Servant of God John Paul II made this urgent task a central point of his far-reaching Magisterial teaching, referring to it as the "new evangelization," which he systematically explored in depth on numerous occasions—a task that still bears upon the Church today, particularly in regions Christianized long ago. Although this task directly concerns the Church's way of relating *ad extra*, it nevertheless presupposes first of all a constant interior renewal, a continuous passing, so to speak, from evangelized to evangelizing.[150]

Not only is John Paul's commitment to implement the interior renewal called for by Vatican II abundantly evident, but also the logic of the pattern of *ES* is evident in many of his addresses, homilies, and writings.[151]

---

149. John Paul II, *CL*, 16, quoting the Synod of Bishops, "The Church." For the complementary view of Ratzinger, see chapter 4, n28.

150. Benedict XVI, *Ubicumque et semper*.

151. A prime example of this is his first encyclical, *Redemptor hominis*, in which John Paul promulgates the program of his pontificate. Following a first and unique part in which he situates his pontificate in relation to Vatican II and the Year 2000, the encyclical's three remaining parts that follow display the pattern of the three paths of *ES*. Part II sets forth the doctrine of redemption in Christ as the revelation of God's love as Good News for man who, made in God's image, is made for love. Part III then surveys the contemporary situation of man to show what the world is like without the love of Christ, and invites his readers to an examination of conscience and to

The preceding discussion demonstrates this: particular subjects and vocabulary may vary, but the logic remains the same.

---

conversion as the way to insert the love Christ into the world. Part IV presents the Church's participation in the three messianic offices of Christ as the way to continue his mission of love in the world. A final article presents the Blessed Virgin Mary as the model of faith by which God makes men his associates in mission.

Conclusion

Ecclesiam Suam, the Logic of Renewal, and the Spirit of Vatican II

THE IMPETUS FOR THIS investigation into *ES* has two main components. The first is the current extensive theological work being done on the interpretation of Vatican II and John Paul II's unflinching call to the Church to exercise assiduous stewardship for the gift of Vatican II. The desire to make known the latter and to contribute to the former motivates a re-reading of *ES*. The turn to *ES* is grounded in the providential place of Paul VI in relation to Vatican II, and especially his original synthesis for understanding the Council, which he sets forth in *ES*. This inspiration finds confirmation in the fact that both John Paul II and Benedict XVI point to *ES* as a key document, if not *the* key document, for their understanding of Vatican II. They also encourage those who heed their appeal to study Vatican II to turn to *ES* as a sure guide to grasping the authentic spirit of the Council.

Part I of this study corresponds to this first impetus. It answers the question, "*ES*, what do you have to say to us today about the renewal of Vatican II?" An analysis of the nature of each of the three dimensions of renewal and an examination of the logic by which they are related yields the fruit of a theology of renewal according to which the Council's goal of a revitalized mission presupposes and is the fruit of a profound renewal or conversion into a more perfect realization of the Church's nature and vocation. While in theological literature the third path of dialogue has received all of the attention and has been isolated from the second path of conversion and the first path of doctrinal penetration, this study confirms the wisdom of John Paul II and Benedict XVI in reading *ES* for the highly ordered whole that it is. The fruit of that wholistic reading is precisely the logic of renewal expounded in Part I, which confirms the uniqueness of Pope Paul's synthesis in *ES*. There is no evidence of any direct influence from another author. However, there is evidence of a gradual realization in Paul's thinking of a compelling logic according to which dialogue relates to personal *metanoia* as fruit to a tree, with a new penetration into the Church's doctrine being the fertile ground of that tree.

A second stimulus to pursue this study is rooted in my knowledge of John Paul II and his commitment to implement Vatican II, the fruit of lecturing on his thought for a quarter of a century. Again, providentially, the same man who as a young bishop outlined a broad-spectrum agenda for the Council in his response to the Ante-Preparatory Commission's sounding of the worldwide episcopate[1] also actively participated in the Council, assiduously implemented it in his own archdiocese, and was elected as pope to succeed Paul VI in implementing the Council. His pontificate and work before becoming pope remain still underexploited sources for discovering the spirit of Vatican II.[2] Many of the themes he develops, even when not explicitly quoting or commenting on texts of Vatican II, are clearly rooted in and develop teachings of the Council. Part II is a sampling of those teachings, the criterion of selection being their relation to *ES*. The principal themes are, first, the law of fidelity to God and of fidelity to man, and second, renewal *ad intra* that projects itself in renewal of mission *ad extra*. These two themes shed a new light on *ES*, indicating that its structure or logic is binomial in nature. Together, the first two paths of doctrinal penetration and conversion constitute the Church's fidelity to God and renewal *ad intra*, while the third path of dialogical mission corresponds to fidelity to man and renewal *ad extra*.

---

1. See Weigel, *Witness to Hope*, 158–60.

2. Rocco Buttiglione's chapter "Wojtyła and the Council" in *Karol Wojtyła* is especially recommendable because it is essentially an exposition of the formation of consciousness and attitudes in *SR*. Many studies that take up John Paul's relation to Vatican II are limited to focusing on his participation in the Council and his influence on the shaping of Conciliar texts. Examples of this are: Williams, *The Mind of John Paul II*; Buttiglione, *Karol Wojtyła*; Dulles, *The Splendor of Faith*. Other studies approach John Paul's relation to Vatican II by way of various subjects. See, for example, Kijas and Dobrzynski, *Christ*; Rowland, "Reclaiming the Tradition." The beginning of McPartlan's study, "John Paul II and Vatican II," focuses on *SR* and the enrichment of faith as the essential purpose of Vatican II, and then discusses John Paul's anthropology and ecclesiology as central to his understanding of Vatican II.

Finally, Part III delves into John Paul's theology of faith, with a focus on how it provides a theological foundation for understanding not only the three paths of renewal of *ES*, but also the three dimensions of programs of formation. Part III (chapter 11) suggests that the logic governing *ES* is so profoundly rooted in the Church's foundations (Scripture) and life (liturgy), and in her understanding of the human person (anthropology) that these are the likely sources of Pope Paul's inspiration. This is why the logic of *ES* should not be considered an artificial theological construct but rather a systematically articulated phenomenology of ecclesial faith and life. While there is no evidence of direct influence of *ES* on the elaboration the three dimensions of formation, the two possess the same essential structure, which is governed by the same internal logic. This is why this study's analysis of the interrelations among the three paths of *ES* has a significant contribution to make to the elucidation of the interconnections among the three dimensions of formation. And since *ES* sketches Pope Paul's vision for the renewal of Vatican II, the institutionalization of the structure and logic of the three dimensions of formation can be taken as evidence of the reception of Vatican II.

As far as I am aware, taking the structure and logic of programs of formation as an indication of the reception of Vatican II is original. The most likely explanation for this being overlooked is that scholarly work on reception focuses on one or another Conciliar document, or on one or another teaching or directive of the Council, or it focuses on finding a hermeneutical key to the Council. With regard to all of these, *ES* has been virtually overlooked, except for the theme of dialogue. This study shows that the reduction of *ES* to the theme of dialogue has impeded the discovery of its true potential to furnish, if not the hermeneutical key to Vatican II, at least one very significant key. This potential of *ES* can only be unleashed by reading the encyclical as the whole that Paul VI intended it to be. Such a reading is precisely the intent of this study.

Given the significance of the theme of dialogue in Vatican II and in the post-Conciliar Church, a partial reading of *ES*, asking of it only what it has to say about dialogue, is understandable. For, how can one demonstrate the reception of the Council considered as a whole, as an event of ecclesial renewal? Some seem to answer that question by calling for synodality to become a more pronounced dimension of the Church's life. This study answers it by indicating that the logic of *ES* as a whole is already deeply imbedded in the Church's life, and that the three dimensions of programs of formation, to the extent that they succeed in imparting that same logic, constitute a privileged institutionalization of the logic *ES* and thus of the spirit of Vatican II. This implies a distinction—but by no means a disjuncture—between the letter and the spirit of the Council and the accurate identification of its authentic spirit.

In discussions about Vatican II and realities inseparable from it, it is not uncommon to find authors place "spirit of" before one or another Conciliar theme.[3] Thus, it is possible and correct to speak of a spirit of ecumenism (or ecumenical spirit),[4] a spirit of collegiality (or collegial spirit),[5] a spirit of renewal,[6] a spirit of dialogue,[7] a spirit of evangelization,[8] etc. Two things must be noted here. First, the meaning of these phrases entails an identification of their doctrinal and theological content and principles. For John Paul II, these various spirits of Vatican II signify specific, content-determined elements of the enrichment of faith, that is, of the consciousness of faith and its corresponding attitudes. Second, while it is helpful to identify major Conciliar themes and their principles, it would be a mistake to think of the spirit of Vatican II merely as one individual theme, a combination of several themes, or even the sum of all of them. The particular doctrinal and pastoral themes relate to the spirit

---

3. In his first series of General Audiences following the Council, December 29, 1965–January 26, 1966, Paul VI does precisely this, identifying a number of "the most evident characteristics of the Council's spirit." He summarizes them: "We have summarily inquired into the spirit of the Council, and it appears that we have been able to identify some salient characteristics, which can be said to have animated the Council with a spirit of fervor and renewal, with a community spirit, with an apostolic, pastoral, missionary and ecumenical spirit, with a spirit of truth and fidelity to the religious doctrine of the Church. There would be many other aspects to consider, which would inform us about the spirit of liberty that blew in the Council, the spirit of modernness, a spirit of interest for the laity and for temporal realities, and so forth. And at the end of the Council, it seemed a duty to identify what had been its properly religious spirit, the source from which so solemnly a religious event had arisen, as an Ecumenical Council intends to be" (Paul VI, "General Audience, January 26, 1966").

4. See, for example, John Paul II, *Ut unum sint*, 31; "Address, August 10, 1993," 3 (with a reference to *UR*, 11).

5. See, for example, John Paul II, *Pastores gregis*, 8 (with references to *LG*, 23; *CD*, 3, 5, 6; *Apostolos suos*, 13); *Ecclesia in Oceania*, 12. *AG*, 6, refers to the "collegial spirit" in which the Church conducts her mission. John Paul refers to the collegial spirit in *Pastor Bonus, Sacrae disciplinae leges, Pastores gregis*, and in several addresses, such as "Address, July 5, 1996," 1.

6. See, for example, John Paul II, "Homily, March 23, 1998," 5 (referring to the Jubilee Year 2000); "Address, October 23, 2003," 4 (referring to the New Evangelization).

7. See, for example, John Paul II, "Letter, September 3, 2004," 2.

8. See, for example, John Paul II, "Address, September 6, 2003," 2.

of Vatican II as so many manifestations of it. As such, they disclose that spirit,[9] but they are not identified with it.

This is why it is very helpful, even necessary, to look for articulations of the spirit of Vatican II in texts in addition to the Council's promulgated constitutions, decrees, and declarations,[10] as well as in post-Conciliar magisterial texts.[11] For, these non-Conciliar texts consider the Council as a whole, while the Council's promulgated texts focus on one subject or another (although some indications about the Council as whole can be found here and there in them). The fundamental continuity of the non-Conciliar texts with the Conciliar texts themselves, and the fact that the authors of the former are major protagonists and eyewitnesses to the Council's preparation, four sessions, and implementation, constitutes

---

9. This is why it is a helpful exercise to identify the many spirits of Vatican II, as Paul VI and John Paul II do, and as O'Malley does in his recent contribution "Deconstructing and Reconstructing a Cliché."

10. To limit an inventory of such texts to those that precede and are contemporaneous with the Council: John XXIII, *Ad Petri cathedram*; *Humanae salutis*; "Address, November 14, 1960"; "Address, June 5, 1960"; *Sacrae laudis*; PA; "Radio Address, September 11, 1962"; "Address, October 11, 1962"; "Address, December 8, 1962"; Vatican II, "Message to Humanity"; Paul VI, "Address, September 29, 1963"; "Address, September 14, 1964"; "Address, September 14, 1965"; *ES*; "Address, December 7, 1965."

11. Among which, I would include: 2nd Extraordinary Assembly of the Synod of Bishops, "The Church"; Wojtyła, *SR*; John Paul II, *RH*; "Address, December 22, 1992"; "Address, February 27, 2000"; Benedict XVI, "Address, December 22, 2005"; "General Audience, March 10, 2010." Because he resolutely committed his pontificate to the implementation of Vatican II, the list of texts in the pontificate of John Paul II could be greatly expanded. For example, in *Dives in Misericordia* he identifies as "one of the basic principles, perhaps the most important one, of the reaching of the last Council" the proposition that "The more the Church's mission is centered upon man—the more it is, so to speak, anthropocentric—the more it must be confirmed and actualized theocentrically, that is to say, be directed in Jesus Christ to the Father. . . . And this is also one of the basic principles, perhaps the most important one, of the teaching of the last Council" (John Paul II, *DM*, 1). The value of post-Conciliar texts such as this derives from their essential continuity with those that are contemporaneous with the Council. In this case, John Paul's insistence that the Church's service to man is essentially a religious one, i.e., to invite man to discover that God alone ultimately fulfills his aspirations to live a fully human life (see *RH*, 4, 13–14, and the numerous references to *GS*, 22 through John Paul's pontificate), corresponds to a central theme of Pope Paul's Address for the Closing of the Council. Theobald's distinction between forty years of preoccupation with an institutional reception of Vatican II, focused on the "states of life, ministries, and structures, as the long series of Roman Synods under John Paul II eloquently witnesses," and, finally, attention to "the question of the internal principle of the Council's *corpus . . . in its totality*" is unfounded ("The Theological Options of Vatican II," 88).

a datum of supreme importance. They constantly describe the spirit of Vatican II in terms of (1) the revealed truth that is the life-giving source and objective measure of renewal—the pastoral expression of doctrine; (2) its goal—a revitalization of the Church's mission through dialogue (New Evangelization); (3) the manner in which this goal is realized—renewal that is both personal (*metanoia*) and institutional (reform). The spirit of Vatican II is the three dimensions of renewal set forth by Paul VI in *ES* and taken as the hermeneutical key to the Council by John Paul II.

When Paul VI thinks of the spirit of Vatican II, he thinks of the "mentality, principle of thought and action, that which gives life—that is, form, attitude, the manner of the soul, the direction of the heart—which in itself belongs to the scope of human psychology, but that, in the order of grace, may well be also pervaded by the action of the Holy Spirit."[12] The texts of Vatican II are the fruit of the human spirits of their authors cooperating in faith with the Holy Spirit. This Vatican II has in common with all ecumenical councils, the decisions and texts of which have "seemed good to the Holy Spirit and to us" (Acts 15:28). This is to say that the texts correspond to the intention of both the Holy Spirit and the human authors.[13] What identifies Vatican II as unique among the councils, and thus as having an identifiable spirit, is comprised by its goals and the means chosen to realize those goals. It is not difficult to correlate the work of the Holy Spirit to the three paths of *ES*. The Spirit is the Church's memory and leads the Church into the fullness of truth (first

---

12. Paul VI, "General Audience, January 5, 1966."

13. This suggests an analogous relation between the assistance of the Holy Spirit in ecumenical councils and the inspiration of the Holy Spirit in Sacred Scripture. The key point is that the intention of the authors, what they intend to communicate, is to be sought in the documents that are the effect of that intention. For a recent discussion of Vatican II on divine and human authorship of Scripture and the notion of the intention of the author(s), see Durand, "Relire *Dei Verbum* dans son histoire," 39–63. In addition to the distinction between the inspiration and the assistance of the Holy Spirit, another important difference between Scripture and Vatican II is that many of the human authors of Vatican II have produced any number of texts that are intended to be commentaries on the Council and are, presumably, rooted in the same intention that produced the Conciliar documents. These include the official *relationes* accompanying the texts and explaining their meaning, as well as properly theological works, and most important for this study, the encyclicals, apostolic exhortations, letters, addresses, audiences, and homilies of the popes of Vatican II (John XXIII, Paul VI, John Paul II, Benedict XVI). The presumption of the unity of intention in these authors, which includes fidelity to the meaning of the original documents, is the justification for turning to non-Conciliar texts as helpful sources for ascertaining the spirit of Vatican II, as well as the meaning of particular texts of Vatican II.

path). The Spirit enlightens consciences and leads people to conversion (second path). The Spirit animates the Church's missionary dynamism (third path).

Ultimately, the spirit of Vatican II is the Holy Spirit speaking to the Church through the bishops assembled at Vatican II, as he spoke to the apostolic Church through the apostles.[14] What the Spirit says to the Church now, as then, is twofold: "repent,"[15] and discern the signs of the times regarding the work of the Holy Spirit.[16] At the same time, the spirit of Vatican II is that which distinguishes it from all of the other councils and events in the Church's life that can be attributed to the Holy Spirit. At Vatican II, the Church engaged in a discernment that includes the various movements that preceded the Council: ecumenical, liturgical, biblical, Marian, missionary, pastoral, patristic, etc., in order to cooperate with the Holy Spirit in taking a giant step forward in the way in which the Church relates to the modern world. The foundation for this Conciliar discernment and cooperation is fundamentally the doctrine concerning the Church. The Church must know herself more precisely in order to be faithful to what God has made her to be and to be faithful to her mission to serve her contemporaries. With the new penetration into this doctrine—especially regarding the Church's unity (ecumenism; universal Church-particular Churches), holiness (universal call to holiness), catholicity (relation to the world: mission and dialogue), and apostolicity (collegiality)—comes the call to renewal through conversion into a more perfect living of this doctrinal penetration.

The importance of what becomes something of an axiom in the pontificate of John Paul II becomes apparent here. In order to fulfill her mission of evangelization and conversion, the Church must first be

---

14. In his "Address, September 14, 1965," Paul VI speaks of the synergy of the work of the Holy Spirit and the efforts of the bishops, based on Acts 15:28. He challenges the bishops to be attentive to what the Spirit is saying to the Church (see Rev 2:7—3:22) as this is first manifested in the movements of their own hearts and minds. Pope Paul takes up this theme following the Council. See Paul VI, "Homily, October 26, 1967"; "General Audiences, January 31, 1968"; "General Audience, April 7, 1975." It is possible Pope Paul's address to the Council and subsequent references to the Holy Spirit speaking to the Church through the Council are the source for the numerous times that John Paul II repeats this theme. See, for example, John Paul II, *RH*, 3; *DeV*, 26; *RMat*, 48; "Address, December 22, 1992," 1; *A Concilio Constantinopolitano*, 10; "Letter, April 8, 1988." The theme is present in his great synthesis of Vatican II, *Sources of Renewal*, written several years before becoming pope (see *SR*, 9–10).

15. See Rev 2:21.

16. See Acts 15:8.

evangelized and converted. This is equivalent to the *ad intra/ad extra* theme, condensing the three paths of renewal. Paul VI first enunciates this theme, and John Paul amply develops it.[17] The *Instrumentum Laboris* for the Synod on the New Evangelization gives a fitting summary:

> Pope John Paul II made the duty to evangelize one of the key points in his vast magisterium, summarizing in the concept of the new evangelization what he systematically developed in many discourses, namely, that this is the task facing the Church today, especially in countries with a Christian tradition. This program directly affects the Church's relation to the outside world, but presupposes, first of all, an ongoing internal renewal, a continuous passing, so to speak, from being evangelized to evangelizing.[18]

Nemo dat quod non habet: "If you are filled with God, you will be true apostles of the new evangelization [which is the desired fruit of Vatican II], for no one can give what he does not have in his heart."[19]

As the Blessed Virgin is the model of Christian virtues and type of the Church, it is not surprising to find John Paul develop the *ad intra/ ad extra* theme Mariologically. Combining his themes of Mary being the first to believe in the mystery of Christ and her being the first evangelizer, the *Lineamenta* for the Synod of Bishops on the New Evangelization succinctly states: Mary "lets herself be fully evangelized, welcoming the Word of God, first in her heart and then in her womb.... In turn, she becomes the first evangelizer."[20] The renewal of Vatican II begins with a humble recognition by the Church that like Mary, the mission entrusted to her is beyond her reach. Mary shows us that the passage from faith as knowledge of God's will (doctrinal penetration) to the fulfillment of God's will (dialogical mission) passes by way of the humility that asks, "How shall this be?" and disposes one to receive God's transforming grace (renewal through conversion).

---

17. See John Paul II, *CT*, 24 (catechized in order to catechize); *RP*, 9 (reconciled in order to be reconciling); "Homily, May 5, 1989" (converted in order to preach conversion); *RMiss*, 47 (converted in order to preach conversion); *RMiss*, 49 (evangelized in order to evangelize).

18. Synod of Bishops, "13th Ordinary General Assembly, *Instrumentum Laboris*, June 19, 2012," 13.

19. John Paul II, "Homily, May 2, 2004," 3.

20. Synod of Bishops, "13th Ordinary General Assembly, *Lineamenta*, February 2, 2011," 13.

Whether *ES* best subsumes and recapitulates the many particular doctrinal and pastoral advances of Vatican II, which can be identified as partial realizations of the spirit of Vatican II, is debatable. But what is not debatable is that *ES* deserves greater attention as an architectonic articulation of the spirit of Vatican II. In virtue of his paschal mystery, Christ sends the "Spirit of truth" to "guide [the Church] into all truth" (John 16:13).[21] With the grace of deeper penetration into revealed truth comes the grace to make an examination of conscience for the sake of conversion into greater conformity to that truth, to *the* Truth, Christ, and with this into a greater participation in his being and in his mission. The unique architectonic articulation of the spirit of Vatican II, in light of which the various spirits of Vatican II are best understood, makes *ES* a prime source for grasping the spirit of programs of formation. Precisely in light of that articulation of the spirit of Vatican II, the post-Conciliar programs of formation, with their three dimensions, appear as significant signposts in the reception of Vatican II.

So long as it is understood in its full depth, the word "pastoral" can be put forward as an apt candidate for signifying the Spirit and various derivative spirits of Vatican II. For, the pastoral dimension of Vatican II, rightly understood, signifies not just the mode of expressing doctrine[22] but the very goal of Council: the revitalization of the Church's mission insofar as this mission is the fruit of conversion into a more perfect conformity to the revealed truth about the nature, identity, vocation, and mission of the Church, that is, participation in the mystery of Christ. *ES* is singular as a development of the Church's consciousness regarding this participation. It is, therefore, a source of unique value for judging the reception of Vatican II in general, and for implementing the programs of formation that so clearly parallel the three paths of renewal. But the true

21. John Paul frequently associates John 16:13 with the texts of the Book of Revelation on the Holy Spirit speaking to the Church (Rev 2:7, 11, 17, etc.).

22. Theobald takes the "pastoralité" of doctrine—"There can be no proclamation of the gospel without taking account of its recipients"—as a key or even *the* key for interpreting Vatican II. Thus, for him it is the spirit of Vatican II. See Theobald, "The Theological Options of Vatican II"; "The Principle of Pastorality at Vatican II" in Faggioli and Vicini, *The Legacy of Vatican II*. In reality, the pastoral way of expressing doctrine is a means to the pastoral goal of Vatican II. Echeverria is right to alert readers to a potential misunderstanding of the "pastorality of doctrine" principle, if it implies a relativizing of doctrine in a Modernist sense, whether Theobald actually takes it this far. See Echeverria "Language, Truth, and Reality"; Echeverria, "History, Unchanging Truth, and Vatican II."

potential of programs of formation to assure the ongoing reception of Vatican II, which entails ongoing renewal, does not lie in the mere material factuality of this parallel. It lies, rather, in the Spirit of Vatican II, the Holy Spirit, who in leading the Church into the fullness of truth, understood as doctrinal penetration (intellectual-theological formation), also leads the Church's members into conversion for the sake of more perfect conformity to revealed truth (spiritual formation), which bears the fruit of a more Spirited participation in Christ's mission (pastoral formation).

In light of the preceding, the study of programs of formation as evidence of the reception of Vatican II, as elucidated in *ES*, confirms that Pope Paul's three paths of renewal are anything but a theological construction. They are, rather, a sketch of the dynamism of the Church's life, which he recapitulates in light of the renewal undertaken by Vatican II. The identity of the Church and of Spirit who speaks to the Church at Vatican II and continues to guide the Church after the Council explains the remarkable parallel between the three paths of *ES* and the three dimensions of formation. The constants are God and the historical revelation that culminates in Jesus Christ, and the dynamisms of human nature common to all whom God calls to participate in the mystery of Christ and the mystery of the Church. These constants explain why the relation between *ES* and programs of formation is one of reciprocal elucidation. To apply Cardinal Wojtyła's principle of integration, "we can rediscover and, as it were, re-read the logic of programs of formation in the logic of *ES*, while we can rediscover and re-read the logic of *ES* in the logic of programs of formation."[23] This is confirmed by showing, as this study has done, that the same elements of the Church's life—biblical, liturgical, theological, anthropological—proposed for understanding the logic of *ES* also shed light the logic of the dimensions of formation.

---

23. See Wojtyła, *SR*, 38–41.

Epilogue

A Parable and Its Explanation

THE EARLIER EXPOSITION OF Pope John's theme of the light of Christ[1] and, later, the theme of fidelity to God and to man as developed by Pope Paul VI and Pope John Paul II, shows the essential continuity in theological vision among these popes. Drawing on the riches of the Catholic tradition and using different language, Pope John's trilogy, light of Christ, light of the Church, light of the nations, anticipates the three paths of *ES*, and the theme of fidelity to God and fidelity man, elaborated by Paul VI and John Paul II, recapitulates the three paths.

In summary, the first path of awareness corresponds to the primacy of doctrine and our fidelity to God. The second path of renewal through conversion is the existential bridge by which the light of Christ becomes, by participation, the light of the Church. The second path also links the two forms of fidelity. Fidelity to the truth of revelation (first path) becomes an existential fidelity to God through conversion (second path), and this bears the fruit of fidelity to man through missionary dialogue (third path). This fidelity to man is fundamentally a witness to the transforming power of God's truth and love, whereby the light of the Church shines into the world to become the light of the nations (*Lumen gentium*) as the Church translates the truth of the faith into a language appropriate for a contemporary audience.

The essentials of this recapitulation of themes, which elucidate the meaning and order of the three paths of *ES*, may be considered a final time with the help of a parable, which will serve as a conclusion to this study.

---

1. See chapter 7 above.

Imagine, if you will, a woman who falls seriously ill. She exhibits a set of symptoms heretofore never encountered. This woman goes from physician to physician in the hope of finding someone with the knowledge and skill to cure her. Everyone she sees runs the same set of standard tests, and the medications they prescribe prove ineffective. No one seems able effectively to diagnose and to treat her condition. With the last of her financial resources, she comes to a specialist who is her final hope. Like those before him, he is unable to arrive at a satisfactory diagnosis or to find an effective treatment. But this last physician takes a special interest in her. Admitting that at this time he has exhausted all options, he nevertheless pledges to keep doing research, to keep consulting other experts, and to keep seeing her. Eventually his perseverance pays off. His research leads him to the director of a research laboratory who has just recently synthesized the drug that his patient needs. He administers the drug and her health is restored.

While the relevance of this parable for this study concerns the physician rather than the patient, it is worth pointing out that the woman, like the woman in the Gospel who, suffering from an incurable hemorrhage, comes to Jesus only after she had tried everything else (Luke 8:43), is in a state of total desperation when she encounters the doctor who would eventually cure her. In our times, and in all times, many people turn to Jesus and his Church only after their search for a meaningful life, a fully human life, leaves them empty, exhausted, and on the precipice of despair. The fact that the Church must, like Jesus himself, always respect people's free will means that no matter how brightly the light of Christ shines through the Church into the world, she can only propose her message and never impose it.[2] If this means that the path for some is to turn to Christ and the Church only as a last resort, then the Church must be as welcoming of them as Christ was to the woman with a hemorrhage. But, this does not mean that the Church need only keep the lights on and the doors unlocked in order to facilitate the journey home. She must actively seek out those who are searching, as the shepherd seeks his lost sheep (Ezek 34:12; Matt 18:12–14; Luke 15:4). This is what Jesus, the Good Shepherd did. In the account of the woman with a hemorrhage, it might appear that she is the one taking the initiative. She comes up behind Jesus and touches the fringe of his garment (Luke 8:44). But her approach and touch would not have been possible had he not already taken the

---

2. See Benedict XVI, *VD*, 105.

initiative to come down from heaven (John 3:13, 31; 6:38, 41, 42, 51) in order to seek the lost (Luke 19:10). "The dialogue of salvation," Pope Paul explains, "was opened spontaneously on the initiative of God: 'He (God) loved us first' (1 John 4:10); it will be up to us to take the initiative in extending to men this same dialogue, without waiting to be summoned to it" (*ES*, 72).

The main point of the parable bears on the physician who symbolizes the Church. In *ES*, Pope Paul likens the Church's relation to the world to that of a physician who does not allow the possibility of contracting a disease to prevent him from coming to the aid of those who are infected.

> Just as the doctor who, realizing the danger inherent in a contagious disease, not only tries to protect himself and others from such infection, but also dedicates himself to curing those who have been stricken, so too the Church does not make an exclusive privilege of the mercy which the divine goodness has shown it, nor does it distort its own good fortune into a reason for disinterest in those who have not shared it. Rather in its own salvation it finds an argument for interest in and for love for anyone who is close to it and can at least be approached through universal effort to share its blessings. (*ES*, 63)

Comparing the Church to a doctor in this way is apt in more than one way. First, the Church continues the mission of Christ. Since Christ compared himself to a physician (Luke 4:23; 5:31), it is natural that the Church should recognize in this imagery a dimension of her relation to the world, that it should be an element of her self-consciousness.[3]

Second, to be a physician is to be a missionary of health for others. If a physician applies what he knows first to himself, it is so that he not succumb to a disease, become incapacitated, and find himself unable to help others. In this way, solicitude for his own health is not solely for his own sake but for the sake of the health of others. This is true for the Church as well. Her self-love is subordinate to love of others. Love of self is not only not opposed to love of neighbor; love of neighbor grows out of love of self: "You shall love your neighbor as yourself" (Matt 22:39). Pope Paul's view is that the Church's consciousness of blessings received from God should not be a cause for triumphalism or separatism, but for reinvigorated missionary love.

---

3. Once again, the principle set forth in *CCC*, 521, applies. The Church's members participate in every aspect of his mystery.

> The love that animates our communion does not separate us from men, nor does it make us exclusivists or selfish. Indeed, because love comes from God, it forms us with a sense of universality. Our truth impels us to love. Recall the admonition of the Apostle: "*Veritatem autem facientes in caritate*"—doing the truth in charity (*Eph* 4:15). And here, in this assembly, the expression of this law of charity has a sacred and ponderous name: it qualifies as responsibility. St. Paul would say urgency: "*Caritas Christi urget nos*"—the charity of Christ impels us (2 *Cor* 5:14). We feel responsible before all mankind. We are debtors to all (cf. *Rom* 1:14). The Church, in this world, is not an end in herself. She is at the service of all men. She must make Christ present to everyone, individuals and peoples, as expansively and as generously as possible. This is her mission.[4]

In other words, the Church's charity impels her toward others [third path] because she knows herself as participating in God's own charity [first path] as a result of being renewed through conversion [second path]. She knows herself as the beneficiary of God's saving love, and therefore she lives in solidarity-communion with all who similarly stand in need of his love. She also lives in solidarity-communion with God, particularly in the Eucharist. Put another way, she knows experientially what grace is. She knows what she would be without it, and this places her in solidarity-communion with all men. She knows the sacrificial nature of the divine love that is the source of grace, and this places her in solidarity-communion with God. This twofold solidarity-communion conforms the Church to Christ, true God and true man, and thereby equips her to participate in his mission of mediation.

Were the Church to shrink from her mission of mediation and withhold the gift of grace from others, this would betray the fact that she has lost her awareness of having been loved by God, that is, her awareness of being what she is by his grace. This would liken her to the unforgiving debtor, whose severity with his fellow debtor indicates that he was never transformed by the experience of having his debt forgiven by his king (Matt 18:27–35). This debtor should have related to his fellow debtor with mercy, as his king had related to him. In other words, the former debtor should be as a king to his fellow debtor, whose plight he knows from experience. After having been let off, he is expected to live in solidarity-communion with the king and with other debtors. This is the lesson of

---

4. Paul VI, "Address, September 14, 1965."

Israel's liberation from slavery in Egypt. God expects his people to treat the widow, the orphan, and the foreigner the way God treated them when they were in slavery in Egypt (Deut 5:14–15; 15:13–15; 24:17–22).

The vocation of the Church of forgiven debtors and emancipated slaves to sin is to be the sacrament of God's efficacious love [first path]. She knows herself as commissioned by God to be for others what he has been for her, to cooperate with him so that his love reaches to other debtors and slaves through her. Her acts of mercy are signs that point to her own encounter with his love in the past, and to the forgiving and liberating power of that same love in the present. The Church is like a physician who, having been healed from a life-threatening disease early in life, dedicates the rest of her life to healing others with the same disease.

The third and fourth applications of the parable bear especially on the second and third paths of *ES*. For example, the parable is relevant to the heretofore undiagnosed diseases corresponding to the Church's encounter with new cultures or new cultural situations in which those she is commissioned to love live.[5] Like the physician who expands his capacity to heal, the Church grows in her understanding of Sacred Tradition as she strives to bring about a genuine inculturation of faith. This entails affirming and strengthening all that is true, good, and beautiful—all that is genuinely human—in the cultures and cultural situations she encounters. It also entails purifying and healing values that are contrary to and threaten human dignity. Developing a theme that Vatican II would make its own,[6] Pope Paul VI puts it this way in his first encyclical:

> Christian life should not only be adapted to the forms of thought and custom which the temporal environment offers and imposes on her, provided they are compatible with the basic exigencies of her religious and moral program, but it should also try to draw close to them, to purify them, to ennoble them, to vivify and to sanctify them. (*ES*, 42)

Like the third, the fourth application of the parable is one that Pope Paul does not develop by way of the medical analogy, yet is most apropos

---

5. See the Pontifical Council for Culture, *Towards a Pastoral Approach to Culture*.

6. There are several verbs associated with the impact of the Gospel on men and their cultures. Verbs associated with what is true, good, beautiful, and genuinely human include: to foster, to take to herself, to perfect, to ennoble, to elevate, to vivify, to sanctify, to renew. Verbs associated with elements that are not compatible with human dignity and genuine human development include: to heal, to purify. See Vatican II, *LG*, 13; *GS*, 40, 49, 58.

for this study. The dedicated physician engages in what could be called professional *aggiornamento*, that is, updating or renewal. He discovers that his current state of knowledge and expertise is inadequate in relation both to his patient's need and his own solicitude as a physician. What begins as a routine diagnosis of the patient ends up entailing a self-diagnosis. In coming face to face with a case he had never encountered, in this confrontation with a new illness, he confronts his own limitations.[7] He makes a critical judgment about his own inadequacy that he could not have made until he encounters a case that requires more of him than he possesses. By expanding his knowledge and expertise, he becomes a better physician and the first beneficiary is his patient.

The necessity of ongoing conversion experienced by the physician corresponds to Pope Paul's second path of renewal through conversion. It thereby complements the theme of fidelity to God and to man, with fidelity to God corresponding to the first path of doctrinal awareness and fidelity to man corresponding to the third path of dialogue (mission, ministry, apostolate, service). What is presupposed and, as it were, left in the background with the theme of fidelity to God and to man, namely, the Church's *ad intra* renewal through conversion, the medical analogy explicitly develops. This renewal *ad intra* is precisely what the bishops at Vatican II recognized must take place if the Church is to reinvigorate her missionary outreach *ad extra* to the modern world.

The Council Fathers's consciousness of the *ad intra/ad extra* duality and the precedence of the former is evident in numerous documents. Perhaps nowhere is this consciousness more incisively formulated than in the first "document" issued by Vatican II. Promulgated nine days after its opening, the "Message to Humanity" clearly sets forth the *ad intra/ad extra* duality in such a way that, with a heightened attentiveness resulting from the preceding reflections, this duality can be seen to correlate to the main lines of the three paths of *ES* and the theme of fidelity to God and to man. To bring out this correlation, in the following paragraph these themes are introduced in brackets immediately following the phrases that correspond to them.

---

7. What the heretofore-undiagnosed disease is for the dedicated physician, the new cultures and cultural situations of her contemporaries are for the Church. The Church constantly reads the signs of the times in order to ascertain or diagnose the threats to human dignity. The teaching of Vatican II is the fruit of such an extensive reading of the signs of the times.

> In this assembly, under the guidance of the Holy Spirit, we wish to inquire how we ought to renew ourselves [second path and renewal *ad intra*], so that we may be found increasingly faithful to the gospel of Christ [first path, renewal *ad intra*, and fidelity to God]. We shall take pains so to present to the men of this age [third path and renewal *ad extra*] God's truth in its integrity and purity [first path, renewal *ad intra*, and fidelity to God] that they may understand it and gladly assent to it [third path, renewal *ad extra*, and fidelity to man]. . . . [W]e as pastors devote all our energies and thoughts to the renewal of ourselves and the flocks committed to us [second path, and renewal *ad intra*], so that there may radiate before all men the lovable features of Jesus Christ [third path, and renewal *ad extra*], who shines in our hearts "that God's splendor may be revealed" (cf. 2 Cor 4:6).[8]

The passage just quoted and many like it clearly indicate that the Council Fathers were primarily interested in the renewal of the Church *ad intra* as the precondition for the renewal *ad extra* of its mission to the world. The aim of this study has been to expound the reasons for this precedence of renewal *ad intra* and for the order among the three paths of renewal.

With respect to fidelity to God and to man, while both dimensions of fidelity are essential, Pope Paul's emphasis lands on fidelity to man. This emphasis in no way implies a reduction of the importance of fidelity to God. Rather, it reflects Pope Paul's conviction that fidelity to God is a fundamental tenet and that the great challenge to the Church at the time of Vatican II was to reinvigorate that dimension of the Church's mystery and vocation that is her mission to the world. For, "the pilgrim Church is missionary by her very nature,"[9] and one of the greatest threats to that mission is the Church closing in on herself and as a result abandoning man in the name of preserving her identity and the purity of her doctrine. The glory of a doctor is in the healing of his patients, not in a self-absorbed reflection on how much wisdom he has accumulated. Here, as always, Jesus is the model: "I am glorified in them" (John 17:10). This external glory deriving from his works and their fruits reflects the internal glory that was his with the Father before the world began (John 17:5).

In his Christmas message just two weeks after the Council's close, Pope Paul takes up the theme of fidelity to man, though without using that expression, to convey the same essential message regarding the

---

8. Vatican II, "Message to Humanity."
9. Vatican II, *AG*, 2.

Church's relation to the world that he set forth by comparing the Church to a doctor. In this instance he bases it on a different theme of Scripture, that of the shepherd whose solicitude for his lost sheep impels him to seek them, and he states that this is "the guiding principle" of Vatican II:

> The dominant mood of the Council was inspired by the gospel image of the shepherd setting out in pursuit of the lost sheep, allowing himself no peace until he has found it. The awareness that mankind, represented with touching simplicity by the straying sheep, belongs to the Church was the guiding principle of the Council. For mankind, by a universally valid decree, does belong to the Church . . . mankind belongs to her by right of love, since the Church, no matter how distant or uncooperative or hostile mankind may be, can never be excused from loving the human race for which Christ shed his blood.[10]

Love is the foundation for the comparisons with the doctor and shepherd. Always, fidelity to man is rooted in charity that becomes active service in behalf of mankind. In his address marking the close of the Council, Pope Paul draws on yet another biblical passage in order to convey this same essential message and to summarize the purpose and spirit of Vatican II. This time he compares the Church to the Good Samaritan.

> Yes, the Church of the council has been concerned, not just with herself and with her relationship of union with God, but with man—man as he really is today: living man, man all wrapped up in himself, man who makes himself not only the center of his every interest but dares to claim that he is the principle and explanation of all reality. Every perceptible element in man, every one of the countless guises in which he appears, has, in a sense, been displayed in full view of the council Fathers, who, in their turn, are mere men, and yet all of them are pastors and brothers whose position accordingly fills them with solicitude and love.
>
> Secular humanism, revealing itself in its horrible anticlerical reality has, in a certain sense, defied the council. The religion of the God who became man has met the religion (for such it is) of man who makes himself God. And what happened? Was there a clash, a battle, a condemnation? There could have been, but there was none. The old story of the Samaritan has been the model of the spirituality of the council. A feeling of boundless sympathy has permeated the whole of it. The attention of our

---

10. Paul VI, "Radio Message for Christmas, December 23, 1965," quoted in Abbott, *The Documents of Vatican II*, 4n7.

> council has been absorbed by the discovery of human needs (and these needs grow in proportion to the greatness which the son of the earth claims for himself). But we call upon those who term themselves modern humanists, and who have renounced the transcendent value of the highest realities, to give the council credit at least for one quality and to recognize our own new type of humanism: we, too, in fact, we more than any others, honor mankind.
>
> Another point we must stress is this: all this rich teaching is channeled in one direction, the service of mankind, of every condition, in every weakness and need. The Church has, so to say, declared herself the servant of humanity, at the very time when her teaching role and her pastoral government have, by reason of the council's solemnity, assumed greater splendor and vigor: the idea of service has been central.[11]

While the similarities are obvious, there is a significant difference between the Good Samaritan and the Church. The Samaritan was on a journey for some kind of business and happened by accident on the man who had been beaten, robbed, and left to die. In contrast, the Church has no other business than to bind the wounds of humanity. The only roads she travels are those on which she knows she will find human beings whose dignity has been stripped by their own misuse of freedom and/or by the malevolence of others.[12] As John Paul II puts it in his first encyclical, man is the path for the Church.[13]

It takes tremendous human and Christian maturity to be attentive to the needs of others. It is always easy to pass by a person in need of being loved and to justify doing so in the name of fulfilling some other responsibility. In a world in which people are ceaselessly striving for more, and who therefore think that they do not yet have enough to be happy, there is no room for taking account of those who have nothing to offer. One thinks of our Lord's words: "For if you love those who love you, what reward have you?" (Matt 5:46).

> And as you wish that men would do to you, do so to them. If you love those who love you, what credit is that to you? For even

---

11. Paul VI, "Address, December 7, 1965."

12. John Chrysostom sees an additional ecclesiological meaning to the parable of the Good Samaritan. The inn to which the Good Samaritan takes the man he found near death is the Church. The Church is the place where mankind recovers the dignity of the likeness of God, that is, of participating in God's life, that is lost by sin.

13. John Paul II, *RH*, 14.

sinners love those who love them. And if you do good to those who do good to you, what credit is that to you? For even sinners do the same. And if you lend to those from whom you hope to receive, what credit is that to you? Even sinners lend to sinners, to receive as much again. But love your enemies, and do good, and lend, expecting nothing in return; and your reward will be great, and you will be sons of the Most High; for he is kind to the ungrateful and the selfish. Be merciful, even as your Father is merciful. (Luke 6:31–36)

The spirituality of the Good Samaritan to serve others out of a love of abundance[14] is the Church's own spirituality. This is that fullness[15] of life that comes with being loved by God in Jesus Christ through the gift of the Holy Spirit. Without this fullness, man experiences himself as needy, and with this experience comes the risk of seeing others in utilitarian terms, that is, the risk of reducing their value to their capacity to meet one's needs. If zeal for mission in the Church, also known as zeal for souls, is not as strong as it should be, this can only mean that too many baptized Christians are not sufficiently aware of the great blessings they have received from Christ. As a result, they repeat the error of the Jews who desired a king in order to be "like all the nations" (1 Sam 8:5, 20), defining their lives and their happiness in secular, worldly terms. When this happens, then they are indeed like the other nations. They too will be in a state of constant agitation and self-occupied restlessness, too busy searching for their elusive fulfillment to take notice of others in need. Christ came into the world as a man living the fullness of God himself (Col 2:9), precisely so that he could love and serve out of this abundance, and he sends those who believe in him as the Father sent him (John 6:67; 20:21).

This is the high standard of Christian perfection, and it explains why Pope Paul places so much emphasis on the second path of renewal through conversion. Like a skilled physician, he engages in a diagnosis—in the language of Vatican II, reading the signs of the times—of the situation in which the Church's mission is disconcertingly languid and ineffective in the modern world. There are three factors that contribute to this: the free will of those to whom the Church is sent; the lack of zeal

---

14. On the distinction between love from abundance and love from need, see Benedict XVI, *DCE*, 3–11. On the connection between Pope Benedict, Paul VI, and Vatican II on the Good Samaritan see chapter 11 above, especially nn6–7.

15. See John 1:16; Eph 3:19; Col 2:10.

for mission and service on the part of the Church's members; the use of ineffective methods.

Regarding the first of these, the Church cannot impose anything but only propose, as has been said. Notwithstanding this, she knows that the truth, beauty, and goodness of the Gospel, and the witness of Christian life, have the power to attract. She also knows that the Spirit of God is at work in secret ways in the hearts of men and women, preparing them to welcome her and her message. She believes that the secret power behind her overt acts of service, witness, and mission is the sacrifice she offers daily for the salvation of the world, and all the prayers of intercession that the faithful unite with that sacrifice. This sacrifice and these prayers are her most efficacious acts expressing her love of abundance, that is, her participation in the fullness of Christ.

The second and third factors fall under the purview of the Church's consciousness and freedom. With Paul VI and Vatican II, the Church examines her conscience and accuses herself of lacking in missionary zeal and of relying for too long on methods of mission and expressions of faith that proved their efficacy in other ages and cultures but are not adequate for the challenges of the New Evangelization. To amplify missionary zeal, the Church engages in an *aggiornamento* of personal conversion, with the goal of producing a more ardent charity. This is the second path of *ES*. In like manner, to improve the efficacy of her service and mission, the Church engages in an institutional, theological, and pastoral *aggiornamento*. This is the third path of *ES*, intended to produce the fruit of conversion both *ad intra* and *ad extra*.

The law of fidelity to God and to man governs the second and third paths of renewal, as it does the first. Pope Paul's emphasis is on fidelity to man as the impetus for personal and institutional *aggiornamento*. This is easier to see for the third path of institutional, theological, and pastoral renewal because these are not ends in themselves but means to the end of a more effective missionary outreach—a new evangelization—both *ad intra* and *ad extra*. With respect to the second path of personal conversion, to say that fidelity to man has a certain priority would appear to reverse the proper order according to which primacy should go to fidelity to God. Is there not great danger in elevating love of man above love of God?

The answer to this important question is that while love of God and thus fidelity to God always retains its primacy, precisely because of this when the Church becomes conscious of deficiencies in love of neighbor and mission this can only mean that there is a corresponding deficiency in love of God. The relation of missionary activity or dialogue and love of neighbor or fidelity to man, on one hand, and love of God or fidelity to God, on the other hand, is causal. Missionary activity is the fruit of love of neighbor, and love of neighbor is rooted in love of God. Thus, when the Church passes a critical judgment with regard to her mission, this triggers a diagnosis that identifies a lack of ardor or zeal as one of two primary factors contributing to her mission's lack of efficacy (the other being the inadequacy of methods). Since this zeal for mission ultimately derives from love of God, the Church engages in conversion in order to deepen communion with God, that is, participation in the life and the mission of Jesus Christ. In this light, love of neighbor or reinvigorated mission is the end to which institutional, theological, and pastoral *aggiornamento* are ordered as means, and it is the occasion for a recommitment to conversion for the sake of deeper communion with God and participation in the life and mission of Christ, which always remains the supreme end. Precisely because this end entails the fruit of love of neighbor and mission, concern for the latter becomes the impetus for a new dedication to fidelity to God.

Another consideration reinforces this primacy of fidelity to God and communion with him in Christ, in other words, holiness. The Church's own zeal, rooted in holiness,[16] has the primacy because it is the source of compelling witness, which is the primary mode of mission.[17] While the Church must attend to the various methods of pastoral activity and to the expression of her faith with a view to the efficacy of her mission, these have a secondary place in relation to witness. Witness is nothing

---

16. John Paul II follows Paul VI in this emphasis on holiness being the source of mission and service. Among the numerous texts that could be quoted are the following two: "Holiness then must be called a fundamental pre-supposition and an irreplaceable condition for everyone in fulfilling the mission of salvation within the Church" (*CL*, 17); "The renewed impulse to the mission *ad gentes* demands holy missionaries. It is not enough to update pastoral techniques, organize and coordinate ecclesial resources, or delve more deeply into the biblical and theological foundations of faith. What is needed is the encouragement of a new 'ardor for holiness' among missionaries and throughout the Christian community, especially among those who work most closely with missionaries" (*RMiss*, 90).

17. All of Pope Paul's references to witness, that is, the life and radiating light of Christians, come in the final part of *ES* on dialogue. See *ES*, 59, 60, 62, 67, 95. The theme of light connects *ES* with the vision for Vatican II of John XXIII. According to this vision, the fruit of the Council would be that the light of Christ shine more brightly in the world and draw people to him.

other than Christian life on display. As Christ revealed the Father simply by living among us, so the Church reveals her communion with God by the life of her sons and daughters, who live throughout the world. This life in Christ is the marvelous work of God, the effect of his love. It is a fully human life, and because all seek a fully human life, it has the power to attract. The good is in things, St. Thomas tells us, and the proper effect of the good is to attract. In this way, witness not only respects people's freedom; it is an appeal to that freedom that carries the promise of expanding it.

This is why in the implementation of Vatican II the post-Conciliar popes emphasize the universal call to holiness as the essential key to the realization of the Council's goals. This shows that in the Church's participation in Christ's mission the primacy goes to final and exemplary causality, while efficient causality is secondary. This presents a great challenge to a culture in which efficient causality is the dominant category. In addition, the connaturality of the bond of communion with God is the source of the *sensus fidei*, which provides an internal auto-critical faculty for maintaining fidelity to God while creatively engaging in pastoral initiatives in order to be faithful to man.[18]

After the preceding examination of the law of fidelity to God and to man as a complement to the three paths of renewal of *ES*, one might wonder if this is still all a bit abstract. If these principles articulate aspects of the spirit of Vatican II and are necessary guides for renewal, and if they have remained largely neglected, as this study claims, are they just for the speculative exercise of theologians, or do they have a place in the Church's daily life? Further, how should we imagine people making the three paths of *ES* and the law of fidelity to God and to man intelligible to our contemporaries through dialogue?

The answer to both questions is based on the realization that the three paths of renewal and the law of fidelity to God and to man are not the content of the Good News that is the basis of the Church's renewal and the message that she brings to her contemporaries. Rooted in and derived from divine revelation, they make explicit what is implicit in it. They are the product of theological reflection on revelation in the historical context of the renewal initiated by Vatican II, placed at the service or ordering and guiding the interpretation and implementation of Vatican II through a New Evangelization. They are structural principles at the

---

18. In *ES*, 37, Pope Paul writes of a connatural experience of the Church.

service of renewal and the transmission of the faith, but not the faith itself.

It is neither necessary nor desirable that all the faithful receive instruction in these principles. What is desirable and indispensable is that those responsible for instructing the faithful, catechists, and candidates for ordination should know these principles and be able to apply them in the production of texts, curricula, and programs of formation for the sake of an integral theological, spiritual, and pastoral formation at various levels. As we have seen, since the Council the Church has consistently set forth her vision for the integral formation of priests, deacons, religious, laity, and catechists based on this threefold structure of theological (or doctrinal, or intellectual), spiritual, and pastoral formation, and these correspond to the three dimensions of renewal of *ES*. Programs of formation that integrate these three dimensions are an institutional expression of the Church's mystery, vocation, and mission in as much as these are realized through awareness of the mystery, ongoing conversion to conform to the mystery, and a missionary dynamism that is always looking for new and more effective ways to be faithful to man by communicating the mystery to others while remaining faithful to God by safeguarding the truth he has revealed. The three dimensions are not principles that are extrinsic to the Church's mystery, vocation, and mission. Rather, they are constitutive elements of her mystery because they are essential dimensions of faith and participation in the mystery of Christ. This has been demonstrated in the discussion of the roots of the three dimensions in the Church's life, in Scripture and in the liturgy. The appendix serves to summarize the data based on which this study claims that the three dimensions of *ES* are principles for ecclesial renewal that are intrinsic to the mystery of the Church.

To take up the second question, the foundational value of the three paths of the renewal and of the law of fidelity to God and to man is verified by the movements in the Church that are producing impressive fruit. The modern apologetics movement is a prime example. For countless Catholics, the desire to respond to a relative or friend who had left the Church or who was going through a crisis of faith became the occasion for a personal renewal and deepening of faith. They quickly discovered that they were not prepared to answer the questions that were put to them. Like the physician in the parable, they went to work to find the answers, many of which they found in the conferences, radio and television programs, tapes, CDs, pamphlets, websites, and books by the likes of Karl Keating, Scott Hahn, Mark Brumley, Rosalyn Moss, Fr. Mitch Pacwa, and Patrick Madrid, to name only a few. Prompted by their love for others, they had to upgrade their own understanding of the faith in order to engage in effective dialogue. And with experience, they became more and more adept at translating the Church's faith into language that their interlocutors could understand. All the while they were acting on their love of neighbor, they remained faithful to God by being faithful to the teaching of his Church.

It has been my privilege to teach many men and women who have had their faith renewed in this way. Not a single one had read *ES* prior to beginning graduate studies in pastoral theology, but nearly all found the study of *ES* to be an illuminating framework in light of which to understand what they had experienced. When introduced to these principles, they immediately perceived their truth and relevance. For them, the three paths of renewal was a lived experience that they could understand more deeply and comprehensively in light of the three paths of *ES*. Faith that is better understood is more fully possessed, more effectively defended, more ardently accompanied by witness, and thus more eagerly and zealously communicated to others. The increasing numbers of the faithful pursuing theological studies and engaging in the various sectors of the Church's mission is a providential opportunity to impart the authentic teaching and spirit of Vatican II for a New Evangelization according to the mind of Christ and the mind of his Church, as these are systematically expressed and unified in the three dimensions of renewal and formation, and in the law of fidelity to God and fidelity to man.

APPENDIX

Three Paths of Renewal
Biblical Foundations and Status as Permanent Features of the Church's Life

THIS APPENDIX HIGHLIGHTS A select number of the more prominent instances in which the pattern of the three paths of renewal can be recognized. The sheer number of these comprises an argument for how the three paths shape the Church's consciousness. This is not a surprise, since divine revelation attests to them. The presence of the pattern in post-Conciliar texts also attests to how deeply the pattern is engrained in the Church's consciousness. This is strongly reinforced by the fact that, with the exception of John Paul II, there is no evidence that the authors of the post-Conciliar texts deliberately adopted the pattern, as if taking *ES* as a foundationally normative reference. Rather, the pervasiveness of the pattern is best explained as being so deeply engrained in the Church's life that it manifests itself almost spontaneously, not as a theological construct, but as a way of life.

Instances of the pattern in Scripture will be grouped together first, followed by a grouping of other texts.

BIBLICAL FOUNDATIONS OF THE THREE PATHS OF THE CHURCH

The Pedagogy of Love

Pope Benedict XVI takes a verse of John's first letter as a summary of what God has revealed and faith adheres to: "We know and believe the love God has for us" (1 John 4:16). God has fashioned man in his own image precisely so that he could make a gift of himself to him. The nature of this gift is such that it can only be received for what it is if it is rightly understood. All God's efforts to make known his love are at the service of man's enrichment of faith, his doctrinal penetration. Further, it is the very nature of God's love that man be enriched by the gift God makes of himself. God's love is performative and transformative. All that man does to cooperate with this transforming love falls under the second path of conversion into a more and more perfect communion with God. Lastly, and in keeping with man's dignity (see *CCC*, 306–7), this communion entails man's participation in God's own mission of love. Otherwise, God would be alone in this mission, and this would wound his love, since it would mean that his gift of self has not been fully received. The definitive sign of communion with God on earth is participation in his mission of saving love.

Moses, David, and Elijah: A Paradigm of Purification through Mission

The lives and missions of Moses, King David, and Elijah display remarkable similarities, which become all the more evident when cast in the frame of the three dimensions of renewal. The paradigmatic pattern that emerges shows that the movement from doctrinal penetration to renewal through conversion to mission is not always linear in the sense that an earlier path is left behind when a succeeding path becomes predominant. It is certainly the case that with respect to a truth that was formerly unknown, the sequence of the three paths is necessary, as with the Blessed Virgin Mary at the Annunciation and in the case of the apostles. The same applies when a previously held truth is understood with greater accuracy or depth, as with Vatican II and the new stage of consciousness of the faith that it occasioned. The sequence that begins with doctrinal awareness and proceeds to renewal through personal assimilation of doctrine and culminates in mission is dictated by the anthropological principle, which was elaborated upon in the second part of this volume.

Nevertheless, the anthropological principle is in no way attenuated by the fact that mission can be the occasion for greater doctrinal penetration and conversion, as is evident in the following examples. The biblical accounts regarding Moses, David, and Elijah open with their commission by the Lord (more background is provided for Moses). It may be presumed that at the time of his calling, each possessed what could be called a prophetic or missionary disposition of faith. In other words, each is the beneficiary of graces that are preparatory for the beginning of his mission, according to what may be taken from Jeremiah as a principle: "Before I formed you in the womb I knew you, and before you were born I consecrated you; I appointed you a prophet to the nations" (Jer 1:5). The definitive paradigm for this is the grace of the Immaculate Conception, which fashioned Mary to be perfectly prepared to receive the grace of divine maternity.

For each one called by God, the providential season of preparation corresponds to the paths of doctrinal awareness and conformity to God's will. Presuming their period of preparation, the lives of Moses, David, and Elijah verify the order of the three paths. Following the biblical accounts of their missions reveals that the third path of mission is, in God's wisdom, the occasion for the continuation and deepening of the first two paths of doctrinal penetration and conversion. For, God does not simply make use of his associates for the sake of others. In his wisdom, the path of mission is also always for his associates in mission a path of doctrinal penetration and a path of conversion.

Moses

While the encounter of Moses with God at the burning bush is the most obvious beginning of his mission, forty years earlier he heeded an interior call and took two initiatives that foreshadow his mission as Israel's liberator. On two consecutive days, he frees a Hebrew from the oppression of an Egyptian taskmaster and attempts to dispel a quarrel between two of the slaves (Exod 2:11–14). The first intervention symbolizes Israel's slavery to foreign powers (bondage *ad extra*), and the second symbolizes the kind of exploitation within God's chosen people that for the prophets is the sure sign of having forgotten the Lord (bondage *ad intra*). This first attempt at mission ends in failure for Moses.[1] Fearing Pharaoh, he flees to Midian, where he undergoes a forty-year period of purification. This is his season of renewal for the sake of the mission that he receives, as

---

1. St. Stephen points to seeing Moses's first interventions as a first attempt to liberate Israel from slavery when he conjectures what Moses was thinking: "He supposed that his brethren understood that God was giving them deliverance by his hand, but they did not understand" (Acts 7:25).

it were for the second time. At the burning bush, God resurrected his deep-seated sense of justice and love for Israel, which he left behind as if his hope had died. His doctrinal penetration comes when God reveals his plan for Israel's liberation. Following this, he is renewed in the power of God's name, the power of his commission, and the power of God's staff. Then, the mission begins, and he takes the good news to God's enslaved people. It should not be assumed that there is no further need for doctrinal penetration or personal purification for Moses. How could his faith in God and his mysterious ways fail to be tested and refined through Israel's hard-heartedness and the Lord's response to it along the way of the journey in the desert? We know that Moses would confront his own capacity to fail in faith. But God's fidelity is greater than Moses' infidelity, and the mission is fulfilled when Israel takes possession of the Promised Land.

David

By the time of his anointing by Samuel, God's grace has fashioned David's heart to be like his own heart (1 Sam 13:14). God's blessing proves to be a two-edged sword. David enjoys early success in victories over Israel's enemies, but this plunges Saul into jealousy and David into a period of persecution. Numerous psalms bear witness to this period of total reliance on the Lord as David's faith is deepened by his experience of the Lord's mysterious ways (e.g., Pss 56; 57), which have led him from the peace and anonymity of the pasture to representing the Lord as shepherd of his people. His triumph appears to be complete as he enjoys rest from his enemies (2 Sam 7:1, 11) and he enshrines the Ark of the Covenant in Jerusalem (2 Sam 6:12-22). Only now he confronts a different kind of enemy, the interior enemy of weakness and sin, which threatens his mission as shepherd of God's people in an entirely different way. David discovers his capacity to despise the word of God (2 Sam 12:9) as his predecessor did (1 Sam 15:23-26), and thereby to contradict his mission as God's surrogate shepherd. A good shepherd lays down his life for his sheep, but David had several of his sheep killed for his own convenience. But God does not default on his word to David (2 Sam 7:8-16). Through his experience of God's mercy, David also discovers that the sacrifice God desires most is that of a humble and contrite heart (Ps 51:17). The depth of David's conversion bears witness to a corresponding doctrinal penetration, i.e., a deeper knowledge of God's mercy. The king who had desired to build for the Lord a temple in which sacrifices to his glory could be offered learns, anticipatorily, that man's very heart is the temple of sacrifice (John 2:21; 1 Cor 3:16–17; 6:19).

Elijah

God has prepared Elijah for his mission by infusing into his heart a zeal for the law (1 Macc 2:58; Sir 48:2) that impels him boldly to stand against the greatest threat of the time to the people's single-hearted devotion to the God who liberated them from slavery in Egypt, planted them in the Promised Land, assured their harvests, and granted them victory over their enemies. The proximate preparation for his mission is the very drought (1 Kgs 17:2–24) that will be the occasion for him to defeat the prophets of Baal (1 Kgs 18:19–40).

As for Moses and David, the initial success of Elijah's mission on behalf of the God of Israel has unanticipated consequences that will be the condition for a deeper conversion on Elijah's part. Elijah, of course, is an icon for the people of Israel; success in mission does not simply entail a triumph over earthly foes, but a deeper fidelity to the One God. Behind this growth is the lesson that suffering in the ways of man and even in the ways of God is unavoidable; but the way one responds to this suffering can be redemptive and part of the overall mission. When Jezebel, patroness of the prophets of Baal, plans to have Elijah killed, the prophet flees, faces death, eats and drinks what an angel provides, and makes a forty-day journey to Mount Horeb, where he is blessed by a theophany and his mission is renewed (1 Kgs 19:1–15). Just as the early and extraordinary triumphs of Moses (the plagues and parting of the sea) and David (victory over the Philistines and the consolidation of the twelve tribes) did not prevent the crises that they would face, Elijah's fantastic feat against the prophets of Baal is no assurance of success in his overall mission to keep pure the faith of Israel. Has his victory been only a momentary triumph? The miraculous provision for his forty-day journey to Mount Horeb and the theophany that takes place there are simultaneously a personal enrichment for him and a consolation to reassure him that God will make his mission fruitful. Personal conversion into a deeper understanding of God's ways and conformity to vocation (second path) are not only inseparable from but are occasioned by the vicissitudes of mission (third path).

The Paradigm of Jesus' Life

With due regard for the human perfection of the assumed human nature of the Incarnate Word, it is still possible to view his earthly life in light of the three paths of renewal. And it is highly fitting that his life and mission should exhibit these three stages, because in this way the fundamental principle of participation in his life is realized: "Christ enables *us to live in him* all that he himself lived, and *he lives it in us*" (*CCC*, 521).

Accordingly, Christ acquired human knowledge of the history of God's dealings with his people through the normal course of instruction and living of the faith that was current at his time. The whole period of the hidden years in Nazareth corresponds to the first path of doctrinal awareness. Above all, Jesus knows himself as loved by the Father and as entrusted with the mission of fulfilling all of God's promises. His baptism and the temptations in the desert are a transition from a life of fulfilling all righteousness in relation to God to fulfilling the mission that the Father entrusts to him. At his baptism, Jesus reveals his solidarity with sinners and a theophany of the Trinity inaugurates his mission of redemption. The Spirit leads him into the desert, where he recapitulates the history of Israel's temptations against faith. This period of forty days are the final preparation for his mission. It corresponds to the second path of conversion into perfect conformity to one's vocation. The remainder of the Gospels bears witness to the mystery of the "dialogue of salvation," the revelation of the full truth about God and the full truth about man through the one who is true God and true man. This dialogue reaches its summit in the paschal mystery. Through his suffering and death Jesus is made perfect (Heb 2:10; 5:8–9), that is, he perfectly fulfills the Father's plan according to which it was necessary that the Messiah suffer and rise to his glory for the sake of the salvation of men (Luke 24:26; Acts 17:3). Through his suffering, death, and resurrection, Jesus exhibits absolute fidelity to the Father, fidelity to man, the triumph of good over evil, and the fulfillment of the paradigm of growth-through-suffering, which is evident in the earlier examples of Moses, David, and Elijah.

The Annunciation

The Annunciation begins with the message that Gabriel brings to Mary, and she receives it in faith. Her initial assent to the Archangel's words provoke a search fully to understand them, as evidenced in what Luke relates about Mary pondering his greeting (Luke 1:29), and in her question "How can this be?" (Luke 1:34). This is Mary's faith seeking understanding, her doctrinal penetration, her journey along the first path. Then follows her being overshadowed by the Holy Spirit and the conception of Jesus (Luke 1:35). This is Mary's journey along the second path of transformation. Then Mary bears witness to what God has done in her and through her, through the Magnificat (Luke 1:46–55), which marks the beginning of her journey along the third path of mission through witness.

Mary's Faith

Based on the biblical witness yet using terms not found explicitly in the Bible, ecclesiastical texts consistently employ three verbs to convey three different dimensions of Mary's faith. Not coincidentally, these three verbs align with the three paths of renewal. Assent: Mary's first response to any word that she knows comes from God is to assent, to hold it as true because it comes from Truth himself. Her assent unleashes the dynamic of faith seeking understanding, especially when she does not at first fully understand the meaning of God's word (Luke 2:50). Mary's habit is to make an abiding place in her memory for the words of God to which she assents (Luke 2:19, 50). Her assent gives rise to remembering and seeking understanding, which comprise her path of doctrinal penetration. Consent: Because God's word is a word of love, he intends to enrich Mary with the graces that are both common to her and to all believers, and with graces that are unique to her. Because by her assent she knows God's plan, she can now consent to his acts of love, which transform her to be precisely what God intends. Her constant consent to God's love comprises her path of renewal through being transformed according to God's plan. Obey: Mary's obedience bears witness to the interior transformation brought about by God's love. She is the paradigm of the "obedience of faith" (Rom 1:5; 16:26; 2 Cor 10:5–6) by which her entire life is a witness to the marvelous works of God.

The Samaritan Woman (John 4:1–42)

The Samaritan woman displays a certain knowledge of faith. She knows the history behind Jacob's well, the difference between the worship of God of the Jews and Samaritans, and the expectation of a Messiah. Jesus leads her to know that he is the awaited Messiah (John 4:25–26). This is the path of doctrinal penetration, which is inseparable from the second path of her conversion, as Jesus leads this woman to realize that her life is far from corresponding to God's will. The fruit of her conversion is the mission that she spontaneously takes on, to invite the townspeople to come to meet Jesus.

The Apostles' Itinerary of Faith

The apostles' doctrinal penetration begins with Jesus' call to follow him. He initiates them into the mysteries of the kingdom of heaven (Matt 13:11). Clearly, they find his life and teaching to be consistent with and to illumine the faith that they inherited from Abraham. His arrest and crucifixion plunge the apostles into a dark night of purification of faith. This is not only a purification of concepts, but a purification of the weakness of the apostles' attachment to Christ. Everything they have learned has to be rethought in light of the resurrection. Their renewal through conversion culminates in Peter's threefold profession of love of the risen Lord (John 21:15–17). Finally, they are able to bear witness to Christ with the boldness (*parrhesia*) that comes with the descent of the Holy Spirit upon them at Pentecost.

The Disciples' Encounter with Jesus on the Road to Emmaus (Luke 24:14–35)

These were disciples who had accompanied Jesus on his final pilgrimage to Jerusalem. They knew his teachings, and they knew all that had happened to him during his final days. But they did not understand the full meaning of his teachings and especially of the final events of his life. The risen Lord, whom they did not recognize, had to open their minds to understand that it was "necessary that the Christ should suffer these things and enter into his glory" (Luke 24:26). This is their doctrinal penetration, corresponding to the first path of renewal. These disciples' words about their new hope point to the second path of renewal through conversion. They are transformed from "We had hoped that he was the one to redeem Israel" (Luke 24:21) to "Did not our hearts burn within us?" (Luke 24:32) and to celebrating the breaking of the bread with the risen Lord. The third path of mission is their bearing witness to their encounter with

Jesus: "And they rose that same hour and returned to Jerusalem.... Then they told what had happened on the road, and how he was known to them in the breaking of the bread" (Luke 24:33–35).

St. Paul

St. Paul attests to religious zeal prior to his conversion. Steeped in the faith-tradition of the people descended from Abraham, he nevertheless is in need of a profound purification of faith—a renewal of his mind (Rom 12:2; Eph 4:23)—in order to discover that Jesus brings the law to fulfillment and perfection. This purification begins with the encounter with the glorified Lord. A miraculous light plunges him into a dark night of faith, of which his physical blindness is a symbol. He emerges from this night of blindness through the graces of baptism and incorporation into the Church of Christ. The rest of his life is defined by fidelity to the apostleship to which the Lord himself commissions him. This fidelity to the Lord is simultaneously fidelity to the Church, to the Gospel, and to all those to whom he proclaims the mystery of Christ.

The Relation of the Allegorical/Christological Sense to the Moral Sense of Scripture

The people and events of Sacred Scripture are not merely historical accouterments, but truthful allegories that enable us to equilibrate our own vision of happiness with the vision of happiness that God has for us. Put theologically, the relation of the allegorical/Christological sense to the moral sense corresponds to the relation between the first path to the second and third paths. The moral sense discloses what it means for believers to participate in the mystery of Christ, which is the reality that unifies all of Scripture. The realization of this participation is called the whole Christ, that is, the Church, Head and body. As Christ's life is oriented to the Father and to the fulfillment of the mission the Father entrusts to him, so the Church's members seek the hallowing of the Father's name, the coming of his kingdom, and the fulfillment of his will *in us*. These petitions clearly presuppose that those who pray them understand what they a praying for, based on what Christ has revealed. This is the first path of doctrinal penetration. For the Church Fathers, God answers these petitions by his kingdom coming, his name being hallowed, and his will being accomplished "in us."[2] This "in us" corresponds to the second path of renewal through conversion. It includes our participation in Christ's mission, especially through witness. This corresponds to the third path, which is also a dimension of the moral sense of Scripture, since it is the realization of our participation in the mystery of Christ.

THE PATTERN OF THE THREE PATHS IN MAGISTERIAL TEXTS

Pope John XXIII, Radio Message, September 11, 1962

Pope John's summary vision for the renewal of Vatican II parallels and anticipates Pope Paul's three dimensions of renewal in *ES*. In his radio address prior to the opening of the Council, Pope John evokes these three paths in the phrase: *Lumen Christi, Lumen Ecclesiae, Lumen gentium*. The light of God becomes the light of men and for men in Jesus Christ, in whom divine revelation is fulfilled and perfected. This revelation becomes the light of the Church and takes the form of the deposit of apostolic faith. It becomes the Church's light through faith, which both grasps the meaning of revelation (first path) and unifies all of life through ongoing conversion that begins with baptism (second path). Then, the Church's light shines into the world through the witness of life and testimony of word (third path).

Vatican II, *Dignitatis humanae*, 2–3

The anthropological foundation for the three paths of renewal is verified in the following sequence regarding man's relation to the truth. The first duty corresponds to the first path of renewal: "It is in accordance with their dignity as persons ... that all men should be at once impelled by nature and also bound by a moral obligation to seek the truth, especially religious truth." The second duty corresponds to the second path of renewal, whereby the truth permeates all human action: "They are also bound to adhere to the truth, once it is known, and to order their whole

---

2. The *CCC* draws from the Church Fathers' emphasis that the holiness of the Father's name comes to be recognized among men through the witness of those who have been transformed by his love, that is, in those to whom Christ has revealed his name. See *CCC*, 2808, 2813–14. The same logic applies to the petitions regarding the coming of the kingdom and the fulfillment of God's will (*CCC*, 2825).

lives in accord with the demands of truth." All of this is in accordance with human dignity, that is, in accordance with human nature. Virtue is rational activity in accordance with the truth, and happiness is rational activity according to virtue. Thus, man's natural dynamism to seek his own happiness makes him a seeker of the truth and moves him to conform all of his activity according to the truth. Finally, because the truth is a common good, it is not possessed precisely as common unless it is being shared (St. Augustine). This leads to the third path, which *Dignitatis humanae* expresses thusly: "The inquiry is to be free, carried on with the aid of teaching or instruction, communication and dialogue, in the course of which men explain to one another the truth they have discovered, or think they have discovered, in order thus to assist one another in the quest for truth."

Vatican II on the Church's Mission

The *Decree on the Church's Missionary Activity* recognizes three stages in the development of a new local Church: "In this missionary activity of the Church various stages sometimes are found side by side: first, that of the beginning or planting, then that of newness or youth. When these have passed, the Church's missionary activity does not cease, but there lies upon the particular churches already set up the duty of continuing this activity and of preaching the Gospel to those still outside" (AG, 6). The planting takes place through the witness to Christ of missionaries and the initiation into the mystery of Christ through the sacraments of initiation. This corresponds to the first path of doctrinal awareness. This is followed by a stage of growth, which corresponds to the second path of conversion into a more perfect conformity to vocation. The final stage occurs when the seeds that were planted mature to full growth and bear the fruit of evangelization. The Church that began by being evangelized becomes an active evangelizer. This is the third path of mission.

The marks of a mature Church are the gift of an indigenous clergy, the witness of holy laity, inculturation of the Gospel, and active missionary endeavors. Regarding the latter, the Decree states: "Since the particular church is bound to represent the universal Church as perfectly as possible, let it realize that it has been sent to those also who are living in the same territory with it, and who do not yet believe in Christ. By the life witness of each one of the faithful and of the whole community, let the particular church be a sign which points out Christ to others" (*AG*, 20). This corresponds to the third path of mission through witness. This final path presupposes the entire process that begins with an initial evangelization of a people in order to bring them to faith and to initiate them into the life of Christ through baptism (the first path of doctrinal awareness) and the constant nourishing of the life of faith through catechesis and the sacraments (the second path of conversion into fuller conformity with vocation).

Pope John Paul II on the Jubilee of the Year 2000: *Tertio millennio adveniente*, 19

John Paul could very well have had *ES* before him when he wrote this section of *TMA*. The first path is exhibited in the statement: "During the Council, precisely out of a desire to be fully faithful to her Master, the Church questioned herself about her own identity, and discovered anew the depth of her mystery." The second path is reflected in the assertion: "Humbly heeding the word of God, she reaffirmed the universal call to holiness; she made provision for the reform of the liturgy, the 'origin and summit' of her life; she gave impetus to the renewal of many aspects of her life at the universal level and in the local Churches; she strove to promote the various Christian vocations." Finally, the third path is evident in the declaration: "On the basis of this profound renewal, the Council opened itself to Christians of other denominations, to the followers of other religions and to all the people of our time."

Pope John Paul II on the Jubilee of the Year 2000: Three Dimensions of Encountering Christ

In *TMA* John Paul calls for a time of immediate preparation for the Jubilee of the Year 2000. The last three years of the second millennium were dedicated to doctrinal penetration, with the subject of each year being one of the Divine Persons, a theological virtue, and a sacrament. 1997: God the Son Incarnate, Jesus Christ; the theological virtue of faith; the Sacrament of Baptism. 1998: the Holy Spirit, the theological virtue of hope; the sacrament of Confirmation. 1999: God the Father; the theological virtue of charity; the sacrament of the Eucharist. The documents of Vatican II and the *CCC* were to be the main points of reference for this entire period of doctrinal penetration.

Throughout the period of preparation for the bi-millennial encounter with Jesus Christ, John Paul called for an examination of conscience and conversion. This would assure the best dispositions so that the Jubilee encounter with God's merciful love in Christ would work the transformation by which all members of the Church would more fully conform their lives to God's will. John Paul participated in Jubilees for virtually every category of member of the Church: bishops, priests, deacons, consecrated life, the elderly, youth, artists, families, sports, disabled, the agricultural world, government leaders and politicians, catechists and religion teachers, university professors, armed forces and police, entertainment world, scientists, craftsmen, sick and healthcare workers, journalists. This Jubilee encounter with Christ and the renewal of commitment faithfully to live out the various vocations in the Church make this year correspond to the path of renewal through conversion.

The hoped-for fruit of the Jubilee is a revitalized commitment to bearing witness to Christ in the New Evangelization. This is to be rooted in a profound spirituality of communion (*NMI*, 43–45). This spirituality takes ecclesial communion, as participation in the communion of the Trinity, as both its origin and its end (*CL*, 32). This corresponds to the third path of mission.

Pope Benedict XVI on the Year of Faith, *Porta fidei*

When Benedict XVI lays out his vision for the Year of Faith, he reproduces the pattern of all renewal. With respect to doctrinal awareness, because the Year of Faith coincided with the fiftieth anniversary of Vatican II, the focus was to be on a rediscovery of the teaching of Vatican II and of the *Catechism of the Catholic Church* (*PF*, 4). Such a rediscovery, or doctrinal penetration, can only result in a summons to "a renewed and authentic conversion to the Lord," because the faith is "a new criterion of understanding and action that changes the whole of man's life" (*PF*, 6). Finally, the fruit of these two will be that "the love of Christ fills our hearts and impels us to evangelize" (*PF*, 7).

Catechism of the Catholic Church, 23

Perhaps the most succinct rephrasing of the three paths of renewal comes in the *CCC*, which has been called the Catechism of Vatican II.

> The Catechism emphasizes the exposition of doctrine. It seeks to help deepen understanding of faith. In this way it is oriented towards the maturing of that faith, its putting down roots in personal life, and its shining forth in witness.[3]

The first act of faith is to grasp the meaning of what God has revealed. As understanding, faith matures both extensively, by assenting to all that God has revealed, and intensively, by a deeper penetration into the meaning of revealed truth (first path). From the outset, the principles of faith give direction to all a believer does, directing the believer's thoughts, words, and actions to God, thereby giving his life a theologal[4] unity. This theologal integration of life becomes more extensive and intensive as faith matures (second path). Finally, the light of faith shines into the world through the witness of life in the Spirit (third path).

Order of the Catechism of the Catholic Church[5]

It should come as no surprise that the order of the first three parts of the *CCC* mirrors the order of the Annunciation and the three aspects of Mary's faith. Part One, on the Church's profession of faith in the mystery of Christ, mirrors the first path of doctrinal penetration. The Church's members' minds are renewed by the truth God has revealed. In this way, the faithful are in communion with God in the truth and based on this they can cooperate with him in the fulfillment of his plan of love, both for themselves (*ad intra*—second path) and for others (*ad extra*—third path). Part Two, on the celebration of the mystery of Christ in the liturgy and sacraments, mirrors the second path of renewal through conversion. In the liturgy and sacraments the faithful cooperate with God in his love

---

3. "Witness" here more faithfully renders the original French and official Latin versions than the "personal conduct" of the official English translation.

4. Though infrequent in English, the word, "theologal," occurs in *CCC*, 2607, 2803, 2686. It is a synonym for "theological," corresponding to the French "theologal." It means "God-centered," as when faith, hope, and charity are called the theological virtues. "Theocentric" is perhaps the best English synonym.

5. The order of the *CCC* reproduces the order of the *Roman Catechism* and prior catechetical works.

for them. Like Mary, they consent to being loved in accordance with what God has revealed about his love. Part Three, on living the mystery of Christ, mirrors the third path of mission through witness to the transforming power of the love that is encountered in the liturgy and sacraments and made known in the profession of faith.

Baltimore Catechism

The *Baltimore Catechism* not only incisively reproduces the sequence of the three paths of renewal, it also very effectively incorporates the question-answer dynamic that is characteristic of the pastoral theology of Vatican II. To the question, "Why did God make you?" the reply is: "God made me to know him, to love him, and to serve him in this world, and to be happy with him for ever in heaven." Knowing God comes first and corresponds to the first path of doctrinal penetration, or what the *CCC* calls understanding of faith. Loving God follows, and corresponds to the second path of renewal, or what the *CCC* calls faith putting down roots in daily life. Serving God corresponds to the third path of mission, by fulfilling the duties of the vocation that God has entrusted to each believer.

THE PATTERN OF THE THREE PATHS IN THE CHURCH'S LIFE AND THEOLOGY

Formation for Clergy, Religious, the Lay Apostolate, and Catechists

As demonstrated earlier, programs of formation include three dimensions, which are nearly always set forth in the following order: Intellectual (or theological) Formation; Spiritual Formation; Pastoral Formation. Intellectual formation corresponds to the path of doctrinal penetration. Spiritual formation corresponds to the path of renewal through conversion. Pastoral formation corresponds to the third path of participation in the Church's mission through ministry, apostolate, witness, and evangelization.

The Order of the Three Theological Virtues

The order among the three theological virtues—faith, hope and charity—is a constant in theological works of the Church's tradition. This order reflects the order among the three paths of renewal. St. Thomas Aquinas, for example, describes this order in the following fashion. Because hope and charity perfect the will and faith perfects the intellect, and because what the will wills must first be apprehended by the intellect, "in the order of generation, faith precedes hope and charity." Faith corresponds to the first path of awareness. With regard to hope preceding charity:

> From the very fact that a man hopes to be able to obtain some good through someone, he looks on the man in whom he hopes as a good of his own. Hence for the very reason that a man hopes in someone, he proceeds to love him: so that in the order of generation, hope precedes charity as regards their respective acts.[6]

Hope aligns with the second path, which concerns the full acquisition of the perfection corresponding to the universal call to holiness, that is, communion with God in charity. Since love of God interiorly impels believers to love those whom God loves, charity aligns with the third path of mission (ministry, apostolate, service).

An established theological tradition provides the foundation for aligning the theological virtues of faith, hope, and charity with the four parts of the *CCC*.[7] Faith aligns with Part I, the Profession of Faith. Here the *CCC* sets forth the Church's understanding of divine revelation and faith as the proper response. It then expounds the Creed to present a summary of the content of the Church's faith. In order to promote a deeper understanding of faith, this recapitulation of the Church's faith is based on Scripture and Tradition, and it takes full advantage of the history of the development of doctrine. This corresponds to the first path of doctrine penetration.

Hope aligns with Part Two, the Celebration of the Christian Mystery, with particular emphasis on the sacraments of faith. In hope, the Pilgrim Church participates in the liturgy of heaven (*CCC*, 1090, 1107, 1130, 1167, 1172, 1405). As true causes of grace (*CCC*, 1084), the sacraments re-actualize the mystery of Christ in the "today" of the Church, in view

---

6. Aquinas, *ST*, I–II, q. 62, a. 4.

7. See Nichols, *The Splendor of Doctrine*, 14; Bradley, *The Roman Catechism*, 28–30, 37–38, 70–71. Important texts within the *CCC* on the order of the three parts include: *CCC*, 1069, 1692, and 2558.

of the eschatological fulfillment of heaven. The Church's encounter in the liturgy with the transforming power of God's love (*CCC*, 1109, 1127) cannot fail to produce a constant growth towards a more perfect conformity of the Church's members with God's will, a more perfect fulfillment of their vocation. The *CCC* repeatedly links the liturgical encounter with divine love and conversion with the mystery of Christ (*CCC*, 1098, 1229, 1248). The constant conversion that characterizes the life of the faithful is especially evident in the Sacrament of Penance and Reconciliation, in which hope in God's mercy is especially prominent (*CCC*, 1431, 1490). This transforming encounter with God's merciful love corresponds to the second path of renewal through conversion.

Part Three on Life in Christ aligns especially with charity. Charity is the fulfillment of all commandments (Rom 13:8–9; Gal 5:14). It is the interior force that impels the Church's members to mission (*CCC*, 851, with a reference to 2 Cor 5:14). It is thus the soul of the apostolate (*CCC*, 864[8]), the essential element of which is missionary witness to Christ (*CCC*, 2044–46). This is the fruit of the graces received in the Church's liturgy. It corresponds to the third path of missionary dialogue.

Rite of Ordination for Deacons

The Rite of Ordination for Deacons incorporates an exhortation that in one succinct sentence includes all three dimensions of renewal: "Receive the Gospel of Christ of which you are the herald; believe what you preach, teach what you believe and put into practice what you teach." The correspondence with the three paths of renewal becomes more obvious by reversing the second and third elements. Believing what a deacon preaches corresponds to the first path, while practicing what is believed and taught corresponds to the second path, and preaching corresponds to the third path.

The Messianic Offices of Christ

As in the first encyclical of John Paul II (*RH*, 19–21), the most frequent ordering of Christ's messianic offices reproduces the order of the three paths of renewal. The prophetic office corresponds to the first path: the

---

8. Here the *CCC* quotes *AA*, 3. It could also have included *LG*, 33, which contains the phrase, "the soul of the apostolate."

foundational attitude of the prophet entails a sense of responsibility for the word of God. Prophets first receive God's word before it becomes a consuming fire that they cannot contain within them (Ps 39:2–3; Jer 20:9). The priestly office corresponds to the second path of renewal for growth in holiness. God's word purifies the one who receives it, making him a living holocaust, and gives rise to the acclamation: "For zeal for your house has consumed me" (Ps 69:9). God's word is effective, causing a transformation in the one to whom it is directed (Luke 1:38) or on behalf of whom it is spoken (Matt 8:8). Finally, the kingly office corresponds to the third path: having been made an acceptable offering to God, a person becomes sacred, set aside for the purpose of fulfilling God's will through fidelity to his vocation and placing his gifts at the service of others.

Faith Formation for Adults

Part II of the U.S. Bishops' Pastoral Plan for Adult Faith Formation in the United States, *Our Hearts Were Burning within Us*, identifies three qualities of mature faith: living, explicit, and fruitful. If the order of the first two is reversed,[9] the sequence mirrors the sequencing of the three paths of renewal. Explicit Faith entails an awareness that it is "rooted in a *personal relationship with Jesus lived in the Christian community*." It is therefore Trinitarian and ecclesial. By such Explicit Faith, a "disciple seeks the clarity and knowledge of faith." This corresponds to the first path of doctrinal awareness. Living Faith also seeks understanding and reflects on the meaning of God's revelation in relation to the believers' lives "in order to grow closer to God." It "leads to deepening conversion," that is, "a deeper appropriation of the Gospel and its power to guide, transform, and fulfill our lives." This corresponds to the second path of renewal through conversion. Fruitful Faith "bears *the fruit of evangelization* . . . the adult disciple bears witness in the world to the gift of faith and to the treasure we have found in Jesus and among the community of his disciples. In this process, the witness of the word is essential, but a living witness in the service of love and justice speaks with special power

---

9. A reversal of the order of the first two is in keeping with the text itself. A "living faith," the bishops declare, is "both a gift of God and an authentically human response—a recognition of God's call in one's life and a free decision to follow this call by accepting the living truth of the Gospel" (USCCB, *Our Hearts*, 50). Clearly, a "living faith" presupposes "a personal encounter with Jesus lived in Christian community" (USCCB, *Our Hearts*, 55).

today." This corresponds to the third path of mission through witness and dialogue.

Three Dimensions of Catechumenal Formation

The Association for Catechumenal Ministry identifies three main areas in the formation of catechumens. Catechetical Formation imparts knowledge of the faith with the explicit intention of preparing catechumens for communion with God in Christ. Liturgical Formation is ordered to a life of ongoing conversion and holiness. Pastoral Formation envisions the catechumen's participation in the mission of Christ, which constitutes a call to conversion and to discipleship for those in behalf of whom it is exercised.

The Order of the Mass

As explained in greater detail earlier, the liturgy of the Mass exhibits the three paths. The Liturgy of the Word corresponds to the path of doctrinal penetration. Through the proclamation of God's word, through the reading of Scripture and the homily, God's revelation continues to renew the minds of the faithful. The essential message of God's love resounds in the Church, and the response is twofold. First, the faithful profess their faith in all that God has revealed by reciting the Creed, the summary of faith. Second, following the example of the Virgin Mary at the Annunciation, they are humbled by God's word and, aware of its demands on them, say, "How shall this be?" This disposes them to enter into the next part of the Mass, the Liturgy of the Eucharist, where they encounter the love of God, in all of its transforming and Christ-configuring power. This is the perfect answer, the only answer, to the question, "How shall this be?" that is, "How shall your word of love be realized in me?" The Liturgy of the Eucharist corresponds to the path of renewal through conversion, by being transformed by God's love. The Concluding Rite of dismissal corresponds to the third path of mission through witness. Transformed by God's love more perfectly to conform to Christ, the faithful bear witness to him most especially by living that fullness of life to which all aspire and thereby attracting them to Christ. Such witness is the essential form of mission.

The Priest's Silent Prayer Prior to Proclaiming the Gospel

Just prior to the proclaiming the Gospel, the priest makes a sign of the cross first on the book containing God's word, and then on his forehead, lips, and heart, saying, "May the words of the Gospel be on my mind, on my lips, and in my heart." A creative flip of the second and third gestures and words results in a perfect alignment with the three paths of renewal. "On my mind" corresponds to the assent of faith and doctrinal penetration. "In my heart" corresponds to the consent of faith whereby what is assented to permeates the totality of one's life. "On my lips" corresponds to the obedience of faith whereby the faithful take up the duties of their vocation in order to participation in the mission of witness to Christ.

Homiletic Directory[10] and the Three Paths of Renewal

Articles 12–13 outline what the Directory calls "a simple yet challenging dynamic." The first dimension of this dynamic is based on the conviction that the homily is "a sort of extension of the proclamation of the readings themselves." Both *proclaim* the Paschal Mystery. "The preacher speaks about the readings and prayers of the celebration in such a way that their *meaning* is found in the death and Resurrection of the Lord." It is natural, then, that "the reflection could well touch on *doctrinal or moral teaching* suggested by the texts," since doctrine and moral teaching are the distillation of the meaning of what God has revealed. This corresponds to the first path of renewal.

The second dimension looks toward the actual celebration of the Paschal Mystery that is proclaimed. The homily "prepares the community to *celebrate* the Eucharist, and to recognize that in this celebration they *truly share in the mystery* of the Lord's death and Resurrection." The homily proclaims the truth of the Paschal Mystery in such a way that the faithful readily perceive its "for me" value (Scripture's moral sense). In this way, the congregation is invited to move *from knowledge* of this mystery *to active participation* in it. Thereby, the first conversion of baptism is fulfilled in the definitive *transformation* of the faithful into and by that in which they believe. This pointing to the Liturgy of the Eucharist corresponds to the second path of renewal.

---

10. Congregation for Divine Worship and the Discipline of the Sacraments, *Homiletic Directory*.

The homily's third dimension "suggests how the members of the community, *transformed* by the Eucharist, can carry the *Gospel* into the world in their *daily lives*. Naturally, the scriptural readings will provide the content and direction for such applications, but the homilist also needs to highlight "the *effect* of the Eucharist itself . . . and its *consequences for daily living* in the blessed hope of inseparable communion with God." The encounter with the paschal charity of Christ is transformative. This *transformation* is the existential bridge by which faith that is proclaimed crosses over to faith that is lived and that by being lived becomes witness and light to the world: "Go and announce the Gospel of the Lord . . . glorifying the Lord by your life." The homily's third dimension corresponds to the third path of renewal.

Mental Prayer and *Lectio divina*

Traditionally understood and practiced, mental prayer and *lectio divina* reflect the sequence of the three paths of renewal. First, corresponding to doctrinal penetration, there is *lectio* and *meditatio*. Second, corresponding to transformation or renewal, there is *oratio* and *contemplatio*. Third, corresponding to mission through fidelity to one's vocation, there is the resolution that St. Francis de Sales recommends. Through the resolution the one who first takes in God's word and then makes it his own projects into daily life the fruits of renewed and reinvigorated communion with Christ.

Select Bibliography

Abbott, Walter M., ed. *The Documents of Vatican II.* New York: Guild/America/ Association, 1966.

Acta Synodalia Sacrosancti Concilii Oecumenici Vaticani II. Vatican City: Typis Polyglottis Vaticanis, 1970.

Alberigo, Giuseppe. *A Brief History of Vatican II.* Translated by Matthew Sherry. Maryknoll, NY: Orbis, 2006.

———. "Vatican II et son héritage." *Études d'histoire Religieuse* 63 (1997) 7–24.

Alberigo, Giuseppe, and Joseph A. Komonchak, eds. *History of Vatican II.* 5 vols. Maryknoll, NY: Orbis, 1995–2006.

Alberigo, Giuseppe, Joseph A. Komonchak, and Jean-Pierre Jossua, eds. *The Reception of Vatican II.* Translated by Matthew J. O'Connell. Washington, DC: Catholic University of American Press, 1987.

Amerio, Romano. *Iota Unum: A Study of Changes in the Catholic Church in the Twentieth Century.* Translated by John Parsons. Kansas City, MO: Angelus, 1996.

Anderson, Floyd, ed. *Council Daybook: Vatican II, Sessions I and II.* Washington, DC: National Catholic Welfare Conference, 1965.

Augustine. *De doctrina Christiana,* I, 1. Corpus Christianorum, Series Latina. Vol. 32, p. 6, lines 10–11.

Barroso, Santiago Díez. "*Ecclesiam suam* (1964–2014): Para un justiprecio de Pablo VI, el Papa 'transfigurado'," *Revista Estudio Agustiniano,* (Part I) 50:1 (2015) 89–138; (Part II) 50:2 (2015) 221–283; (Part III) 51:2 (2016) 213–263; (Part VI) 51:3 (2016) 535–589.

Barthélemy, Dominique. *God and His Image: An Outline of Biblical Theology.* Translated by Aldheim Dean. London: Chapman, 1966.

Bauer, J. B., ed. *Encyclopedia of Biblical Theology. The Complete Sacramentum Verbi.* New York: Crossroad, 1981.

Bea, Augustin. *The Word of God and Mankind.* Chicago: Franciscan Herald, 1967.

Benedict XVI, Pope. "Address to the Roman Curia, December 22, 2005."

———. "Address to the Participants of the Plenary Assembly of the Congregation for the Doctrine of the Faith, February 10, 2006."

———. "Address to the Participants at the Ecclesial Convention of the Diocese of Rome, June 5, 2006."

———. "Address to the Participants in the International Symposium of Secular Institutes, February 3, 2007."

———. "Address to the Participants in the Plenary Assembly of the Pontifical Council '*Cor Unum*,' February 29, 2008."

———. "Address to the Participants of the International Meeting of Priests, June 10, 2010."
———. "Address to Bishops of the Episcopal Conference of India, September 8, 2011."
———. "Address to Representatives of the Council of the 'Evangelical Church in Germany,' September 23, 2011" [Italian].
———. "Address to Young People in Germany, September 24, 2011."
———. "Address to Bishops from the United States of America, November 26, 2011."
———. "Address to the Roman Curia, December 22, 2011."
———. "Address to Bishops Taking Part in the Meeting Organized by the Congregations for Bishops and for the Eastern Churches, September 20, 2012."
———. "Angelus, October 2, 2011."
———. "*Ecclesia in Medio Oriente*, September 14, 2012."
———. "General Audience, March 10, 2010."
———. "General Audience, February 16, 2011."
———. "General Audience, October 24, 2012."
———. "General Audience, February 27, 2013."
———. "Homily during Visit to Brescia and Concesio, November 8, 2009."
———. "Homily for the Solemnity of *Corpus Christi*, June 7, 2012."
———. "Homily for the Opening of the Year of Faith, October 11, 2012."
———. "Inflight Interview with Journalists, March 23, 2012."
———. "Message at the End of the Eucharistic Concelebration with the Members of the College of Cardinals, April 20, 2005."
———. "Message for World Mission Sunday, January 6, 2011."
———. "Message to Bishop Luis Collazuol, on the occasion of the 80th anniversary of Catholic Action Argentina, April 4, 2011."
———. "Message for Lent, 2013."
———. "*Ubicumque et semper*, September 11, 2010."
Benedict of Nursia. *Holy Rule*. Translated by Boniface Verheyen. Grand Rapids: Christian Classics Ethereal Library, 1949.
Bernard of Clairvaux. *Bernard of Clairvaux: Sermon on the Song of Songs*. Translated by Kilian Walsh. Kalamazoo, MI: Cistercian, 1971.
Bradley, Robert. *The Roman Catechism in the Catechetical Tradition of the Church. The Structure of the Roman Catechism as Illustrative of the "Classic Catechesis."* Lanham, MD: University Press of America, 1990.
Bretzke, James T. *Consecrated Phrases: A Latin Theological Dictionary; Latin Expressions Commonly Found in Theological Writings*. 3rd ed. Collegeville, MN: Michael Glazier, 2013.
Bulman, Raymond F. and Frederick J. Parrella, eds. *From Trent to Vatican II: Historical and Theological Investigations*. Oxford: Oxford University Press, 2006.
Bushman, Douglas. "Pope Paul VI on the Renewal of Vatican II as an Act of the Church Drawing from Her Treasure Things both Old and New." *Nova et Vetera*, English Edition 9:2 (2011) 361–393.
———. "General Introduction." In *The Sixteen Documents of Vatican II*. Edited by Marianne Trouvé. Boston: Pauline, 1999, xv–xxvii.
Buttiglione, Rocco. *Karol Wojtyła. The Thought of the Man Who Became Pope John Paul II*. Translated by Paulo Guietti and Francesca Murphy. Grand Rapids: Eerdmans, 1997.

Camadini, Giuseppe, ed. *"Ecclesiam Suam" première lettre encyclique de Paul VI. Colloque international, Rome 24-26 octobre 1980.* Roma: Instituto Paulo VI, 1982.
Carlen, Claudia, ed. *The Papal Encyclicals 1740-1981.* 5 vols. Ypsilanti, MI: Pierian, 1990; McGrath, 1981.
Catechism of the Catholic Church. 2nd ed. Washington, DC: United States Conference of Catholic Bishops—Libreria Editrice Vaticana, 1994, 1997, 2016.
Catholic Church. *The Code of Canon Law: in English Translation.* London: Collins, 1983.
Chadwick, Henry. "Paul VI and Vatican II." *The Journal of Ecclesiastical History* 41/3 (1990) 463-469.
Chenaux, Philippe, ed. *Giovanni XXIII e Paolo VI: i due papi del Concilio.* Rome: Lateran University Press, 2013.
Chenu, M.-D. "De commercio inter Ecclesiam et mundum secundum constitutionem 'Gaudium et spes' (n. 44)." In *Acta Congressus Internationalis de Theologia Concilii Vaticani II. Romae diebus 26 septembris-1 octobris 1966 celebrat.* Edited by Adolfus Schönmetzer. Rome: Typis Polyglottis Vaticanis, 1968.

———. "Le Message au Monde des Pères Conciliaires," *L'Église dans le Monde de ce Temps, réflexions et perspectives.* Vol. 3. Edited by Yves Congar and M. Feuchmaurd. Paris: Cerf, 1967.
Chinnici, Joseph P. "Reception of Vatican II in the United States." *Theological Studies* 64 (2003) 461-494.
Clifford, Catherine E. *Decoding Vatican II: Interpretation and Ongoing Reception.* New York: Paulist, 2014.
Colombo, Giuseppe. "Genesi, Storia et Significato dell'enciclica 'Ecclesiam Suam.'" In *"Ecclesiam Suam" première lettre encyclique de Paul VI. Colloque international, Rome 24-26 octobre 1980.* Roma: Instituto Paulo VI, 131-160.
Congar, Yves. *Le Concile de Vatican II. Son Église, Peuple de Dieu et Corps du Christ.* Paris: Beauchesne, 1984.

———. "Reception as an Ecclesiological Reality." In *Election and Consensus in the Church.* Edited by Giuseppe Alberigo and Anton Weiler. New York: Herder & Herder, 1972.

———. "Sur la trilogie: prophéte-roi-prête." *Revue des sciences philosophiques et théologiques* 67 (1983) 97-115.
Contat, Alain. "L'ermeneutica del Vaticano II e la metafisica della partecipazione." *Alpha Omega* 17/3 (2014) 485-541.
D'Ambrosio, Marcellino. "*Ressourcement* theology, *aggiornamento*, and the hermeneutics of tradition." *Communio* 18 (1991) 530-55.
De la Soujeule, Benoît. "Tout récapituler dans le Christ." *Revue Thomiste* 98 (1998) 591-630.
De Liguori, Alphonsus. *Uniformity with God's Will.* Translated by Thomas W. Tobin. Rockford, IL: Tan, 1977.
De Lubac, Henri. "Commentaire du préambule du chapitre I." *La Révélation Divine.* Unam Sanctam, 70a. Paris: Cerf (1968) 244-245.
De Mattei, Roberto. *The Second Vatican Council: An Unwritten Story.* Translated by Patrick T. Brannan, Michael J. Miller, and Kenneth D. Whitehead. Edited by Michael J. Miller. Fitzwilliam, NH: Loreto, 2013.
Delhaye, Philippe. "Nature and Grace in the Theology of Vatican II: A Note on Caffarra's 'Marriage as a Reality in the Order of Creation and Marriage as a Sacrament." In

Contemporary Perspectives on Christian Marriage. Edited by Richard Malone and John R. Connery. Chicago: Loyola University Press, 1984, 285–296.

De Margerie, Bertrand. *Christ for the World: The Heart of the Lamb*. Translated by Malachy Carroll. Chicago: Franciscan Herald, 1973.

De Sales, Francis. *Introduction to the Devout Life*. Translated by John K. Ryan. New York: Image, 1972.

Dhanis, Eduardo. *Acta Congressus Internationalis de Theologia Concilii Vaticani II. Romae, diebus 26 septembris–1 octobris 1966 celebrati*. Rome: Typis Polyglottis Vaticanis, 1968.

Dondaine, H.-F. *Saint Thomas d'Aquin, Somme Théologique: La Trinité*, I, Questions 33–43. Paris: Cerf, 1962.

Doré, Joseph. *Introduction á L'Etude de la Théologie*. 2 vols. Paris: Desclée, 1992.

Dulles, Avery. *A History of Apologetics*. San Francisco: Ignatius, 2005.

———. *The Splendor of Faith. The Theological Vision of Pope John Paul II*. New York: Herder & Herder, Crossroad, 1999.

Dulles, Avery, et al. *Toward a Theology of Christian Faith*. New York: Kenedy & Sons, 1968.

Dupont-Fauville, D. "Une herméneutique pour Vatican II. *Nouvelle revue théologique*, 134/4 (2012) 560–579.

Durand, Emmanuel. "Relire *Dei Verbum* dans son histoire . . . Pour surmonter une fausse division entre exégèse scientifique et théologie." *Transversalités* 2 (2018) 39–63.

Duroux, Benoît. *La Psychologie de la Foi chez Saint Thomas d'Aquin*. Tournai, Belgium: Desclée, 1963.

Echeverria, Eduardo. "History, Unchanging Truth, and Vatican II." *Catholic World Report* (October 18, 2018).

———. "Language, Truth, and Reality. Revisiting *Veritatis splendor* on its 25th Anniversary." *Catholic World Report* (August 5, 2018).

Faggioli, Massimo. *A Council for the Global Church: Receiving Vatican II in History*. Minneapolis: Fortress, 2015.

———. "The Future of Vatican II." In *Vatican II: A Universal Call to Holiness*, ed. Anthony Ciorra and Michael W. Higgins. New York: Paulist, 2012, 267–289.

———. *Vatican II: The Battle for Meaning*. New York: Paulist, 2012.

Faggioli, Massimo, and Andrea Vicini, eds. *The Legacy of Vatican II*. New York: Paulist, 2015.

Famerée, Joseph. "XIII International Study Interview. For a Church 'Experienced in Humanity'. Paul VI Interpreter of Vatican II." Paul VI Institute, Concesio-Brescia, 23–25 September 2016. *Revue Theologique de Louvain* 48/2 (2017) 298–300.

Famerée, Joseph, ed. *Vatican II comme style: L'herméneutique théologique du Concile*. Paris: Cerf, 2012.

Fitzmyer, Joseph. *The Anchor Bible: Romans*. New York: Doubleday, 1993.

Flynn, Gabriel, and Paul D. Murray, eds. *Ressourcement: A Movement for Renewal in Twentieth-Century Catholic Theology*. Oxford: Oxford University Press, 2012.

Francis, Pope. "Address to Representatives of the Communications Media, March 16, 2013."

———. "Address to the Students of the Jesuit Schools of Italy and Albania, June 7, 2013."

———. "Address to Seminarians and Novices, July 6, 2013."

———. "Address to the Bishops of the Episcopal Conference of the Netherlands, December 2, 2013."
———. "Address to the Bishops of the Episcopal Conference of Poland, February 7, 2014."
———. "Address to the Bishops of the Episcopal Conference of Bulgaria, February 13, 2014."
———. "Address to the Bishops of the Episcopal Conference of Rwanda, April 3, 2014."
———. "Address to the Community of the Pontifical Leonine College in Anagni, April 14, 2014."
———. "Address to the Bishops of the Episcopal Conference of Burundi, May 5, 2014."
———. "Address to Rectors and Students of the Pontifical Colleges and Residences of Rome, May 12, 2014."
———. "Address to the 66th General Assembly of the Italian Episcopal Conference, May 19, 2014."
———. "Address to the Bishops Taking Part in the Seminar Organized by the Congregation for the Evangelization of Peoples, September 20, 2014."
———. "Address to Visitors of Mary Theotokos Shrine (Loppiano), May 10, 2018."
———. "Address to Teachers and Students of the Alphonsian Academy Higher Institute of Theology, February 9, 2019."
———. "Address to Participants in the General Chapter of the Pontifical Institute for Foreign Missions, May 20, 2019."
———. "Address to the Delegations of Missionary Institutes of Italian Foundation, September 30, 2019."
———. "Angelus, February 2, 2014."
———. "Angelus, July 29, 2018."
———. "*Antiquum ministerium*, May 10, 2021."
———. "*Evangelii gaudium*, November 24, 2013."
———. "General Audience, November 19, 2014."
———. "Letter to the Bishop of Assisi, April 16, 2017."
———. "Letter to Mrs. Angela Merkel, June 29, 2017."
———. "Letter to Cardinal Fernando Filoni, October 22, 2017."
———. "*Lumen fidei*, June 29, 2013."
———. "Message for the World Day of Prayer, September 1, 2016."
———. "Message for World Mission Day 2017."
———. "Message for the 1st World Day of the Poor, November 19, 2017."
———. "Message for the 2nd World Day of the Poor, November 18, 2018."
———. "Morning Meditation, March 7, 2014."
———. "Morning Meditation, March 16, 2017."
———. "*Summa familia cura*, September 8, 2017" [Italian].
———. "*Veritatis gaudium*, December 27, 2017."
Gaffney, James. "On Parenesis and Fundamental Moral Theology." *Journal of Religious Ethics* 11/1 (1983) 23–34.
Gaillardetz, Richard R., and Catherine E. Clifford. *Keys to the Council: Unlocking the Teaching of Vatican II*. Collegeville, MN: Liturgical, 2012.
Garrigou-Lagrange, Reginald. *The Three Ages of the Interior Life*. St. Louis: Herder, 1947.
———. *The Three Ways of the Spiritual Life*. Rockford, IL: Tan Books, 1977; original French 1933.

Gregg, Samuel. *Challenging the Modern World. Karol Wojtyła/John Paul II and the Development of Catholic Social Teaching*. Lanhan, MD: Lexington, 1999, 2002.

Gregory the Great. *The Book of Pastoral Rule*. Translated by James Barmby. In *Nicene and Post-Nicene Fathers*. Second Series. Vol. 12. Edited by Philip Schaff and Henry Wace. Buffalo, NY: Christian Literature, 1895.

Grisez, Germain. *The Way of the Lord Jesus*. 3 vols. Chicago: Franciscan Herald, 1983.

Grisez, Germain, and Russell Shaw. *Personal Vocation. God Calls Everyone by Name*. Huntington, IN: Our Sunday Visitor, 2003.

Grumett, David. "Henri de Lubac: Looking for Books to Read the World." In *Ressourcement: A Movement for Renewal in Twentieth-Century Catholic Theology*. Edited by Gabriel Flynn and Paul D. Murray. Oxford: Oxford University Press (2012) 236–249.

Guillet, Jacques. "La typologie de l'Exode dans l'ancien et nouveau Testament: Le thème de la marche au désert dans l'ancien testament." *Recherches de science religieuse* 36/2 (1949) 161–181.

Hamer, J. and Y. Congar, eds. *Vatican II: La Liberté Religieuse*. Paris: Cerf, 1967.

Hartman, Louis. *Encyclopedic Dictionary of the Bible*. New York: McGraw-Hill, 1963.

Hebblethwaithe, Peter. *John XXIII: Pope of the Council*. London: Chapman, 1984.

Heft, James L. *After Vatican II: Trajectories and Hermeneutics*. Grand Rapids: Eerdmans, 2012.

Heschel, Abraham Joshua. *God in Search of Man: A Philosophy of Judaism*. New York, Farrar, Straus & Cudahy, 1955.

Hughson, Thomas. "Interpreting Vatican II: 'A New Pentecost.'" *Theological Studies* 69 (2008) 3–37.

International Theological Commission. *Sensus Fidei* in the Life of the Church, 2014.

John XXIII, Pope. "Address on the Celebration of the Second Ecumenical Vatican Council, June 5, 1960." *The Pope Speaks* 6 (1960) 231–239.

———. "Address to Members of the Pontifical Commissions and the Secretaries Preparing for the Second Ecumenical Vatican Council, November 14, 1960." *The Pope Speaks* 6 (1960) 376–385.

———. "Address on the Opening of the Second Ecumenical Vatican Council, October 11, 1962" [Italian].

———. "General Audience, August 1, 1962" [Italian].

———. "*Humanae salutis*, December 25, 1961" [Italian].

———. "Radio Message, September 11, 1962" [Italian].

John Chrysostom. *In Genesis* 3, 8 (Homily 17, 1): *Patrologia Graeca*. Vol. 53, Col. 134.

John of the Cross. *The Collected Works of John of the Cross*. Translated by Kieran Kavanaugh and Otilio Rodriquez. Washington, DC: ICS, 1991.

John Paul II, Pope. "*A Concilio Constantinopolitano*, March 25, 1981."

———. "Act of Consecration to the Virgin of the Thirty-three, May 8, 1988."

———. "Address to the 3rd General Conference of Latin American Episcopate, January 28, 1979."

———. "Address to the Catholic Laity in Portugal, May 12, 1982" [Italian].

———. "Address to the Young People of Scotland, May 31, 1982."

———. "Address to Members of the Pontifical Academy of Sciences, October 23, 1982."

———. "Address on the Occasion of the Delivery of the 'International Paul VI Award' to Hans Urs von Balthasar, June 23, 1984."

SELECT BIBLIOGRAPHY 373

———. "Address to the Cardinals and Collaborators of the Roman Curia, June 28, 1986" [Italian].
———. "Address to the Academic Body of the Catholic University in Lyon, France, October 7, 1986" [French].
———. "Address to the Bishops of the Church in New Zealand, November 23, 1986."
———. "Address to the Leaders in Catholic Health Care, September 14, 1987."
———. "Address to the Central Committee for the Marian Year, February 2, 1988" [Italian].
———. "Address to Participants of the National Convention of Italian Catechists, April 25, 1988" [Italian].
———. "Address to the Italian Bishops, May 3, 1988" [Italian].
———. "Address to the Catalan Pilgrims in Spain, December 5, 1988" [Catalan].
———. "Address to the Tribunal of the Roman Rota, January 28, 1991."
———. "Address to the Religious Women of the Basilicata, April 28, 1991" [Italian].
———. "Address to the Hungarian Seminarians, August 19, 1991" [Italian].
———. "Address to Convention Participants Organized by the European Community Episcopate, October 11, 1991" [Italian].
———. "Address to H. E. Mr. Sinthu Sorasongkram, Ambassador of Thailand to the Holy See, November 19, 1991."
———. "Address to Scholars Participating in the Study Week on 'Resources and Population,' November 22, 1991."
———. "Address to Participants in the 35th Conference of the Canon Law Society of Great Britan and Ireland, May 22, 1992."
———. "Address to the Bishops of the Episcopal Conference of Scotland, October 29, 1992."
———. "Address to the Cardinals, to the Pontifical Family, to the Curia and to the Roman Prelature, December 22, 1992" [Italian].
———. "Address to Participants of the European Episcopal Conferences' Council Meeting, April 16, 1993." [Italian].
———. "Address to Representatives of Christian Churches and Ecclesial Communities of Jamaica and the Caribbean, August 10, 1993."
———. "Address to Participants in the '4th National Ultreya of the Cursillos in Christianity,' May 6, 1995" [Italian].
———. "Address to Members of the Central Committee of the Holy Year and to the Representatives of Episcopal Conferences of the Whole World, February 16, 1996" [Italian].
———. "Address to the Bishops of Tanzania, February 20, 1996."
———. "Address to the Bishops of Myanmar, July 5, 1996."
———. "Address to representatives of the Federation of Christian Organizations for International Volunteer Service, February 22, 1997."
———. "Address to the Alsatian Gypsies, March 21, 1997."
———. "Address to the Cardinals, Papal Household and to the Roman Curia, December 22, 1997."
———. "Address to the Bishops of the Episcopal Conference of the United States of America, October 9, 1998."
———. "Address to the Priestly Fraternity of St. Peter and Pilgrims in Rome for Recent Beatification, October 26, 1998."
———. "Address to an International Symposium on the Inquisition, October 31, 1998."

———. "Address to the Bishops of New Zealand, November 21, 1998."
———. "Address to the Pilgrims from the Diocese of Vigevano, April 17, 1999."
———. "Address to the Bishops of Canada, September 25, 1999."
———. "Address to the Conference Studying the Implementation of the Second Vatican Council, February 27, 2000."
———. "Address to the Members, Consultors and Staff of the Pontifical Commission for the Cultural Heritage of the Church, March 31, 2000."
———. "Address to the Bishops and Apostolic Administrators of Albania, February 3, 2001."
———. "Address to Representatives of the World of Culture, September 24, 2001."
———. "Address to the 6th Public Session of the Pontifical Academies of Theology and of St. Thomas Aquinas, November 8, 2001."
———. "Address to the International Catechetical Congress, October 11, 2002."
———. "Address to the Bishops of Brazil, November 26, 2002."
———. "Address to Members of the Pontifical Commission for Latin America, March 27, 2003."
———. "Address to Members of the Council of European Episcopal Conferences, May 8, 2003."
———. "Address to the Bishops of India, September 6, 2003."
———. "Address to the Bishops of the Philippines, October 9, 2003."
———. "Address to the Bishops of England and Wales, October 23, 2003."
———. "Address to the 3rd Group of French Bishops, December 18, 2003."
———. "Address to the Bishops of the Ecclesiastical Provinces of Baltimore and Washington (U.S.A.), April 29, 2004."
———. "Angelus, November 5, 1995" [Italian].
———. "Angelus, August 2, 1998."
———. "Angelus, August 8, 1999."
———. "*Apostolos suos*," May 21, 1998."
———. "*Centesimus annus*, May 1, 1991."
———. "*Dilecti amici*, March 31, 1985."
———. "*Ecclesia Dei*, July 2, 1988."
———. "*Ecclesia in Oceania*, November 22, 2001."
———. "*Ex corde Ecclesiae*, August 15, 1990."
———. "*Fidei depositum*, October 11, 1992."
———. "General Audience, October 17, 1984" [Italian].
———. "General Audience, June 5, 1985" [Italian].
———. "General Audience, October 2, 1985" [Italian].
———. "General Audience, December 18, 1985" [Italian].
———. "General Audience, May 7, 1986" [Italian].
———. "General Audience, November 12, 1986" [Italian].
———. "General Audience, April 13, 1988."
———. "General Audience, March 18, 1998."
———. "General Audience, August 9, 2000."
———. "General Audience, June 25, 2003."
———. "Homily for the Inauguration of His Pontificate, October 22, 1978."
———. "Homily during the Apostolic Journey to the Dominican Republic, January 25, 1979."
———. "Homily for Holy Mass with Bishops of Europe, June 20, 1979."

———. "Homily for the Inauguration of the Academic Year of the Pontifical Roman University, October, 15, 1979" [Italian].

———. "Homily during the Apostolic Journey to Davao, Philippines, February 20, 1981."

———. "Homily for the Holy Mass at St. Frances of Rome Parish, November 29, 1981" [Italian].

———. "Homily for the Concelebration at the 'Laval' Catholic University, Québec, September 9, 1984" [French].

———. "Homily during the Apostolic Journey to Santo Domingo, October 11, 1984" [Italian].

———. "Homily during the Apostolic Journey to Venezuela, January 28, 1985" [Spanish].

———. "Homily during the Apostolic Journey to Australia, November 27, 1986."

———. "Homily during the Apostolic Journey to Poland, June 13, 1987."

———. "Homily for Holy Mass at the New Basilica of Oropa, Biella, Italy, July 16, 1989" [Italian].

———. "Homily during Pastoral Visit in Campania, Italy, May 24, 1992" [Italian].

———. "Homily during Apostolic Journey to Philippines, January 13, 1995."

———. "Homily during Pastoral Visit to Bologna, Italy, September 27, 1997."

———. "Homily for the Beatification of: Fr. Elías del Socorro Nieves, Fr. Giovanni Battista Piamarta, Fr. Domenico Lentini, Mother Mary of Jesus and Sr. Maria Teresa Fasce, October 12, 1997."

———. "Homily for the Conclusion of the Special Assembly for America of the Synod of Bishops, December 12, 1997."

———. "Homily during the Apostolic Journey to Nigeria, March 23, 1998."

———. "Homily during Apostolic Journey to Malawi, May 5, 1989."

———. "Homily during Apostolic Journey to Romania, May 9, 1999."

———. "Homily for the Inauguration of the Academic Year 1999-2000, October 15, 1999."

———. "Homily for the Opening of the Academic Year for Ecclesiastical Universities, October 22, 2000."

———. "Homily for the Jubilee of the Apostolate of the Laity, November 26, 2000."

———. "Homily for the Jubilee of Catechists and Religion Teachers, December 10, 2000."

———. "Homily on the 41st World Day of Prayer for Vocations, May 2, 2004."

———. "Letter to Cardinal Joseph Ratzinger, April 8, 1988" [Italian].

———. "Letter to the President of the Association of Central African Bishops' Conferences, May 2, 2002."

———. "Letter to Cardinal Walter Kasper, September 3, 2004."

———. "Message for the 22nd World Communications Day, May 15, 1988."

———. "Message to Seminarians in Spain, November 8, 1982." [Spanish]

———. "Message to the Youth of Curaçao, Netherlands Antilles, May 13, 1990."

———. "Message for the 33rd Day of Prayer for Vocations, 1996."

———. "Message for World Migration Day, 1997."

———. "Message to the Young People of Cuba, January 23, 1998."

———. "Message to the Staff and Residents of the Rennweg Hospice, Vienna, June 21, 1998."

———. "Message to the Prefect for the Congregation for Oriental Churches, November 1, 1999."
———. "Message for the World Day of Prayer for Vocations, April 25, 1999."
———. "Message for the World Day of Prayer for Vocations, May 14, 2000."
———. "Message for the World Day of Prayer for Vocations, May 6, 2001."
———. "Message to the President of the Immaculata, September 18, 2001."
———. "Message for Brazil's Lenten 'Campaign of Fraternity 2003,' January 4, 2003."
———. "Message for the World Day of Prayer for Vocations, May 11, 2003."
———. "Message to the Bishop of Mantua on the Occasion of the 12th Centenary of the Diocese of Mantua, June 10, 2004."
———. "*Mulieris dignitatem*, August 15, 1988."
———. "*Pastor Bonus*, June 28, 1988."
———. "*Pastores gregis*, October 16, 2003."
———. "*Sacrae disciplinae leges*, January 25, 1983."
———. "*Salvifici doloris*, February 11, 1984."
———. "*Sapientia Christiana*, April 15, 1979."
———. "*Sollicitudo rei socialis*, December 30, 1987."
———. "*Ut unum sint*, May 25, 1995."
———. "*Veritatis splendor*, August 6, 1993."
———. "*Vita consecrata*, March 25, 1996."
Kaplan, Grant. "Vatican II as a Constitutional Text of Faith." *Horizons* 41/1 (2014) 1–21.
Käsemann, Ernst. *Commentary on Romans*. Edited and translated by Geoffrey Bromiley. Grand Rapids, MI: Wm B. Eerdmann's, 1980.
Kijas, Zdzislaw Jósef, and Andrzej Dobrzynski. *Christ, Church, Mankind: The Spirit of Vatican II according to Pope John Paul II*. New York: Paulist, 2012.
Kobler, John Francis. "Introduction to the Thought of Vatican II." *Chicago Studies* 44/1 (2005) 82–100.
———. *Vatican II and Phenomenology. Reflections on the Life-World of the Church*. Dordrecht: Martinus Nijhoff, 1985.
Küng, Hans, Yves Congar, and Daniel O'Hanlon, eds. *Council Speeches of Vatican II*. Glen Rock, NJ: Deus/Paulist, 1964.
Lamb, Matthew, and Matthew Levering. *The Reception of Vatican II*. Oxford: Oxford University Press, 2017.
Latinovic, Vladimir, Gerard Mannion, and Jason Welle, eds. *Catholicism Opening to the World and Other Confessions: Vatican II and Its Impact*. Cham, Switzerland: Palgrave Macmillan, 2018.
Latourelle, René. *Christ and the Church. Signs of Salvation*. Translated by Sr. Dominic Parker. Staten Island, NY: Alba House, 1972.
———. *Man and His Problems in the Light of Jesus Christ*. New York: Alba House, 1982.
Latourelle, René, ed. *Vatican II: Assessment and Perspectives Twenty-Five Years After (1962–1987)*. Vol. 1. New York: Paulist, 1988.
Latourelle, René, and Rino Fisichella, eds. *Dictionary of Fundamental Theology*. New York: Crossroad, 1994.
Laurentin, René. *L'Enjeu du Concile: Bilan de la Première Session*. Paris: Editions du Seuil, 1963.
Lesquivit, Colomban, and Xavier Léon-Dufour. "Pasteur et Troupeau." In *Vocabulaire de Théologie Biblique*. Paris: Cerf, 1970, 917–921.

López, Angel Pérez. "Karol Wojtyła's Thomistic Understanding of Consciousness." *The Thomist* 79 (2015) 407-437.

Lyonnet, Stanislas. "La 'loi naturelle' et la 'règle d'or' évangélique (Rm 2:14-15 et 13:8-10)." In *Le message de l'épître aux Romains*. Paris: Cerf, 1971, 47-55.

Mannion, Gerard, ed. *The Vision of John Paul II. Assessing His Thought and Influence*. Collegeville, MN: Liturgical, 2008.

Marchetto, Agostino. *The Second Vatican Ecumenical Council: A Counterpoint for the History of the Council*. Translated by Kenneth D. Whitehead. Scranton, PA: University of Scranton Press, 2010.

Marie-Eugene of the Child Jesus. *I Want To See God* and *I Am a Daughter of the Church*. Chicago: Fides, 1953.

Martelet, Gustave. *Les idées maîtresses de Vatican II. Introduction à l'esprit du Concile*. Paris: Desclée de Brouwer, 1966.

McCarthy, John F. "The Second Vatican Council: A Needed Interpretation." In *Living Tradition*, no. 148 (September, 2010).

McPartlan, Paul. "John Paul II and Vatican II." In *The Vision of John Paul II. Assessing His Thought and Influence*. Edited by Gerard Mannion. Collegeville, MN: Liturgical Press, 2008.

Merton, Thomas. *The Ascent to Truth*. New York: Harcourt, Brace, 1951.

Melloni, Alberto, and Christoph Theobald, eds. *Vatican II: A Forgotten Future? Concilium* 2005/4 (2010).

Montini, Giovanni. "*Pensiamo al concilio. Lenten Pastoral Letter*, 1962 [Italian]."

Murphy, Joseph. *Christ Our Joy: The Theological Vision of Pope Benedict XVI*. San Francisco: Ignatius, 2008.

Murray, John Courtney. "This Matter of Religious Freedom." *America* (January 9, 1965).

Nichols, Aidan. *The Splendor of Doctrine. The Catechism of the Catholic Church on Christian Believing*. Edinburgh: T & T Clark, 1995.

Nicolas, Jean-Hervé. "Amour de soi, amour de Dieu, amour des autres." *Revue Thomiste* 56 (1956) 5-42.

Oddie, William, ed. *John Paul the Great: Maker of the post-conciliar Church*. San Francisco: Ignatius, 2005.

Olson, Carl E. "The Art of Imaginative Apologetics. An Interview with Dr. Holly Ordway." *Catholic World Report*, July 5, 2017.

O'Malley, John W. "Deconstructing and Reconstructing a Cliché—Vatican II as a 'Pastoral Council.'" In *Catholicism Opening to the World and Other Confessions: Vatican II and Its Impact*. Edited by Vladimir Latinovic, Gerard Mannion, and Jason Welle. Cham, Switzerland: Palgrave Macmillan, 2018.

———. "Developments, Reforms, and Two Great Reformations: Towards a Historical Assessment of Vatican II." *Theological Studies* 44 (1983) 373-406.

———. "'The Hermeneutic of Reform': A Historical Analysis." *Theological Studies* 73 (2012) 517-546.

———. "Reform, Historical Consciousness, and Vatican II's *Aggiornamento*." *Theological Studies* 32 (1971) 573-601.

———. "The Style of Vatican II." *America* 188/6 (2003):12-17.

———. "Trent and Vatican II: Two Styles of Church." In *From Trent to Vatican II. Historical and Theological Investigations*. Edited by Raymond Bulman and Frederick Parrella. New York: Oxford University Press, 2006.

———. *Vatican II: Did Anything Happen?* New York: Bloomsbury T. & T. Clark, 2007.

———. "Vatican II: Did Anything Happen?" *Theological Studies* 67 (2006) 3–33.
———. *What Happened at Vatican II?* Cambridge, MA: Belknap Press of Harvard University Press, 2008.
Paul VI, Pope. "Address on the Opening of the 2nd Session of the Second Ecumenical Vatican Council, September 29, 1963" [Italian].
———. "Address to the Pontifical North American College, December 20, 1963" [Italian].
———. "Address on the Opening of the 3rd Session of the Second Ecumenical Vatican Council, September 14, 1964" [Italian].
———. "Address to Members of the 'Consilium ad Exsequendam Constitutionem de Sacra Liturgia,' October 29, 1964" [Latin].
———. "Address to Representatives of the Christian Churches and Communities of India, December 3, 1964."
———. "Address to Participants at the 3rd Congress of the Federation of Italian Religious Hospitalers, April 23, 1965" [Italian].
———. "Address to the 7th General Assembly of 'Caritas International,' September 10, 1965" [French].
———. "Address on the Opening of the 4th Session of the Second Ecumenical Vatican Council, September 14, 1965" [Italian].
———. "Address to the United Nations Organization, October 4, 1965."
———. "Address on the 10th Anniversary of C.E.L.A.M., November 23, 1965" [Italian].
———. "Address during the Last Meeting of the Second Vatican Council, December 7, 1965."
———. "Address to the General Chapter of the Discalced Carmelites, June 22, 1967" [Italian].
———. "Address to Graduates of Catholic Action, August 28, 1968" [Italian].
———. "Address to the Secretary General of the United Nations Organization, April 28, 1969."
———. "Address to a Group of Newly Ordained Priests from the North American College, December 20, 1969."
———. "Address to Participants in the 21st Italian Biblical Week, September 25, 1970" [Italian].
———. "Address to the Ambassador of Malta to the Holy See, February 4, 1971."
———. "Address during the Pilgrimage to Subiaco, September 8, 1971" [Italian].
———. "Address to the New Ambassador of Costa Rica to the Holy See, August 7, 1972."
———. "Address to His Eminence Archbishop Paavali, November 11, 1972."
———. "Address to a Group of Newly Ordained Priests from the Pontifical Beda College, April 9, 1973."
———. "Address to the Sacred College, June 22, 1973" [Italian].
———. "Address to the Diocesan Leaders of Social Communications, November 17, 1973" [Italian].
———. "Address to Members of the Pontifical Biblical Commission, March 14, 1974" [French].
———. "Address to the President's Council of the C.E.I., May 9, 1974" [Italian].
———. "Address to the New Ambassador of Ireland to the Holy See, December 19, 1974."

———. "Address to the Sacred College and the Roman Prelature, December 21, 1974" [Italian].
———. "Address to Members of the Diplomatic Corps Accredited to the Holy See, January 11, 1975."
———. "Address to the "Work Camps for the Youth" of Florence, November 4, 1975" [Italian].
———. "Address to Bishops Participating in the Theological *Aggiornamento* Course of the C.E.I., November 14, 1975" [Italian].
———. "Address to the Sacred College, June 21, 1976" [Italian].
———. "Address to the Sacred College and the Roman Prelature, December 20, 1976" [Italian].
———. "Address to the Ambassador of Haiti to the Holy See, June 10, 1977."
———. "Address on the Occasion of the Canonization of Bishop John Neumann, June 20, 1977."
———. "Address to the Bishops of Yugoslavia, November 21, 1977" [Latin].
———. "Address to the Diplomatic Corps Accredited to the Holy See, January 14, 1978."
———. "Address to the Students of the Pontifical Scots College, March 4, 1978."
———. "Address to the Participants of the 26th General Assembly of the Major Superior Union of Italy, April 15, 1978" [Italian].
———. "Address to the Italian Collaborators of the Mother Teresa of Calcutta Missionaries, May 6, 1978."
———. "General Audience, August 5, 1964" [Italian].
———. "General Audience, November 25, 1964" [Italian].
———. "General Audiences, December 29, 1965" [Italian].
———. "General Audience, January 5, 1966" [Italian].
———. "General Audience, January 12, 1966" [Italian].
———. "General Audience, January 19, 1966" [Italian].
———. "General Audience, January 26, 1966" [Italian].
———. "General Audience, July 27, 1966" [Italian].
———. "General Audience, September 7, 1966" [Italian].
———. "General Audience, March 8, 1967" [Italian].
———. "General Audience, January 31, 1968" [Italian].
———. "General Audience, April 3, 1968" [Italian].
———. "General Audience, July 10, 1968" [Italian].
———. "General Audience, December 4, 1968" [Italian].
———. "General Audience, January 15, 1969" [Italian].
———. "General Audience, May 7, 1969" [Italian].
———. "General Audience, January 14, 1970."
———. "General Audience, July 15, 1970" [Italian].
———. "General Audience, August 12, 1970" [Italian].
———. "General Audience, September 30, 1970" [Italian].
———. "General Audience, March 24, 1971" [Italian].
———. "General Audience, April 14, 1971" [French].
———. "General Audience, July 12, 1972."
———. "General Audience, January 16, 1974" [Italian].
———. "General Audience, February 20, 1974" [Italian].
———. "General Audience, August 7, 1974" [Italian].

———. "General Audience, April 7, 1975" [Italian].
———. "General Audience, April 30, 1975" [Italian].
———. "General Audience, August 6, 1975" [Italian].
———. "General Audience, December 15, 1976" [Italian].
———. "Homily for the 3rd Sunday of Lent, March 13, 1966."
———. "Homily for the Synod of Bishops Inaugural Ceremony, September 29, 1967" [Italian].
———. "Homily on the Visit of Patriarch Athenagoras I, October 26, 1967" [Italian].
———. "Homily on a Visit to the Shrine of Namugongo, Uganda, August 2, 1969" [Italian].
———. "Homily for Ash Wednesday, February 11, 1970" [Italian].
———. "Homily for the 'Gen' New Generation Conference, March 2, 1975" [Italian].
———. "Letter to Cardinal Alexandre Renard, October 22, 1972" [French].
———. "Message for the World Day for Missions, 1966" [Italian].
———. "Message for the World Day for Missions, 1967" [Italian].
———. "Message for the World Day for Missions, 1974" [Italian].
———. *"Mirificus eventus,* December 7, 1965" [Italian].
———. *"Populorum progression,* March 26, 1967."
———. *"Quinque iam anni,* December 8, 1970" [Italian].
———. "Radio Message, December 23, 1965" [Italian].
———. *"Sanctitas clarior,* March 19, 1969" [Italian].
Pieper, Josef. *"Divine Madness": Plato's Case against Secular Humanism.* Translated by Lothar Krauth. San Francisco: Ignatius, 1995.
———. *In Tune with the World: A Theory of Festivity.* Chicago: Franciscan Herald, 1973.
Peri, Vittorio. "Appunti per un'indagine sull'ecclesiologia di Paolo VI. Titoli di originalità dell'*Ecclesiam suam*." *Rivista di Storia e Letteratura Religiosa Firenze* 17/3 (1981) 409–450.
Pitre, Brant. *Jesus and the Jewish Roots of the Eucharist.* New York: Doubleday, 2011.
Pontifical Council for Culture. "*Toward a Pastoral Approach to Culture*, May 23, 1999."
Pontifical Council for Social Communications. "*Communio et progressio*," May 23, 1971."
Pottier, Bernard. "Vatican II et Jean-Paul II." *Nouvelle Revue Théologique* 107/3 (1985) 361–375.
Pottmeyer, Herrmann. "Continuité et innovation dans l'ecclésiologie de Vatican II." *Les Églises après Vatican II: Dynamique et prospective.* Edited by G. Alberigo. Collection Théologie historique, 51. Paris: Beauchesne, 1981, 91–116.
Prat, Ferdinand. *The Theology of St. Paul.* 2 vols. Translated by John L. Stoddard. Westminster, MD: Newman, 1952.
Ratzinger, Joseph / Pope Benedict XVI. *Behold the Pierced One: An Approach to Spiritual Christology.* Translated by Graham Harrison. San Francisco: Ignatius, 1986.
———. *Church, Ecumenism and Politics. New Essays in Ecclesiology.* New York: Crossroad, 1988.
———. *Dogma and Preaching. Applying Christian Doctrine to Daily Life.* 1st ed. Edited by Michael J. Miller. Translated by Michael J. Miller and Matthew J. O'Connell. San Francisco: Ignatius, 2011.
———. "Freedom and liberation: The anthropological vision of the instruction *Libertatis conscientia*." *Communio* 14 (Spring 1987) 55–72.

———. *Gospel, Catechesis, Catechism: Sidelights on the Catechism of the Catholic Church*. San Francisco: Ignatius, 1997.

———. *Introduction to Christianity*. Revised edition. Translated by J. R. Foster. San Francisco: Ignatius, 2004.

———. *Jesus of Nazareth. From the Baptism in the Jordan to the Transfiguration*. Vol. 1. Translated by Adrian J. Walker. San Francisco: Ignatius, 2008

———. *Jesus of Nazareth. Holy Week: From the Entrance into Jerusalem to the Resurrection*. Vol. 2. Translated by Philip J. Whitmore. San Francisco: Ignatius, 2011.

———. *Jesus of Nazareth. The Infancy Narratives*. Vol. 3. Translated by Philip J. Whitmore. New York: Image, 2012.

———. *Milestones: Memoirs 1927–1977*. Translated by Erasmo Leiva-Merikakis. San Francisco: Ignatius, 1998.

———. *On the Way to Jesus*. Translated by Michael J. Miller. San Francisco: Ignatius, 2005.

———. "On the Meaning of Sacrament." Translated by Kenneth Baker. *Fellowship of Catholic Scholars Quarterly* (Spring, 2011) 28–35.

———. *Principles of Catholic Theology: Building Stones for a Fundamental Theology*. Translated by Sr. Mary Francis McCarthy. San Francisco: Ignatius, 1987.

———. "Reform from the Beginnings." *30 Days* (November, 1990) 62–69.

———. *Salt of the Earth: Christianity and the Catholic Church at the End of the Millennium. An Interview with Peter Seewald*. Translated by Adrian Walker. San Francisco: Ignatius, 1997.

———. *Spirit of the Liturgy*. Translated by John Saward. San Francisco: Ignatius, 2000.

———. "Sources and Transmission of the Faith." *Communio* 10 (Spring 1983) 17–34.

———. "The Ecclesiology of Vatican II." *Communio*, 13 (Fall, 1986) 239–252.

———. *The Feast of Faith. Approaches to a Theology of the Liturgy*. Translated by Graham Harrison. San Francisco: Ignatius, 1986.

———. *The Nature and Mission of Theology: Essays to Orient Theology in Today's Debate*. Translated by Adrian Walker. San Francisco: Ignatius, 1995.

———. *The Theology of History in St. Bonaventure*. Chicago: Franciscan Herald, 1971.

———. *Theological Highlights of Vatican II*. New York: Paulist, 2009, 1966.

———. *To Look on Christ: Exercises in Faith, Hope and Charity*. New York: Crossroad, 1991.

———. *Truth and Tolerance: Christian Belief and World Religions*. Translated by Henry Taylor. San Francisco: Ignatius, 2004.

Ratzinger, Joseph and Vittorio Messori. *The Ratzinger Report: An Exclusive Interview on the State of the Church*. San Francisco: Ignatius, 1987.

Ratzinger, Joseph, and Karl Rahner. *Revelation and Tradition*. Quaestiones Disputatae 17. New York: Herder & Herder, 1966.

Ratzinger, Joseph, and Hans Urs Von Balthasar. *Mary, the Church at the Source*. Translated by Adrian Walker. San Francisco: Ignatius, 2005.

Riccardi, Andrea. "40th Anniversary of *Ecclesiam Suam* by Pope Paul VI." *L'Osservatore Romano*. September 1, 2004.

Routhier, Gilles. *Vatican II Herméneutique et réception*. Montréal: Éditions Fides (coll. Héritage et projet, 69), 2006.

———. "Vatican II: Relevance and Future." *Theological Studies* 74 (2013): 537–554; reprinted in *50 Years On: Probing the Riches of Vatican II*, ed. David G. Schultenover. Collegeville, MN: Liturgical, 2015.

Rowland, Tracy. *Ratzinger's Faith: The Theology of Pope Benedict XVI*. Oxford: Oxford University Press, 2009, 27–48.

———. "Reclaiming the Tradition: John Paul II as the Authentic Interpreter of Vatican II." In *John Paul the Great: Maker of the post-conciliar Church*. Edited by William Oddie. San Francisco: Ignatius, 2005.

Ruddy, Christopher. "*Ressourcement* and the Enduring Legacy of Post-Tridentine Theology." In *Ressourcement: A Movement for Renewal in Twentieth-Century Catholic Theology*. Edited by Gabriel Flynn and Paul D. Murray. Oxford: Oxford University Press (2012) 185–204.

Rush, Ormond. *Still Interpreting Vatican II: Some Hermeneutical Principles*. New York: Paulist, 2004.

Rylaarsdam, Richard. *John Chrysostom on Divine Pedagogy: The Coherence of his Theology and Preaching*. Oxford: Oxford University Press, 2014.

Sacred Congregation for Clergy. "*Ratio Fundamentalis Institutionis Sacerdotalis - The Gift of the Priestly Vocation*, December 8, 2016."

Sacred Congregation for Divine Worship and the Discipline of the Sacraments. *Homiletic Directory*, June 29, 2014. Rome: Libreria Editrice Vaticana, 2015.

Sacred Congregation for the Doctrine of the Faith. "Letter to Bishops the Catholic Church on Certain Aspects of Christian Meditation, October 15, 1989."

———. "*Mysterium Ecclesiae*, June 24, 1973."

Sakwoski, Derek. *The Ecclesiological Reality of Reception: Considered as a Solution to the Debate Over the Ontological Priority of the Universal Church*. Roma: Tesi Gregoriana, Teologia, Band 204, 2014.

Schnackenburg, Rudolf. *The Gospel according to John*. 3 vols. Translated by Devin Smyth et al. New York: Crossroad/Seabury, 1980, 1982.

Schönborn, Christoph. *Chance or Purpose? Creation, Evolution and a Rational Faith*. San Francisco: Ignatius, 2007.

———. *Creation and Evolution: A Conference with Pope Benedict XVI in Castel Gandolfo*. San Francisco: Ignatius, 2008.

———. "The Divine Economy Interwoven Through the New Catechetical Work." In *Reflections on the Catechism of the Catholic Church*. Chicago: Midwest Theological Forum, 1993, 75–83.

———. *Introduction to the Catechism of the Catholic Church*. San Francisco: Ignatius, 1994.

———. *Living the Catechism of the Catholic Church. A Brief Commentary on the Catechism for Every Week of the Year*. Vol. 3: *Life in Christ*. San Francisco: Ignatius, 2001.

Schüller, Bruno. "The debate on the specific character of a Christian ethic: some remarks." In *Readings in Moral Theology, No. 2: The Distinctiveness of Christian Ethics*. Edited by Charles E. Curran and Richard A. McCormick. New York: Paulist, 1980.

Schultenover, David, ed. *50 Years On: Probing the Riches of Vatican II*. Collegeville, MN: Liturgical, 2010.

Schurmann, Heinz. "Les Charismes Spirituels," *L'Église de Vatican II*, Tome II. Edited by G. Barauna. *Unam Sanctam*, 51, B. Paris: Cerf, 1966, 541–573.

Sensing, Tim. "Towards a Definition of Paraenesis." *Restoration Quarterly* 38/3 (1996) 145–58.
Simpson, Peter. *On Karol Wojtyla*. Belmont, CA: Wadsworth, 2000.
Spicq, Ceslaus. *L'Épitre aux Hébreux, II. Commentaire*. Paris: Gabalda, 1963.
———. *Théologie morale du Nouveau Testament*. 2 vols. Paris: Gabalda, 1970.
Stacpoole, Alberic, ed. *Vatican II Revisited by Those Who Were There*. Minneapolis: Winston, 1986.
Starr, James, and Troels Engberg-Pederson, eds. *Early Christian Paraenesis in Context*. New York: de Gruyter, 2004.
Suenens, Léon-Josef. "A Plan for the Whole Council." In *Vatican II Revisited by Those Who Were There*. Edited by Alberic Stacpoole. Minneapolis: Winston (1986) 88–105.
Synod of Bishops. 2nd General Extraordinary Assembly. November 24–December 8, 1985. "*Message to the People of God*, December 8, 1985" [Italian].
———. 2nd General Extraordinary Assembly. November 24–December 8, 1985. "The Church, in the Word of God, Celebrates the Mysteries of Christ for the Salvation of the World, *Final Report*, December 8, 1985."
———. Special Assembly for America, November 6–December 12, 1997. "Encounter with the Living Jesus Christ: The Way to Conversion, Communion and Solidarity. *Instrumentum laboris*, December 12, 1997."
———. Special Assembly for America, November 6–December 12, 1997. "Encounter with the Living Jesus Christ: The Way to Conversion, Communion and Solidarity. *Lineamenta*, 1996."
———. 13th Ordinary Assembly. October 7–28, 2012. "The New Evangelization for the Transmission of the Christian Faith, *Lineamenta*, February 2, 2011."
———. 13th Ordinary Assembly. "The New Evangelization for the Transmission of the Christian Faith, *Instrumentum laboris*, June 19, 2012."
———. 13th Ordinary Assembly. October 7–28, 2012. "The New Evangelization for the Transmission of the Christian Faith, Final Propositions, October 27, 2012."
———. 13th Ordinary Assembly. October 7–28, 2012. "Message to the People of God, October 28, 2012."
Teresa of Avila. *The Interior Castle*. In *The Collected Works of St. Teresa of Avila*. Vol. 2. Translated by Kieran Kavanaugh and Otilio Rodriguez. Washington, DC: ICS, 1980.
Theobald, Christoph. "The Theological Options of Vatican II: Seeking an 'Internal' Principle of Interpretation." In *Vatican II: A Forgotten Future?* Edited by Alberto Melloni and Christoph Theobald. London: SCM, 2005, 87–107.
The Roman Missal. Third Edition. United States Conference of Catholic Bishops, 2011. Authorized translation of *Missale Romanum ex decreto sacrosancti oecumenici Concilii Vaticani II instauratum auctoritate Pauli Pp. VI promulgatum Ioannis Pauli Pp. II cura recognitum. Editio typica tertia, reimpressio emendate*. Città del Vaticano: Typis Vaticanis, 2002, 2008.
Thils, Gustav. "… en pleine fidélité au concile du Vatican II," *La foi et le temps* 10 (1980) 274–75.
Thomas Aquinas. [Unless otherwise noted, the English translation of the following works of St. Thomas can be found online at the Aquinas Institute, Inc. at <https://aquinas.cc>.]
———. *Commentary on Aristotle's* De Anima.

―――. *Commentary on St. Paul's Letter to the Galatians.*
―――. *Commentary on St. Paul's Letter to the Romans.*
―――. *Commentary on the Gospel of John.*
―――. *Disputed Questions on Truth (De veritate).* Translated by Robert W. Mulligan. Chicago: Regnery, 1952.
―――. *Summa Contra Gentiles.* Translated by Anton C. Pegis et al. New York: Hanover House, 1955–57.
―――. *Summa Theologiae.* Translated by Fathers of the English Dominican Province. London: Benziger, 1947.
Tillard, J.-M.R. "L'Église relit sa catholicité devant Dieu et l'ensemble des baptisés." In *Vatican II and Its Legacy.* Edited by M. Laberigts and L. Kenis. Leuven: Leuven University Press (2002) 107–128.
United States Council of Catholic Bishops. "*Our Hearts Were Burning Within Us.* November 17, 1999."
Vanhoye, Albert and Jean Corbon. "Connaître." In *Vocabulaire de Théologie Biblique.* Paris: Cerf, 1970, 199–204.
Vargas, Michael. "Administrative Change in the Fourteenth-Century Dominican Order: A Case Study in Partial Reforms and Incomplete Theories." In *Reassessing Reform: A Historical Investigation Into Church Renewal,* edited by Christopher M. Bellitto and David Zachariah Flanagin, 84–104. Washington, DC: Catholic University of America Press, 2012.
Vatican II. "Message to Humanity, October 12, 1962," [Latin] *Acta Synodalia Sacrosancti Concilii Oecumenici Vaticani* I/I. Rome: Typis Polyglottis Vaticanis, 1970–1999, 254–256; [English] *The Documents of Vatican II. In a New and Definitive Translation with Commentaries and Notes by Catholic, Protestant and Orthodox Authorities.* Walter M. Abbott, S.J., General Editor. New York: Herder and Herder / Association Press, 1966, 3-7.
Vincent of Lérins. *Commonitorium. Patrologia Latina.* Vol. 50, Cols. 639 and 667.
Von Balthasar, Hans Urs. *The Glory Of The Lord: A Theological Aesthetics.* 7 vols. Edited by Joseph Fessio and John Riches. San Francisco: Ignatius, 1982–83.
―――. *In the Fullness of Faith: On the Centrality of the Distinctively Catholic.* Translated by Graham Harrison. San Francisco: Ignatius, 1988.
―――. *Love Alone Is Credible.* Translated by David L. Schindler. San Francisco: Ignatius, 2005 (Original German 1963).
―――. *Prayer.* Translated by A. V. Littledale. New York: Sheed & Ward, 1961.
Vorgrimler, H. *Commentary on the Documents of Vatican II.* 5 vols. New York: Herder & Herder, 1967–69.
Weigel, George. *The Courage to Be Catholic. Crisis, Reform, and the Future of the Church.* New York: Basic, 2002.
―――. *Witness to Hope. The Biography of Pope John Paul II.* New York: Cliff Street, HarperCollins, 1999.
Wicks, Jared. *Investigating Vatican II.* Washington, DC: Catholic University of America Press, 2018.
Williams, George Hunston. *The Mind of John Paul II. Origins of His Thought and Action.* New York: Seabury, 1981.
Wiltgen, Ralph. *The Rhine Flows into the Tiber: The Unknown Council.* New York: Hawthorn, 1967.
Wojtyła, Karol / Pope John Paul II. *The Acting Person.* Boston: Reidel, 1979.

———. *A Catechesis on the Creed.* 4 vols. Boston: Pauline, 1996–1998.
———. *Crossing the Threshold of Hope.* New York: Knopf, 1994.
———. *En Esprit et en Vérité. Recueil de textes 1949–1978.* Translated by Gwendoline Jarczyk. Paris: Le Centurion, 1980.
———. *Love and Responsibility.* Translated by H. T. Willetts. San Francisco: Ignatius, 1993.
———. *Memory and Identity: Conversations at the Dawn of a Millennium.* New York: Rizzoli, 2005.
———. *Person and Community. Selected Essays.* Translated by Theresa Sandok. Catholic Thought from Lublin. Vol. 4. New York: Lang, 1993.
———. *Sign of Contradiction.* New York: Crossroad, Seabury, 1979.
———. *Sources of Renewal: The Implementation of Vatican II.* Translated by P. S. Falla. San Francisco: Harper & Row, 1980.
———. *The Way to Christ, Spiritual Exercises.* San Francisco: Harper, 1984.

www.ingramcontent.com/pod-product-compliance
Lightning Source LLC
Chambersburg PA
CBHW071238300426
44116CB00008B/1083